J. F. (John Francis) Campbell

Life in Normandy

Sketches of French Fishing, Farming, Cooking, Natural History, and...

J. F. (John Francis) Campbell

Life in Normandy

Sketches of French Fishing, Farming, Cooking, Natural History, and...

ISBN/EAN: 9783744777933

Printed in Europe, USA, Canada, Australia, Japan

Cover: Foto ©ninafisch / pixelio.de

More available books at **www.hansebooks.com**

LIFE IN NORMANDY.

Printed by R. Clark

FOR

EDMONSTON AND DOUGLAS, EDINBURGH

LONDON . . . HAMILTON, ADAMS, AND CO.

CAMBRIDGE . . MACMILLAN AND CO.

DUBLIN . . . M'GLASHAN AND GILL.

GLASGOW . . JAMES MACLEHOSE.

LIFE IN NORMANDY

SKETCHES OF FRENCH FISHING
FARMING, COOKING, NATURAL HISTORY
AND POLITICS
DRAWN FROM NATURE

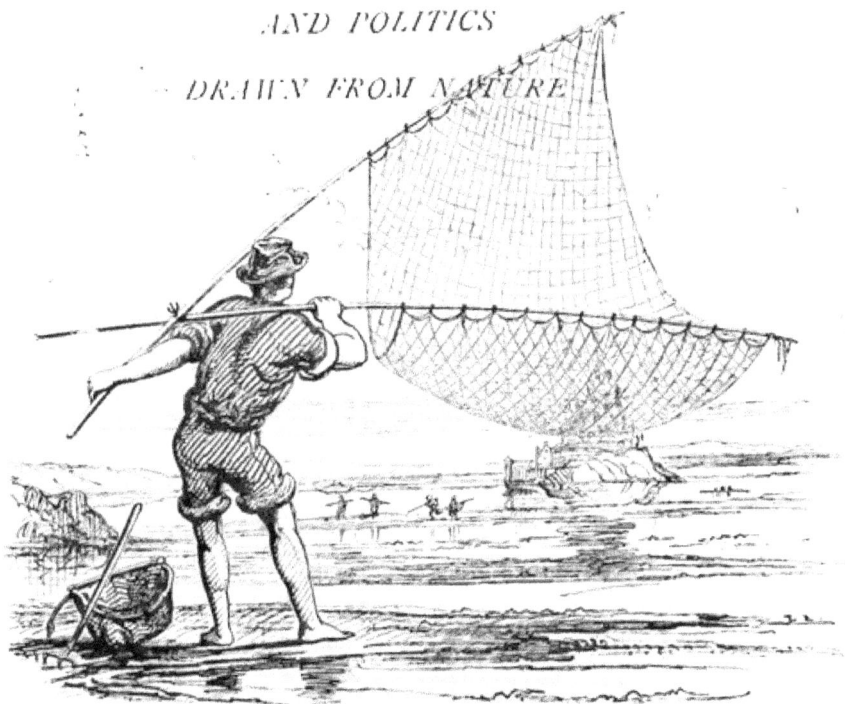

EDINBURGH: EDMONSTON & DOUGLAS

MDCCCLXV

PREFACE TO THIRD EDITION.

THE book for which this preface was written in 1862 was favourably received by the press and by the public. The Publishers have now decided on printing a third edition in a cheaper form ; and the Editor is anxious to carry out the Author's intention by making his work more accessible to those for whom it was chiefly meant. It was meant for people who catch or earn their food, and who cannot afford cooks : classes who may take a hint from French house-wives, who feed their families well on very small means. The book itself has been reprinted, because it seemed beyond an Editor's province to alter a work which has been well received. With the exception of a few short inter-polations, and some changes in the casting of sentences here and there, the original manuscript was published at first. With a view to cheapness, lithographs from sketches made by the Author's son, and by his wife, are omitted, and a portrait of the Author is substituted. It is a copy of a pencil-sketch made by Saunders more than thirty years ago.

In some respects the work has been misunderstood.

A few friends at home and abroad have vainly sought for Hope, Cross, and the Marquis, and for some record of the émeute at Granville. The natural history is fact; the framework, fiction founded on fact. Hope and Cross are creatures of the Author's imagination; so are the French men and women with whom they converse; but those who knew the Author of " Life in Normandy" know that Hope and Cross think his thoughts and narrate many of his adventures; while those who know the fisher-folk of Granville, Norman gentlemen, farmers, and tradesmen, also know the originals of these pictures of real life. The adventure on the quicksand never happened as described, but many similar adventures occurred there; and the Author describes his own sensations when he paints those of puppets on his stage.

Many years ago, while shooting seals in the West Highlands on a strand which rivals the Grève in size and danger, the Author of " Life in Normandy" was surprised by a rising tide. He ran for his life: the firm sand began to move as the tide rose, feet sank, and the footstep filled as the foot rose: to use his own expression, he ran to the river in the middle of the sand, because drowning was a cleaner death than smothering. It was a case of real peril, the peril so well described in the book; a peril which the Editor understands, for he too has felt that Highland quicksand sucking him in. A boat which chanced to pass rescued the sportsman, and by his special desire no guest of his ever went seal-shooting on that strand without having a boat on the channel which runs through it. In spite of the boat the feeling of sinking into a hole, which fills with heavy sand and holds fast, is one which could only be described from experience, and it is truly described in this book.

The episode of the refugee is founded on the narratives

of real men.   Atrocities which were perpetrated in 1848 are unfit for publication; many of them never were published; but they were narrated at Avranches by men who marched to Paris and who returned triumphant as described. One, in particular, spoke of shooting "Reds sitting" in their lairs in a wood; and his reason for so doing was, that he had seen pockets stuffed with the eyes of his dead comrades.

Exception has been taken to hunting eels with a dog and a pickaxe.   Those who object would probably shake their heads at the notion of truffle dogs, but truffle dogs and eel dogs are authentic as pointer dogs, though not so common.

A returned sailor once entertained his mother with his adventures, at her special desire.   "Mother," he said, "I have been to the West Indies, and there I saw sugar mountains and rivers of rum."   "Ay, Jock, that's the place that we get a' our sugar and rum from, I ken that weel eneuch."   "Well, mother," said he, "we came round by the Red Sea, and one morning when we pulled up the anchor we found a wheel fast on it."   "Ay," said the mother, "I have read a' aboot Pharaoh and his host, nae doot it was a wheel aff a chariot."   "Well, mother," said Jock, "I have seen fish flying in the air like birds."   "Jock," said she, "haud yer whisht, and dinna tell lees to yer auld mither."

With this old story I leave this edition of "Life in Normandy" to those who can distinguish a mosaic from a gilt frame—a framework of fiction from facts which give value to an amusing story.

J. F. CAMPBELL.

LONDON, *April* 1865.

PREFACE TO FIRST EDITION.

THE following pages were written for pastime in 1848, by a Highland gentleman resident in Normandy, at the suggestion of an honoured friend, who named the subjects of French Cookery, Fishing, Natural History, Farming, Gardening, and Politics. It was suggested that ingenious foreign devices and engines for ensnaring, growing, and gathering food, and for making it eatable, might be so described as to benefit the poor at home, whose single dish of potatoes might easily be varied at small cost. It was argued that a good cheap dinner at home would tempt a poor man from bad dear drink abroad, and that a poor Scotchman's wife might be taught to do that which poor wives do elsewhere. And, as even salmon, when raw, are nasty, while well-cooked marrots, cuttle-fish, limpets, frogs, snails, and maggots, are eaten and relished, so instruction might be seasoned and made agreeable with sketches from life in Normandy, such as it then was.

The suggestions were taken, the papers were written and sent, and they are now published,—though both the author and his friend have passed away,—because it was their wish, and in the hope that the object which they aimed at may be attained.

"There are as good fish in the sea as ever came out of it;" and many a barren Scotch strand might yield a good harvest if men only knew how to reap it and use it.

In Hope and Cross, and their conversations about France and

the French Revolution, it is easy to recognise the mind of the experienced, liberal, clear-sighted politician, who knew the meaning
of political gratitude; who tolerated all forms of religious worship,
though he steadfastly adhered to his own, at home and abroad ;
who could foresee that communism, disorder, and a French
republic would lead to well-defined rights of property, stricter
order, and something like despotism ; and who held that the
rigid system of protection which placed a custom-house at the
gate of every petty town, levied dues on every basket of eggs,
and even planted sentries over sea-water, to guard the salt
monopoly, must give way to more liberal measures.   The empire
and the tariff of our day now prove the sagacity which predicted
a change in the direction of monarchy and free trade.

Those who knew the writer need not be told his name.
They will recognise the generosity whose chief luxury was to
give pleasure to others, and the chivalry of the gentleman who
was courteous to a bare-footed fisher-girl as to the highest in
the land.

Those who knew provincial France some fourteen years ago
will recognise the country gentleman of old Norman and Breton
type, who has so much in common with his Norse and British
relations.   They will know the warm, adventurous, hospitable,
polite nature that still delights in love and war, danger and hard-
ship ; in riding, sailing, shooting, fishing, country life, good living, and good fellowship ; and which in the olden time made
vikings and gallant knights, hospitable chiefs, good soldiers, and
minstrels, of Norseman and Norman, Celt and Saxon.

They will also recognise some characteristics of other classes.

If there be a shade of caricature, it is evenly applied to
friend and foreigner, and there is no gall in the ink.   " The
Marquis" cooked a dinner;—but it was for his friends, and
if he ate his full share, he earned it by wading for it like a
man.

Men, and their manners and customs, are lightly sketched,
but from nature, and on the spot :—the habits of animals are

described from close observation by one who always delighted to watch them and catch them, without caring much for their long book names or for learned theories.

The lithographs in the first edition are copied from rough sketches made on the spot ; and if the volumes do no more, they may at least serve to amuse the reader, and perhaps remind him of an old friend.

EDINBURGH, *December* 1862.

CONTENTS.

CHAPTER I.

FÊTE-DIEU, JUNE 1848.

CHAPTER II.

FRESH FROM PARIS.

CHAPTER III.

A TRIP TO CAROLLES.

CHAPTER IV.

STRAND FISHING, ETC.

CHAPTER V.

AN ESCAPE.

CHAPTER VI.

THE EBB TIDE AND A LATE DINNER.

CHAPTER VII.

STONEWALL FISHING.

CHAPTER VIII.

AN EVENING AT MONSIEUR PIXEL'S.

CHAPTER IX.

A NORMAN BREAKFAST AND A STROLL.

CHAPTER X.

LOST ON THE GRÈVE.

CHAPTER XI.

A STORY OF THE REVOLUTION OF 1848.

CHAPTER XII.

THE MARE DE BOUILLON.

CHAPTER XIII.

THE MOLE AFTER A GALE.

LIFE IN NORMANDY.

CHAPTER I.

FÊTE-DIEU, JUNE 1848.

DREADFUL NEWS!" exclaimed François, a French lad about :venteen years of age, as he rushed into his master's room.

Mr. Cross, the said master, was a Scotch gentleman who had ved for some years in France. He had originally come to the untry for the health of a sister, but she having died at Nice, ₂ left the south, and since that time he had resided in various ɔrthern provinces; latterly he had established himself in Nor- andy, where everything was cheap and everybody poor. A ɔor man, therefore, could not be looked down upon for being , the same position as his neighbours; indeed, poverty in ngland being wealth in Normandy, Mr. Cross, with a small in- ₂pendence, found himself the great man of the quiet little ɔwn where he lived.

François, his servant, had been taken, when a boy, from the oundling Hospital; he had served at first as the piper's man's ee laddy used to serve in a Highland establishment—that is to ₃y, he did everybody's work, both in the house and out of it, ; well as his own, and thereby acquired a universal knowledge ⁚ household operations. The cook made him learn and execute l her duties, beginning by shelling peas, and ending by looking ter her stews and côtelettes, while she flirted with the gardener, ₂ wasted her time by talking for ten ordinary women on market ₁ys. The housemaid made him wax and *frotter* the floors,

B

dust the rooms, and occasionally make the beds ; and if he ever had a spare moment, the gardener was sure to find him employment in watering, weeding, or arranging the flowers. He had been engaged to assist Mr. Thomas, an old and faithful servant, who had been many years the attendant both of Mr. Cross and his father. François' own duties were therefore to clean lamps, shoes, and knives, and to carry water from the well ; water-pipes and pumps being an unknown luxury in that part of France. Thomas, though faithful, was old ; François was young and clever ; and he soon learnt to clean plate and brush clothes so well, that the faithful Thomas, after a while, only watched to see that his master's comforts and interests were not neglected or injured by the mal-performance of his young assistant. Under such schooling, it is not surprising that François learnt to be a good servant, with a very general knowledge of all the branches of household work. The boy had the national gaiety of his countrymen. Early broke in to hard and constant labour, he avoided their great faults, idleness and frivolity ; taken from the Foundling Hospital to this new routine of duty, constant employment was to him a change for the better ; for he was well fed, well clothed, and had a comfortable bed to sleep on—comforts unknown before, and so much prized that he was always cheerful. In passing through a French town, therefore, let no one feel shocked at seeing a string of two or three hundred children, all foundlings, marching through the streets ; let him forget that the Foundling Hospital bears the stamp of giving facility to immorality, and rather suppose that it is a useful national seminary for providing good domestic servants for those who may require them ; and in this he will not be disappointed, provided he takes them young enough, before their spirits are broken and soured by ill-treatment. Six months before the time we mention, poor old Thomas had been gathered to his fathers. François, being promoted to his place, would no longer submit to do the work of the whole household ; the consequence of which was, that a meeting took place which obliged Mr.

Cross to have a general clearance. After this he found that he was better served by François, one old woman, who was both cook and housemaid, and a man once a week in the garden, than when he had the larger establishment under old Thomas, who, though honesty personified, was an Englishman, and therefore no match for the clever roguery of the Normans. Such was the state of Mr. Cross's household, when François burst into his room, announcing that there was dreadful news from Paris !

Mr. Cross sat up in bed and rubbed his eyes, not much frightened by the intelligence. He was accustomed to hear the superlative degree applied to all sorts of news ; he had heard it on the 23d of February, and in May, when it was used in all the extremes of horror ; and before either of these two eventful months he had listened to the same amount of hyperbolical exaltation, when the news of the capture of Abd-el-Kader had arrived in France. It was therefore in a very quiet tone that he inquired what was the matter.

" There is an émeute in Paris ! the streets are barricaded, the troops and the people are fighting, and thousands of people and soldiers have been killed ! is not that affreux ?" exclaimed the lad.

" Bad enough," said his master, " if it be true. And where, pray, did you hear this fine story ?"

" I was going, as monsieur had ordered, to the tailor's, and I met Philippe, who was with me in the hospital, and who is now in the printing-office of the Gazette, and he told me that he had seen the telegraphic despatch which was just sent in to be printed. I heard the drum going through the streets as I returned, so it must be true."

" It looks as if it were. So give me my clothes and hot water : I will get up and go and see for myself."

The news was true enough, and for the next two days rumours were afloat at every moment. The faces of the English residents looked long, and flight was the universal theme of conversation. The third day was Sunday, and the little English chapel was full : fear is a great promoter of devotion. The service was over,

and the clergyman had given out his text, when the loud sound
of drums beating the générale was heard below the windows.
The congregation became fidgety, the parson preached in vain ;
indeed, Cross afterwards declared that he saw him turn over two
pages of his sermon at a time, and no one found him out, nor
did he correct his mistake, for he, honest man, as well as his
non-hearers, was more taken up with the émeutes in the streets
than the pious emotions of the heart.   His sermon was uncommonly short, and the rush from the chapel when he concluded
was so rapid as to be barely decent.   Once at the door the
movements became more decorous, for as it rained servants were
in waiting with umbrellas, and from them it was learnt that a
number of the National Guards were about to march for Paris
to assist the Government in restoring order.   Most of the ladies
walked quietly home, but many of the gentlemen went to the
Place Valhubert to see the muster.   The crowd there was very
great ; almost all the National Guards were under arms and
drawn up, although only a part had volunteered to march to Paris.
Among these were, however, almost all the principal gentlemen
of the place.   They were a motley crew ; few had uniforms,
and the rest had dressed themselves in clothes to stand the
weather.   Shooting-jackets preponderated, nevertheless they
were a serviceable-looking body of men, and they looked well
and gay.   Under the eyes of men who valued them as protectors
of order, and of women who admired their courage, it would have
been impossible for a Frenchman even to look anxious.

Nothing can be done in France without a little theatrical
display.   In France they have rather too much of it, in England
certainly too little.   The French error is the best, for every man,
whether he allows it or not, loves in his heart to have his services appreciated, and the bravest will not meet death less bravely
if fair faces and bright eyes have cheered him on his path, and
may weep for him if he falls.

Following the usual custom, the volunteers were marched
round the Place that every one might see them.   Then they

formed a hollow square ; the tricolor was blessed and handed to
the officer ; speeches were made by the authorities, ending of
course with " be brave, be Frenchmen ;" and then they were
re-formed and marched off, the band playing " Mourir pour la
patrie." The whole National Guard followed, together with
half the inhabitants of the town, who marched the first mile
with them towards Paris, only leaving them when they mounted
into the long waggons which had been ordered to await them on
the road. " Soyez braves, soyez Français," were the concluding
words which had been addressed to the soldiers by the authorities ; " Soyez braves, soyez Français," were the first which
were applied by the coachmen to their horses as they started at
a trot ; but the latter added, " Allez toujours, Br-r-r-igands,"
with a dose of whip—which addition the French quadrupeds
bore in a manner that showed they were used to it.

The rain had ceased, and the sun was bursting forth as the
large escort turned to regain the town. When the concourse
reached the Place where the military had so lately been mustered,
the scene was greatly changed, for the sunbeams glittered not
on musket barrels, but on the vestments of a procession of priests.
These vestments shone in all the splendour of gold and silver
brocade. In front were borne high in air the embroidered ban-
ners, long waxen torches, and the silver cross. A band of choristers came next, marching on either side of the street, the
centre of which was filled by little girls dressed as angels, having
garlands on their heads and baskets of flowers in their hands.
The flowers they scattered from time to time in front of a canopy
which followed. The canopy was covered with embroidery and
silver lace ; it was carried by four priests in splendid dresses,
and beneath it walked an old man similarly dressed, and bearing
the consecrated Host in his hands. Immediately in front of the
canopy, and on either side, marched a number of boys waving
censers of incense. These were of silver, and they glittered
brightly while they gave forth their fragrant smoke as they were
tossed in the air by their bearers. All were thus thrown at the

same moment, time being kept by a man dressed in black and white robes, with a high square cap on his head, who gave the signal and the time to both choristers and incense-boys, by opening and shutting a box made in the form of a book. Every time it shut it made a hollow sound, which could be heard at a good distance. More priests followed ; then a troop of Sœurs de Charité and Bonne Sœurs, and behind them a crowd of women. Among these could be seen a few old men, but not one young one—devotion being decidedly not the fashion among the young men in France. Still, on joining the procession, the crowd paused and uncovered, to allow it to move on, but took advantage of every cross street to escape to their homes.

On entering the streets, Cross saw that from one end to the other they were hung with white sheets. Here and there those in front of a house might be seen with a broad black edging sewn round, to mark that the inhabitants of that house had lost a relative and were in mourning.

"What ceremony is this?" asked Cross of an old man. " Sacré hérétique" was the only answer which the old rascal condescended to give. Cross knew him to be a drunken vagabond, who kept a cabaret and let out horses and carriages for hire. He was somewhat astonished at hearing this burst of Catholic zeal from such a quarter, for he did not know that about a month before, this venerable good-for-nothing had been upset when returning home drunk, and had been nearly killed. When confined to his bed, his wife had thought it a good opportunity to administer a little spiritual consolation. Her priest was sent for, he had been properly lectured, and as a sign of his reformation, he was ordered out to carry a candle and march in the rear of the procession.

> " The devil was sick, the devil a saint would be ;
> The devil got well, the devil a saint was he "—

held good in this instance, for the same evening Cross saw his pious friend sitting in front of his own door as drunk as a Norman, and swearing at his wife as loudly as ever.

Though Cross could get no answer from this worthy, one of the Sœurs de Charité lifted her head and answered—

"It is one of the great ceremonies of our Church, my good gentleman—to-day is the Fête-Dieu."

Cross recognised in the soft voice and sweet expression of the Sœur de Charité a person who had called on him some time before to request a donation for the society to which she belonged. Knowing the great good which they did, admiring the truly Christian feeling of these women, who are ready to nurse all who are sick or in affliction, Cross had given her a handsome donation. She answered his question sweetly and gently; there was no tone of reproof in her voice; true to what she believed to be right, she could still respect the belief of another. "What a difference," thought Cross, "exists between that drunken old sinner and this mild Christian woman,—as great as the difference I have just seen between the two parties who have so lately been on this spot. Prayers and hymns now sound here instead of drums, trumpets, and rude oaths; and the smell of incense fills the air in place of the sulphurous odour of gunpowder that pervaded the atmosphere less than an hour ago."

Though Cross had been several years in France, it so happened that he had never witnessed the ceremony of the Fête-Dieu. One year he had been ill himself; on another he had been confined by the illness of his sister; on a third by her death. He therefore resolved to follow the procession now; and respect for the Sisters of Charity made him do so with less inclination to find fault with what seemed to him a mummery.

On advancing into the town they came to a shop the front of which had been taken out. The interior was dressed with an altar, on which stood candelabras, numerous lights, and flowers in quantities, both real and artificial, and a crucifix. The whole interior of the room was adorned with moss, evergreens, and garlands of flowers, arranged with great taste.

Here the procession stopped; the priest lifted the canopy and

entered the chapel, bearing in his hand the Host, and followed
by a number of his brother clergy. Prayers were said and sung,
and then the large collection of nosegays lying before him was
blessed. One after another they were lifted from the altar, each
was pressed on the gilded case in which the sacrament was carried, and then laid down again, to be claimed by the parties who
had left them there.

Cross looked at the Sisters of Charity. " The Lord forgive
me," he said to himself, " if I am unjust ; but this is awful nonsense. Can any rational being believe that this mummery gives
any value to these flowers ? and yet what right have I to find
fault with their absurdities, and forget that the same faith which
places value on withered flowers because they have been blessed
by a priest, leads these excellent women to sacrifice every hour
of their lives to works of love and charity !"

The ceremony ended at this Reposoir, the procession again
moved on for a couple of hundred yards, till they came to a place
where four streets met. Here a chapel was raised in the middle
of the open space. It was beautifully made of white linen,
moss, and evergreens, twisted into pillars, with a roof of laurel
leaves that looked like scales. Within again was an altar surrounded with rare plants in pots, and covered, like the first, with
garlands, lights, bouquets, and a cross. The same ceremonies
took place—the only alteration being, that a number of pretty
little girls scattered flowers before the priest as he ascended the
steps of the altar, and two others held china vases in their hands,
from which a stream of fragrant smoke issued. These stood at
the bottom of the altar steps, and there remained while the service was chanted. When this was ended, Cross thought he had
seen enough, and as the procession began to move, he slipped
into one of the side streets to take his way homewards. When,
however, he entered the main street that led towards his house,
he was surprised to see that a number of Reposoirs had been
raised at short intervals along the whole length of the street.
He could not help stopping to examine and admire these struc-

tures, for the ingenuity and taste displayed in the arrangement of very simple materials was quite extraordinary. A number of young women and girls were employed in giving the finishing touches to the works, and some stood with a lantern and taper ready to light the candles at a moment's notice. Several young men were looking on, but doing nothing.

"By whom are all these made?" asked Cross of a young Frenchman whom he saw standing among the spectators.

"You may see," he answered; "all the young girls in the country have been at work preparing for to-day. They have been employed for some weeks to make what will be seen for only a few hours; but they work with pleasure, for not one of them fails to believe that, according to the work they do, so is their prospect of getting a husband increased; and if they do not work, they are firmly convinced they have no chance of being married for a year."

"That explains what puzzled me much," said Cross; "for many a hand and many an hour must be required to arrange those various-coloured mosses in such elegant patterns. But who makes all the wood-work?"

"That," replied the Frenchman, "is made once for all. When taken down this evening it will be laid aside till next year; the boards and posts will be placed in the neighbouring houses, and will be covered with some fresh device this time twelve months."

Cross bowed, thanked his informant, and proceeded home. In the evening, when he came out to stroll through the streets, not a vestige remained of any of the chapels or altars. The scene was again changed; groups of men in blouses were walking; some few singing the Marseillaise, but most of them looking anxious; gentlemen were standing at the corners of the streets conversing, and a considerable crowd was collected watching the telegraph, whose arms were working, conveying and receiving some fresh intelligence from Paris. Presently a shout was heard from the end of the street, and all hastened to learn

the cause : it was a long line of waggons and carriages laden
with National Guards, who were hastening to Paris from four of
the more southern towns to lend their aid to the cause of order.
Cross narrowly observed the faces and actions of the crowd
which was pouring in from every side to see them pass, and the
examination was satisfactory, for the approbation and pleasure
displayed proved that communism was at a discount in Normandy, and that the discontented in one city, large though it
was, must yield to the will of the nation.

During the next two or three days, great anxiety was felt
and expressed regarding the volunteers who had marched for
Paris ; the telegraph, and such newspapers as were printed,
reported that order was restored, but private letters arrived from
Paris stating that several assassinations had taken place, and
that some of the National Guards from the country had been
shot while on duty. These anxieties, however, did not last long,
for most of those who had gone wrote to announce their safe
arrival. Many of these letters—those at least which were
written to male friends—were read aloud, and were found to
contain much more ample details of the ridiculous misadventures
of the writers and their companions, than of the horrors which
they had gone to witness and suppress ; but, by degrees, all
that had taken place was made known, either by the public
prints or private letters. Then people began to breathe more
freely, and to talk loudly in behalf of order and against the
domination of the refuse of France, who thought proper to ruin
their country by raising émeutes in the capital. Grapeshot,
gunpowder, and wholesale extermination of these miscreants,
poured from the mouths of all who had anything to lose; and
not a few talked of the propriety of marching *en masse* to Paris
to destroy the hornets' nest by burning it to the ground, as the
only means of restoring peace to France.

A few days more passed, and matters became quieter, and
then the news arrived that the services of the National Guard
from the country could be dispensed with, and that the volun-

teers were to be dismissed and return to their homes. The
town was in great commotion on receipt of this intelligence.
Their friends were to arrive the following day, and it was
unanimously resolved that they should have a public reception ;
accordingly, on the following morning all was bustle. At one
o'clock, the National Guard who had remained at home, the
artillery company with their guns, and the fire-brigade, mustered in the Place Valhubert, and from thence marched with
bands of music to Pont, to receive their friends on the spot
where they had taken leave of them so short a time before.
Short as that time had been, great was the change in the minds
of those who now went to welcome their townsmen. When
they had gone to bid them adieu, depression and anxiety were
on the countenances of all, but now they bore a triumphant
look : the cause of order was in the ascendant ; their lives and
(what a Norman values more) their *livres* were safe ; they considered the volunteers to be heroes, who had assisted in this
good work ; for they felt, and justly felt, that although few of
the country National Guards had actually been engaged, yet the
moral impression given by their march to the capital had done
as much for the establishment of order as the more bloody
deeds of those who actually fought at the barricades. All eyes
were therefore bright, all hearts were gay, and the military
music sounded merrily as they marched down the hill. And
on this hill was many a fair face, and many an aged form. The
young came to meet lover, brother, or husband ; the old to
catch the first glimpse of a son's form, and to contend with the
young for the first glance of his eye. Mingled with the better
class were hundreds of the peasant women, dressed in their
high white caps and gaudy-coloured handkerchiefs. They gave
a striking effect to the edge of the steep hill on which they
were grouped ; and behind them were mustered masses of the
farmers and peasants, dressed in their blue blouses. No young
men of the upper classes were there, for they were in the ranks,
which had just left the town ; but a few old gentlemen stood

near the ladies, like them watching for the return of a son or a
relative.

From the height where all were thus assembled, the village
of Pont could be clearly seen. Every eye was turned in that
direction, and at length a universal buzz and clapping of hands
gave notice that the flag was hoisted, to intimate that the
comers were in sight at Pont. Two minutes after, a shout told
that they were in sight from the hill. The shout, for a French
one, was good ; but, after all, it was but a poor concern. There
is nothing that strikes the ear of an Englishman more forcibly
than the difference between the cheers of a British and a French
crowd. The cheer of the French is a sort of irregular roar, and
sounds tame in comparison with an English cheer ; but, to make
up for this deficiency, the French beat the English hollow in
their cries of anger. The shout of an angry British mob resembles the roar of a bull, while that of a French one is like
the scream of demons let loose. No one was angry on this
occasion ; all were pleased and highly excited, for the cheers of
the men were unusually good, and the women pressed forward
to the very edge of the road, waving their handkerchiefs to the
still distant party. A quarter of an hour elapsed, which seemed
like an age to the watchers ; then came the waggons in which
the troops had travelled ; and the drivers, having no enemy to
beat, as a matter of course beat their horses. After the waggons
there was a pause for a minute, and then the band turned the
corner, playing right heartily ; but the sound of their instru-
ments was drowned in the roar of a salute from the cannon at
the top of the hill. In a few seconds the band had passed, and
then the heroes of the day were close to the anxious gazers.
First came six of the Garde Mobile of Paris ; they were natives
of the town, who had distinguished themselves in the contests
in the streets, and had received ten days' leave of absence to
conduct their townsmen to their homes. They were all mere
lads, but they had fought, and fought well. One, in particular,
had greatly distinguished himself. A year before, he had been

the ill-used apprentice of a hair-dresser, from whom he had run away ; he was now returning, hailed as a hero, with a laurel wreath hanging from his bayonet. All the muskets of the Garde Mobile were thus adorned with wreaths, while those of the volunteers had a nosegay and a branch of laurel stuck in their barrels. All these passed rapidly by, having barely time to return a glance or a nod to the vivas and waving of handkerchiefs of their fair friends. Behind them followed the rest of the local troops, and then came the rush of the crowd to get a place in the Place Valhubert, where the volunteers were to be mustered and addressed before being dismissed.

Such an opportunity for a little theatrical display was not likely to be lost by the officials. It was done, and well done ; for there are no people in the world who do this better than the French. The people were paraded and praised in a neatly-turned speech by one ; they were re-praised and re-paraded by a second ; and a third received back their flag, and gave them yet another laudatory oration, and then they were dismissed ; and though, to our colder natures, so much parade and praise may look like braggadocio and nonsense, it is well judged in France ; for, once dismissed, the embracing was endless. There was not a gamin in the streets, when he saw the laurel wreaths, that did not wish to enlist in the Garde Mobile ; nor a single National Guard who was not ready to march to the devil, instead of to Paris, in the hope of being so paraded, so praised, and so kissed on his return. As for the Garde Mobile, their only difficulty was how to meet the innumerable invitations that poured on them from every side. Poor boys ! if they could march to Paris, it was more than they could do to go to bed. Some slept where they supped ; others were carried shoulder high to their quarters by men not much more sober than themselves ; thus making another escape for their lives, seeing that it is a question which was the greater danger, a shot from an insurgent in Paris, or a fall on the pavement from the shoulders of their friends at home.

The morning after their arrival came an order for a funeral mass in all the churches in France, which was to be celebrated in honour of those who had fallen in defence of the government. This order was proclaimed through the streets by the drum. The day following, Cross's servant brought him a scrap of paper, which looked very like the little dirty butcher's bills which were weekly laid on his table ; but on examination it proved to be an invitation to attend the funeral procession and service ; the parties to meet at the préfecture, and march in form to the church of St. Gervais, where the ceremony of the funeral mass was to be celebrated. Never having seen anything of the sort, Cross hastened to don a suit of black, stuck a sprig of cypress in his button-hole, and walked off to the place of meeting.

At the door he was met by the dignitaries, dressed in black and wearing scarfs of tricoloured silk either over the shoulder or round the waist. It is wonderful what a number of office-bearers there are in every French town; all were now mustered in full fig, and to each a bow must be given. In the large room another party of officials met him ; these were the professors of the college, with gowns and square black caps. The trencher caps of our own collegiate dignitaries are so odd in the eyes of foreigners, that we have no right to laugh at similar oddities on the heads of the learned in other lands. The inside of the heads of these teachers of youth are so well garnished, we presume, that the outside must be absurdly clothed to mark the difference. More bows, of course, were made to each of these, and it was no easy task to go through them, for, like the civic officials, there seemed to be a preposterous number of professors in proportion to the number of scholars to be taught. Behind the professors were ranged the invited guests, but liberté and égalité were evident, for there stood, side by side, the ancient nobles of the land with the butchers, bakers, and grocers of the town. More bows still, and when Cross's neck was half broken by such constant bending, he at last drew up against the wall to watch the arrival of any other guest. Punctuality is not a French virtue; if so, it was not now practised, for it was after waiting a full hour past the appointed time that the sound of a military band was heard. Immediately afterwards the National Guard marched into view and drew up in front of the door.

A roll of drums gave notice that all was ready. The officials marched off, beginning with the sous-préfet and ending with a junior professor ; the guests followed as they could ; the band struck up " Mourir pour la patrie ;" the cortége moved off, and Cross found himself, with two or three of his countrymen, walking behind the butchers and bakers of the town.

" When we invite foreigners to attend our public ceremonies," said an old general officer to Cross, " we always offer them some place of distinction ; but I suppose they mean this as a compliment, we have seen their backs in action and they are giving us another sight of them."

Cross laughed ; he did think that, for a nation which pretends to be the most polite in the world, it was somewhat odd to allow strangers to be jostled by the riff-raff of the town.

The old General, having vented his spleen, recovered his good humour and marched on, but his equanimity was again rather disturbed when, on entering the church, he found that no seats had been reserved. Every one was seated, except the half dozen English gentlemen who had been invited. After a while a lady made room in her pew for the General ; the rest of the English were obliged to stand, and, as the church was tremendously crowded, and the day intensely hot, this was no joke. Cross was interested in watching the ceremony, and did not therefore so much care for the fatigue, as by standing he had a better opportunity of seeing what was going on.

The first entry into the church was striking to any one who witnessed such a ceremony for the first time. Seats having been reserved near the altar for the dignitaries, the band, and for all the invited guests, except the English, every other corner of the church was crammed with females, among whom might be remarked about a dozen of *old* men. The priests and choristers stood in front, close round the altar, all dressed in their glittering costumes ; a little further off were ranged the boys in white and black dresses, each holding a silver incense-vessel in his hand. The walls round the altar were hung with black festoons, and on it burnt a number of tall wax tapers, and close to the railing stood two highly-gilt antique reading-desks, with large folios open upon them.

As the procession entered the church, the band ceased to play, and the drums struck up a rōw-dōw—rŏw-dŏw-dŏw, all striking at the same moment. The noise on entering the vaulted roof of the church was deafening. They marched on, two and two, opening out into single file as they passed the bier which stood in the centre of the aisle, and joining again when they had passed it. On reaching the altar they filed off to the right and left, and formed lines behind the incense boys, continuing to beat the same rōw-dōw—rŏw-dŏw-dŏw, till the aisles were completely filled by the National Guards. They then gave a roll that made noise enough to bring down the roof of the church, had it not been built of solid materials, and the service began. The first part was impressive, for the beautiful music of the Roman Catholic service, with the sight of so many women seemingly rapt in devotion, must strike every feeling mind with serious thoughts, and Cross, though bred in a simpler and very different form of worship, felt that just respect for the belief of others, which he claimed for himself. As the service advanced, however, two or three circumstances occurred which rather shocked his Calvinistic ideas of propriety. At two or three different periods during the service, the band struck up in full chorus. At first they confined themselves to playing bits from various operas, but afterwards they played waltzes and polkas ; and during this most dancing music one priest was still reading at the desk, two or three more were bowing low from time to time and walking around and across the reader and the altar. This struck him considerably, but he felt still more astonished when the period arrived for the elevation of the

Host. The bell rang first, then resounded the voice of the colonel giving the word of command ; all the soldiers presented arms and knelt on one knee, while the drums struck up a most deafening roll. When the sacrament was taken the drums ceased, the voice of the colonel was again heard, and the soldiers resumed their places. A great number of candles that surrounded the bier were then lit, the priests approached, some prayers were chanted, and the service was over. The dignitaries left their places, and again led the way from the church as they had entered it, followed by the same guests. They re-formed in the front of the church, the sous-préfet at the head, to conclude the ceremony by once more marching in procession through the streets.

"Hang their humbug !" said the old General to Cross, " I have had enough of this ; suppose you and I fall out of the ranks and cut them. Keep this side of the street ; we will pop down the first lane and be off."

" With all my heart," answered Cross ; " for, to own the truth, I am nearly done up by standing so long in such awful heat."

" You may say that," said the General ; "and if a young fellow like you feels it so much, you may judge how I would have suffered if that worthy lady had not made room for me. But here is a fine narrow lane, so give me your arm, and we will cut the concern."

Cross gave his arm, and they entered the narrow lane as the General had proposed ; it was in shade, and when once fairly entered on, they paused to enjoy the refreshing coolness.

" I say, Cross," said the General, " you have been in Italy as well as myself. These Frenchmen do not manage matters so well as the Italians. In Italy, though I thought them a set of blockheads to believe in saints and relics, yet I never went into their churches that I did not feel a respect for them ; but faith, here, with their drums and trumpets, I feel no respect for either priests or people ; and the young men seem to care as little for

C

their priests as I do, for there was not one young fellow present
except those who were obliged to be there on duty."

"I agree with you, General, in thinking that there is far
greater solemnity and decorum in the church service as it is
performed in Italy ; but we have no right to judge by what we
have seen to-day ; neither you nor I have ever seen a public
military funeral in Italy, and therefore we cannot draw a comparison. As for your critique on the absence of young men, I
have made the same remark before. I have frequently gone
into the churches to hear the music at high mass, and have
always been struck by never seeing any of the young men of the
better class at church. You will see a number of the elderly
peasants and a small sprinkling of the young ones, but never
since I have been in this country have I seen a young man in
society at church. If they do go at all, it must be very early in
the morning, or late at night, for I have never seen them there."

Thus talking, they had resumed their walk. Strolling gently
down the lane, they had now reached the end where it opened
into the market-place. The sun was striking hot and bright into
the open space, and they paused again, disliking to face the heat.
In front of them sat a group of the peasant women in their high
caps ; before each was a table on which were spread fruits of
various sorts, and beside them were ranged baskets containing
vegetables. Each woman held over her head a large red umbrella,
which shaded herself and her goods from the force of the sun's
rays ; but the light passing through the umbrella gave colour to
the shade it afforded, tinting cap, table, fruit, and baskets, with
varied shades of red.

"That is very picturesque," said Cross ; " I wish I was a
painter !—what a picture might be made of what is now before
us !—the grouping is so good, and the colouring so rich, both
in brilliancy and shade."

" You don't surely call those caps pretty ?" exclaimed the
General.

"Not pretty, certainly," replied Cross ; " but yet I think

hem picturesque. Individually, I agree in thinking them
rightful, but in groups, those high white cones make beautiful
nes ; and ugly as we may consider them, they have stood a
ood long test, more especially in a country where the fashion
f dress is so often changed. You will see this same cap cut
n the oldest tombstones ; and we know that the wife and
idies of the court of William the Conqueror were thus be-
ecked, and the Icelandic cap has much the same form as some
f these. But you need not fix your eyes entirely on the Nor-
ian cap : there is a group of prettier and quieter head-gears
om other parts of the country now crossing the market-place ;
nd if you look to the left, you may see that line of Granville
ips which the fish-women wear. The reflection of the red
mbrellas on their white turban-like head-dresses is quite
riental ; they, at all events, have the double charm of being
idividually pretty and highly picturesque. And see, there is
ertainly a countryman of ours, who is admiring either the
omen or their wares, for he has been standing staring at them
nce we have been here. He is a new comer, I think—nay,
ow I am certain, for I see the mark by which to recognise a
esh-arrived Johnny Bull ; don't you see he has a Murray under
is arm ? Suppose we go and reconnoitre him, and, at the same
me, see what fish remains unsold."

"By all means," said the General ; and they proceeded to-
ards that part of the market appropriated to the sale of fish.
he stalls were almost cleared, but large slices of skate were
ill hanging over the sides of small tubs ; a few fresh-water fish
nd some red gurnet were lying on the tables, and baskets of
ockles and oysters were standing on the ground. When they
ame near the stall by which the stranger was standing, they
iw that on that table lay a salmon of about fourteen pounds
eight, and the owner was undergoing a cross-examination from
he Englishman as to where it was caught, and when. The
tranger turned when they were close to him ; Cross sprang
orward, and as he seized his hand, exclamations of recognition

and pleasure at meeting were exchanged. The General took his
leave ; but before he went, Cross introduced the stranger as
" my old friend, Mr. Hope."   When the General was gone, a
volley of questions followed from Cross.

"I am so glad to see you, my dear fellow, and the pleasure
is so unexpected. When did you come ? where did you come
from ? where are you staying ? and what the deuce brought you
here ?"

" I may return the compliment," answered Hope, " and say
truly, I am right glad to see you ; and then for your questions
—I will answer them *seriatim*.   I came last night ; I come
from Paris ; I am staying at the inn hard by ; and I have come
here because I saw the name of this town on a large placard at
the Diligence Office, with an intimation that I could come here
in twenty-six hours, on payment of a certain number of francs ;
and here I am.   Now I must ask you one question in return :
Are you settled here ?"

Cross answered in the affirmative.

" Then that decides me," said Hope ; " I too will stay.   The
sight of that salmon had nearly determined me to do so, but
now my mind is quite made up ; for it cannot be a bad place
where a man may catch a salmon now and then, and have an
old friend to talk to.   However, we can talk of our friends and
ourselves by-and-by.   In the meantime I must hear a little
more about this salmon, for I never expected to see such a short
thick fish in France.   A fellow like that would give sport on a
line."

" This one I suspect had no such chance," replied Cross,
" but has been caught in the stake-nets.   Salmon, however, are
often taken in the rivers with the fly.   There are two streams
close to this town, but I have very seldom heard of the salmon
rising in the warm weather.   Early in the season they take very
well.   Just now you must content yourself with fishing for
smaller fry.   Trout, large dace, chub, and bleak, may all be taken
with the fly a few miles up the river ; and if you choose to con-

escend to bait-fishing, you may lie on the grass and pull out
y the dozen the finest gudgeons I ever saw."

"That will do for me," said Hope; "for I am quite contented
ɔ catch any fish, and in any way. I have met men who were
uch epicures in fishing, that they considered it a degradation
ɔ fish for anything but salmon. For my part, I can sit in a
unt and rake for gudgeons when nothing better offers. The
nly difference is, that when I take to a punt on the Thames I
ke to have a paper of sandwiches or a pie, with a bottle of
ine and some iced soda-water for companions. When I fish
or salmon, I only insist on a small flask of whisky or brandy in
ɪy pocket to strengthen my inward man, and drink a pleasant
ɔiling to my captives."

"If that is your feeling," said Cross, "you may do very
ƿell here, for you may have your creature comforts on the grass
s well as in a punt, with this additional gratification, that you
an drink your bottle of champagne for half-a-crown instead of
ɪalf-a-guinea, and if you are bent on higher game, half a day
ƿill take you into Brittany, where the fishing is really good, and
ɔu may drink your brandy and pay for it with sous instead of
ɦillings."

"Bravo!" answered Hope; "I always thought you a pleasant
ellow, but you have risen a hundred per cent in my estimation,
ɔr, to tell you the truth, I was a little low. Driven out of
ʔaris, and too poor to live in London, I was thrown on my
ɹack; but you have set me on my legs so well, that when I
ɪave eaten a bit of that salmon, Cæsar will be himself again!"

"Well, then," said Cross, "you shall eat it with me. I will
ɹuy the half of it, and shew you where and how I get on here,
ɪnd you, in return, shall tell me all your news. Fresh from
ʔaris; you must have much to tell if you were there during all
ɦese late horrors."

"In truth, you may well call them horrors. But I shall
ɹequire some dinner, and a glass of wine, before we speak of
ɦem. Let us stick to salmon and fish just now; we will not

talk of Paris till the evening. First let us get a bit of this fish, then you shall shew me your quarters, and help me to find some for myself, for those I now inhabit are not very clean or comfortable, and I don't like bagmen, above all, French bagmen, for my companions at table. Such a set of ruffians as I met at the table-d'hôte breakfast this morning, reminded me too strongly of the fellows I saw grinning over the barricades, to be pleasant."

"I shall be delighted to help you," said Cross. "I will buy the fish, and we must have a few oysters and cockles for sauce, as there is no chance of getting a lobster to-day."

"Oysters in June!" exclaimed Hope; "did any one ever hear of such an idea? Have they no close-time here?"

"I don't think they have," said Cross, "for you always see oysters every market-day throughout the year, and I eat them as others do, and find them very good. I suspect that those which are now sold are what are cast up by the tide. The women call them *Gite de marée*, which I do not understand, unless it is a corruption of *Huitres de marée*—oysters of the tide. These may be fish that do not breed, and therefore remain good when others are out of season, for the fishermen do not dredge for them during the summer months, yet the markets are always well supplied with those which the girls collect at low tide on the sands, and, as I tell you, I have always found them very eatable."

"That is an advantage," said Hope, "they have here over us in England, and I shall be glad to try them, for an oyster is always a good thing. As you have invited me to dinner, you must let me send you your dish of fish."

"No, no, my good fellow," said Cross, "I am too good a patriot to allow a new comer to buy anything in a Norman market till he knows a little more of the people; why, if you were to try and deal with that old lady you would raise the market for the next six weeks, by giving her what she asked, and thus get yourself into a scrape with me and the rest of your countrymen. So, you must e'en condescend to eat your fish, as well as the rest of your dinner, at my expense to-day."

" As you will," replied Hope ; " I remember you always liked to have your own way, so I will not interfere. Provided I have a bit of that fish I shall not quarrel with the person who procures it."

Cross had a wrangle with the fish-woman, which lasted some five minutes ; bought the salmon and a few dozen of oysters, sent them home to his house, and then took Hope's arm to follow his purchase and show him the way.

" Do you often buy fish in the market?" asked Hope laughing. " You seem to be pretty well up to the trade."

" I do now and then, for fun, take a turn through the market," answered Cross, " and then I buy fish, fruit, or flowers, if I see any that tempt me. I have not lungs to make a practice of it ; I keep a cook, however, who is a Norman, and to hear her speak you would think she was a daughter of Boreas. She buys everything for the house, which is much the best way. She cheats me of course, but in moderation, and allows no one else to do so, which I consider being in a very comfortable position. You remember the story of Lord Grey and his Greek courier?"

" No," said Hope, " I don't remember it."

" Why, he said he had found a treasure equal to the Pitt diamond ; and when asked what it was, he answered that he had found a courier who cheated him comfortably. That is exactly my position with my cook, and if you fix yourself here, I hope you may be equally fortunate. But here is my house, to which let me bid you welcome."

The two friends entered the door. Hope examined the house, furniture, and different arrangements, and declared that, though not so gay and smart as a Paris lodging, he thought everything fully as comfortable, and then he asked whether there was any chance of finding the same accommodation for himself. Cross explained that he could show him plenty of houses very

like his own, which he could take with only the bare walls ; the
furnishing must be arranged with another party, who would put
in any quantity of furniture that might be required, charging
rent according to the number and quality of articles supplied.
Hope then inquired if, being a single man, he could not find
some family with whom he might board and lodge ; but Cross
recommended him not to try such a plan, as the loss of temper
he must endure would be but ill repaid by the saving of trouble.
" You may find," he said, " what you want ; but you would be
very uncomfortable in changing all your own habits to suit those
of your host or hostess.   They think their own manners and
customs charming ; you would find them provincial, and think
them detestable.   John Bull is a variety of the genus homo that
has his own ways, and understands the word *comfortable* better
than any other being on earth ; he should therefore always have,
what I advise you to secure, a home of his own.   A very short
time will suffice to get all you want in order, and in the meanwhile I can give you a room and something to eat, which, though
not very splendid, is, at all events, better than your inn.   A kind
welcome must make up for deficiencies."

After some little demur Hope accepted the offer ; and after
drinking a glass of wine and water they sallied forth in search of
a house.   There was no difficulty in finding one, for the panic
caused by the Revolution had driven away most of the English
families.   Hope's arrival was therefore a godsend to the householders and dealers in furniture.   Before six o'clock all his
arrangements were made, on payment of a sum one-third less
than the rent which Cross paid for the same accommodation,
with a promise that everything should be in order in three days.
Hope instantly wrote for his servant to join him, with his plate
and linen ; and then sat down to Cross's snug little dinner, with,
as he said, a feeling of comfort and security which he had not
felt for months.

CHAPTER II.

AFTER dinner Cross began the conversation, being anxious to hear, from an English eye-witness, what he had seen and thought of late events in Paris. Hope was no longer unwilling to speak.

"Tell me," said Cross, "what you felt during all these events; and if the reports are true which we have heard and seen in the newspapers regarding all the horrors which they describe. Is it true, for instance, that the women showed such brutal cruelty in the last outbreak ?"

"Strange to say," answered Hope, "in no newspaper have I seen horrors mentioned such as I have witnessed with my own eyes. I say strange, for, in general, the caterers for the public rather exaggerate than mitigate such deeds. The French, of course, do not like to publish the account of atrocities that are disgraceful to their nation; but I am surprised none of the English newspapers have mentioned one which drove me out of Paris. I was present when an old woman was seized who had been seen actively engaged on one of the barricades. She was searched to discover if she had any cartridges concealed on her person, and from her pocket was taken a handkerchief saturated with blood, which, when opened, was found to contain a number of tongues, eyes, and other parts of the human body, which this monster had cut off with her own hands, from the persons of some unfortunate Gardes Mobile, who were taken at the barricade where she was placed. I tell you, Cross, the expression of that wretch's face, and the contents of her pocket, have never been absent from my mind, night or day, since I saw them. I could not remain in the same town where such demons were loose, for I heard, and I believe, that many other women had acted in the same brutal manner as this fiend. She boasted that with her own hands she had mutilated all the unfortunate lads of the Garde Mobile who were taken prisoners at the barricade where she was stationed, and she had left them to bleed to death. As a great many of their bodies were found thus mangled, I believe the confession to be true. I stood the first outbreak. I saw, it is true, men with the look of fiends ; men, the like of whom I never saw before, and some of my friends who have lived in Paris all their lives knew not from whence they came, though they stream into view in all great commotions of that capital ; but these were men, not women. Their appearance and their deeds of blood did not give that feeling of shuddering horror which that old wretch's pocket gave me. I saw almost an infant shoot a man, and have his own brains blown out for the act ; I heard of one poor devil being tied between two planks, and then sawn in two. I have seen, with my own eyes, hats full of poisoned bullets taken from the insurgents ; indeed, I have got some dozen of these which I can show you. All this I saw, and yet I was unwilling to leave Paris, and give up the house which had cost me so much trouble and expense to put in order. But this old fiend's look I could not endure ; I could not eat, I could not sleep ; the streets seemed to smell like a slaughter-house, and the very moon and stars had a red tinge in my eyes. I could bear it no longer, and I resolved to be off; the only question was, where ? and this doubt, as I tell you, was answered by my accidentally seeing a large placard stuck up at the door of a diligence office, stating that there was such a place as this, which the expenditure of a few hours and a few francs would enable me to reach. I went home, consulted Murray, took my place, and alighted here last night. The sight, this morning, of a fresh-caught salmon cheered me up, for it recalled the memory of young and happy days : and now, thanks to your pleasant company and good dinner, I am myself again, and can think of killing fish, not men."

" And I," said Cross, "am truly glad if I have been of the least use, or comfort, to such an old friend. The only thing that astonishes me, is that you, who used to like the country and country pursuits, should have set yourself down in a great city like Paris ; you were a great lover of flowers, a dabbler in natural history, as well as a sportsman, when I first knew you."

" All true, my dear fellow," answered Hope ; " but I am not rich enough now to do all that I used to do. Sporting I was fain to give up ; but flowers I could still enjoy in the greatest perfection in Paris ; then, for natural history, or other branches of science, if I could not possess the living objects, I could see them preserved in the museum, and I could converse with men who talk well on these subjects ; and, let me tell you, that a clever Frenchman is a very agreeable companion. The most able, and therefore to me the most agreeable, are to be found in the capital. But since I am driven from thence, I shall resume my old ways ; and with your help, I hope to be able again to begin the practical, if I give up the theoretical study of birds, beasts, fishes, and flowers."

" And here," said Cross, " you will have a tolerably good field to practise upon, for, although the birds are not very numerous, there are many different kinds. Animals are scarce, but the variety of fish is considerable, and we are rich in plants and insects."

" To begin with fish, then," said Hope ; " you must tell me about the habits of the salmon here. Are they the same as with us in the North ? when do they begin to run ? when do they spawn ? when does the fry come in ? have you sea-trout and finnocks in any quantity, and at what time do the grilse arrive ? for if they are at all like what they are with us, I may yet get a grilse or two this year, if not a salmon."

" You ask a number of questions," said Cross, " which I will try to answer as best I may ; but in truth it is not easy to

do so, for there is a considerable difference between the seasons
here and at home. In the first place, great quantities of the best
fish come into the rivers in December; the largest shoals of fry,
it is true, arrive at the same time as with us, namely in April,
but they differ in appearance from ours. They have the same
bright silvery belly, but the back, instead of being a greenish
black, is here a dark straw colour, when fresh taken out of the
water, which darkens as they die. I cannot help thinking that
this is a beautiful provision of nature to protect them from their
enemies. The great shoal of fry hang about the foot of the
streams, and these have the light colour on their backs; but
those that go higher up the river are exactly like ours at home.
Now here, the bottom of all the embouchures of the rivers is a
light-coloured sand, and I have asked myself if it be possible
that these fish, like moths, have the power of gaining the colour
of the bed on which they rest and feed. I should wish much
to know if such is the case at any of the English rivers. Generally speaking, in Scotland the mouths of the streams are
gravelly, or where there is sand it is dark in colour, and there
the salmon-fry have dark backs; but here, the tide leaves miles
of river flowing through white sand, and here the salmon-fry
have yellow backs in spring. I say in spring, for, strange to
say, in this country there are two periods when the fry come
into the rivers: the greater quantity, as I have already told you,
arrive at the same time as with us in the North; but there is a
second shoal, which comes in about the last week of October or
beginning of November. I took a considerable number last
November; they were undoubtedly salmon-fry, and they had
dark backs like our own."

"Fish often change colour," said Hope. "I once looked
into a newly-made pond in a public garden in Germany, where
the water was clear and the bottom of various shades. There
was dark mud in some places, and light gravel newly thrown in
at other spots. The pond was full of fish, and I noticed that
whenever one moved from one place to another, he showed

dark or light, as the case might be, against the background, and amongst his fellows ; but after he had rested a while he assumed the shade of the ground on which he rested. Not being a fish, I cannot say whether they did it on purpose or not ; but I suspect the change of shade is in some way produced by light. Dead trouts can have no will in the matter, and they change colour in the most extraordinary way. Sometimes they mark each other ; sometimes a leaf, or the basket, or anything else, marks the skin with a pattern. The dry skin is of a different shade from the wet skin. In short, I suspect that fish change colour for the same reason that men do, whatever that may be. A miner has a pale complexion, a mountaineer has a cheek as brown as his own hills. One is 'bleached,' and the other 'sunburnt,' and men and women can blush and turn pale, sometimes to very good purpose. They get red when they are hot, and icy blue when they are cold, and it may be useful to look blue on blue ice, but all this men generally do without any exercise of their will. At all events, fish change colour, and to very good purpose, for they are harder to see when they take the shade of the bottom ; and so it may be a provision of nature for their protection from the enemies who are provided for their destruction, and who must, in their turn, look out for themselves, or make provision for some other. Think of that, Cross, when you use your wits to tempt a trout with a fly, and then devour him. There is a great deal to be learned before we can give reasons for anything, even for a change of colour in man or fish."

"Did you count the rays on the fins ?" asked Hope.

"I did," replied Cross, "and found them quite correct. They had also the black spot on the gill, and the mark, on which I lay great stress, for ascertaining the difference between the young of the salmon and that of the bull-trout. A practised eye can distinguish a difference in the form, for the fry of the salmon has one easy even swell in the belly, while the fry of the bull-trout is more aldermanic in shape ; he is more pot-bellied, and has a sort of notch under the gills, from which the swell of the belly springs.   To observe this, however, requires, as I said, a practised eye, and requires also that the fish should be examined when fresh taken, for they lose this distinction when they have been dead for any time.   My mark is a much simpler, and, to my mind, a much surer test; it is this : The scale of the young salmon is so tender, it is like the bloom on a plum, which you cannot touch without removing, while the scale on the trout is much firmer.   In taking a salmon-fry off your hook, your hand is silvered over with a substance which is so fine you can hardly see that it is composed of minute scales ; whereas, with a trout, the scale, though it comes off, does so in a much less degree, and you can clearly distinguish that what sticks on your hand are scales.   Put both fish in the water when you have killed them, and you will see the shape of your fingers clearly marked on the salmon in a sort of blue colour, quite free from any shining speck, while on the trout you will find that the scales are only partly removed, and that many still remain adhering to the parts which your fingers have pressed.   I tell you I give great weight to this test, and I tried it and every other I knew, on the fry taken in November, which stood them all ; and therefore I feel confident that they were salmon-fry, and that there are two seasons in France, though but one in Britain, at which salmon must spawn, and fry run.   I do not like to speak positively on this point, for fish are a difficult study ; and it requires close watching for years before being able to affirm decidedly about them ; but now that you are here, we may observe them to-gether, and come to a surer result—two heads being better than one.   As for grilse, I do not believe there is a man in the country that knows the difference between a grilse and a salmon. There are a good many grilse sold about this time of year, and they are all called salmon.   These are taken in the stake-nets, for the salmon, or grilse, will not rise in the hot weather ; and the river is so full of roots of trees that it cannot be fished with nets; which is fortunate, for, if it could, there would not be a fish left in the water."

" Thank you," said Hope, " for your information ; I shall be delighted to assist you in your researches ; but till then, I should not quite wish to leave the river alone. I have seen fish rise well in hot weather if tried after sunset, or just as the sun is rising, and perhaps one of my small gaudy flies might tempt them."

" We may try, at all events," replied Cross ; " but there would really be no use in doing so till we have some rain ; the rivers are too sleepy to afford sport without a fresh in the water, or a stiff breeze."

The friends continued to converse thus for an hour or two, discussing birds, fish, and flowers, but never returning to the painful scenes Hope had witnessed. He was tired and went early to bed, it being arranged that they should try one of the rivers after the first fall of rain ; and that till then they should make little excursions to see the country, and visit the different nursery gardens, to examine the beautiful roses and carnations. for which the place was famed. The weather was too sultry to go far, and Hope wished to superintend the arrangements of his house, so that the next four days were spent chiefly in lounging about the nursery gardens. On the fifth, Hope was installed in his new abode, his servant having arrived with his baggage ; but, by way of welcome, a most tremendous thunderstorm and a deluge of rain burst on the town half an hour after he had taken possession.

" That is an awful flash," said Hope, as a clap of thunder resounded, shaking the house to the foundation. " I hope it will not frighten the fish; for this rain will make a fresh in the river, and we are to try what we can do to-morrow."

" Aye," answered Cross, as he looked out of the window ; " if the rivers are not too large and overflow their banks. When it does rain here, it is no trifle ; we seldom see such torrents in England, though often in Italy."

In the evening the storm ceased, and the two friends went out to take a walk. The town being placed upon a height, they could see that the meadows below, on either side of the river, were under water; while, from being thus situated on a hill, the streets were scoured by the tremendous rain, so that the pavement looked as clean washed as if it had been a Dutch instead of a French town. Cross pointed this out to Hope, saying that he ascribed the great healthiness of the place mainly to this cause; rain in Normandy not being unfrequent, and when it did come, it came with such force that it proved a first-rate scavenger, purifying in a wonderful manner the narrow dirty streets of the older part of the town.

The next morning the day was clear and bright during the early part, but the afternoon was cloudy, and as the river had fallen to nearly its usual size, the two friends dined early, and started, rod in hand, to begin a little above the village of Pont, to fish from thence to the sea-line, and back again. One sea-trout, two common trout, and a few chub were all that rewarded their labours, when they reached a rapid, at the place where the river entered the Grève, a great sandy plain, which is covered by the sea at spring tides, but through which the river continues to wind for miles when the tide is out. On this plain, however, it is not safe to fish, for the sand is so quick in parts that hundreds of people have been lost in attempting to cross it, and never seen again. Here Hope began to fish with great care; he hooked and landed a large sea-trout, and had just raised a fine grilse, when three or four lads, who were watching them from the other side, began to throw handsfull of the white sand into the water, splashing it, and making it white and dirty. Hope remonstrated, and asked the lads to stop, but the only reply was a shout of laughter, and a double quantity of dirt thrown. Three men, who were filling carts with the sand for manure, joined the boys when they heard the noise they made. Hope requested them very politely to stop the boys from doing that which could be no amusement to them, but spoiled his fishing, when one of the men, for answer, jumped into the river, and kicked up the sand with his feet, making the water perfectly

white ; a second cheered on the boys, and a third struck up a
song, the chorus of which was—

> " Sur la France l'Anglais
> Ne regnera jamais "—

in which boys and men joined after the first couplet.

"Come away," said Cross, " we shall do no good now. I
know these fellows ; they are the leaders of all the blackguards
in the place."

" The French themselves make a bad job of ruling France.
I would like to break some of their heads before I go !" exclaimed Hope.

" No doubt of it," replied Cross, "and so should I. You
and I could lick the whole boiling of them ; but if we knocked
one of them down the others would be witnesses against us, and
we should find ourselves to-morrow lodged at the expense of
the Republic, and in quarters that Inspector Hill has never
examined. The Justice of Peace will make no allowance for
any provocation you may receive ; and if you strike a Frenchman before witnesses you are quite sure to see the inside of a
prison. But if we could get them out of sight, and then break
their ribs, they would have no remedy, for no man can be a
witness in his own cause. This I know, for a young countryman of ours enticed a fellow who had been insolent to him into
a stable ; he shut the door and half killed him, and the Frenchman could get no redress for his two black eyes and bloody nose,
because he had no witness. Just now, we know not how many
eyes are looking on, so we may as well go down to that dyke
where there is a deep hole and a bit of a stream."

Hope bit his lip but walked on, as Cross proposed. As they
reached the head of the stream they saw a fish rolling on the
shallow. Hope pulled out a good length of line and cast ; but
as his line fell on the water a stone plunged beside it. The
same boys were close behind them on the other side of the water.
Just as the stone fell, Hope and Cross saw a large fish cross the
shallow and dash into the deep pool.

D

" The scoundrels !" exclaimed Hope, " if that would not try
the patience of Job, I do not know what would."

" I agree with you, and yet we must submit," said Cross,
" for if I knocked one of them on the head with this stone,
there are those three rascals standing by their carts to see what we
do, so we must just grin and bear it.   Our only chance is to go
up the hill a little way ; there is a lane by which we may make
a short cut to the bridge ; and perhaps, now that the sun is low,
we may come better speed up the river than we did in the afternoon."

Hope absolutely ground his teeth, he was so angry ; but he
yielded to his younger companion, and left the river.

" Did you see that fish ?" asked Cross, when they were fairly
in the lane and beyond the sound of the derisive cheers which
their persecutors gave on seeing them walk off.

" To be sure I did," replied Hope ; " and I think I had a
good chance of catching him, if those scoundrels had left us alone."

" Well, if it is any comfort to you, I do not think you had
any chance," said Cross.   " I suspect he was burning from the
lice ; did you not see the white mark on his tail as he passed us ?"

" Yes, I saw it," said Hope, " and knew at once it was either
a wound or the louse mark ; but I have seen fish rise very well
when so marked.   In some of the small rivers in the west of
Scotland, the fish, after a long term of dry weather, are often
marked in that way.   They cannot get into these small rivers
without a spcat, so they lie about the mouths till rain comes ;
if this is long delayed, the lice get so firmly fixed on them, that
they eat a hole on the dorsal fin.   As these torments cannot live
in fresh water more than a few hours, they fall off as soon as the
fish is fairly in the river, and the spot where they have been
looks white in the water.   I daresay it is not very comfortable
for the poor fish ; but still it does not prevent their rising, for I
have caught several so marked in the same day."

" What curious-looking creatures these sea lice are," said
Cross ; " did you ever look at them through a microscope ?"

"Yes, once," replied Hope; "but my instrument was bad. They look like tadpoles, with the heads squeezed flat, and a small hole in the centre of the flat part, just opposite the tail, which, I suppose, is the mouth. These are the animals which drive the salmon out of the sea into the rivers; there is another, which fixes on them in the fresh water and drives them back again into the sea. Did you ever examine these?"

"No," said Cross, "I have not; and though I have looked at a good many kelts, I never saw any lice on them."

"Perhaps you did not look in the right place," returned Hope. "The sea louse fixes on the outside of the fish, and drives him to the river—the river louse, or rather leech, fixes on the inside of the gills, and drives him back to the sea. I have examined these last pretty accurately, and I know they do not live an hour in salt water. The creature is a thin semi-transparent leech, with small bright red rings, alternating with the transparent portions for the whole length of the body. This is their appearance when alive and fixed on the gills of the fish; but when you put a kelt into salt water, they fall off in a very short time, and then they become of a dirty yellow colour. This fact I know, for I once kept a kelt in a tub of salt water for about three hours, and then turned him out. In pouring off the water, some of these yellow creatures caught my eye; I examined them, and found that there were thousands of them in the tub. Not feeling quite sure if they had, or had not, been in the water before I had put the fish in the tub, I repeated the experiment, pouring the water through a sheet by way of filter, and then placed another kelt in the water with the same result. This fish was very sick, for I examined the gills before I put it in the tub, and, I have no doubt, hurt it in so doing; but the result was the same. I saw myriads of these red and white animalcules on the fish at first, and I found them dead and dirty yellow in the water after I let the fish go."

"These two creatures, then," said Cross, "act as flappers to quicken the instinct of the salmon. The first tells him to go to the rivers to breed, the second sends him to recover his strength and flesh by sea-bathing. How do you explain the assertion that is made, that salmon do not eat in the sea, and that nothing is ever found in their stomach when they are caught ?"

"Nothing in the world more simple," said Hope. "A salmon, like many other creatures, vomits when pursued or frightened, on the principle, I suppose, of ' take my money and spare my life.' Did you ever go on a rock where Solan geese were breeding ? It is a very absurd sight, and a case in point. A Solan goose sits with one foot on her single egg. If you approach her, she stands up, still holding her foot on the egg, stretches out her neck, and disgorges the contents of her crop. As soon as you move away, she recovers her property and swallows what she has just put down. A salmon, I know, goes through the first process, for I have seen it done."

"How was that ?" asked Cross.

"I was on the sea in a boat," answered Hope, "rowing, one bright calm day, along some rocks near the mouth of a salmon river, when I spied one of the poaching nets used by the High-landers. To conceal these nets, they use bunches of the large button sea ware instead of corks as floats; but the water was so clear that I saw not only the net, but everything at the bottom of the sea, as clearly as if I had been in a room. We went towards the net, and, in so doing, started a salmon, which dashed into it. I saw the salmon strike and entangle itself, and in a moment begin to vomit a number of tiny herring fry. I could see them quite distinctly, for we were exactly over the fish. I pulled up the net as fast as I could, and in a second the salmon was in the boat. So quick was I, that there were upwards of a dozen of the fry still in his mouth, although he had been ejecting a shower of them as I drew him to the surface. Of course there was nothing in his stomach; but the idea of saying that salmon do not eat is ridiculous. I have myself caught scores with a worm, and thousands are so taken every year, which sufficiently proves that they eat; but when they find themselves fast on a hook or in a net, they disgorge like the Solan goose, or as the salmon did that I have just described, and thus nothing is found in their stomachs when they are opened."

"Your theory, I allow, is good," said Cross, "and what you tell me quite settles the question in my mind. Now, turn to your left and you are at the river again, and as I hope far from our tormentors."

Hope turned, and they reached the river at a bend. He took a few casts, hooked and landed a chub, and continued his way up the stream.

"Where can all these leaves and grass come from?" he asked; "it is very annoying."

Cross pointed a few yards up the river; there stood the same boys, heaving the grass, leaves, and reeds that the flood of the preceding day had left in various cracks in the bank into the water.

"Confound them," exclaimed Hope; "this is really past endurance." He stooped and picked up a large stone.

"Ah-h-h, sacré-é goddam," shouted the boys.

"Take that, you confounded French frog," cried Hope, as he launched the stone with all his force.

The leader put his hand to his shoulder and gave a howl, which proved that both the direction and force had been good. The rest of the boys ran away.

Cross was laughing heartily. "Come along," he said; "we must be off as fast as we can, or we shall have the whole village on our backs. You have settled that fellow for a while."

Hope was quite satisfied with himself, and wound up his line.

"That has done me a world of good," he said. "I do not think I could have slept if I had not had a rap at one of those vermin. My only wonder is that a young fellow like you can bear their insolence."

"Why, to say the truth, I find it difficult," answered Cross.

"I only resist because I know that just now these fellows would have the best of it. It is dangerous at any time in this country to strike a man; at the present moment it would be folly. 'When the pot boils, the scum is on the top,' is an old proverb which is most true in France just now. Even here, in this quiet place, where there are not many blackguards, the magistrates are so afraid of these few, that an Englishman has no chance of justice or fair play should he get into a row with any of them. So we had better step out, for the worst characters in this part of the country are the carters who live in this village, and if we remain we are sure to get into a scrape."

"Discretion is the better part of valour," said Hope; "so come along."

The two friends walked briskly forward for some distance along the banks of the river, and were in the act of turning into a little path that led towards the hill, when Hope suddenly stopped.

"Come along," said Cross. "I see a crowd beginning to gather on the bridge. I have no doubt they are looking after us."

"I cannot help that," replied Hope; "I saw a kingfisher come out of a hole in that high bank, therefore I am sure she has got a nest, and if I am obliged to fight half the town, I must have a look at it."

"Mark the place," said Cross, "and we will come another day; we have got no spade, so we shall only get into a useless row, and see nothing, if we wait now."

"I believe you are right," said Hope, reluctantly; "as we have no spade, we may as well move on, but it is very provoking. I have been all my life hunting after kingfishers' nests, and I have never found but three: one when I was a boy at Eton, one in Northamptonshire, and one in Italy, in a small stream running into the Lago Maggiore. Every one of these nests was different, so that I am most anxious to find another, to ascertain if they always differ in the form or not."

"I hardly think you can prove this now," said Cross, "for so late in the year you are not likely to find a nest, although you may see a bird come out of a hole."

"There you are wrong," answered Hope, "for I found the nest in Northamptonshire in the month of July, and it had five eggs in it. I was fishing for perch with bait, and I saw a kingfisher come out of a hole, as I did just now. I got a spade, dug upwards of a yard into the bank, and found the eggs; for in this instance there was no nest, but only a few very minute white bones, mixed with the earth around them."

"And how did you find the other two nests?" asked Cross, "for you have been more fortunate than I have been. I have seen thousands of kingfishers, and have shot dozens, yet I never found a nest."

"And a great many naturalists are in the same position as yourself," answered Hope. "Some people say that the kingfishers enter their nests below water, but this I doubt. They may perhaps take possession of an old rat's hole, so near the water's edge that in floods the entrance may be under water. Thus the first brood may be sometimes destroyed, and the parent birds may breed a second time, which will account for finding nests with eggs so late in the season, and yet find young birds ready to fly at a much earlier part of the year. If these birds bred twice a year they would be much more numerous than they are, but, being comparatively scarce, I am led to think that they only breed a second time when their first nest is destroyed either by rats or floods. Now, the first nest I ever saw was in the month of May. It was discovered quite by accident. Instead of fishing, I was swimming in the Thames, when I observed one of those beautiful little birds dart out of a hole close to me. I told two of my schoolfellows of my discovery, so we provided ourselves with a landing-net, and next day we went to try and catch the bird as she flew out, but she escaped us then, for we saw her fly away when we were some yards distant from the bank. I suspect that they hear footsteps at a great distance when any one approaches their nest, and that they go at once, which is the reason they are so seldom perceived coming out of their holes. As I tell you, this lady escaped us that day, but as we were resolved to obtain her, one of my companions proposed that we should climb out of our dame's house at night, and at all risks make sure of our prize. Though such an expedition was a sort of high treason against the laws of Dr. Keat and Eton College, the temptation overcame all fears of birch. We agreed to go, and having provided a boat, a landing-net, and a spade, as soon as everybody was in bed we clambered over the garden paling, took our way to the river, got into our boat, and dropped gently down the stream till we came to the bank where the nest was. There the boat was softly pushed to the shore, and the bag of the landing-net was fixed over the mouth of the hole. When this was completed, we no longer cared about keeping silence ; we landed, and began to dig away the bank from above. This work had not continued many minutes when we heard the harsh disagreeable notes of the mother, who had darted from her nest and was screaming in the net, in which she was fairly entangled. The poor bird was soon placed in one of our hats, over the top of which a handkerchief was tied, and she was then deposited in the locker of the skiff, which operation was performed by one of my companions, who got his fingers well bit before it was accomplished. The mother being thus secured, we resumed our digging, which took us so long that day was breaking before we arrived at the nest. We worked very carefully for fear of injuring it, and well worthy was it of our trouble, for when at last we reached it, we saw something that looked like the carved ivory balls that are sent from China. One side only was open, and within were three young birds nearly full fledged. This prize was placed first in a pocket-handkerchief, and then in a hat ; the boat was rowed back to its hiding-place, and we took our way home across the fields, and re-entered our dame's house without discovery ; but we were so delighted with our success, that we were quite prepared to take a flogging without a murmur, had we been missed. I ought to mention, that before we came away we saw in the faint light what we called the ' other old one,' namely, the male kingfisher, flying backwards and forwards before the place we had disturbed, which I remember now, for it convinces me that these birds are greatly attached to their young. We did our best to make up to our captives for the loss of parental care ; the father was not likely to come to them, and the mother killed herself against the cage, before we were out of school that morning, leaving her offspring to our sole care. Whether we took too much, or too little, I don't know, but the whole of them were dead in three days, in spite of all the minnows and prickle-backs that we crammed down their throats. However, in death we did them every honour, for we clubbed our money to pay a certain Mr. Joe Cannon for stuffing them ; the young ones were then replaced in their nest, and the mother was perched by their side, on a bit of root ; and as a mark of maternal tenderness, she had a minnow fixed in her mouth. The nest, in this instance, was very curious and beautiful ; when cleared from the sand that adhered to it, it looked brilliantly white, and, on close examination, it proved to be made of myriads of small fish bones, glued together with a browner substance. It was nearly circular, having only one side open ; the top, bottom, and sides, were all composed of the same substance ; the inside was covered with some of the light sandy soil which surrounded it, and which adhered to the bottom ; the outside was beautifully white, and looked, as I said before, like carved ivory or lace. In the nest which I found in Northamptonshire, I have already told you, there were only eggs ; they were deposited at the end of a hole four feet deep, and were lying on sand, mixed with a few small bones ; and I may mention, by the by, a circumstance which I have never seen remarked by any naturalist—namely, that the shell of these eggs was thinner and more tender than that of any other which I ever saw. There were five eggs in the nest when I found it ; but with all the care I could take, two of them were broken before I reached home."

"You said that you had found three nests," said Cross, "what was the third like?"

"That is just what I am going to tell you," replied Hope. "When I was in Italy, I one day crossed the Lago Maggiore in a boat to see the famous fig orchards. The season of the year you may know by my telling you that the figs were colouring, and had a bluish tint. As I was walking out of one of these orchards, where the trees are said to be of great age, I saw two men, one of whom was carrying a silk flue net without any corks on it. The other had two long poles on his shoulder. I asked them where they were going to fish, and they answered that they were going to catch birds, not fish. I proposed to go with them, to which they agreed; so I followed till we came to a small river with rows of pollard trees and bushes lining either side of it. Here the men stopped, and one of them crossed the stream, taking one end of the net in his hand and drawing it after him. When across, he fastened it to one of the trees on his side, and the man who remained with me did the same to the other end which he had retained. The net thus remained tightly stretched across the river, the bottom just touching the water, the upper edge about four feet and a half above it. The trees and bushes overhanging the stream threw a shade on the spot, so that the net was hardly perceptible at a few yards' distance. When all was thus arranged, the man on my side bade me lie down and hide myself where I could watch what took place. I did so. First, they each took a pole and made a circuit, keeping a good distance from the water, and approaching it again when they had gone about four hundred yards up the stream; then they began to shout and beat the bushes with the poles, advancing rapidly towards me as they did so. Before they had completed half the distance, I saw two or three kingfishers dart past like bullets from a gun, and in the next moment I heard the same harsh screaming notes that had struck my ear on our night-excursion from Eton College. I raised myself and saw the bright green colours of the birds fluttering in the net;

the men still advanced, and then I saw, one after another, the
rapid flight, and black-and-white plumage of about six or seven
water-ouzels, which dashed past me and struck the net as if a
stone had been thrown against it.   These gave but one scream,
and hung quietly in the sort of bag which they had made for
themselves.   The kingfishers continued to struggle and cry till
the men came up, and then the noise of the poor birds was soon
hushed, for the net was loosened on one side and pulled to the
other, and each bird, as it came to hand, was seized, a spike was
stuck into the back of its head, and it was thrown on the ground,
to give one more flutter and die.   The net was then spread on
the ground, each bird was cautiously taken out of the bag he had
made for himself, their ruffled feathers were smoothed, and they
were carefully laid out in a basket.   I asked what use was
made of these birds, and was told that they were valued for
their skins, the kingfishers especially.   The skins of the water-
ouzels were used to line muffs and cloaks, and their flesh was
eaten, but no one ate the kingfishers.   When this first beat was
over, we went on for a quarter of a mile higher up the stream,
where the same process was gone through of hanging the net ;
the men went away as before, and I was again left to watch.   It
was while I was thus lying waiting that I found the third nest.
Before me was a steep bank of red clay, out of which a number
of the roots of the trees were sticking.   Suddenly I thought I
saw something move under one of these roots ; I kept my eye on
the spot, and a second time I felt sure I saw some object.   When
the men began to advance and shout, I was so intent in watching the other bank, that I did not perceive a kingfisher fly past
me ; but I heard his scream when caught, and at the same
moment I saw the brilliant colour of another dart from under the
root, pass me like a flash, and join its screams with those of the
first, for it too was caught in the same snare.   I need not repeat
that the operation, before gone through, of spiking the heads of
the captives, and basketing them, followed ; no mercy was shewn,
and in two minutes after the men had come up, all was over with

the birds that had been taken.   But while this process was going
on I had slipped into the stream and had waded across, nearly
up to my middle ; and sure enough, when I reached the other
side, I saw a small round hole under the root from whence I had
seen the second kingfisher dart.   Spade I had none, but the bank
was composed of a very soft, sandy clay.   One of the men came
across to see what I was doing, and with his knife he made a
sort of spade out of a bit of wood, with which I dug away the
earth, and soon arrived at the nest, for the hole was barely a foot
deep in this instance.   When I reached the nest, I found four
young birds, not long hatched ; there was no use in leaving them,
for I had a certainty that the mother was no longer able to take
any further care of them, seeing that I knew she was safely deposited in my companions' basket ; I therefore dug the nest
carefully out.   It was composed of similar materials to the one I
had found on the banks of the Thames, but the colour was of a
dirty yellow, instead of white, and the form was different, being
round like the nest of the hedge sparrow, except at the back, and
there it rose, with an irregular edge, about two inches higher
than the front.   The bottom, front, and sides were quite hard,
but the part that rose behind was soft, and broke easily under
my fingers when I lifted it from the ground ; but on the next
morning, when I again examined it, I found that what had been
soft the day before was then dry and hard.   I mention all these
circumstances rather at length," continued Hope, " wishing to
draw your attention to them, because from them I have formed
a theory as to the habits of kingfishers, which I believe to be
correct.   Great difference of opinion has existed regarding these
birds, both amongst ancient and modern writers.   The ancients
supposed that the nests were made of foam that would float on
the water.   Modern writers say very little about them, but relate the diversity of formation that has been observed, without
assigning any reason for the difference.   Now, I believe that I
can explain this difference from the observations I have made on
the three nests just described.

" First, the tender quality of the eggs explains their being laid on soft sand. Secondly, I am convinced that the nests are entirely formed from the castings of the birds, for when carefully examined, it will be seen that the whole mass 'is composed of the bones of small fish ; the darker part may be the partially digested scales that are ejected with the bones, and which, when dry, form the cement that glues the whole together. I have no doubt these birds cast like hawks, for during the three days that our young kingfishers lived at Eton, they did so, daily ejecting quids of white, lumpy matter, which at the time, we, in our ignorance, considered as a sign that they were not in good health. We did not then know that hawks cast up the feathers and fur which they swallow with more digestible food, and therefore we did not reason, as I do now, that if hawks eject feathers and fur, kingfishers may do the same by the bones they swallow. But to go on : The nest which I found with eggs, was no nest at all. Bewick, I think, describes one that he saw having six eggs, which had a nest, but he does not say whether these eggs had been sat upon, or were fresh laid. The eggs I found were perfectly fresh, and there were only five of them ; now, if six is the number they generally lay, my birds had not finished laying. If the eggs referred to by Mr. Bewick had been sat upon, the theory I have formed, and which I am going to tell you, remains correct. It is this—that these birds take possession of a hole in which they deposit their delicate eggs, and gradually raise a nest around them by their castings. If I remember rightly, Bewick describes the nest he saw as being round and flat, like that of a chaffinch ; now, if these eggs had been sat upon, there would have been from eighteen to twenty-one days, during which time the castings of the parent birds might have accumulated sufficient material to build such a nest as he describes. The nest I saw in Italy was deeper than this of Mr. Bewick's, and there was the commencement of the wall at the back ; but then, be it remembered, the birds were hatched, and must have been so for some days. The difference in the size of that nest may therefore be explained by the greater quantity of castings accumulated during that time, not only from the parents, but also from the young brood ; and this idea is confirmed by remembering what I told you of the first nest which I saw on the banks of the Thames. There the birds were nearly ready to fly, and there the habitation was nearly round, which may be accounted for by the building up of the great increase of castings which must have been deposited during the time these older birds were growing to maturity. Tell me now, what do you think of this theory ?"

" Why," replied Cross, " it seems to be a very probable solution of a doubtful question, and it will certainly give a fresh zest to my search for nests."

" You may be more fortunate in that respect than I have been," said Hope, " if you take as much trouble ; but do you know, it is upwards of twenty years since I found the last nest, and I have never been near a river which kingfishers frequent that I have not watched them for hours, both early and late, and yet I have never been able to see any other go into a hole. They have the cunning of Old Nick, and always contrive to evade my sight. Indeed I cannot help thinking that they do not always confine themselves to building on the banks of rivers, for I watched for many days a pair that came to fish at a small rapid. I saw these birds catch their fish and fly away with them in their mouths. Instead of following the river, they always flew across a field. I observed that in their flight they invariably passed close by a hollow ash tree, and after that I lost sight of them. I hid myself in the hedge near this tree ; the first day they came close by me ; I know not whether I was seen or not, but they turned round the tree and flew straight back to the river, and though I went there several times afterwards, I never got another glimpse of them."

" You marked well the place whence the bird came just now ?" asked Cross.

" Exactly," answered Hope.

" Well, to-morrow, or next day, we will dig it out," said Cross ; " it will give me great pleasure to assist you in your researches ; and if you require any further examples, we can watch them in the river to the north of this ; they are more numerous there, and the fishing is better there also, only the people are more troublesome, and we have further to go. Have you seen many of these birds in Scotland ?"

" No," replied Hope, " not many ; but I have seen one or two at a time in several places. I have seen them in the Tyne, in the Findhorn, and in various parts of the West Highlands. A pair, for two years, frequented a pond in a garden in one of the Western Isles ; but, apparently, they never bred, for only one pair were ever seen, and at the end of the second year they vanished."

" I never," said Cross, " saw the nets used in the way you describe, but I have seen something of the sort done for catching woodcocks. If our poachers knew the plan, they might spoil many a good day's shooting. The way I saw it done was this : A net, such as you describe, was hoisted up and suspended between two trees, in a narrow ride in one of the large woods near Ostia. Just as the sun was setting, one man remained concealed at the foot of one of the trees, holding a line in his hand by which he could hoist or lower the net at pleasure ; two other men with dogs then went to a distance, and beat the wood very quietly. This set all the woodcocks in motion, and as it was flitting time, when once on the wing, they flew about, dashing up one opening and darting down another. If they chanced to enter the ride, where we were posted, they were sure to be taken, for they seemed never to see the net, but went headlong into it. Whenever they became entangled, they made a great noise, which struck me as remarkable ; for when shot, woodcocks die without a sound ; even when caught by a dog they give no cry, but in the net they invariably did so. The man who held the line always allowed them to scream and struggle for a while before lowering the net to wring the birds' necks. I asked him his reason for so doing, and he told me that these cries alarmed the other birds, and prevented their alighting to feed, and that, as they flew about to see where the danger was, they were pretty sure to pass into the ride where he was waiting for them. I can only say that the plan was very successful, for I saw nine taken in the hour that I remained to watch the process."

"I have heard," said Hope, "that pigeons are caught in this way also, but I never had the luck to see how it was done. I am sure, however, that great quantities of wood-pigeons might be taken any night in autumn, in our woods, by merely hanging a net across some of the openings or rides at sunset."

"I am sure they might," answered Cross; "but it was not wood-pigeons, but a sort of turtle-doves that I saw caught in Italy. I was present on two occasions when an immense number were killed. The method was much the same in both instances, but the situation was different. The first was in a large wood near Florence; a net was hung across a road in the wood which ran nearly north and south. In two high trees near this road stages were raised from which the whole country could be commanded, and in these stages boys were hid, having with them several stuffed imitations of birds with their wings out-spread. These were made with a weight towards the head, and had a string, about a yard long, fastened to the tail. This string the boy held in his hand, and whenever a flock of pigeons was seen in the distance, he whirled the lure round his head and cast it towards the net; the string acted like a sling, enabling the boy to throw the lure to a great distance, the weight in the head making it fly straight forward like a shuttlecock. If the lure was seen by a flock of pigeons, they were sure to turn towards it; if they did not turn, it was because that the first cast had not been seen, and the same boy threw a second or a third time till the birds came towards them. The second boy always remained still until the flock were quite close, then he also threw a lure straight towards the net. The art consisted in judging the proper moment when to throw, in throwing in the right direction, and without being seen himself; for when this was well done, the whole flock were sure to go headlong into the trap. On the first occasion, I saw many hundreds taken; on the second, there was nearly a cart-load killed; as I told you, the method was different, in so far that the place chosen was a narrow valley to the south of Naples. There were several boys and men employed in casting lures, who concealed themselves in small huts built of turf. The head man threw the last lure with great skill. The net was suspended between two rocks, and I saw upwards of a hundred pigeons fluttering in it at the same moment."

"I should like to see that for once," said Hope, "but it must be sad butchery. These Italians are most ingenious in their method of catching every sort of bird; the quantity of quails they take in the long nets which they set along the coast is quite surprising."

"I never saw that done," said Cross, "but, on one occasion, I saw the quails arriving, absolutely alighting in the town of Naples, so exhausted that they might have been knocked down with a stick; indeed I did catch two or three with my hat on the rocks by the Castel dell'Ovo."

"They do not kill the quails as they catch them," said Hope; "they put them into long narrow boxes, and feed them on hemp and other seeds till they are fat. They are such pugnacious little rascals, that they give them no space to turn or move; as they fatten, they draw up a slide, giving an inch or two at a time, to allow for the expansion of flesh, but no more; for if any one bird could turn, he would instantly kill his neighbour. You know that the Chinese fight quails in the same way that they used to fight game-cocks in England not long ago."

"I am aware of that," replied Cross, "but I wished you to tell me what sort of net was used for catching them in Italy."

"Simple enough," answered Hope. "The net is about a yard

E

deep, but of great length; the bottom of this is pegged to the
sand, close to the edge of the sea ; the top is hung on small
notches cut in sticks, about two feet and a half long, which are
stuck upright about a foot before the net, and about three yards
apart.   When the net is set, it is thus made to stand up, being
suspended on these sticks ; but as the upper part rests only on
the notches, a very slight blow knocks it off, and then it falls
on the sand, covering with its meshes whatever chanced to
strike it.   I remember once lying for hours among some sea-
ware, watching one of these snares ; at every moment I saw the
little jerk, and then a portion of the net fall ; but I never could
distinguish the birds, they flew so fast and so close to the water.
I never perceived one till I followed the proprietor and saw him
put his hand under the net at every place where it had fallen,
lift up a quail and deposit it in a large hollow gourd that he
carried instead of a basket, and then hang the net again on the
notch in the stick.   The net of which I speak was more than
half a mile long, and the owner spent the whole day in walking
gently from one end of it to the other, gathering the birds, and
as he reached each end he emptied his gourd into a number of
long narrow boxes with canvas tops and fronts, which were
ranged in readiness.   All the boxes were provided with seed
and water-troughs, and the Padrone told me that if the canvas
front was shut down, so as to prevent the birds from looking
about, they were such bold little fellows, that they would eat
and drink freely ten minutes after they were taken."

"That method of snaring," said Cross, "is simple enough,
but it can only be practised where the birds arrive in the great
flights like those which alight on the Italian coast.   There are
considerable flights in the southern coasts of France; but in
this part of the country there are only a few bevies.   I have,
however, seen here some large flocks of pigeons that resemble
very closely those in Italy, only that they appear smaller.
They are called La Tourterelle.   A great number of these breed
in England.   They leave our shores about the end of August,

but they remain much later here, for I saw several large flocks
going in a south-eastern direction in the last week of October.

"You mentioned just now that the Chinese spent their
time and lost their money in fighting quails; here the little
blackguard boys gamble by fighting stag-beetles. These creatures
fight like fury, tearing each other to pieces; and you need not
be surprised if some day you find one thrown on you by some
of the gamins : it has been done to myself and some others of
our country men and women. If a stag-beetle gives you a pinch,
it is no trifle, for I never saw such large ones as there are here,
and this year they are very numerous. You may see and hear
scores of them whirring past you every evening. But here we
are at the road ; turn to your left ; we will go by the steep
path ; it is shorter, and we have less chance of meeting any of
the blackguards who may have followed us from Pont Gilbert."

"Shew the way," replied Hope, "and I will follow."

Cross turned into a narrow path that wound up the steep
face of the hill on which the town was built. Trees and shrubs
had fixed their roots in the crevices of the rock and shallow soil,
gaining sufficient nourishment to grow to such a size as to shade
the path and mask the view. They did not take many minutes
to reach the top, where, being free from shrubs and above the
trees, a most extensive prospect opened before them. Hope was
delighted with the scene, and not sorry to pause and admire it ;
for although the ascent had not been long, it was very steep,
and quite sufficient to make a pause agreeable to a gentleman
who had spent so many months in the idleness of a Paris life.
Once on the top, therefore, they paused to breathe and look
about them.

"It is a beautiful view," observed Hope, whenever he had
recovered breath enough to speak.

"It is indeed," said Cross ; "and I am not sorry that we are
now here to contemplate it, instead of being down there," and
he pointed to the river.

"I see," said Hope, and he counted seventeen men and four

boys who were returning towards the bridge; "do you think those fellows have been looking after us ?"

"Not a doubt of it," answered Cross ; "and before we go down there again, we must make peace with those vagabonds. I know two of them ; one is the postman, the other a shoemaker, and as they are the strongest men and good-tempered fellows, though great blackguards, I will give them a few fish-hooks and a franc or two to make them keep the rest in order : till that is done, we must not repeat our visit to the river."

"I have no patience with you," exclaimed Hope ; "knuckling down to these scum of the earth is too revolting. I would much rather get two or three of our countrymen, and see if they dare touch us."

"Revolting enough, undoubtedly," answered Cross ; "but remember the good old proverb, 'It is better to flatter than fight with a fool.' If Louis Philippe had followed this plan, he would still have been on the throne of France : and suppose we did lick these fellows, as I allow we might do, they would only revenge themselves on the first of our countrymen or countrywomen whom they found alone. No, no ; I am all for making a friend of the shoemaker by getting him drunk, and leaving him to settle with his companions. I tried the soothing system at Ducey with great success, although they were all on fire there against us, merely because an Englishman was present when a nice, half-cracked young Irishman chose to fire a pistol at a set of scamps who were throwing leaves and dirt into the river to spoil his fishing, just as they did to you to-day. I believe they thought he was English, but he astonished them by blazing right into the middle of his tormentors. They ran away, but we got the blame, and no one could go near the place afterwards without being robbed and insulted, until I bethought me to order some wine from a radical wine-seller, who was the leader of all the rows ; and since then, I am privileged to go there in peace, though the war still holds good against Englishmen in general."

" Well, perhaps you are right," said Hope, " and I give you credit for your judgment and temper ; so if this river is closed against us for a while, you must shew me the other, and introduce me to your friend. Just now, I may console myself for being driven away from my sport by looking about me while there is light enough to admire this view, which is certainly very beautiful, with the purple tint falling on that immense extent of rich wooded country ; and with this pretty garden which we overlook as a foreground, the picture is really charming. What thousands of roses they have ! I am not quite sure that I admire the square patches in which they are planted, though thus crowding them together enables you to compare the many different colours and shades of colours that are mingled side by side. I see a number of children moving about among the beds. Are they gathering flowers for bouquets ?"

Cross watched the children for a moment ; each carried a bag, and they were carefully examining every separate flower, and picking something from them which they put into these bags.

" No, no," he replied. " They are not pulling the flowers ; they are preserving them, and their occupation is rather a curious one, for it serves a double purpose. These children are employed in at once saving these beautiful roses from destruction, and preparing food for the ducks that they rear. There is here a small beetle, not the rose-beetle of England, the Cetonia aurata, but one of the cockchafer tribe, that attacks the roses and devours them. At times they come in such quantities that they would not leave a rose or a hollyhock untouched, these being the two flowers they principally destroy. Ducks are very fond of these insects and grow very fat and large by eating them. Gardeners, therefore, generally rear a brood or two of ducks, and their children collect the beetles to give to them. If a gardener has no ducks of his own, or no children, he allows any whom he knows to be careful to come and gather them, and there are always plenty anxious to avail themselves of that per-

mission. The children you see are thus employed. You may
see more boys shaking the trees and picking up something from
the ground ; they are collecting the common cockchafer, which
they use for the same purpose ; the ducks eat them most greedily,
and grow very fat on them ; but when fed on the common cockchafer, that food gives a strong smell and disagreeable flavour to
their flesh ; so much so, that no one will buy the birds till they
have been kept for some time after on boiled buckwheat or
other grain, which purifies them. The smaller sort of beetles,
however, that these children are gathering from the roses, fatten
the ducks without giving them a bad smell or flavour, and therefore they are at a premium and eagerly sought for. Feeding
ducks on cockchafers is said to make them lay a great number
of eggs. It might be well, therefore, if the plan were introduced
into England for feeding the breeding birds of our cottagers. I
own I should not like to eat one fed on such nasty food, even
if it should not give a bad taste to the flesh ; but for breeding
birds, and to increase the supply of eggs, I think the system
would be highly advantageous to our poor. In the neighbourhood of Windsor, for instance, I have seen such quantities of
these insects that I could have filled a large sack in an hour or
two. Here, the practice of seeking them is universal ; there is
not a garden or a public walk where children are allowed to go,
that you may not see them, bag in hand, shaking the trees, and
gathering the cockchafers as they fall."

"Your hint may class with the *utile*, though not exactly with
the *dulce*," said Hope ; "therefore I shall remember it. But
look ; can you tell me what bird that is ? I thought at first it
was a robin of some strange variety ; but now I see it is not
one. The red on the breast is darker, and there is a yellowish
colour on the side ; the bird, too, is smaller and more slender in
the form, and there is a white line on the edge of the tail. See,
there are two ; and they have some young ones following."

"Ah !" answered Cross, " I am glad you have pointed it out,
and that I can repay you for your information regarding the

kingfishers. That little bird is very scarce in England, and not
very common here. I have seen it several times, however, in
this part of the country, and in great numbers in the south.
Bewick calls it the Dartford Warbler, and Buffon the Pittechou.
It has a very pretty note, and, like the robin, it gives the sign
of fine weather by sitting on the highest twig of a bush and
singing, when rain has ceased and the day is clearing up."

"They are very pretty birds," said Hope, "and I am afraid I
am barbarian enough to wish to kill a couple for the sake of their
skins, as I have never seen one of them before, either dead or
alive. But they are going to roost, and we may as well go home,
as the light is failing fast."

Cross assented to this proposition, so they bent their steps
towards the town. They had not gone far along the first street
when they heard the rattle of a carriage behind them. They
drew to one side to allow it to pass. When the conveyance
overtook them, the driver pulled up, and hailed Cross by his
name. Hope then saw that two of his countrymen occupied a
sort of half gig, half cart, in which he observed some fishing-
rods and baskets.

"What sport?" asked the driver, whose tongue announced
him to be an Irishman, and whose breadth of shoulders marked
him as a most useful friend in a row.

"Very little," answered Cross, "but it might have been
better;" and he then, in a few words, related their adventure.

The Irishman burst out laughing.

"By the holy poker," he exclaimed, "we have had just such
another turn up with the blackguards. We went about four
miles above Ducey last night—we had good sport there—and
again this morning, and nobody disturbed us; but this afternoon,
two chaps thought proper to molest me just when the trout
were rising. Well, one of them got hold of my rod and broke
it, for which I knocked him down, and threw his friend into
the river; upon which they walked off, swearing like blue
blazes, and I set to work to splice my rod. It was rather a long

job, and I had hardly finished it when our landlord, an honest
fellow, came down to beg us to be off as fast as we could, for
the two blackguards were raising the country, and that we
should be murdered. We refused at first ; but then he changed
his tune, and declared that the people would burn his house for
giving us shelter, and he really seemed in such a fright that we
agreed to go. He had brought our gig and traps to the road,
hard by, so we forthwith put up our tackle and started, and faith,
none too soon, for we saw forty or fifty fellows, with pitch-forks
and scythes, coming down the road headed by our acquaintances.
We met four or five more going to join them, who did not
venture to stop us, but contented themselves with sending a
volley of stones after us when we had passed. Fortunately
they were precious bad shots, for none of them touched us. I
just gave them a bit of my mind and drove off, as I thought
fifty to two, without mentioning pitch-forks and scythes, was
rather too long odds to be pleasant."

"Were you trespassing on those people's land, that they
molested you ?" asked Hope.

"Their ground !" exclaimed the Irishman ; " they never had
a shovelful of land among the whole boiling ! why, the river is
government property, and I have leave from every proprietor on
both sides of the stream. It is nothing but dirty jealousy ; the
blackguards cannot make or throw a fly themselves, and they
can't bear to see a man that can. If there was law or justice,
no man would be allowed to molest a gentleman when he is
amusing himself with a quiet day's fishing, and hurting nobody.
If they had any civility, they would not come fifty to one, on a
stranger, who had mastered two of them already."

"I am sorry for this," said Cross ; "for now it is quite impossible for us to see this river."

"Take some of our fish, then," said the Irishman ; " if you
cannot see the river, you may as well taste what comes out of it,
and we have far more than we can use ; we have nearly four
dozen of trout, besides dace and gudgeon."

Cross accepted the offer, for he was anxious that Hope should see the sort of fish which the river afforded. A dozen trout and as many gudgeons were therefore put into his basket, and the two parties separated.

The fish were produced at dinner ; they were well shaped and handsome in appearance, but soft and not well flavoured.

" Well, it is a bore," said Hope, " being prevented from fishing any of the rivers ; but in the eating way, we suffer no loss, for I cannot say much for the quality of these trout for the table."

" In the spring," said Cross, " they are excellent, and by that time we must hope that something like order will be restored to the country. In the meanwhile, we must go some distance for a day's fishing, or find some other way of passing our time."

" Is there no sea-fishing ?" asked Hope ; " I should like much to know something of the coast, and the produce of the sea hereabouts. We may find some other curiosity, besides that of oysters being in season all the year round."

" I will make inquiries," answered Cross ; " but for a few days we must content ourselves with looking at the country, or watching some of the birds or insects. If you care for entomology, this part of France is tolerably rich in insects. Among other things, there is a great variety of dragon-flies ; I killed one the other day, that I never saw before, it had a death's head, and a body as thick as my little finger."

The friends continued thus to converse on various subjects, till it was time to retire to bed. Two days after their adventure, armed with a spade, they returned to the river, with the intention of digging out the kingfisher's nest. The hole was situated very near the water, and had a high bank of soft sand above. They commenced to try to undermine it, but the sand was so soft, that after making a hole, less than a foot deep, the bank from above rolled down, bringing several tons weight of earth, which nearly fell upon them. Nothing daunted, they again resumed their exertions, but had not proceeded long, when they heard the voice of a man remonstrating in no measured terms. Cross turned at the sound and recognised a small farmer, a dealer in butter, to whom the land belonged. To him Cross explained the object of their labours, and the farmer very good-humouredly replied, that the search might be extremely interesting to them, but ruinous to him, for he found it difficult enough, as it was, to prevent the river from carrying away his land, and that if they seconded its encroaches by continuing to dig, the first flood would cause him great damages. The man spoke with so much good temper, that both Cross and Hope at once felt the propriety of yielding to his remonstrance by abandoning their work.

"It is a confounded bore!" said Hope, as he walked off. "It seems as if there was a charm against my ever being able to prove or disprove my theory regarding kingfishers' nests!"

CHAPTER III.

" What say you to a trip to Carolles ?" said Cross, entering the room where Hope was sitting. " We can find very good quarters, as there is a tolerable cabaret, where they have a table-d'hôte, at which you may dine at two o'clock ; they will give us a bit of dinner very comfortably at a later hour should we prefer it, or if you would like to be still more quiet, there are several houses wherein you may have rooms, and the mistress will cook for us. The houses are not quite such as you would expect to find in an English bathing-place, yet still, many of the best French families go to Carolles and to the other fishing villages along the coast, and rough it for a few weeks for the benefit of sea-bathing. I mention Carolles in preference to any other village, because it is within easy distance of the Mare de Bouillon, where there is very fair trout-fishing, and as you wish to learn the method of fishing on this coast, you will be able to see the different modes of sea-fishing, and also get a few days' whipping at the river, or on the lake."

" By all means let us go," said Hope ; " how shall we go, and what things should we take with us ? It is exactly what I wished to see. You young fellows don't care for your comforts, but I am old enough now to like to get a good bed and a good dinner, as well as good sport, and by your description I shall get all of these at Carolles. I am very anxious to see the manners and customs of the population on this part of the coast, so when shall we start, and how ?"

" Why, for the when, I say to-morrow, for it is full moon

the day after, and there is little or no fishing here except at spring tides ; if we start to-morrow, you will be able to see the coast fishing for three or four days, which should be ample time to satisfy your curiosity ; and as to the how, I will secure a covered cabriolet and a horse, with a lad to take care of the beast and drive us. You can take with you all the clothes you require, and as you like your comforts, there can be no harm in taking a few bottles of wine and a pie. Good brandy you can always get, and cider in these little villages is always better than in the larger places, for they never put any water into it in the country, which they always do in the towns. These liquors satisfy me, but we may take a few bottles of good wine for a treat. As for eating, there are ducks, chickens, and eggs in every house, mutton, and of the best, is to be got now and then, and they always have bacon, which, when new, is excellent, though I allow it is rancid when kept for any length of time, and at this season fruit and vegetables are so abundant and so good that you may feast like an alderman, even without the fish which we may catch or buy."

"Bravo ! that will do ; you shall be Commissary-General ; and, let me tell you, I have always considered the commissariat as a highly honourable portion of the military service, for judging by myself, I am sure I should never fight well on short commons. I shall therefore leave all to your guidance ; name your hour, and I shall be ready to a moment."

"At eight, then, we shall start, for although we have not far to go, the roads are execrable, and it is as well to have a long day before us to ensure finding good quarters, and getting everything in order before night ; and as we pass through St. Jean de Thomas, we may as well spend an hour or two there, to see that village and the country round it."

"I like your plan amazingly, so, while you make arrangements for the journey, I will look over the tackle, and choose a couple of rods ; but as there is no use in taking more than we want, you must tell me what sort of flies to select."

" Why, for flies, I am as much in the dark as you are, for the natives rarely use them, they almost always fish with worms or maggots ; but you can never go far wrong in trusting to black and red palmers. Of these you have a goodly stock of all sizes in your trout book. By taking that book and a couple of fifteen-feet rods, we shall be able to do something. I will take a few small gaudy sea-trout flies, as I hear that a Frenchman had a very good day's sport with them last week ; so now, good-bye till dinner-time."

At dinner the two friends met again. Cross reported that the conveyance was ordered and the supplies prepared ; and Hope shewed his fishing-basket and rods properly packed, with fly-hooks, reels, and lines in the basket, and the preparation he seldom neglected for the creature comforts, namely, a flask with a sliding cup, and a sandwich-box, which resembled and was worn like a cartridge-box.

Upon the principle of victualling the garrison, a regular Scotch breakfast was prepared, and next morning, at eight to a minute, the carriage drove up to the door. It was a cabriolet with a hood, with very long shafts, and very large wheels ; it was drawn by a little black stallion, not above fourteen hands high, and from the length of the shafts and the height of the wheels, he looked much smaller than he really was ; the driver, a sharp-looking boy of twelve years old, was seated on a bit of board at the foot of the apron, with one foot resting on each shaft. He came up to the door at a rattling trot, and sprung from his seat as he pulled up, giving a familiar nod to the gentlemen at the window.

The carpet-bags were tossed into a sort of case on the top of the hood, and a leather cover buckled over them ; the bottles and a large pie, with sundry smaller articles, were packed below the seat, and the driver with another nod and grin announced that all was ready, and summoned the party to take their places.

When Hope came down to the door the diminutive appearance

of the horse struck him more forcibly than when he had seen
it from the window.

"Surely," he said, "you don't mean to tell me that this
wretched little beast is able to take us over twelve miles of such
roads as you have been describing."

"No fear of him," answered Cross, "he would go three
times the distance without being tired, as you will see, and as
for bad roads he is accustomed to them, and will go through
places that would puzzle our fine English horses. You must be
quite aware that a Scotch Highland pony will carry you safely
through a moor in his native country, where an English blood
horse would be either stuck fast or smothered in the first ten
minutes. So it is with the horses in this country ; the main
roads are in general excellent, but the cross ones are disgraceful
to a civilized land. My little friend here is well accustomed to
them, not only here but also in Brittany, where they are even
worse than those we shall see to-day ; you can ask the boy
when we start, for a description of the roads in Brittany ; he is
an intelligent little fellow, and can give you a very tolerable
description of the country ; but don't let us waste time.
Jump in."

Hope clambered round the wheel into the cabriolet, the boy
holding down the end of the shaft and whistling to his horse.
Cross followed and seated himself by his friend's side, and then
the boy gave another whistle, and let go the end of the shaft,
which immediately rose up in a line with the horse's ears, and
the cabriolet was only prevented from falling back with its load
by the broad leather strap that passed under the horse's belly.

"This will never do," said Hope, "we shall be over in five
minutes, for if we get a jerk going up hill we shall lift that
little brute off his legs."

"No fear," answered Cross ; "wait till the boy is up and you
will see that we make a splendid balance."

The boy sprang up, clawed up the reins, which were tied by
a leather thong to the apron, gave a sort of squeal and cracked

his whip, and the little horse dashed off at good ten miles an
hour; the cabriolet, when he was in his place, was so justly
balanced, that a very few pounds' weight on the end of the
shaft would turn it either up or down.

"There," said Cross; "didn't I tell you how it would be.
To do the French justice, there are no people in the world who
understand loading a pair of wheels as well as they do. Their
carriages in country places are abominable things to look at, but
the large wheels and the way they are hung enable them to
carry greater weights than we can contrive to stow on our
smarter conveyances. Their horses also are much better than
they look, but they are shamefully used, for, generally speaking,
the French are not good to their beasts; often, indeed, they
treat them so brutally that I wish some French Martin of Gal-
way would spring up and bring in a bill for the prevention of
cruelty to animals; even my little friend here, who is an exception to the general rule, and who really takes great care of
his horse, will, before the day is over, swear every oath and call
him every abusive name that you can find in the French
language."

As Cross said this, the lad turned down a narrow steep lane,
just wide enough to admit the wheels of the carriage, wretchedly
paved with round uneven stones, and with a gutter in the middle,
down which the horse skated at the same rapid pace.

"Where the deuce are you going? go gently," said Hope.

"Don't be afraid," said the boy; "it's the shortest way, and
Noir never falls."

Just as he spoke, the horse slid for a yard or two, but kept
his legs like a cat; the boy, however, to prove the truth of
what Cross had just said, immediately began a string of oaths,
in which "sacré," "cochon," and "br-r-r-i-gand," were frequently
heard. This continued till they had reached the bottom of the
lane, making three very sharp turns before they regained the
broad highway. Once more on the smooth road, the boy began
to squeal and whistle to his beast, calling him by names of

affection ; then cracking his whip, he turned and looked back
to his passengers, saying with a grin—

"Is he not a good beast my horse ?"

"He seems so," answered Hope ; "but you have a good way
to go, and you must not press him so hard."

"It is all down hill for the next mile, and we must make
the most of the good road while we have it," said the boy, as
he gave another crack with his whip and whistle, while the little
horse trotted briskly down the hill ; the road was good, and he
went as firm as a rock without the slightest slip or stumble.
When they reached the bridge at Pont Gilbert the boy pulled
up on the centre. The water looked white and was covered
with foam.

"Look," said the boy, "the tide is up ; we shall have it
very high to-morrow, since it is so high to-day. Did the gentleman ever see the tide come up ? Strangers think it curious,
and the English often come here at spring tides to see the Great
Wave."

"What does he mean ?" asked Hope.

"Why, the rise and fall of the tide along the whole of this
coast is very great, being about forty-four feet at spring tides.
It comes in very rapidly, and there are banks on the Grève
which apparently retard the flow for a while, for all of a sudden
you may see a sort of wall of water pass over them, and this
rushes up in a mass two or three feet high, and roars up under
the bridge. The mass of water as it rolls along gathers up the
white muddy soil over which it passes, and it is that which
makes it look so white, and the great force with which it comes
creates the foam with which you see it is now covered. The day
after full and change of the moon this wave comes up exactly
at nine o'clock, and many people make it an object for a walk
to come up here and see it pass."

"I daresay," said Hope, "it is well worth seeing if it is anything like a wave I once saw in the river Findhorn. I was
fishing there. The day was cloudy, but we had no rain ; it

had, however, rained very heavily in the hills. Fortunately I had a man with me who knew the river, for on a sudden I heard a sort of hollow roar of water, and I felt an increase of breeze coming down the river. 'Run for your life, and up the rocks,' roared my companion, and he dragged me away, not even allowing me to pick up my fishing-basket; and as I saw him in such a desperate hurry and fright the panic seized me also, and I made the best use of both hands and feet in clambering up the steep face of the rock. I had not got up many steps when I heard a noise like thunder behind me. I turned and saw a wall of water tumbling along. I got one glimpse of my poor fishing-basket just as the wave reached it; it was only a glimpse, for in the next moment the torrent was roaring six feet deep where it was lying, and where I had been standing a minute before. It was one of the grandest and most appalling sights I ever beheld, and I thought for many a day after of what my companion said when the red furious stream splashed against the rocks close below our feet. 'Whaur wad ye hae been if I hadna made ye rin?' he said, as he pointed to a large rock that was rolling along before the torrent. Ah! where, indeed, thought I; and it made me think more seriously than any half-dozen of the best sermons I ever heard. This cannot be so grand a sight as that, but it may recall it to my memory, and I shall make a point of coming to see it before I leave the place. In the meantime, let us go on."

Crack went the whip, and away they trotted, keeping the same pace half-way up a long though not very steep hill.

"Go gently, my friend," said Cross, "we see your beast is good, and in our country we say, never ride a willing horse too hard."

"Ah, sir," said the boy, "is he not a good beast? and now that there is no commerce, he keeps himself, my father, my mother, and me."

"What do you mean by no commerce, my friend?" asked Hope.

F

"Why, sir, my father kept a cabaret, and my mother and I traded in fowls, ducks, pigeons, and game. I have a cart, very light and very convenient, and, sometimes by myself, and sometimes with my mother, I went all over this country, and all over Brittany, to purchase from the farmers and sportsmen their poultry and game, and we sold it again at a good profit in the town. But now nobody buys anything, and I don't know what they live on; so my commerce is gone. I am obliged to let my horse to others, as I cannot use him for myself, and happily they know he is good, and he is seldom idle, which is fortunate, for my father is very ill, and my mother does not like selling cider to the people, for they talk so loud now, and make so much noise, that it makes my father worse, and then she scolds them, and they don't come to us as they used to do."

"How do you mean, my friend, that the people don't buy anything now? surely people must eat now as well as formerly?" said Hope.

"I suppose they must eat something, because they don't die," replied the boy; "but they don't eat poultry and game, unless they can get it for less than I pay for it, and that won't do, you know. The farmers don't understand why the republic that was to make them all so rich and happy should make them sell their chickens and ducks for less money than they got when Louis Philippe was here; then they have more taxes to pay—forty-five per cent more on the land—and (between us) they are wishing to have a king back again; only don't repeat it, for they would send me to Mont St. Michel if they knew that. I quite agree with them in thinking that if Louis Philippe was a tyrant, we have Henri Cinq, or even Napoleon's nephew, to make a king of; and I believe that if we had a king again, they could sell their birds, and I could afford to buy them."

"So you are a royalist, my little friend?" said Hope; "do you find that many of the farmers are of your opinion?"

"Everybody almost wants some change; for since the republic every one is poorer than before. Some few wish to see

a red republic, because they have nothing, and never had anything ; they say that they ought to have a share of other people's
property.   I don't know much of these people, for they never
buy poultry or sell it, but I see them sometimes in the cabarets,
and I hear what they say.   There are not many of them, and
everbody else is against them ; but still these are the people
that talk the loudest, and make the greatest noise ; this keeps
the proprietors in a state of alarm, and nobody buys anything,
and when they sell anything, they hide their money.   I hear
that in England you have grand seigneurs who have thousands
and thousands of acres that belong to them, and they have
farmers to whom they let their land.   This is not so here.   We
have farmers like you, but not many, who pay rent.   Almost
all our farmers have their own properties, which they cultivate,
and a great many people have only a house and garden ; but
this they do not wish to lose or even to divide with the com-
munists ; and when the friends of a red republic and the com-
munists talk so loud in the cabarets, they are frightened that
this division of property may take place, and they wish for a
king to protect them and act with firmness.   Some, whose
fathers were soldiers, or who served under the emperor themselves, wish for Napoleon's nephew ; others wish for Henri
Cinq, but none of these speak out, for they will not trust each
other ; they only complain, and say they wish for a change.   I
cannot tell you what change they would like, but I should like
to have Henri for my king ; for the emperor was always
having conscriptions ; and perhaps his nephew might like fighting, and making us fight all the world, as the great emperor
did.   Glory is a very fine thing, but I like commerce better."

"Bravo ! my little friend," said Hope.   "I think your
taste excellent, for it agrees with my own ; and if many of your
countrymen think like you, your country will soon exceed all its
former greatness."

"Not till they get a better mode of working their land,"
said Cross, "and till they find out that time is money.   Just

look at the crops on either side of the road—how bad they are ;
and yet, perhaps, there is no better land in Europe than that
through which we are passing.   Look at the ploughs, which
only scratch and do not plough the land.   Draining or deep
ploughing is never thought of, and the consequence is, that sixteen or twenty bushels an acre is a large crop with the farmers
here, while with ordinary management the land would yield
forty ; they have little or no green crop, consequently they have
no manure ; their hay meadows are covered with rushes, and some
with stagnant water ; in short, nothing can be worse than the
agriculture of this country, and this is the more remarkable from
the fact that nothing can be better than the way in which they
work their small gardens, from which the produce is enormous.
Look, for instance, at this field, and at the garden taken off from it."

Cross pointed to a house built in the corner of a field by the
road-side, with a small garden behind and at one side of it.
The garden was surrounded by a row of pear and plum trees,
the branches of which were nearly breaking with the weight of
fruit.   The garden itself was crammed with most luxuriant
vegetables, with French beans fourteen feet high, and loaded
with pods, and with various sorts of cabbages of different ages ;
the cottage walls were nearly hid by vines and apricot trees,
also laden with fruit.   The field was divided into strips bearing
various crops, like run-rig in the Highlands of Scotland ; the
crops were wheat, oats, barley, buckwheat, and Siberian buckwheat, with two or three small patches of potatoes and beetroot,
and all the crops were bad, and foul with weeds.   The field
was ploughed into ridges about five feet wide ; no pains had
been taken to give a free run to the water, so that there was no
crop in the furrows, which made the field look as if it was laid
off with narrow paths at every five feet.

" Look at the difference," said Cross, " between that garden
and that field.   The soil is the same ; the climate is the same ;
and yet how different is the result in crop.   The garden,
luxuriant as it looks, is now bearing its second crop ; where

the cabbages are growing so well, it has already produced beans and early potatoes—in short, the produce from these little spots is very great, while that from the field is comparatively nothing, and all owing to the difference of management. The gardens are thoroughly drained and trenched to a great depth, while the rich land in the field is sour with water, scratched with a plough, and never cleaned from weeds."

"The difference is very marked, certainly," said Hope ; " but where the deuce is the boy going ?"

This remark was made as the carriage turned into a narrow lane, the first fifty yards of which were tolerably smooth, and then the little horse suddenly plunged up to the shoulders into a hole, and drew the carriage after him, which sunk up to the naves of the wheels. " Allons, march, cr-r-r-ré- br-r-r-r-igand," said the boy, as the poor little beast scrambled out on the other side, and twisted a little to one side in dragging the carriage out again.

" Where the devil ARE you going ?" exclaimed Hope, who had received a good thump on the back when they sank into the hole.

" To Carolles, through St. Jean de Thomas," replied the boy, with perfect naïvete ; " was not that where monsieur wished to go."

" Certainly," said Hope, " but is there no other way but this ?"

" Yes, sir," answered the boy ; " there is another road, but it is not so good as this, indeed it is hardly safe."

" And pray do you call this safe ?" said Hope, as one of the wheels sank into another hole—the carriage leaning over as if it never would again recover the perpendicular.

" Oh yes, sir, quite safe ; carriages are never 'emptied' on this road, but they sometimes are on the other."

" Well, I'm only a passenger," said Hope, " but go gently or I shall be pounded to a jelly."

" Don't be afraid," said the boy, and for the next quarter of a mile they jogged along in silence, twisting about to avoid the worst holes, and sometimes making the horse wade up to the shoulders through them, so as to allow the wheels to remain on the firmer ground.

"Hope," said Cross, "this reminds me of a Highland road in the West, where a friend of ours vowed that he once found a muddy man sounding a hole with the butt end of a driving whip. He asked him what he was doing, and he replied, 'Sir, I have found my hat, but I have lost a horse and gig somewhere here.'"

"Ah," said Hope, "there is a post-road in the north Highlands which runs for twenty miles along the bank of a lake. A lad who carried the letters up or down every day for some years was asked by a lowlander, who did not know the country, whether he rode or drove. 'Ride!' said the lad, grinning; 'there's pairts o't a man himsel' wull no be vary canny on;' and it was true, for in some places the path was hardly fit for anything but an active kid in good condition, and that 'road' was then the only land communication between the east and west of that part of Scotland, and the postman got small pay for 'travelling it.'"

"Do you see that château?" said the boy, turning round and pointing to a large house at a short distance from the track (for road we cannot call it).

Slush, slush went the two wheels into two holes, jerking the passengers out of their seats.

"Mind where you are going," said Hope, with an exclamation. "I wish you would look at the road and not at anything else; you have nearly bumped my inside out."

"Oh, by our Lady, yes!" said the boy; "but it is nothing; there we are out again. I beg your pardon, but I could not help asking you to look at that house, because it belongs to one of my best customers; but, poor gentleman, he cannot buy any more partridges, for some of the people in Paris who held his money are bankrupt, and they give him nothing, so he cannot afford to go shooting and buying partridges."

" He may not choose to buy your birds if he is poor," said Hope, " but why should he not shoot his own game if he likes ? Powder and shot are not so dear as to prevent his taking a shot if he wishes it."

" Ah, you don't understand," said the boy ; " monsieur is very generous, but he is a bad shot ; every Sunday he went out shooting, and sometimes twice a week, but as he killed very little himself, and liked to make presents of his game, he always sent word to me the day before, and I hid ten or twelve partridges and a hare or two, in places we agreed upon, and he picked them up. He paid me very well, and, to say the truth, he was right to do so, for I always gave him fresh birds, although sometimes I was obliged to go as far as Brittany to get them, when he wanted to have a good day."

The quiet way in which this explanation was given tickled Hope so much, that he quite forgot the badness of the road in the merry laugh it created. " Well," he said, after he had finished his laugh, " that is the best account of French sporting I ever heard—and is this the only way he can reach his house ?"

" Yes," said Cross, " this is his only road, and they are certainly queer people. I once asked why he did not mend some of these holes. Two days of a horse and cart, with four men to fill and empty them, would make the road passable ; but no—it was not his business—the commune were bound to mend the roads, and he would rather run the risk of breaking his carriage every day than mend the road for others."

" But why," said Hope, " does not some man of influence get all the country round to turn out for a day and mend the whole road ? if this is the only way they have of going to market, it would be worth their while to work for a month, instead of a day, and they would gain the whole value of their time."

" You are quite right," answered Cross ; " but yet you cannot convince them of so plain a truth. Every farm, every hamlet, every commune is jealous of the other, and they would

rather suffer any inconvenience themselves than put their hand
to a work which would benefit their neighbours. The government of France have been shamefully negligent in attending to
the minutiæ of agriculture. Without the interference of government these improvements never will take place, and they are
most short-sighted in not doing so, for nothing can be easier.
As they have an army of official men scattered in every corner,
they have only to issue an order to make these men call out
every man without exception to execute one or two days of
statute labour, and you would have all these cross-roads at least
in passable order, and gain millions a year to the country ; and
here comes a proof—draw into the ditch, boy, and let this
waggon pass."

The boy did as he was bid, and even then left barely room
for the coming cart to pass. It was one of the long carts
mounted on two enormous wheels, and drawn by two horses
and three bullocks ; a horse led, then came three bullocks, and
a second horse in the shafts. It came rolling and plunging
along the road like a boat in a heavy sea. Immediately behind
the cart rode four or five men, and a sack, about a quarter full,
was placed behind each rider.

" What a nice smell of fruit," said Hope.

" Yes," said Cross ; " the cart is laden with fruit, and the
half of it is mashed to a jelly before it reaches Granville. I
hear the people have made a great deal of money this year by
their plums, and they would have made four times as much if
they had but a road to convey them along ; as it is, three-
quarters of the best of the fruit is mashed, and is sold for half
nothing to the pastry cooks to make into preserve."

" And those people behind," asked Hope, " what have they
got in their sacks ?"

".Oh, that is wheat or some other grain which they are
carrying either to market or to the mill ; they seldom take
more than two bushels at a time, which must cause a great deal
of trouble and also great loss of money by the waste of time in

taking so small a quantity to market every week, instead of
taking a ton or two in a waggon. But one of the greatest faults
they have in this country is, that they put their whole crop
into barns. You will not see a single hay or corn stack. The
inevitable consequence of which is, that unless the season is remarkably fine, both hay and corn are apt to be musty, and the
expense of farm-buildings is enormously and uselessly increased."

The cart was now alongside. Hope learned that the terms
"sacré," "cochon," and "brigand," were common to both horses
and horned cattle, for the driver gave one of the bullocks a kick
with his heavy sabot that might have broken his ribs, and
applied these terms of affection to the unfortunate beast. The
smell of the fruit was very sweet, and the destruction was
evident, for the juice was running through the baskets to the
ground. These baskets were filled with apricots, green gages,
and large blue plums, and were piled one over the other in the
cart, which stopped as it came alongside the carriage.

"Will you sell some of your fruit to us?" asked Cross,
making a bow to one of the men on horseback. He was dressed
in a black velvet hunting-cap, a blue blouse, coarse woollen
trousers, and sabots.

"The gentleman will do me much honour by taking as many
as he pleases," said the farmer, making a bow and waving his
hunting-cap, as if he were the master of the buck-hounds receiving the prince. A quantity of fruit was selected from the
different baskets and handed to the gentlemen; no payment
would be accepted, the farmer declaring he was too much
honoured by seeing them eaten.

Hope asked him if it would not be a good thing to have the
road mended.

"Excellent," answered the farmer; "and you will see in
our commune we are doing something; but what is the use?
for we have a league and a half to go through these holes, and
therefore we only lose our time, as in the winter this road is
quite impassable. To be sure this year we need not mind, for

we shall have no cider ; but, thanks to the Virgin, the plums and pears are famous, and we can get something for them before the bad weather comes on. I have the honour to wish the gentlemen good morning." With another flourish of the cap and a low bow he rode on, and the boy set his horse in motion.

"How comes that old cock to wear a hunting-cap ?" asked Hope ; "he looks for all the world like a whipper-in gone mad."

"Why," answered Cross, "an English gentleman some years ago rode his horse over a district of this country for a match ; he wore a jockey cap. Since then there have been races, at which, also, the riders were dressed as they are with us ; so, by way of looking sporting, everybody who has a cart-horse to trot a match considers it right to wear a hunting-cap ; and many who have no horse at all think it knowing to pretend that they have, and find it cheaper to buy a cap than a horse. That old fellow is very well off, and really has horses, and good ones, for he generally wins the farmers' stake for trotting, and though he wears sabots and a blouse, he marks his love for the turf by sporting his hunting-cap on all occasions."

Use makes us accustomed to almost everything ; Hope, who was far from comfortable at first, got reconciled to his shaking when he saw that it was quite possible to go with one wheel up to the nave in a hole, and the other on the bank, without being upset, or "emptying" the carriage, as the boy expressed the process. So they jogged along, admiring the rich country, and bemoaning the ignorance of the people in not making more of it. They passed a small stream, on the banks of which a dozen very handsome women were washing clothes by hammering them on a stone with a wooden beetle.

"Hilloa," said Hope, "we have got into the land of beauty. I have not seen a good-looking woman since I have been in Normandy, and here we have a regular covey of beauties."

"Ah," answered Cross, "we are getting near St. Jean de Thomas, and these must have Granville blood in their veins.

All the women there are handsome, although I agree with you in thinking that Normans in general are not famed for good looks. They tell me the Granville people are of Spanish origin ; and their black eyes and graceful carriage confirm the supposition."

Five minutes more brought them to the top of a hill, and before them they saw the straggling village of St. Jean de Thomas buried in orchards, with a low well-wooded hill to the north, and a promontory stretching to the westward, which completely sheltered it from all winds but the south and the south-west. In the last direction stood Mont St. Michel, rising from its sandy bed and forming a marked and picturesque object in the distance.

"Faith," said Hope, "what a snug little place to spend the winter in ! it must be so warm ! and being so near the sea, and so well sheltered, I should say it must be a capital place for delicate lungs."

"I am afraid not," answered Cross, "for, from the want of draining, the flats to the south are a perfect marsh during winter, and I hear there are often agues in consequence ; besides which there is not a decent house in the village. You may see the best, and judge if an English family would put up with such accommodation in a place which is inaccessible in the winter. Such a spot in England, with such shelter and so much beauty, would be converted into a little paradise ; but we must wait a while before we see the capital expended here which would be necessary to drain the bottom and build houses fit for English Christians to live in. Some of our countrymen, and many rich French people, do come here and rough it for a few weeks, for the sake of sea-bathing, and almost every house has its lodgers."

They were now crawling into the village ; the road allowed no faster pace. The houses stood detached from each other in their gardens, where the trees were loaded with fruit of all sorts, and they looked gay and pretty as the bright sun shone on the many colours which the fruit-trees and house-leeks gave

to their fronts and roofs. All the houses were either thatched
or covered with shingle; there was not a slate in the whole
place.

"The ladies are coming in from bathing," said the boy,
"so the tide must be a good way out."

"How do you know?" asked Hope; the boy had spoken to
no one.

The boy pointed with his whip to the various doors as they
passed, and at each there hung at least one pair of blue trousers
and a short blue blouse. They swung in the gentle breeze, being
suspended by a string, and having a stick stuck into the waistband to keep them open.

"Whatever they do in the rest of France," said Hope, "I
see the ladies wear the breeches here."

"Yes," answered Cross; "there are no bathing-machines, so
the ladies, both here and at all these small bathing-places, walk
down in the dresses you see, and put them off when wet, either
in small sheds or on the open beach. The dress has a great
advantage over the bathing-gown of England, for it allows the
ladies to swim, which many of them do very well."

After passing through the greater part of the village, the
carriage was pulled up at the entrance to a yard, and the two
friends alighted.

"As we must rest the horse here for a little, you may as
well look at the house," said Cross; "you will see the sort of
way in which people live here. An English family have hired
this one, which is one of the best in the place, and are to be here
in a day or two; but as it is empty at present we can see everything without interfering with any one." He led the way, and
Hope followed, into a dirty court-yard. The house stood before
them, covered, like all those they had passed, with vines and
apricot trees. Over the door was a branch of the apricot loaded
with its rich yellow fruit, and round all the windows hung
numberless bunches of grapes, still small and green; the roof
was partly of thatch, partly shingle, but all covered with

parasitical plants, the varied colours of which, with the festooning of the vines, gave a very picturesque look to the building. Two sides of the court were surrounded with offices, the lower storeys of which were used as drinking-places, or as stables and cow-byres; the upper were used as barns, and many of them were now filled with hay. In the centre of this yard rose a mound from which grew a beautiful walnut tree that gave promise of a most abundant crop, and its rich green foliage might have afforded a delicious shade to the inhabitants of the house could they have approached it dryshod; but this was out of the question, for all the dirty water from the houses, and the drippings from a spring, ran into the hollow space between it and the buildings, causing a mass of dirty and unsavoury mud, which spread so near the house that there was only a narrow path left between it and the mud. This mud, unsavoury as it was, was useless even for manure, for the spring running into it washed away whatever might be valuable for enriching the farm, and the road into the yard was the drain along which this filthy stream found a vent. Behind, and to the right of the house, was the garden, shewing the same extraordinary luxuriance of vegetation, both in fruit and vegetables, which was remarked of all the gardens they had passed. While they were looking at what we have just described, a woman came out of the house bearing two large brass pans, which she filled at the spring, the overflow from which, as we have before described, ran through the yard. As this spring rose considerably above the level of the house, twenty feet of pipe would have brought an abundant supply of water to the kitchen, and the same length of drain would have carried off the superabundant water, thus saving constant labour to the servants, and rendering the place clean, tidy, and wholesome.

"Talk of French civilisation," said Hope; "I will be hanged if this does not beat Celtic indolence. You may see the same sort of carelessness among the lowest orders of Welsh, Irish, and Scottish Highlanders, but not among the better class. The proprietor of this place, you told me, is rich, is in the employment of the government, and considers himself enough of a gentleman to call me out, if I told him what I think of his dirt and ignorance."

" C'est la mode du pays," answered Cross; " and as we are not their schoolmasters, we must take them as we find them; but now for the house."

The kitchen had two doors, entering directly from the yard, without any porch ; it formed the whole lower part of the house, being about thirty-five feet long by thirty wide. In front of the door by which they entered were two beds, beautifully clean, with gay patch-work quilts spread over them. These beds were sunk into the wall, and had a large cupboard between them, which served as a sort of pantry for containing provisions. On the left were two windows, and between them a rack filled with plates and dishes, with a long table below nearly as long as the room ; another long table stood in the centre of the kitchen, and at this a woman was employed in shredding the leaves of some cabbages for making soup. As she cut them she pulled a string which ran through a small pulley on the ceiling, the other end of the string being fixed to a basket in the shape of a flat bee-hive, neatly made of very close wicker-work. When the string was pulled it raised this basket, and within, or rather below it, stood one of the large brass pans she had just filled at the spring. Into this pan she threw the cabbage leaves as they were cut, a quantity of other vegetables being already there ; it looked very clean and bright. There were two other baskets exactly of the same form and similarly arranged, standing at equal distances on the table.

" What is the use of these baskets ?" asked Hope.

" Don't you see ?" answered Cross; "they serve as dish-covers to keep off the flies and dust, which they do admirably ; and the same plan would be of great use in our best kitchens, for it is very handy and highly effective. The dinner as it is prepared is left under these baskets till it is time to place it on the fire, and when it is dished it is again put there till served on the table, by which means no flies or dust can ever touch the food."

"Well," said Hope, "it is always more agreeable to praise than censure, and as I have been abusing the dirty yard, I am delighted to be able to praise what I now see, for it certainly gives an air of great cleanliness. And this cabbage soup—is it good? I have heard much of it, but never have tasted it."

"Its goodness is a matter of taste," replied Cross. "I like it myself, and it must be very nutritious, for many a strong fellow eats nothing else but this soup and bread. It is very much the same as that which Soyer has been making for the Irish. After the cabbage has been boiled for a considerable time, some bits of bread and onions, fried in butter or fat, are added to the soup, and it is ready ; or they begin with the grease and onions, then add the cabbage and water, and when it has boiled for a good while they throw in the slices of bread, and serve. If the peasantry look dirty in their persons, they are never so in their cookery or their beds ; in these departments they are scrupulously clean. Their bed and table linen is coarse, but very nice, and they have a great quantity of it ; for here, as in Scotland, they consider a large quantity of linen as a mark of respectability and wealth."

"Well," said Hope, "that knowledge must always be a great comfort to a stranger visiting the country ; for a man may bear a great deal of untidiness out of doors and will put up with very humble fare when he is sure that that fare is clean, and that he will have a good bed on which to stretch his limbs at night. I like their fire-place, too, for it reminds me of the comforts of the old English farm-house." As he spoke he pointed to the right side of the room where the fire-place was built, projecting into the room, with a settle on either side of the fire, which burnt under the large open chimney. The fire was small, of wood burning on dogs, with a large heap of ashes ranged round it. "They could not cook much dinner at such a fire as that," said Hope.

" I beg your pardon," said Cross, " for there you are wrong ; you would be astonished to see the number of dishes they can cook at that little fire, with the assistance of the charcoal stoves, which you see in the dresser."

" Charcoal stoves ?" said Hope ; " I don't see any."

" Look here," said Cross ; and they went to the long table against the wall in front of one of the windows. They there saw four holes, six inches square, lined with brick, and having a small iron grating at the bottom ; some Dutch tiles were let into the table around the holes.

" Do you call those stoves ?" asked Hope.

" Faith do I," answered Cross, "and each of them will dress you a dish fit for a king. These holes are filled with charcoal, and a pan placed over them, standing on a low trivet, so that a very small quantity of fuel gives ample heat to dress most excellent dishes. I assure you our countrywomen might take useful lessons from the women here in economy of fuel in their kitchens. Let us look at what they can do with these small holes in a table, and that small fire.

" First then, these stoves will give you four entrées for your first course, and as many for your second ; then on the fire they hang the pot for the soup, which is kept warm in the hot ashes ; when it is taken off, vegetables and fish take its place ; in the front they can roast as well as we can with our large coal fires ; and then they have also a contrivance which I would fain see introduced into the Irish and Scottish cottages, where peat is burnt, for peat embers would be as good as the wood embers used here. The contrivance I allude to is this, it is called a ' four de campagne.' "

Cross pointed to a circular iron box, which looked like a bushel measure, standing with the mouth downwards, and having a projecting rim about four inches broad, fixed on to the bottom.

" What is the use of that ?" asked Hope.

" Why, it makes a very good substitute for an oven ; it will bake rolls, tarts, and pies remarkably well. The dish is put down on a trivet, which is placed on the hot stones close to the fire ; this 'four' is then put over it, the hot embers are piled around it, and the top is also filled to the upper part of the rim with embers. Whatever is placed inside is baked nearly as well as in an oven. They are very cheap, being made of thin sheet iron ; and if our people had them, and would learn to use them, they would be of great use. Many a nice little dish might a wife prepare to greet her husband's return after a hard day's work, and with no trouble, for, once put in order, they require very little looking after ; and they will cook best exactly the sort of dishes which are within the reach of a Highland peasant, such as fish pies, bacon and potatoes, or eggs, fish, butter, and potatoes, beat into a pudding."

"If these things will do all you say," answered Hope, "you are quite right, and if we understand out-of-doors work better than the French, I see we may learn a great deal from their indoor habits ; but here is a regular girdle, like what the Irish and Scottish peasants use for making oat cakes."

"You are right," said Cross, "and they use it for nearly the same purpose. They do not make oat cakes, it is true ; but they make a sort of scones of the flour of the buckwheat, which are called gallets ; they are made exactly like oat cakes, and when you taste them you will allow they are very good."

"Well, as you command the commissariat, if you produce them as part of your stores, I shall devour, and report my opinion ; in the meantime, let us see the rest of the house."

On the same side of the room as the door by which they entered rose a steep wooden stair. It began and wound round to the same side as the fireplace, and under this staircase was a third bed, as clean as the other two. They mounted the steps and entered the upper room through a door at the top. This apartment was the same size as the lower room, and had a second staircase to ascend to the upper storey. It resembled the kitchen, with this difference, that the staircase out of the second room

was hid from view by wooden panels, while in the kitchen it
was open, having only a hand-rail. A portion of this upper room
was also cut off by a wooden partition, which concealed three
bed-places which exactly resembled three state-rooms in a steam-
boat. The furniture was primitive enough, but the room looked
gay with the scarlet and white curtains that hung round the
windows, and the beds, like the others, were beautifully clean.
This, however, was the whole accommodation of the best house
in the village ; for the upper flat was only a granary and store-
room, and was full of lumber, and casks containing various kinds
of grain.

"For a family," said Hope, "this is no great things, but in
a sporting country two or three men might get on famously. Is
there any shooting here ?"

"Shooting you can hardly call it, for everybody carries a gun.
If you or I were to shoot a sparrow in the hedge, we should
forthwith be asked to produce our porte d'armes ; but they are
not so strict with each other. Every one, therefore, shoots, and
of course the game cannot be plentiful. Still there are a sprinkling of hares and partridges ; and in the beginning of the season
you may always pick up a few brace of birds. In the winter, I
hear there are always woodcocks and snipes, and quantities of
shore-birds, such as curlews and dottrel. There are ducks in
the streams, and there are large flocks of widgeon on the Mare
de Bouillon. Of the winter shooting I can only speak from
hearsay, for the roads here are then quite impassable. If you
have seen enough of the house, we may as well take a look at
the ruin of an old castle on the hill. There is not much to see
in the ruin itself, but the view from it is worth looking at ; and
the castle they say was once a stronghold of the Montgomeries."

Hope expressed his willingness to go wherever he was led ;
so they started up a little steep track to the shoulder of the
hill, where they found very small remains of what had once
been a place of strength, and had been the home of the mighty
dead. The building greatly resembled in structure some of the

old forts in the West Highlands of Scotland. There were the
ruins of the same sort of square tower, forming one quarter of a
quadrangle of lower buildings ; but little remained, and that
little would soon vanish, for all the walls were too much under-
mined to continue long standing. The situation must have
been chosen before the use of artillery was known, for as a place
of strength it would be useless in modern days, being commanded by higher ground on three sides ; but these heights
added greatly to its comfort and beauty as a residence, for, in
the way of comfort, they sheltered it from all winds but the
south, and being covered with walnut, chestnut, and oak trees,
their rich and varied foliage tended greatly to increase its beauty.
Below the hill lay the village buried in its gardens and orchards,
and further off stretched the rich and wooded plain through
which they had passed ; while on the right was the sea, with
Mont St. Michel rising against the blue horizon, and the shore
of Brittany in the extreme distance. The view was certainly
lovely.

Hope showed his admiration by exclaiming, " What a
paradise of a place might a man make here with taste and
money !"

While they were thus standing and gazing before them, a
hoopoe lit on a green knoll, the debris of a portion of the fallen
ruin ; he was close to them, and as he spread his crest in the
sun, the colours showed bright on the beautiful little bird.

" Bless me !" said Hope, " there is a hoopoe ! I never saw
one alive before."

" They are common enough in this country," answered Cross ;
" and if you listen you may hear the note of another very pretty
bird that is uncommon in England—I mean the oriole ; there
are great numbers of them here. Their note in the earlier part
of the year is most pleasing ; I like it better than that of almost
any other bird, though it has not the charm of the nightingale,
which sings when all else is still. The nest of both birds is
curious. I have never seen it mentioned in any book of natural

history, but I have remarked that the hoopoe lines its nest with the nastiest filth, and the smell is abominable. The instinct that dictates this I cannot explain, unless the fermentation of the filth keeps up the warmth in the eggs when the bird is off the nest. Everybody knows that if you clean out your pigeon-house you will have no young pigeons, but a hoopoe requires something nastier still than its own dung with which to line its nest."

" Your remark," said Hope, " is curious ; seeing these pretty birds and watching their habits, gives a further charm to such a place as this."

" I agree fully in your remark," answered Cross; " for a lover of natural history may find amusement in almost any place, and the study of nature's works is so absorbing, that if once begun, it will make many an hour pass lightly that otherwise might hang heavily on our hands. Birds, beasts, and insects too, are most abundant and most varied in such places as this, for the beauty which wood, hill, and water give to our eyes, affords the shelter and food necessary for the support of animal life. But I see troops of people wending to the shore. We are come to look at the fishing, not to prose about natural history, so if you have seen enough of the view, let us go down and see what the fishermen are about—first securing our quarters for the night. The horse must now be rested, and it will not take us long to reach Carolles."

CHAPTER IV.

FROM the height where they stood, the line of road leading to the shore was partially visible. It wound along the bottom of the hill, edged with a fringe of fruit-trees, through the spaces of which, groups of men, women, and children were seen all hastening in the same direction. All carried baskets on their left shoulders, and many bore nets which were rolled round poles about eight or nine feet long.

"Come along," said Cross, "the tide is far enough out now; and if you make haste you will see all the different modes of fishing on the shore." He led the way as he spoke, directing his course down a steep path, which passed through a bank of dwarf whin to the road below. Just as they entered the whin cover, a covey of twenty-three partridges rose at their feet; the young birds were well grown, but still they were of such an age that it was impossible for a sportsman to mistake the old birds—of these there were two, and twenty-one young ones.

"Bless my heart," said Hope, "there is a fine covey! it is the largest I ever saw; if the birds breed in that fashion in this country, they ought to have the finest shooting in the world."

"*Ought* is a very fine word," answered Cross; "but where every man carries a gun, and where, in spite of the laws to the contrary, little or no respect is paid to close-time, it is quite impossible for game to be plentiful; if the ground was at all preserved, it might easily be so, for these large coveys are by no means rare. Last year, very near this place, I found one that had twenty-four birds, being one more than that we have just seen. The great quantity of buckwheat which is grown here is the only thing that prevents the total extermination of game; for the people are furious at any person going through this crop. It is always sown late, and is never cut till the middle or end of September; consequently, the birds, who have the instinct to know where they are safe, always take to the fields of buckwheat the moment they are sprung, and their persecutors dare not follow them there. A certain number thus escape and supply breeding birds for next year. I believe it is this same buckwheat, or sarrasin, as it is here called, which renders them so prolific; for, in harvesting this grain, a great deal is shaken and falls to the ground, which gives considerable feeding during the autumn and winter. There is also another variety of buckwheat which is grown here; the peasants call it Siberi, being a contraction of Siberian buckwheat. This they grow for the feeding of their poultry and pigs, and excellent food it seems to be, for the fowls lay an immense quantity of eggs; and I believe it is from this feeding that the poultry acquires the flavour which I have heard you praise so much. This grain gives food to game very early in the year; I have remarked that in the corn-fields its grains are perfectly formed and full by the first week in May; and I own I have often felt astonished that in our own country, where we think ourselves so learned in the art of rearing game, this Siberian buckwheat has never been introduced; if it has been I have never seen it."

"What is its peculiar advantage?" asked Hope.

"Why," answered Cross, " I have already told you that the grain is fit for food in the first week in May—very shortly after they have sown their oats and barley—these are the crops that are generally sown after buckwheat, or this Siberi. A few grains of buckwheat always spring up the second year; but in a crop after Siberi, Siberi still seems to be the only crop sown, so great is the quantity that comes up. However severe the winter, it appears never to injure the vegetative powers of this hardy grain; indeed, where once sown, it becomes a perfect weed and sticks in the ground with as much pertinacity as wild mustard. As poultry and game seem to prefer it to any other food, and as it is always either growing, or lying on the fields, I think it would be invaluable to our game preservers."

" Well," said Hope, " it is not a bad wrinkle, and I thank you for the hint. I will take a parcel of the seed with me, and enlighten my sporting friends when I go home. But whom have we here ? I did not know that your fishermen wore such smart black moustaches."

This remark was made as they reached the road; for while Cross had been lecturing on the merits of Siberi, they had continued their progress down the hill, and when Hope declared his intention of enlightening his sporting friends in England on the subject, they had arrived at the hedge that lined one side of the way. About twenty yards from the place where they stood, Cross saw five men advancing from the town. They were all dressed very much alike, namely, in blue trousers and jackets. Two of the party wore old straw hats, that looked as if they had been stolen from some scarecrow ; the other three had on foraging caps, that had certainly seen good service ; none of the party wore stockings ; some had wooden sabots, the others, shoes to'match the hats and caps. Each of them carried a good-sized basket fixed on the left shoulder, and these were roughly but very closely plaited. The man who led the way had on his right shoulder a net with very small meshes, which was twisted round two poles about eight feet long, and at the end of each of these poles was fixed the curved end of a sheep's horn, the outer side of which was polished quite smooth. The remaining four followed in pairs ; they too had nets and poles, but only one net and one pair of poles to each couple. The ends of the poles rested on their shoulders, and a considerable quantity of net was rolled round the centre, the weight of which was divided between the two ; the ends of these poles were also covered with a bit of horn, and as they walked the clink of a chain could be heard, keeping time to the sound of their steps, and mingling with their laughter and conversation. The mouths of all were garnished with fierce

black moustaches, and cigars in full smoke. Ten seconds brought
this party in line with the gap in the hedge where Cross and
Hope were standing. An instantaneous halt took place, and a
shout from the whole voices at once of, "Ah, my dear Cross!
here you are! how happy I am to see you. When did you
arrive?"

Cross returned the greeting of his friends, and told them that
he was showing the country to his friend Hope, whom he begged
to make known to them, and whose great object, he mentioned,
was, among other sights, to see the mode of fishing practised in
Normandy.

"Then, pray come with us," said the gentleman who was
leading when they came in sight, "pray, come with us; we are
going to fish; you will bring us good fortune and shall share our
spoil."

Cross explained that they must first return to the village, to
give directions about their conveyance, and secure quarters
at Carolles, where they meant to stay if they could find apartments.

"Don't let that prevent your joining us," said the gentleman
who wore the worst of the two shocking bad hats; "I am at
Carolles, and if a double-bedded room will serve you, there is
the best in the town now vacant, for our friends Adolph and
George René have this moment told me that they must return
to Rennes, and have charged me to arrange with our landlord,
and intimate their departure. My servant will be here in a
second, and I will make him secure the room for you, and your
boy can drive him there if that will suit you." Cross looked at
Hope, and receiving a nod of assent, he at once accepted the proposal, and then more formally presented his friend to the party.
Hope was somewhat surprised to find that the wearers of the
straw hats were gentlemen of the best families in Normandy;
and of the other three, two were officers in a cavalry regiment,
and the third a gentleman whom he had often heard mentioned
as one of the most agreeable people in the district. Four of them

were quartered in the village; the other, as we have already mentioned, was at Carolles; they were there to take the baths, as they said, meaning thereby, swimming for an hour while the tide was in, and wading in pursuit of prawns and small soles for two or three hours whenever the tide was out.

As the Marquis de ——— had promised, his servant joined them almost immediately; he received the joint instructions of his master and Cross, and when he turned to execute them, the whole party started for the shore.

Hope took his place by the side of the Marquis de ———, and Cross walked in front with the Baron de ———. Hope, while he talked with the Marquis, had his eye fixed on the coil of net that wound round the poles, the ends of which were resting on the shoulders of the Marquis and his companion, one of the cavalry officers; the clinking of the chain caught his ear again, and on looking he saw that a considerable quantity was twisted in the net, and a number of loops hung on either side of the pole, which was shaken by the motion of the bearers, and one loop, striking against the other, caused the sound which he heard.

" What do you expect to catch to-day ?" asked Hope of the Marquis.

" The same as usual," he replied ; " bouquets, chevrettes, crabs, and soles."

" What are bouquets and chevrettes ?" asked Hope.

The Marquis spoke a little English, so he answered, " Bouquets are what you call prawns ; chevrettes are shrimps ; in Paris and in most parts of France, prawns are called salicoques, and shrimps crevettes, but here they bear the names of bouquets and chevrettes ; crabs and soles of course you know."

" And is it with the same net that you catch all these varieties ?"

" O yes, the same net will catch them all. We have a great variety of nets, but all work for the same end. For example, you see my friend has one different from ours—every one to his taste. He likes to have a net that he can manage himself, for he likes to work round the rocks, as he says the prawns are largest there, and I like to fish with the one we are carrying, because I know we always catch more than he does, and I am very sceptical as to his getting the largest ; and beside the two which you see, the women have nets like those which I saw for catching shrimps in England. There is also another sort which has two poles ; they are joined in the centre with an iron pin, and open and shut like a pair of scissors ; a net is fixed to one of the ends of this cross, and when they wish to use it, these scissors are opened so as to stretch the net quite tight, and a cross bar is fixed, which keeps it in that position ; this done, the women push the net before them in the same way that they do in your country."

"What difference is there between the net you now describe and the one which Monsieur le Baron is carrying ? I see it has two poles."

"Why, this—the poles are not joined, and the net is much wider ; it requires a good deal of strength to keep them well open, and then they are about eight feet wide. They are kept open when on the flat sand, but when going through narrow places in the rocks, the fisherman has the power of contracting the width to suit the size of the channel through which he wishes to pass."

"And the horns fixed on to the ends of the poles, of what use are they?"

"If the points of the poles were left bare, they would be constantly catching against every small stone, or sticking in the sand ; these curved horns slip smoothly along the bottom, and prevent a great deal of hard labour."

"And what sort of net have you got ? it seems a great deal larger."

"Oh, mine is the net ! for, although it is hard work to use it, still it catches so much more that the extra labour is well paid for. This net is ten yards wide. My friend takes one pole and I the other, and we march along, sweeping ten yards at once, in-stead of eight feet."

" And what is the use of that chain which is hanging in festoons below the pole ?"

" Oh, the chain ? I should hardly have thought you need inquire. Soles, shrimps, and prawns all sink themselves into the sand, and they require to be scratched, to make them jump ; with a long net like this, they would lie still and allow the net to pass over them, we should catch hardly anything without the chain, but it scratches the sand, and everything that is started falls back, and we are sure to find it in the bag which trails behind."

" But why these festoons ?"

" The festoons are everything. In the first place, they help to make the bag which holds the fish ; in the second, if the chain was straight, a good deal of the fish would pass below it, which they cannot do when it hangs in loops ; and last of all, it pre-vents the net from rolling. You must be aware that, in shal-low water, in dragging a net which has the common rope and lead to sink it, the net rolls, and you lose all your fish ; but when it is fixed to a small chain, and is arranged in loops, or festoons, as you call it, the net never rolls ; indeed it is quite impossible for it to do so."

" But how do you contrive to preserve the form of these loops, for they must become straight as you drag it along ?"

" Not at all. The net is made wider before it is finished than when it is set in. For instance, this net and chain are fourteen yards long when straight, but we can only sweep ten yards with it, now that it is finished. I will describe the way in which it is arranged for use. A net fourteen yards long, having a purse in the centre, is fixed to a small chain, also fourteen yards long : you then take a strong cord, or small rope, and stretch it very tight, and mark it off with thirty marks, each mark exactly a foot apart. The centre of the chain is then fixed to the centre of this cord ; this done, you measure two feet of

the chain on either side, and fix the places so measured to the
first one-foot mark on either side of the centre. This of course
makes a bow or loop in the chain one foot wide and six inches
deep ; you then continue working on, measuring a certain quantity of chain, and fixing each bit, as it is measured, to one of the
marks on the cord, till the whole is fastened. I ought to tell
you that the quantity of chain measured is lessened each time ;
for instance, the two centre loops are two feet, those next them
are twenty-two inches, the third twenty, the fourth nineteen,
and so on, gradually diminishing an inch each loop till the whole
is finished. The cord and the chain are then made fast to the
bottom of the poles as you see, and the ends of the net are also
stretched, and attached to them ; and then the top line is fastened three feet from the bottom, and you have a net ten yards
long, fit for work. All this you will see when we begin to work,
and will understand the process much better by one glimpse
than by a day's explanation."

"I think I understand it," said Hope, "but I shall be all
the wiser when I see the nets in operation."

At this moment a number of young girls ran past them ; they
were laughing merrily, though their clothing was of the lightest.
All of them had the universal baskets fixed on their left
shoulders ; some of them held in their hands forked sticks, some
a long iron crook, some hand-nets in the shape of a racket, and
some had nothing at all but nature's weapons.

"What are these ?" asked Hope, "and where are they
going ?"

"Fishers going to fish, like ourselves," answered the Marquis.

"And what do they expect to catch?" said Hope.

"Those strong girls with the forked sticks are the boldest
fishers here ; they go farther out than any of us ; they are going
in search of oysters, which they find in the beds of sea-grass.
They wade up to their waists, and raise the oysters very dex-
terously with those sticks. The younger girls with the hand-

nets are going in search of prawns, and sometimes they take a
great many. When the tide goes out, there are a number of
cracks and holes in the rocks, which remain full of water.
Some of these are of considerable depth, and these girls wade
through them, and scrape the sides and bottoms with those small
nets : if there is a prawn in the hole, they are sure to catch him.
Though either you or I would not get a dozen in a day, these
monkeys will half fill their baskets before the tide turns."

" And these with the iron crooks, what are they ?"

"They are crab-hunters : they, like the girls with the hand-
nets, search the holes in the rocks ; they either know the holes
well, or have much better eyes than I have ; for you will see
them presently dragging the crabs and spider-crabs from their
hiding-holes with great success ; and if you like to try your
hand at it, I will back any one of them to catch a score for
every one you take."

" And these little things ? are they going to fish, or do they
only go to carry what the others take ?"

" O no ; they do not carry for others ; they are going on
their own account, and will have as good a back-load as any of
the others. They are cockle-pickers, and even in that there is
a great art, for, till you are taught, you would not find one,
though these little brats may be filling their baskets all round
you."

" I know that trade," said Hope ; " I have learned to know
a cockle's eye from practising in Scotland, and I don't think they
would beat me much there. Have you any razor-fish on this
coast? for I have been taught how to see them too, which is a
more difficult accomplishment."

" I have never seen any of them taken," said the Marquis,
" although I am sure there must be plenty, for the coast is
covered with their shells."

" Well, I will try my hand at it some day, if I stay here ;
and if I succeed," said Hope, " I shall be able to teach these
poor little girls a new mode of filling their baskets."

Thus talking, they reached the strand, and began picking their way towards the rocky point that stretched a good way out to sea.

"We are in capital time," said the Marquis, "for the point is not dry yet, and we shall have the first of this ground, though they have been at work for an hour to the westward."

The promontory along which they were moving rose to a considerable height, and from the base of the cliff low rocks projected for some distance into the sandy waste; to the southward, the strand was exposed for a great distance, showing how far the tide had already fallen, and groups of figures could be seen scattered along the shining surface of the wet sand. The figures were clearly defined even up to the base of the rock where Mont St. Michel lifts his lofty aged head. Although those in the distance seemed mere specks, yet in the bright sunlight and on the glittering expanse they were so clearly marked that Cross declared he could distinguish the universal basket on their shoulders, and could tell who were using nets and who were gathering oysters.

The whole party stepped briskly along the sand skirting the projecting rocks, till they came nearly to the point of the promontory; and there the waves still rippled against the rocks, so that it was necessary either to mount these or to take to the water and wade.

"There is no use, gentlemen, in getting wet just now," said the Marquis. "as you have no nets to keep you in exercise ; the water is still pretty deep at the point, so I advise you to go along the rocks—there is a view worth seeing when you get to the end. You can look at that, and we will join you on the other side and show you what we get, for we will not lift the nets till we come to you."

"I must have a look at your nets and see you start," said Hope, "and then we will follow your advice."

The Baron took his net from his shoulders, unwound it, and opened it to its full width. His elbows he placed against his sides, and grasped the poles about three feet from the upper end, sunk his hands on a level with his hips, holding the net tightly stretched and open, while the upper end of the poles nearly met behind him. He was ready in a moment, and marched into the water, pushing his net before him, and keeping as close as he could to the heel of the projecting rocks. The Marquis and his companion also unwound their net, so that Hope saw it exactly as it had been described; each took a pole and advanced into the water, pushing the pole before them, and by leaning in opposite directions, keeping the net stretched to its utmost extent. Hope had kept his eye on the proceedings of the Marquis, and had not observed what the other two gentlemen were doing, but he now saw them trudging into the water in exactly the same manner as the Marquis and his friend, and was aware that there was no difference in the mode of proceeding. The Baron, with his single net, as we have already said, kept close to the heel of the rocks; the others kept further out, the Marquis and his friend taking the outside, and in two minutes they were all toiling along up to their waists in the water.

When they were once started, Cross and Hope mounted the rocks and proceeded in the same direction.

There was a good deal of short seaware growing, which was very slippery, so that they were obliged to pick their steps and tread only on the bare spaces. By attention to this it was very easy to walk, although the surface was very rugged and broken, for the bare rocks looked like a continuation of immense sponges, which slightly broke under their feet as they walked, giving them so firm a hold that to slip was impossible if they avoided the seaware.

"What rum-looking rocks!" said Hope. "I wish I had a hammer; I should like to take a bit home and examine it more closely, for it is like Madrepore or coral rocks."

"Never mind the rocks just now," said Cross; "you can get a bit of that at any time, and it would not be fair to detain

our friends, as they have promised not to empty their nets till
we join them."

Hope walked on, still keeping his eyes on the rocks at his
feet, till he was roused by a merry shout of laughter close to
him. They had just passed over a ridge rather higher than any
they had yet seen, and had come unexpectedly on some of the
party of girls who had passed them on the road. These were
the crab-hunters, and the girls with the hand-nets.

When Hope looked up he saw that the rocks were now
flatter, but were broken up by crevices of various depths, from
ten to fifty yards long and of irregular breadth, rarely, however,
exceeding six feet. In these crevices the girls were wading;
some whisking their little nets rapidly along the bottom or
weed-befringed sides, tossing whatever they caught into their
baskets; while others were moving along more slowly, carefully
lifting the weed, and poking their iron hook into every hole.
When Hope had raised his eyes, he saw that the laugh had been
created at the expense of one of these crab-fishers, who had been
so much occupied in searching a split in the rock that she had
forgotten that she was standing at the edge of a very deep hole,
into which she had slipped. She was laughing with the rest,
though up to her arms in the water. "It is nothing, it is nothing," she said; "see what a fine one I have got; and these
gentlemen, I am sure, will buy it: it is a real good one, and so
heavy." She stretched out her hand, in which she held the
large spider-crab which she had just taken, and which had made
her forget the deep pool.

"We will come back to you presently," said Cross, "and
perhaps buy your crabs, but we have not time just now;" then
calling to Hope, he continued, "we must get on or they will be
round the point before us."

Cross led the way, and Hope followed. Half a minute more
spent in walking brought them to the point, and when they had
clambered up a steep ledge the view opened upon them. On
this side, as on the other, they saw an immense expanse of wet

shining sand ; but here several masses of flat red-looking rocks
broke the sameness of the view, and several hundred men, women, and children, were seen, either wading in the distant blue
water, or scattered over the rocks or on the sand. In the far
west were the rocks of Chausey ; and in front was another promontory, on which stood the town of Granville—the spire of the
church, the barracks, and the houses in the old town forming a
broken sky-line—while the masts of the ships in the harbour
could be distinctly seen cutting against the houses in the lower
part of the town. The sea was dotted with the white sails of
many of the three-masted luggers which the fishermen of Granville use for trawling. The day was so bright and beautiful that
even an uglier scene would have seemed fair ; and now there was
so much life and movement, that Hope would fain have paused
to look and admire for a while a panorama that gave him so
much pleasure ; but Cross hailed him again, and pointed to their
friends, who were nearly round the point ; so on they went as
fast as the nature of the ground would permit them, and arrived
at the edge of the water just as the fishermen reached the land.

"Very good," said the Baron, examining his net ; " I have
some famous ones ; there is nothing like the single net when it
is well handled."

"Capital ! capital !" said the Marquis, who had shortened
the net, and who was now looking into the bag which he
carried in his hand. "Bah ! don't talk of your single net—
look here !"

"And look here," said the other couple, who were shaking
the contents of their bag into the flat portion of the net.

Hope and Cross did look, and saw that in each net there
was a considerable quantity of prawns, shrimps, soles, and a few
crabs. Many of the prawns were extremely large, and the
shrimps were very fine. The crabs were rather larger than a
man's fist ; the soles were all small, none being larger than a
man's hand, and many not half that size, but there were a great
many of them.

"Mine are decidedly the finest," said the Baron, who looked somewhat vexed at discovering that the double-handed nets had certainly caught four times as much as he had.

"Never mind who has the best," said the Marquis; "let us sort the fish and be off; we shall have both good and plenty if we do not waste our time."

"Yes, yes," cried the rest; "we shall have a capital day; so to work."

The best of the soles were selected and emptied into one basket, the crabs were put into another, and then the prawns and shrimps were thrown together into the other empty ones. The Baron insisted on keeping his own apart, to prove that he had caught the finest. A handful or two of wet sea-weed was thrown into each basket, and the gentlemen prepared to start again. The Baron was first, and walked off; the Marquis stopped for a moment to pick up the soles that were too small for use to throw them into the sea again.

"My friend is a little vexed," he said, "because I cannot convince him that ten yards will fish more ground than eight feet; but though he is an obstinate droll, he fishes well, so we won't tease him."

While the nets were being emptied all eyes had been fixed on them, and Hope had not thought of the tide, but now that the Marquis turned to renew the fishing, he saw with astonishment that it had fallen so rapidly that they were now upwards of three hundred yards from the water, although five minutes before they had stood absolutely in it when the nets were lifted.

"The tide falls fast here," said Hope.

"And it rises faster," replied the Marquis, "which we must remember, for when it turns we can fish no more. So adieu for the present."

The Marquis and his friend walked straight out to sea. Cross and Hope took their way towards one of the masses of rock round which a number of men and boys were busily engaged in digging in the sand.

" Are those people gathering bait ?" asked Hope.

" Some of them are," answered Cross ; " those, for instance, whom you see on the dry ridges of sand ; but the greater part of them are seeking sand-eels, or lançons as they are here named ; they are excellent eating, and we will buy some.   There are two sorts of lugworm that they find in the sand, one of which is much more prized by the fishermen than the other.   The one they value I have not remarked on our coasts, though it may be there ; it is larger than the common lug, and has a large lump in the middle.   When they dig them up, the fisherman tears off the tail and squeezes the inside out.   The worm then looks like a narrow strip of raw beef ; the fishermen tell me that the brills and bass take this bait, but that only flounders and plaice take the common lugworm.   We will look at them, and you will see how they find and distinguish the two sorts ; but, first of all, let us watch them catching the sand-eels.   I daresay you have often seen them caught on our coast ; there, as you must know, they are taken by drawing a blunt sickle through the sand at the edge of the sea ; here, at night, these girls catch them also much in that way, only they use a two-pronged fork instead of a sickle.   In the day-time, however, they catch them by digging circular trenches in the wettest parts of the strand, as you will see."

" We have forgotten the crab-hunters," said Hope.   " I should like to have seen more of their way of working.   I wish to see all the different modes of fishing, and all the varieties of fish they catch."

" Well, you have a good deal yet before you, but you need not be afraid of not seeing both the hand-nets and crab-hunters at work ; they will be out here soon, for they are sure to come here as soon as they have searched all the crevices where we left them, and these rocks before us are more productive, as they are further out to sea, and the crevices are more numerous. If you look behind, you will see the girls are nearly at the end of the rock where we came down to the strand ; when they

get there, they will follow in the line we are now going, and
you will have plenty of time to see them at work."

Hope agreed to be guided, and they stepped out towards
the diggers. He was surprised, as they walked, to find that the
distance was so great; the people apparently were quite close to
them, yet it took several minutes' sharp walking to reach the
spot where they were at work, so deceiving was the flat wet
surface over which they moved. When they did reach the
place, they found a number of people—men, women, and boys—
all engaged exactly in the same way. Each held in his hand a
spade about six inches wide and ten deep, with a long straight
handle; the blade of the spade was a good deal bent, so as to
prevent the sand from slipping off. The two friends stationed
themselves beside an old woman with a good-natured face. She
wore very short petticoats, and showed a pair of uncommonly
stout legs, and as she dug they soon saw that she had arms to
match. The sand, where they joined her, was very wet, and
small streams filtered from the rock, making some places more
soft than others. These were the spots which were especially
selected, and the mode of operating was by beginning on the
side nearest the sea, and throwing out a narrow trench, two or
three spadesful wide, forming a ring about six feet in diameter;
this she did with great rapidity, and every now and then a little
bright speck would be seen in the sand she threw out, upon
which she pounced like lightning, and then flung the little
silver wriggling thing into the basket, which for this sport was
not worn on the shoulder, but was generally placed in the
middle of the circle being made. When one circle was completed, another was commenced immediately before it; when
that was finished like the first, a third was begun, and ended
exactly in the same way. The old lady then went back to the
place she had begun upon, and turned over the whole of the
sand which had remained undisturbed in the centre of the rings,
and she took a considerable quantity. She worked with great
speed, and was certainly in capital condition, for she neither

drew a long breath, nor seemed the least heated by the exertion.

Hope asked her why she dug the rings, and then came back again.

" My good gentleman," she said, " the lançons are sometimes deep, and then we don't get them, but when we make this ring it fills with water, and they come nearer the surface ; so when we dig again we turn them out and fill our baskets. Will you buy mine ? you shall have them cheap."

" How much," said Cross, " do you ask ?"

" Whatever the good gentleman pleases," she replied.

" Oh, nonsense, Marie," said Cross ; " any price is no price ; tell us what you expect, and perhaps we shall buy."

The old woman looked at Cross ; she seemed to think he was an old hand, so after a pause she said, " Will the gentleman give me a sou the dozen ?"

" That is more than they are worth, you know, Marie, but if you keep them for us, we will give you a sou the dozen for all you catch to-day."

" I will keep them," said the old lady, " and thank you."

" Shall we go and watch them dig for lugworms ?" said Cross ; " we shall just have time to see them and then return to meet the crab-hunters, who, you may observe, are now coming here, as I said they would."

" Allons ! marche !" said Hope ; " but tell me, do you know that old lady with the stout legs ? for you called her Marie."

" Not I," replied Cross ; " but nine-tenths of these old bodies are called Marie, and are dedicated to the Virgin. The others have very fine names, such as Euphrosyne, Angela, or Seraphine. I made a dash at Marie, and was right."

" Poor old Marie ! I think you drove a hard bargain with her. A sou a dozen is surely not much, especially as you tell me that fish is dear here."

" She is very well off at a sou the dozen ; it is double the price she would get from any one else, for though it is true that

any large fish is sold very dear in comparison with other things
in the country, yet small fish are cheap; you may get half a
basketful of sardines for five sous, and they will ask you five
francs for a bass of six or seven pounds weight.   It is a
curious thing for a people that understand good eating, but
they seem to prefer a coarse fish, if he be large, to those delicate
little things.   I believe the cooks are such lazy brutes that
they don't like the trouble of cleaning such small things, and so
spoil them in dressing, to disgust their masters.   The girls with
the hand-nets will very likely get some of these sardines, and
if they do, we will take them home, and you shall say if they
are not equal to, if not better than, whitebait."

" I never tasted a bass," said Hope ; " is it a good fish ?"

" Yes," replied Cross, " it is at least not a bad fish, and if you
are anxious to taste one, we may easily gratify you.   The tide is
now very nearly low enough for the people to examine their nets
and lines, and they are pretty sure to have some bass or bar as
they call them, and you may get a tolerably good one for a franc
and a half, or two francs; but here we are on the dry sand.   Now,
look; that boy is digging for the common lug; you see he is
digging straight on in a place where the casts are numerous.   We
need not look at him, but here comes this old fellow, who, you
see, is only digging every here and there.   He is looking for the
sort of lug I described to you.   If you remark there are hardly
any castings where we now are, and the holes are in pairs from
one to two feet apart; these are made by the worm which they
prize; each worm has two holes, and it seems as if they enter by
one and go out by the other, for they are always found between
these two holes.   There appear to be a good many here, so I will
hail the old fellow and you shall see."

Cross called to the old man—"There are a number here."
The old man came towards them.   "Thank you, sir," he said,
" this looks well."   He immediately stuck his spade into a hole,
and a small quantity of sand and water was raised in another
hole about two feet distant.   "There is one here !" he ex-

claimed, and began to dig in the line between the two, opening deeper as he got towards the centre; when there, he dabbed down his hand and drew forth an ugly-looking animal, about ten inches long, the half of which was of a dark muddy red, and twice the thickness of the other, which was of a dirty yellow colour. They had not long to examine it, for in an instant the old fellow tore off the yellow part, squeezed a quantity of nasty-looking stuff out of the big end, threw it into his basket, and then began at another hole with the same result.

"What are you going to do with these?" asked Hope.

"We are going to bait our lines; and it is nearly time to start, for here comes my wife and son, and if we do not look sharp, some one may take our fish."

"Have you any lines set just now?" asked Hope.

"Yes, and nets too, and we are going to set more. You see my wife and son with their burden; they have my best tree-mell and some lines. My little boy and myself have fresh bait to put on the hooks that we set yesterday, for to-morrow is the great marée."

"His best tree-mell! what does he mean?" asked Hope.

"Surely you must know," answered Cross, "the tree-mell is our trammell, or fluc-net; we must have learnt this mode of net-making from the French, for trammell is evidently the trois-mailles, or three meshes, which exactly describes the net."

"You are right," said Hope, "the large meshes in the strong nets, which form the two walls, with the fine net of small meshes which hangs between them, are certainly three meshes. Live and learn; and to-day I have had a lesson, for I now know that the English trammell is the Norman tree-mell. But how do they set their nets and lines, for I see no boat?"

"They don't require a boat, and, indeed, I don't believe there is such a thing on any part of the coast between Granville and Pontorson, for I never saw one. The fishermen choose a place on the sand, generally where the castings of the lugworms are most numerous, or where the ground is marked by the water-runs,

and there they spread their nets or set their lines ; this they do
when the tide is at the lowest, and there they leave them till the
tide goes out again.   They then go to them, unhook any fish that
have taken the bait, rebait the lines, and again leave them.   The
nets are set in the same way, similarly left and examined.   They
have three days once a fortnight that the ebb is very great, and
during these three days these people work very hard ; for they
come along these dreary sands and examine their nets and lines
both now and during the night tide, when they have to rebait
their lines, pick and clear the nets from weeds and dirt, and
smooth them out if they are at all entangled; and all this in a
very short space of time, for they dare not remain on the shore
when the tide turns, especially at night, for often the wave comes
—that is to say the tide—in with such a sudden rush that if it
were to overtake them, they must inevitably be drowned.   When
you talk of a boat you forget the great rise and fall of the tide
here ; and I must remind you that the nets which these people
set now on the dry sand will have seven fathom of water over
them when the tide is full."

"That is true," said Hope ; "I had forgotten the greatness
of the tides.   I should like to go out and see what these people
have caught."

"We had better put that off till to-morrow," said Cross, "as
you wish to see the crab-catching.   The highest tide is to-morrow,
and the nets catch most at these tides, for the fish are most on the
move then ; whereas the first day of the high tides is always best
for crabs, as they do not move about so fast.   The girls do not
seek them much during the neap tides, so that they have ten or
twelve days to accumulate in the holes.   My advice, therefore, is
that we see what the girls are about to-day, and to-morrow we can
observe the nets and lines."

"So be it," said Hope ; "but just let me have one look at the
net before we start, for the old woman and the man are quite close
to us."

This was true : a tall elderly woman, showing the remains of

great beauty, and wearing the picturesque Granville cap, was within
a few yards of them ; she was carrying one end of a long hand-
barrow, on which a quantity of net was piled so high that it completely hid a fine handsome lad who was bearing the other end.
When they came up to the old man they put the barrow down
on the sand and began to rub their hands.

"That must be heavy," said Hope, addressing the woman, who
had bowed very gracefully to the two strangers.

"O no, gentlemen," she replied, "it is not heavy now, for it
is dry, and we have always hope that it is to bring us something
to buy bread, which makes it feel light ; but when the grand
marée is over, and we have to take it to the shore, if we are disappointed in our hopes and catch little, then, indeed, we remember that it is wet and heavy, for our hearts are heavy too, and
we know that we are poor, and shall be ill off till the next grand
marée."

"Had you any luck with the morning tide ?" asked Cross.

"Yes, sir, we did very well, and I sold them all, except one
nice bar and a brill, which the boy has in his basket ; as we did
so well, I can sell them very cheap."

"Let us see them," said Cross ; then speaking in English to
Hope :—

"You wished to taste a bar, we may as well let this old lady
cheat us as anybody else."

The young man took the basket from his shoulder ; it was
much larger than those usually carried, and was quite full of little
bundles of straw ; each bundle was about four inches long, and
two in diameter ; they were twisted very neatly round with a
single straw, so that they were quite hard and firm ; there were
at least a hundred of them in the basket. The young man emptied them out on the sand, and below lay a bass about four pounds
weight, and a very fine brill.

"There, gentlemen !" said the woman, "I can let you have
these beautiful fish for five francs—you will not often get such a
bargain."

"Bargain do you call it?" said Cross; "where did you leave your conscience, madam? do you think it rains francs, that we can give you five francs for two wretched things like those?"

"Wretched do you call them?" answered the lady, raising her voice; and sticking her finger into the gills of the fish she plunged them into the water that had filtered into one of the holes her husband had dug in seeking for worms. "Look at them! and if you have any sense you must allow that you never saw better."

"Then since they are so beautiful, you had better keep them," said Cross; "let us go."

"Ah, sir," said the woman, lowering her voice; "look at them again, you will see you are mistaken; the fish are beautiful, and if you look you will make me an offer."

"Well," said Cross, "as it is the first day of the tide I will be generous; I will give you three francs for the fish, provided you send them to Carolles for me."

"Give them to the gentleman," interposed the old man, "and let us go; we shall have some one robbing our nets."

"Who allowed you to speak?" said the woman to her husband, and putting her arms a-kimbo; "if you are to interfere you may sell the fish yourself, for I shall go home."

The husband looked penitent and said not another word.

"Make it three and a half," said the woman, turning again to Cross, "and you shall have them."

"Not a liard beyond three francs," said Cross, and began to walk away.

"Stop! stop!" said the woman, "here comes the little boy; give him five sous for carrying them and you shall have them."

Cross turned and produced his purse; he counted out the three francs and gave them to the old lady, who immediately tied them in the corner of the handkerchief which she wore round her neck.

"I have given away the fish," she said, smiling; "but you will give me a better price another time."

" Yes, a fairer," returned Cross ; " for I cannot afford to give such extravagant prices every day."

The woman laughed and shook her fist at Cross. " Here," she said to a boy who ran up, " take these fish to Carolles ; the gentleman will tell you where, and he will give you five sous. Take care that you show them to me when I come home ; no cider, remember, unless these good gentlemen give you a cup for being quick."

The boy, who seemed in great spirits, nodded and answered, " Yes, mother ; and see here," he continued, holding up a basket, " see what 'Phrosyne has given me—is she not good ? there is enough for to-day and to-morrow."

The woman looked in the basket, and then clapped her hands. " She is indeed good," she said ; " this is a lucky day."

Hope looked in the basket also ; he saw a large mass of dirty, black-looking jelly lying at the bottom of the basket, and two or three dozen of very small sand-eels.

" What nasty-looking stuff is that they are clapping their hands about ?" he asked.

Cross looked also ; " It is a lot of small cuttle-fish," he said ; " they make the best bait in the world for catching other fish ; one of the girls with the hand-nets has caught them, I suppose, and has given them to the boy. Will you show the sepias to this gentleman ?" The boy put down his hand and raised it half full of the black stuff ; this he took to the hole full of water, where he rubbed and squeezed it for a few seconds. When Hope looked again he saw that the boy was holding up six or seven transparent-looking fish about as long as his finger ; the body of the fish was like an elongated transparent bag, the eyes were very large, and in front of them protruded a bunch of feelers from half an inch to an inch long, which were also semi-transparent. When the boy dipped them again into the water, Hope saw that they had a sort of silvery lustre that shone very brightly. He at once recognised them as the same fish which he had seen in such quantities at Naples, and which are so much

valued on our own coast as bait for cod-fishing. He had never
before seen them so small, and he took one into his hand to
examine it; he could not feel the bone which he had always
seen in the large ones.

"Good-day, gentlemen," said the woman; "we are fortunate
to get them, for if any fish come in, we are sure to have good
luck to-night." She stooped to lift the end of her barrow, and
the young man, who had replaced the little bundles of straw in
his basket, lifted the other; while the boy emptied the much-
prized bait into the old man's basket, who marched away with
his wife and eldest son, leaving the little boy to wash his basket
and the fish, and to carry them where he might be directed.
These directions Cross gave him, and then led the way towards
the rocks.

"What a handsome old woman that was," said Hope, "and
what a soft voice she had, even when she was scolding you and
her husband. All her motions were very graceful, but her voice
struck me as so very different from the harsh utterance of the gene-
rality of the peasant women I have heard speaking in this country."

"I believe," said Cross, "that her voice was peculiarly
musical, but I do not know if it would have struck you forcibly
anywhere else. It was the contrast that made it so evident,
after listening, as you have lately, to the harsh strained voices of
the Norman peasant women. This old lady is evidently a Granville woman, and her graceful carriage, handsome face, and black
eyes, mark her Spanish origin, or, if not Spanish, at all events
show that they come from some other blood than the very ordi-
nary-looking people that live around them; they never steal,
these Granvillites, and are so far honest; but they are such
rogues in making a bargain, that I believe, if they are not
Spanish, they must be one of the lost tribes of Israel."

"Talking of bargains," said Hope, " I felt half ashamed when
you were having such a wrangle with the poor woman, and
abusing her fish so shamefully. Half-a-crown for such fine fish
was surely not much."

"I agree with you," said Cross, "they were not dear, as fish sell here; yet still I gave more than I might have got them for. A Granville woman always asks more than twice what she will take; and as for wrangling, my dear fellow, I always like to be respected by the people of the country where I may chance to live. If I had been weak enough to give that worthy lady the five francs she asked, she would have pocketed my money and held me in utter contempt; as it is, she has gone away with a sort of respect for me, and had I beat her down to two francs, instead of three, she would have made me a curtsey whenever she saw me."

Hope laughed. "What a snap she gave her husband for telling her to give us the fish! she seems to have broken him in pretty well."

"Not more than other Granville women do; they all keep their husbands in tremendous order; they say, and, from what I have seen, I believe it is true, that no Granville man dare call his soul his own in his wife's presence."

"The same thing is said of most fishing villages," said Hope, "for the wife holds the purse, and therefore thinks herself authorised to keep her husband, as well as the house, in order."

"Yes, but," said Cross, "in Granville this authority is not confined to the fishermen; it is a place of considerable commerce, and the shopkeepers' wives keep as tight a sovereignty as the fisherwomen. All the porters there are of the fair sex, and if a man were to offer to carry your trunk, these gentle creatures would throw him over the quay."

"After such a description," said Hope, "in spite of their beauty, I should rather prefer choosing a wife elsewhere. But, by the by, I forgot to ask you what is the use of these little bundles of straw that the son had in his basket?"

"Those are the sinks," answered Cross, "with which the lines and nets are kept in their places."

"Sinks?" said Hope, "straw for sinks! that is something new."

"I was wrong to call them sinks," said Cross, "for in fact they are a sort of anchors. There are string loops fixed at every yard along the bottom of the nets, and at every two or three fathom of the lines; into each of these loops one of those straw bundles is fixed; a hole is then made in the sand, six inches deep; the straw is pushed into the hole, and with a tramp of the heel the straw is covered, by which arrangement both nets and lines are so firmly fixed in their place, that neither fish nor sea can move them."

"It is a capital plan," said Hope, "but can only be of use on a coast like this, where the rise and fall of the tide is so great."

"I am not so sure of that," said Cross; "there are a great many places on the coast of Britain where the sea goes out a long way, and where, I am sure, the same thing might be done with advantage, especially at the mouths of small rivers, where salmon and sea-trout frequent. You may make the net take any shape you like with these straw anchors, which is not easily done with leads or stones. When we go to see how they are set to-morrow you had better look carefully at the way it is done, and we must also see the fisheries which are made with stones, and which are the most productive mode of fishing on the coast. But here we are at the rocks; and all the girls seem so busy, I suspect they must have good success, so you will see them in all their glory."

CHAPTER V

THE rocks up which they now scrambled rose like an island in the plain of sand, and resembled the mass over which they had already passed. The general surface, however, seemed flatter as they first looked over it; but as they advanced, Hope saw that the crevices were more numerous and longer. The rocks were also more covered with marine plants; but, wherever they were bare, they showed the same sort of spongy-looking texture which had attracted his attention at the promontory. Here and there a point rose higher than the general surface, and these points, when examined, proved to be masses of bastard clay-slate. One point especially rose considerably higher than any of the rest, and looked of a lighter colour than the surrounding mass.

The girls were scattered about, two of them generally wading together in the same hole, one moving rapidly, drawing her little hand-net first on one side and then on the other; while the second was proceeding more slowly, lifting up the sea-weed and carefully searching under every stone and in every hole with her iron hook. When the two friends reached the first pair, Hope recognised in one of them the same little girl who had fallen into the water when they had first seen them.

"I am glad you are come," she said, "for you will buy my crabs; and I have got some very fine ones. Shall I show them to you?"

"Let me see them," said Hope.

The little girl stepped out of the water, took off her basket, which seemed very heavy, and placed it on the rock beside the two friends.

" I only said perhaps I would buy them," said Hope.

" Ah, but the other gentleman-looked as if he would," said the little girl ; " and when you see them you cannot help wanting them, they are so good." As she spoke she sat down and spread out her petticoat, into which she dropped six or eight crabs which she picked out of the basket. Almost the whole of these were the spider crabs, with one or two of the common crab among them ; the largest was about twice the size of a man's fist.

" Let me look at one of these brutes," said Hope ; " they are very ugly."

" Yes, but they are very good," said the little girl; " just feel how heavy this one is," and she handed up one of the largest of the spider crabs.

Hope looked at it. A common crab is no beauty, but the one he held in his hand was a hideous animal ; the body was very much thicker than the common crab ; the claws were very small, and the legs were covered with a sort of spines and a quantity of small marine plants. The back shell was also covered with the same sorts of plants, some of which were two inches long. Hope put it down in a small water-hole, where it lay tolerably still, and then looked like a stone or a bit of the surrounding rock covered with sea-weed, for the weed floated away from it when it was in the water, and no unaccustomed eye could have guessed that it was a living creature.

" They must have precious sharp eyes to distinguish that animal in these deep holes," said Hope, " or, when seen, to know that it is a crab, and not a bit of the rock."

" They have uncommonly sharp eyes," answered Cross, " but they do not trust altogether to their eyes. If you take the hook from the girl and touch that fellow under the belly, you will see that he will resent your interference, and grasp the weapon, holding it so tight that you may lift him out of the water. That is the way in which they are taken, for in general they are lying in holes where even our friend's pretty black eyes would never see them. A poke with the iron rod, however, finds them out, and their irritability of temper proves their destruction; for they grasp the iron and hold on till they are removed by the fisher, and sent to recover themselves, or fight it out with a dozen or two of companions in a basket."

Hope took the hook from the little girl and tried the process. He put the hook under the crab, which immediately seized it; he then raised and held it out to the little girl, who looked up as she stretched out her hand to seize the animal by the back.

" She certainly has very pretty eyes," said Hope, "and they look soft and gentle though they are so dark."

" She is no doubt a Granvillaise," said Cross; "and soft as her eyes may look, I will warrant, when she is old enough to be married, that she will keep her husband in as tight order as the handsome old dragon we met just now."

" Well, she does not seem as if she would," said Hope, "and she looks and moves so gracefully, I could hardly believe she had spent her young life in picking cockles, or hauling up crabs with an iron rod. But though she is so pretty and graceful, I am sure her game does not resemble her, for I cannot conceive anything more ugly or ungraceful than a spider crab: are they good to eat? I should doubt it, for my part, and think he must have been a brave man, or dreadfully hungry, who was induced to eat the first."

"I have heard your last remark made," said Cross, " about oysters, lobsters, and many other good things. Ugly as these creatures are, they are very good to eat. The people of the country prefer them to the common sort. You must have eaten partan-pie in Scotland, and the Scotch must have learnt that dish from their allies the French, for that is one of the ways of dressing them here. Another is to mix the meat after it is boiled with fine herbs, oil, and vinegar, and serve it cold in the shell. You shall try both these ways if you choose to buy this girl's basket, and while you are making your bargain I will go and see what the other girl is doing up in the corner of that crevice. I suspect she has got a shoal of what they call sardines, and if so, I will get some to let you taste them."

Cross walked away, and Hope made the little girl empty out her basket; she had about sixty crabs of both sorts, and all sizes. Hope selected two dozen of the finest, and asked the price.

The little girl looked at him with soft pleading eyes, and answered, "They are very fine, the gentleman will give me two francs."

" Two francs," said Hope to himself, " two francs are equal to twenty pence—twenty pence for twenty-four crabs! less than a penny apiece; that surely is not dear, and Cross cannot laugh at me, so I will give it ;" then addressing the girl he said, " if I give you two francs you will take them to Carolles for me."

" O, yes," replied the girl, her eyes sparkling and a smile playing round her mouth, " give me the two francs and I will take them home for you."

" But if I give you the money now, perhaps you will not take them," said Hope, thinking himself very sharp.

" Oh," said the girl, " who would ever suspect me of being so dishonest ? If you do not like to trust me, I will wait till you come to the house, and you can see them before you pay me."

" No, no," said Hope, " I will trust you ; there is the money, and you may take the crabs home when you like; for if you are a rogue your face belies you."

" I will take them directly," said the girl, " and thank you ; but see, the other gentleman is beckoning to you."

Hope looked and saw Cross waving to him : so he walked towards him, leaving the little girl to replace her crabs in the basket. Hope felt rather proud of his bargain, and thought to himself that Cross had been unjust towards the Granvillaise— if the little girl was one—for she had asked a very moderate price for her wares, and had agreed to carry them home into the bargain, and that without the slightest wrangle. When he got near Cross, he asked what he had got to show.

"There are a great lot of these cuttles here," answered Cross, "and it may interest you to see them make use of the provision which nature has given them for their defence. I have sent the girl to drive them up to this end, and when she begins to use her net, you will see how, in a moment, they will make the water as black as ink, by ejecting the sepia from their ink-bags : they move very slowly in the water, and every fish, even the very prawns, attack them: this power of hiding themselves by darkening the waters seems their only protection against so many enemies, and they are richly gifted with this weapon of defence. You will see after they are taken and well washed that they are quite empty and transparent—yet if you put them back and leave them undisturbed in the sea for ten minutes, you will find that they are again charged, as full as ever, with this black fluid. I have thought when I saw the experiment tried, that it might be a source of great profit to a paint-maker, if he could discover the chemical compound of a fish's stomach, that can so rapidly convert sea-water into this pitchy ink."

The girl was walking very slowly towards them, holding her net in both her hands, and striking it gently on the top of the water.

"Here they are," said Cross ; "do you see them ?"

Hope looked. He observed a number of shining objects moving in the water with a sort of little jerk. He told the girl to stand still, and then he saw indistinctly the shape of the cuttle-fish ; when the girl advanced, he again saw them move with a jerk, but he could not distinguish whether they moved with their head or tail foremost : he thought it was the latter, but he found it impossible to say which ; for when they moved they threw out a small jet of the black liquid, that darkened the water so much, they were quite obscured.

The girl now came forward and made two rapid sweeps of

the narrow corner with her net : after each sweep she emptied her net on the back, and lifted each time two or three large handsful of the nasty jelly-looking stuff, which they had before seen in the boy's basket. The water was as black as ink.

"They will not move now," said the girl; "and I shall get them all." She then again swept her net several times deeper and slower through the water, emptying a good quantity at each sweep on to the first heap ; at last the net came up empty.

"I think we have them all now. Would you like me to wash them ?"

"Do, if you please," said Cross, "and then we can count them. As they have got no sardines to-day, I will try to buy them, for I can tell you they are very good, and the Christians here like to eat them quite as well as the fish do. This girl tells me she never before saw so many taken in one day as they have caught now ; the fishermen prize them so highly for bait, that it is not always fair to buy them for eating ; but to-day we shall not injure the fishermen, as they have more than will bait all their hooks ten times over ; and strange to say, they never think of salting them. I am quite sure, if they did salt them, that they would be quite as good for bait, after a night's soak-ing, as the fresh ones ; but this they never do, whether from carelessness or the high price of salt, I cannot say."

"Are they really such good bait ?" asked Hope ; "or is it only fancy in the fishermen ? "

"No, no ; there is no fancy in it, they seem to attract be-yond any other bait. There are holes in these rocks where small lobsters hide, and perhaps there may be one now. I will make the girl try, if she has brought her sniggle with her, and you will see him come out and follow one of these cuttles into the net."

Cross bought the whole lot for ten sous, and offered the girl ten sous more if she would try to catch a lobster, for he saw that she had a sniggle-stick stuck into the string of her petticoat In England, when boys go sniggling eels, they take a straight switch with a sharp point, on to which the end of a lobworm is stuck, and instead of a hook they put on a worsted needle firmly fastened in the centre ; but on the coast of Normandy they use a long narrow hook, the shank of which, when baited, they stick into a hole on the point of a stiffer stick than that used with us. To prevent the line from catching they also bore a hole through this stick about two inches from the point ; through this hole the line is drawn and held tight in the hand while they are fishing, which is a much better arrangement than ours, for the line is never entangled in the weeds, roots, or rocks, and when you do hook a fish you have far more power to draw him from his haunt.

The girl at once agreed to try all the lobster holes she knew, and immediately produced her line and stick ; she took the largest and brightest cuttle-fish she could find and baited her hook.

" You must carry these sepias for us," said Cross.

" They will blacken my bouquets," said the girl ; " but never mind, I can wash them again, and I will put some weed to keep them separate."

" They can blacken nothing now," said Hope ; " they are as bright as silver, and seem all dead."

" No, no, they are not dead," answered Cross, " they are not so easily killed ; and, dead or alive, they will not be ten minutes in that basket till they are as black as ever; but after the next wash-ing, I hope they may keep bright, and we will taste them, for when well fried they are excellent, and they resemble in taste, but are better than, the most delicate tendons de veau ; by the by, did you buy any crabs, and what did you pay for them ?"

" O yes," said Hope ; " I bought two dozen, and very reason-able I found the little girl; she asked two francs, and I gave them at once."

Cross burst out laughing. " Well done, little Granvillaise !" he exclaimed.

" What are you laughing at ?" asked Hope, rather piqued.

"Why, to be honest," said Cross, "at the way that little monkey has done you; and I will be bound she enjoyed the joke and has laughed much more heartily than I have; she would gladly have sold you all she had in the basket for one franc, and you have given her two for the half of it."

"Never mind," said Hope; "she is welcome to the extra franc and the half of the fish, for I doubt, with all the other things we have got, if we shall be able to eat even a quarter of the two dozen crabs she has taken home."

"You are right," said Cross; "too much crab is heavy food, so we shall scarcely get through your two dozen, and you must forgive my laughing, only remember that you must not trust pretty pleading eyes in the head of a Granvillaise, be she woman or be she child, unless you are prepared to pay for looking at her eyes, instead of for the fish she has to sell you. But come along, the girl is on before us."

They found the girl at the end of one of the deepest crevices; her arm was plunged up to the shoulder in the water, and when they looked down they could see that she was poking the end of her stick into a narrow split in the rock.

"There is something here," she said; "I think it is a lobster; but he is shy, and I have not seen him yet, and he does not pull hard." She drew the stick gently back, and they saw something follow the bait.

"What was that?" asked Hope.

"Only prawns," said the girl, "but they are very large, so we will have them;" she plunged the other arm into the water and held the net close to the bottom; she then again pushed the bait into the hole and drew it out very slowly.

Hope could now see four very large prawns following the cuttle and giving it a strong jerk by seizing hold of the feelers; the girl continued to draw back the bait till it was over the net, which she suddenly raised, and the whole four were safe in the bag. "There," she said, "they are worth the trouble, for they are enormous."

And so they were, for Cross declared they were the largest he had ever seen. Though he knew that the largest were generally found thus hid, like lobsters, in the deep narrow cracks of the rocks, still he had never seen any so large as the four just taken.

"I had no notion that a prawn would take a bait in that way," said Hope.

"It is only on a coast like this that you can see it done," said Cross; "but you must be aware that they take bait, if you only remember that along the south coast of England the fine prawns are not caught with nets, as they are here, but with flat baskets, which are baited with fish-heads, and set like lobster-pots."

"True, true," said Hope; "but never having seen them following a bait before, I had forgotten that they must eat as well as everything else. Are there any more holes," he said, addressing the girl, "where you expect to find a lobster?"

"O yes," she replied, "plenty; but lobsters are scarce at this season; we find a great many more in the spring."

At the next hole which they tried the bait was pulled from the stick and drawn back into the hole with great force.

"It is an eel," she said, "and I have him." She held the line tight in one hand and the stick in the other, and pulled steadily, and with considerable force, for a second or two; all at once both hands were raised, and an eel of considerable size was wriggling in the air at the end of the stick.

The girl wrapped the line quickly round the stick, pulled out a coarse knife, cut out the hook, and popped the eel into her basket, all in ten seconds. It was then that Hope saw the merit of passing the line through the hole in the end of the stick, for, by drawing the line tight, the eel had no power of moving or entangling the line by twisting himself round it.

"A French sniggle is certainly the best," said Hope; "and if I were young enough to go back to Eton, or to care for sniggling eels, I should certainly follow the French plan."

The two friends followed the girl, while she tried several other holes. A second eel was taken, and a few more large

prawns. At the last place which the girl declared to be likely
for a lobster they did get one. It was very small, and was
caught exactly in the same way as she had taken the prawns.
The bait was drawn slowly back, till the lobster came above the
net; which was then quickly raised, and the lobster was flap-
ping his tail in the bottom of it. This Cross bought, and, together with the large prawns and cuttles, it was put into the
basket of the old lady with the stout legs, who had been
employed to dig sand-eels. She was then approaching, after
just finishing her day's work, having tried the wet places along
the whole length of the rocks, and with great apparent success,
for her basket was one-third full.

"How many have you?" said Cross, when he saw her.

"Without counting, give me two francs," said she, "and I
will take them home."

Cross looked at the basket. "At a sou a dozen, you are
not unreasonable. I did not calculate, however, on getting so
many, or on paying two francs for sand-eels; but, as I made the
bargain, I must take them. We can give away what we do not
want, and they are capital for breakfast." It was therefore
agreed that she should take them, with the lobster, cuttle-fish,
etc., to Carolles. All these, as we have already said, were put
into her basket, and away she marched, looking highly pleased
with her day's work. The cuttles, as Cross had foretold, were
as black as ever, and underwent another washing and squeezing
before they joined company with the brilliant little sand-eels.

The spot where this transaction took place was the outer
end of the mass of rock. The hand-nets and crab-hooks were
still busily employed behind them; immediately below, several
little children were engaged knocking something off the rock;
a number more were seen scattered over the expanse of sands
that stretched between the two friends and the sea; in the
water marched troops of prawn-fishers; and still further out
they saw the heads and shoulders of the oyster-catchers; while
here and there on the sand a man or a woman could be seen

with a dog following. These dogs did not attract Hope's notice at the time, and Cross made no allusion to them.

"What are those little things picking off the rocks?" asked Hope. "Are they periwinkles?"

"No," answered Cross, "it is not periwinkles they are gathering, but limpets. When I told you all these little things were going after cockles, I was wrong; I forgot the limpets. The people here never use periwinkles, but the poor people consider limpets to be very nutritious food. They stew them with some butter or grease, and put them into their soup. Taste differs in different countries; for with us, limpets are only used for bait, and the people eat periwinkles. Here, periwinkles are never looked at, and limpets are prized as good food for man. I rather suspect the French are right, and that, if our people were better cooks, they would find that limpets do not deserve to be despised by our poor. Our friend the Marquis is a great gourmand, and a capital cook. If you remind me, we will consult him on this head, as his opinion may be relied on ; and we need not wait long to ask the question, since, if I am not mistaken, I see him coming with his friend, for I see two people carrying a double-handed net between them."

"Till they reach us," said Hope, "let us look at the limpets these brats are gathering; they may be of a different sort from ours, and thus be better eating."

"I think they are exactly the same," said Cross; "but, as you look more minutely at these things than I do, you may perhaps see some difference that has not struck me."

They went towards the children, each of whom had a square-pointed knife with a thick back; some had, in addition, small wooden hammers, others only a stone in their right hands. The edge of the knife was applied always on one side and never on the top of the shell; a little sharp tap was given, either with the hammer or the stone, and the fish fell at once. Hope examined the contents of one of the baskets; the greater part of the limpets were exactly like those on the British coast, but some had much smoother shells, which were marked with bright coloured rings, some purple, some red, some yellow; all the children, however, agreed in affirming that those smart fish were exactly the same in quality as their sombre brethren, and that all were excellent in soup.

While they were talking and examining the basket, the Marquis and his friend had been approaching them; he hailed them when about fifty yards off, asking them how they got on and whether they were amused. The two friends then advanced towards him, asking what sport he had had.

"Capital," said the Marquis; "I shall be ruined in buying baskets to send them to my friends, for when we have chosen the best for ourselves, I have enough for twenty others."

Cross whispered to his companion, "We shall share the best, as he never neglects number one." The two friends then examined the basket, which contained a prodigious quantity.

Both offered their congratulations on his good sport.

"It is wonderful," said the Marquis, "and I almost wish it was not so good, for my back will be broken before I get home, and I am rather anxious to be there; for, since I am to have the honour of dining with you, I should not like that our land-lord gave you a bad dinner, so I shall give him a little advice myself. I like to keep my hand in practice in that fine art, for if things grow much worse here I have some thoughts of offer-ing myself to some of your grand seigneurs, who, I hear, pay for a good cook at a rate not unworthy the notice of a poor French marquis."

Cross laughed at the joke; Hope took what was said for gospel, for he did not know, as Cross did, that the Marquis was a legitimist and as proud of his rank and old blood as any Welshman; indeed, being a Breton, he had Welsh blood in his veins; but the intention of assisting the cook Cross knew was no joke, and he was therefore well aware that they would have as good a dinner as the provisions of the place could afford.

"Mr. Hope and myself," he said, "feel grateful for the

interest you take in our nourishment ; and, since you are going
to our quarters, will you allow me to recommend to your notice
the fish we have sent home, in hopes that you will give the
proper orders to the cook ?"

"With the greatest pleasure," said the Marquis. "Pray,
what have you sent?"

Cross enumerated the various sorts, and mentioned that his
friend had never tasted cuttle-fish.

"Ah, then, I will see to them myself," said the Marquis,
"and I hope he will not be disappointed ; but with so much
before us I will lose no time."

"Before you go," said Hope, "will you have the kindness
to tell me if limpets are good to eat ?"

"For want of better," said the Marquis, "they allow themselves to be eaten : they are a little hard, and require time and
attention; but with this they are nutritious, and by no means
to be despised by a person who is a judge ; and they should suit
the English taste, for they are improved by being a little
peppery."

Hope thanked the Marquis, adding that he wished to
enlighten his countrymen on some points of good eating, which
they had hitherto neglected, among others limpets and cuttle-
fish; and since he had heard his opinion on limpets, knowing
him to be such good authority, he should take the earliest opportunity of correcting the ignorance which had hitherto been
displayed in Britain by overlooking such an article of nutriment.

The Marquis gave a bow and a smile. "If you take the
merits of limpets on mere report, I hope to allow you to judge
for yourself regarding cuttle, and have no doubt as to the result."
He then marched off. The water, while he was standing, had
dripped into his sabots, from which it squirted as he walked.
With his old ragged straw-hat, sand-besprinkled blue flannel
trousers, and wooden sabots, he looked as little like a marquis
of ancient lineage as well could be.

"He may be a great man and a good cook," said Hope, " but he looks as little like either as anything I ever saw."

"Wait till you see his dinner and himself to-night, and you will change your opinion," said Cross; "in the meantime, if you wish to try if you can find cockles as well here as in Scotland, we had better be off."

They turned to walk towards the children who were far out on the sand, and as they did so, they saw close to them an old woman, followed by a dog. The old woman carried the usual basket on her left shoulder, and on the other a pickaxe with a very long handle. The dog was white, with long hair and a bushy tail, twisted up with a double turn, which he carried on one side of his back; he had a long, sharp, foxy-looking face, with bright black eyes, and his ears stood very erect, and were pointed.

"Here is something worth your seeing," said Cross ; "I had forgotten this sort of fishing, and as I am sure you will think it more interesting than cockle-picking, we will follow this old lady, and see what sport she gets. I know the dog; it is one of the best on the coast."

"The dog!" said Hope. "What has a dog to do with fishing?"

"Everything," said Cross, "in this sort of fishing, as you will see if you follow."

"But tell me," said Hope, "what are they going to fish for?"

"Eels," replied Cross ; "and by the blue colour of the dog's face, and the weight of the old lady's basket, they have had very good success already."

Hope stepped out and overtook the old woman ; he asked permission to see what she had in her basket.

"Willingly, my good gentleman," said she; and lifting up the sea-ware, he saw that the basket was half full of conger-eels, about as long as his arm.

"And does your dog catch those eels?" asked Hope.

"O no, sir; the dog finds them," she answered, "and I catch them. If you like to come on a little, there is a very good place near this, and you shall see how it is done."

"By all means let us go," said Hope; "fishing for eels with a dog and a pickaxe is something new, and quite beyond the common."

The old woman led the way along the outer edge of the rocks, till she came to a place where the sand ran for a considerable distance into the body of the rocks, which rose rather steeply on either side of this sandy estuary. The sand, however, was not smooth, for in all directions little mounds rose up, breaking the level.

"Go and seek, good dog Trompette," said the old lady, when she had entered this creek.

The dog started off, hunting in all directions. In a quarter of a minute he stopped at one of the little lumps, and began to scratch and whine like a terrier at a rat-hole.

"See! he has one," said the woman, as she ran towards the dog, brandishing her pickaxe. When she reached the place, she looked which way the hole ran, and then began tearing up the sand, which rose in lumps at every blow. After eight or ten strokes out tumbled a conger-eel about the same size as those in her basket; the dog and his mistress made a dash at it; the biped got it; the woman flung it with great force on the hard sand, and then quietly put it in her basket with the rest of her load, shouting, "Seek again, Trompette."

Trompette obeyed, and in this way, within five minutes after entering the creek, the dog found, and the mistress dug up and basketted, three of those eels. After this there was an interlude, the dog still hunting, and the old lady remaining stationary, with Cross and Hope beside her.

"He is a capital dog that of yours, madame; you call him Trompette, I think?" said Hope.

"Yes, sir; his father was called Trompette, and all his puppies were called Trompette after him. The father got the

name because his tail was twisted like a trumpet ; and you see
my dog's tail twists like one too."

" And are there any young Trompettes ?" asked Cross.

" O yes; a great many," replied the woman.   " I have got
two, and I call them both Trompette."

" Well," said Hope, in English, " if there are different gene-
rations of Pepper and Mustard on the borders of Scotland, I see
there are Trompettes of all ages on the shores of Normandy.
And pray, madame," he continued, addressing the old lady,
" have you much difficulty in breaking these dogs to hunt
eels ?"

" None at all ; we take a young dog out with an old one
once or twice, and we let them worry the eel, or perhaps eat
one, and then they will hunt quite well ; but some of them
have finer noses than others, and of course these are the best."

" And is this talent confined to the famille Trompette, or
are there other dogs that do the same ?"

" Other dogs are taught," said the old lady, " but my dog's
family do it at once."

" And in what sort of ground do you hunt for these eels ?"

" In ground like this," she said, lifting up a lump of the
sand with her pickaxe.

As she did so, Hope saw that there was something curious
in the sand ; it was, in fact, exactly like the rocks over which
they had been walking, only quite soft.

" Ha," said he, " I must have a look at this. Here, madame,
you have shown me something new to-day, and take this to
drink in return for the pleasure you have given me."   He gave
her a franc, and she, after returning a volume of thanks, began
to walk away.

Hope called after her, " Before you go, just knock me off a
bit of that rock, if you please."

She did as she was asked, and then continued her way, followed by her dog, to renew her search in the next creek in the
rocks.

"Well," exclaimed Hope, "this eel-hunting with a dog is the funniest sight I ever saw, and well worth coming all the distance to see; and now let me have a look at the ground where they find them, for it seems equally curious."

On examination, they perceived that the whole ground was composed of small tubes, laid side by side, exactly like honeycomb; the tubes seemed to be composed of some glutinous substance in which shell-sand was sticking.

"I should like to get a sight of the insect that makes these tubes; it must be something like those which form the coral rocks."

He sought in vain, however, in the mass before him; the insect was deeper down in the sand, and they had nothing with which to dig deeper.

"Come to the place where the eels were found," said Hope; "the hole is deeper there, and I have little doubt that the congers are in search of these pipe-makers when they bury themselves in the sand."

They went to the spot where the last eel had been found; it was close by the place where the old woman had knocked off a good number of bits of the rock; and here they were more fortunate, for in the very first sandy lump which he broke, Hope saw twenty or thirty long worm-looking creatures draw themselves back into their holes. The whole lump was soon detached from the rock, and the object of his search was before him.

The creatures were worm-like; the lower half, or tail, being considerably thinner than the upper half; this upper half had rings on it, that at first looked like legs; at the head there was a slight increase of size, and the end, or mouth, was somewhat like a lamprey's; the colour was a pale yellowish-brown.

"I have seen a good deal that is new to me to-day," said Hope; "these among the rest. Each of these pipes seems to contain an insect, and if so, what countless myriads must there be on this coast; and how little would we think, in casting a

glance on this vast plain of sand, that it was teeming with life
so varied and innumerable ! If I do not mistake, the rocks are
living too, for almost all we have passed over to-day look like
indurated masses of the same formation as this sand. I will
soon see, by looking at what the old lady has knocked off for me,
whether I am right in this supposition ; at all events I feel convinced that the conger-eels bury themselves in search of these
insects. If I were near the basket again, I would cut one open
to examine what it has in its stomach."

The broken rock was quite close ; a few steps brought them
to it, and the first glance proved that Hope was right ; the rock,
like the sand, was composed of tubes, lying closely joined together. At one place where the pickaxe had struck, a very
large fragment had been broken off ; the softer spongy substance had split and fallen, showing that it was a superstructure
raised on a foundation of clay slate. The mass that had fallen
had peeled from this harder rock, and enabled the friends accurately to examine the formation, and they could plainly see that
the tubes were continuous for several feet. The surface of the
mass exactly resembled a large sponge, swelling into lumps or
sinking into hollows ; but on more minute examination, the ends
of the tube, which in a sponge would be soft, were here formed
of small particles of silex and broken shell, stuck together by
some glutinous substance.

"It looks," said Hope, "as if these creatures, on leaving
their holes, got covered with this sand, and scraped themselves
clean on the edge when they went back."

"Yes it does," replied Cross ; "and with the sand they must
leave some of the slime from their bodies, for the edge, which
is quite soft, is sticky to the touch."

"So it is," said Hope ; "and I suppose it hardens by exposure,
and thus forms these rocks ; let us try to get hold of some of the
insects again, and feel if they are sticky or slimy."

A lump of the rock was broken, and like the sand it was
found to be swarming with the same insects. Those in the rock,

however, were rather darker in colour and smaller than those they had examined on the flat sand ; and they were confirmed in their idea as to the formation of the rock, by finding that a glutinous substance issued from them when they were rubbed between their fingers.

Hope and Cross remained some time quite absorbed in examining the form of the rock and the creatures within it. Hope was in the act of breaking off some small bits to carry home with him, when Cross suddenly gave a loud shout, calling out—"The Lord have mercy on us ! I forgot the tide, and here it comes !"

Hope turned towards the sea and saw a stream of water running at a rapid pace, and covering the sandy creek where the eels had been found. Not aware of the danger, he said quite quietly—"Faith, so it does ; I suppose we had better be off."

" If we can," said Cross ; " by crossing the rock we may yet be in time." He looked rather pale as he spoke, and Hope seeing his alarm hastened to follow him ; for the moment Cross ceased speaking he scrambled up the rocks, and began walking as rapidly as he could across them towards the nearest shore ; but the pace was necessarily slow, for the roughness in some parts, and the slipperiness in others, obliged them to pick their steps ; the numberless crevices, which had been a source of amusement an hour before, now served still further to retard their progress, for they were forced to make many a detour to get past them. At last they reached the highest point, and could see before them.

" Thank God !" said Cross, " the sand is not yet covered, but we must run for it."

The sand was in fact still visible, but small lines of blue water could be seen marking and breaking the surface.

They hastened on, Hope looking at these lines, which seemed rapidly to increase in breadth ; but he was soon obliged to keep his eyes on the ground, for in looking up he had placed his foot on a bunch of weed, slipped, fell, and got a severe shake, besides cutting his hands.

K

In three minutes more, however, they were at the edge of the sand, but when they reached it, they saw that the sand was now in stripes, the water in sheets.

"We shall do yet," said Cross, "for, thank God! here is a girl before us." He began to run rapidly, and Hope followed.

They proceeded thus for about two hundred yards, when they saw the little girl (the same from whom Hope had bought the crabs) coming hastily towards them. She reached them before they had advanced many more paces, and as she ran she called out something which they could not at first understand, for she was so much out of breath.

When she was close to them, they could distinguish that she said, "The wave! the wave! it is coming; turn, turn, and run, or we are lost!"

They did turn, and they saw, far out to sea, a large wave rolling towards the shore. Blown as they were, they yet increased their speed, as they retraced their steps towards the rocks they had just left.

The little girl passed them and led the way; the two friends strained every nerve to keep pace with her, for, as they neared the rock, the wave still rolled towards them; the sand became gradually covered, and the last ten steps were up to their knees in water, but they were on the rock.

"Quick! quick!" said the girl; "there is the passage to cross, and if the second wave comes we shall be too late."

She ran on for a hundred yards till she came to a crack in the rock, six or seven feet wide, along which the water was rushing like a mill-sluice.

"We are lost," said the girl; "I cannot cross, it will carry me away."

"Is it deep?" asked Cross.

"Not very," she said, "but it is too strong."

Cross lifted the girl in his arms; he was a strong big man; he plunged into the stream, which was up to his waist. With a few strides he was across, and set the girl down; he then held on by the rock, and stretched out his hand to Hope, who was following like an experienced wader, taking very short steps, and with his legs well stretched out, to prevent being swept away by the force of the water ; Hope grasped the hand thus held out to him, and in another second the two friends were standing by the girl.

"That is tremendous," said Hope ; "if I had not seen it I never would have believed it."

"It is indeed," said Cross ; "and in winter or in blowing weather, the tide-wave comes in with far greater force than this we have just seen."

"Come on, come on," cried the girl. "Holy Virgin ! we were nearly lost."

The little girl again led the way to the high point of lighter coloured rock which Hope had remarked in the morning. When they had reached it, she said, "We are safe now ;" and she pulled from her breast a string of beads with a crucifix, and began to tell the beads. The two friends looked on in silence ; perhaps they too were returning thanks to heaven, although they held no beads in their hands.

After a few minutes thus spent, the girl looked up and smiled to Cross. "Thank you," said she, "for lifting me over ; I could not have crossed by myself ; and," she continued, "the second wave has come, and it is all water now."

The friends looked ; all around them was the wide sea ; they were on an island which each moment became less ; and this island was three quarters of a mile from the shore.

"I am afraid, sir, you will be cold," said the little girl. "We are quite safe here, for this point is always above water except in a storm ; but we shall have to remain here for three or four hours before we can go to the shore."

"Cold or hot," said Cross, "we may be thankful we are here. But what made you forget the tide, for you must know the coast so well ?"

"I did not forget it," she said, "but I feared you would be

drowned as you are strangers; and I thought I should be in time to tell you, but I was too late, and the wave came."

"And did you risk your life to save us?" said Hope, the tears starting into his eyes.

"I thought at any rate I should get here," she replied. "As you are strangers you would not know that it is always dry here, and on the strand you would be lost; so I came to help you, for the gentleman was kind, and gave me a good price for my crabs; so I hoped I should be in time to warn you, but I was very nearly too late."

Hope took the little girl in his arms and kissed her. "Never say a word against a Granvillaise again as long as you live," he said to Cross, "for this child shows that they are brave and generous. If they drive a hard bargain you see they are grateful, instead of laughing at their customers; and for this little creature's sake I shall love and respect them even if they do bully their husbands;"—then speaking in French to the girl he continued, "We owe you our lives, you brave little creature; so I thank you in the meantime, and hope to do more hereafter. But how came you to know we were here?"

"I took your crabs to the inn, and the bourgeois gave me some bread for the rest that I had in my basket. As I came back I met Angela on the hill. She was tired, and she asked me to carry some of her oysters; and while I was dividing them between her basket and mine I saw you below. I knew it must be you, for only strangers would stay so long out here at spring tides. I ran away at once, and forgot that I had her oysters, and that the bread for my mother was on the grass. I remembered the oysters when I had run a good way. They are heavy, and I wished I had left them, for I could not run so fast with them on my back."

"She is a brave little thing," said Cross, "and shows she has presence of mind to see, and promptitude to act. She shall have all the money in my pocket."

"And in mine too," said Hope, "but it is not much, and we

must do something more for her. I wonder what she would most like in the world."

"Ask her," said Cross.

Hope did so.

"To have a dress," she said, "to wear when I go to mass, just like the one Angela's sister had on last Sunday, with a beautiful silver crucifix like hers."

"You shall have it," said both Hope and Cross together; "but I wish," continued Hope in English, "she had asked something else than dress."

"Though she is a little heroine," said Cross, "still she is French, and therefore a slave to finery; and, heaven knows, she is lightly enough clothed just now to make her covet something better to wear. Poor thing, she must be very cold." He asked her.

"Yes," she replied, "I am a little cold; for I am hungry."

"And I have left my sandwich-box in the carriage," said Hope; "another proof, if any were wanting, that no one should ever move without the commissariat. Poor little thing, she will have long to wait, and, to say the truth, I feel that a good breakfast will not last all day."

"Have you got your flask?" asked Cross.

"Yes, by the by, I have got that," answered Hope; and he produced it from his pocket.

"We shall do very well then," said Cross, "for I have got half-a-dozen Jersey biscuits, which fortunately are in my breast pockets, and therefore dry; we shall take the liberty of making free with Miss Angela's oysters, which, with a drop of your brandy to wash them down, will stop a gap till the tide turns. Have you got your knife?" he asked of the little girl.

"Yes, sir," she said, and held up a coarse square-headed clasp-knife covered with rust; as well it might be, for it was hanging to her side by a string, and had been trailing for many a day in the sea.

"Count Angela's oysters, then," said Cross, "that we may pay her for them when we get on shore ; for we will eat them, and you shall have a share."

The little thing laughed amazingly, and seemed to think the plan a capital joke ; she emptied the basket on the rock, opened her knife and an oyster in a moment, and handed it to Cross, who in return gave her two biscuits, and the same to Hope.

The girl smiled as she bit one of the good solid captain's biscuits, and then held up another oyster ready opened to Hope.

" Eat that one yourself," he said. " I will take the rest."

She did as she was bid, laughing right merrily as she said— " Poor Angela ! she did not think she was giving us our supper when she asked me to carry her oysters."

Hope then took his share, Cross followed, and the little girl was again desired to take her turn and swallow another of the oysters, which she opened as fast as they could eat.   This continued for several rounds, the girl always laughing heartily when she was desired to take her turn, apparently thinking that every fresh oyster was a new and excellent joke.

" Now," said Cross, " a small drop of your bottle, just to keep these fellows warm, and then to work again.   Much as I like oysters, I never knew how good they were till to-day."

Hope produced his flask, and offered the little girl the first sip.

She put her lips to the cup and then returned it.   " It is too strong," she said ; " if it was cider I would have drunk it and been grateful, but for this I must only thank you, for I cannot drink it."

Hope and Cross pressed her in vain even to taste it again, but she refused.   As they had no objections to the strength, they practised what they preached, and swallowed a good modicum to their great inward comfort, and then resumed their attack on the biscuits and oysters, never stopping again till all were finished.   Another sip from the flask completed the feast.

" There," exclaimed Cross, " there is an end of that ; we have passed, in my estimation, a very pleasant ten minutes, but they are the only agreeable ones we shall spend for some time, if they are not the last; the water is narrowing our territory every moment, and if the tide rises much more, we shall have to swim for it yet."

The girl, though he spoke in English, understood by his eye that he was speaking of the tide.

"There is no fear," she said; "for even if the water reaches us, it has no force now, and the points are always dry."

"Cold comfort," said Hope, looking at the small sharp-pointed rocks that rose about a couple of feet above where they were sitting; they were just high enough to afford a slight shelter from the wind, which they now felt to be cold enough. Their island, however, was still about twenty yards across; the tide was rising more slowly, but it was rising. The food and brandy had warmed the men, but the little girl looked very cold; she was trying to give another turn to a ragged black silk handkerchief which she wore round her neck. The two francs which Hope had paid her, which had excited her gratitude and saved their lives, were tied in one corner; so worn was the handkerchief, however, that the colour of the metal could be seen through the silk.

"Here," said Hope, "put this round your neck;" and he produced from his pocket a gaudy, scarlet, silk pocket-handkerchief, with a black edge.

"O no, sir," she said; "it is so handsome, I am afraid it will be spoiled."

"No, it will not," said Cross, "the gentleman gives it to you; so you will take care of it;" then speaking in English, he said to Hope, "as the corner of their handkerchief is always their purse, we may as well club what money we have to furnish the one you have given her; the idea of her riches will do more to warm her than dry clothes and a fire."

"I have not above twenty francs in my pocket," said Hope, "but to those she is heartily welcome."

"And I have not so many," said Cross; "here is all I have, just seventeen francs; but join them with what you have, and tie them whole in the corner of your handkerchief, then put it round her neck, and I will warrant that she will be as warm as a toast, and think herself a second Rothschild."

The money was clubbed—it proved to be forty francs—and was tied as Cross recommended in the corner of her handkerchief. The girl watched the proceeding, and when Hope passed it round her neck, she blushed with delight, kissed both their hands, repeating several times, "How beautiful! how generous, how kind you are to give me so much!" and after looking at her treasures for a while she said, "How jealous Angela will be, and how happy my mother."

"We must not let Angela be jealous," said Cross, "for she is to tell us where her sister got her smart dress; this gentleman and I have promised that you shall have one like it; so you must bring Angela to see us to-morrow, that we may give her a handkerchief also in payment for the oysters, and then she will help us to get the dress we have promised."

"O happy day! happy day!" she said, clapping her hands; "Angela will be so pleased."

"If we ever get ashore," said Hope, for a wave at that moment rolled past, and the water began to run along the little platform they were sitting upon; they all rose and mounted on the rocky points, where they clustered, supporting each other. Another wave came, it appeared only like a ripple, but when they looked down the water was a foot deep where they had previously been seated. There was silence for a while; another wave came— the water was within six inches of their feet.

"It is a terrible high tide," said the girl, "but if we hold together, we shall not be washed away."

"That is true," said Cross; "and as we are wet already we need not much care."

Hope's face was towards the shore. "There are a great many people clustering on the point," he said; "it is always a comfort to know that our fellow-beings take an interest in us, and I suppose those people are watching us."

The little girl turned to look ; a faint sound of a cheer was heard, and they could see the people on shore waving their hats and handkerchiefs.

"They think the tide has turned," she said, "and they are shouting to cheer us."

She was right ; the tide had turned. Another wave came and wet their feet ; but when it had passed, the water had fallen, and in five minutes more the platform was again dry !

CHAPTER VI.

WHEN the bare surface of the rock was seen, the whole party gladly descended from the point round which they had been clinging so uncomfortably during the last quarter of an hour.

"Grâce à Dieu!" exclaimed the little girl; "I was frightened; were not you?"

"The time seemed very long," said Cross; "and, to own the truth, I was calculating how long I could have kept my feet on that slippery ledge if the water rose much higher."

"And I," said Hope, "am glad to be again standing on this flat surface, wet though it be. We never know the full value of anything till we have lost it; and, as a case in point, I little thought, twenty minutes ago, that I should be glad to be standing here still. And stand we must, for, cold as it is, we should not mend our position by settling down in the puddles which the sea has left."

The light began to fail, and they kept their eyes turned towards the shore. All their hopes were fixed in that direction; for although the white sails of the fishing-boats could be seen to seawards returning to port, they knew that they were hastening to seek the shelter of the mole at Granville, and that there was no chance of any assistance on that side. Five minutes after they had reached the platform, they saw the large group of people disperse from the high point where they had been collected. A few now only remained on this elevated station; the rest were collected in smaller groups, each group being at some little distance from the other.

"They are gone to the market now," said the little girl. "I am sure they have been thinking of us, for they are very late. Old Marie de Coutance will be very cross, for she is always in such a hurry to be off before it is dark."

"What market do you mean?" asked Hope, "and who is Marie de Coutance?"

"There are people from the different towns who come here to buy what we catch; three of them are called Marie, and so, to distinguish them, they are called after the town they come from. Marie de Coutance comes from Coutance; she is always cross, and always in a hurry, for she has a long way to go; but she gives good prices, so she has many who sell to her. You see she has plenty near her now; that is her station, the farthest to the left."

"How do you know her station at this distance?" asked Hope.

"Because every one always goes to the same place. The station next to her belongs to Mons. Aufoé. We call him Aufoé de Paris, although he comes from Granville; for he buys all the prawns he can get, and sends them to Paris; and the people like him, as he always gives the same price, and will take all you have without any trouble; so a great many go to him, as you may see, for he has the largest party at his station; and you can see beside him his two horses with the large panniers. Whatever he buys just now, will be boiled and sent off to Paris by the diligence to-morrow morning."

"There is a good deal of method in that arrangement," said Cross.

"There is indeed," replied Hope; "and it explains to me what I did not before understand—I mean the way in which all the fish are disposed of; for the quantity must be very great, if the hundreds we have seen fishing to-day only caught a very small portion each. It proves the truth of the assertion, that demand creates supply. If the same organised market could be established in the west of Ireland, or even in Scotland, there would not be so great a complaint against the indolence of the people as now ; for were there a few Mons. Aufoés de Londres or de Dublin scattered in their fishing-stations, the people would rush to the sea, as they do here, and in time they would learn to extract and spread the riches which now lie untouched and unsought for in her fruitful bosom."

" Why," said Cross, " we have the same sort of people, and on a much larger scale ; what do we call our fishcurers who buy thousands of pounds' worth of herrings every year from our fishermen?"

" I call them very useful people in their way," said Hope, " and they prove the truth of what I have said ; they buy herrings, and the herring-fishing is fostered, but there are no people to buy and send off to market the shoals of fish which might be caught and sold fresh, for the consumption of our large towns. What employment would be given, what wealth could be gained, by the capture and sale of the myriads of fish which hang on the coasts of Britain, more especially on the west coasts of Ireland and Scotland !"

" I daresay you are right," said Cross, " but I have never thought much on the subject ; I have been more taken up in observing the different modes of catching those I have found best to eat ; and see there is one of your friends, a spider crab ; he has come out with the tide, and is now employed in scraping our oyster shells."

Hope looked where Cross was pointing. In eating their oysters the shells had been thrown into a hollow in the rock ; this now stood full of water about six inches deep, and on the centre of the heap of white shells lay something like a bunch of small sea-weed.

" It is a crab," said Hope, " for I saw him move, and we may pass away the time by watching his movements."

" You must keep very still then," said Cross, " for if we move he will not."

They remained very quiet, and after a while, they observed

the animal slip very slowly from one shell to the other, evidently eating any small remnants of fish that remained.

"I wonder what they live on in general," said Hope, "for it is not often, I suspect, that people come out here to eat oysters."

"I imagine," replied Cross, "that they catch fish for themselves, for I once saw one who had a live fish in his claws. I cannot help thinking that nature has given them this covering of sea-ware on their shell as much to aid them in the pursuit of their prey as to protect them from enemies. Their motions are so slow that they could never catch anything so nimble as a fish, unless the fish went to them; it is for this reason that I think their covering is given to aid them in procuring their food. There are a vast number of fish who hide themselves under stones—such as sea-loach, bullheads, and rock-fish or sea-perch; all these go under every stone they pass; now, if you are deceived in thinking this crab a stone or a bunch of sea-weed, we may well suppose that a fish may make the same mistake. If they did so, and ran under him as they do under other stones, they would find themselves, as the Yankees say, in a very unhandsome fix; for the crab has only to grasp as he does the iron hook, and it is all up with poor fishy, whatever sort he may be; besides which the crab may be able to snap up some of the insects that make these rocks, and serve them right, since looking at them nearly converted us into food for fishes. If we had been drowned, I have no doubt some of these beauties would have found us out and had a taste of us; practically answering your question as to what they live on by eating a bit of you."

"What a horrid idea!" said Hope; "the very thought of being eaten by a brute like that makes me colder than ever."

"Phoo! nonsense," said Cross; "what would it signify? How go the lines?

'A good fat priest is a dainty meal,
And I'll have my share with the pike and the eel.'

I suppose any stout gentleman would do as well as a priest:

and for pike read crab, and the lines will do ; and why should
they not try how you tasted ? You have been making very
anxious inquiries regarding their flesh, and as they cannot speak,
it would be quite fair that they should put the question practically ; but thanks to our little friend here, they have been
balked for this time."

"You are a horrid fellow," said Hope, "and you have quite
prevented my having any wish to taste these creatures."

"You are very dainty," replied Cross ; "I only wish I had a
few well dressed, and I would make an example of them ; for,
to say the truth, in spite of our oysters I feel horridly hungry.
I could even eat a dish of eels, which I never very much liked,
for I was told a story that quite put me off touching them."

"And what might that be?" said Hope ; "it must be something very bad."

"Why," said Cross, "the story of the widow and her
drowned husband."

"I never heard it," said Hope.

"Oh, you dear innocent creature !   What a pleasure it is to
find a grown gentleman who does not know one's old stories!"

"I can afford you that pleasure," said Hope, "for I am fully
grown and never heard it ; so pray tell it to me."

"Why, you must know then," said Cross, "that there once
lived a man and a wife who were not on the best terms. One
fine morning the man was missing, and nothing could be heard
of him for a fortnight. The wife pretended to be in great distress, so much so that when his body was at last found in a fish-
pond near the house, no one liked to tell her, more especially as
the finding was accompanied with what they thought would
shock her dreadfully ; namely, that when the poor fellow was
pulled out of the water a great quantity of eels fell on the grass
from his body ; the fact was he was full of them !

"At last a friend undertook to break the intelligence, and
receive the widow's instructions. This he did, not omitting to
mention the eels. The story told, he asked what were her

wishes, as he was anxious, together with the rest of her friends, to obey her orders.

"The widow removed her handkerchief from her eyes, and murmured out, 'Send home the eels and *set him again*—I am very fond of eels.'"

"You nasty fellow," said Hope, "I am half frozen already, and your story makes my flesh creep; I am fast losing what little warmth I had."

"I am sorry I told it then," said Cross, "for I am as cold as a frog myself, and have been talking nonsense to pass the time and to try to make us forget where we are. Since my stories make you colder, let us move about a bit; our territory is becoming larger; quite enough to have a short race. I will give you ten yards and run you a hundred."

"That would have done very well in the morning," said Hope, "but I am much too stiff for anything of the sort just now; you forget that your younger blood does not cool as fast as mine, for I have twenty years the start of you."

"Well, let us walk then; take my arm and we will make the round of our island; it will be something to do and keep us in motion."

"We must not forget our little friend here," said Hope, "although she is as quiet as a mouse, and never complains."

"We will ask her to come with us," said Cross, "but as I told you, she has forgot cold and hunger; she is admiring your silk handkerchief and the five-franc pieces in the corner—she is building castles in the air, and thinking how she shall expend her riches; but we may as well disturb her dreams and make her join our walk, for she will be able to tell us when it will be safe to start from our present kingdom—Marie," he called.

"Did you call me?" said the girl, starting from her reverie; "my name is not Marie, I am Matilde."

"And a very pretty name," said Cross; "will you come with us and tell us how much longer we must stay here?"

"Willingly," she replied; "but there is not much use yet,

for when the tide turns it goes out quickly for a little and then stops a while ; after which it falls very fast. The back wave has not come yet, and till then we must not think of moving."

" To prevent being benumbed we must follow my first plan then," said Cross, " and make the tour of our island."

He took Hope's arm and they began their walk, but it was no easy job, for it was now nearly dark, and they stumbled and slipped at every step. Cross insisted on going on, and dragged Hope with him ; after groping and stumbling for a considerable time they found themselves again on their old platform. Hope was bored to death, tired, and out of breath; but they were no longer cold, and they had got over a good portion of their time. They could no longer distinguish what was on the shore, but the line of the high promontory could be seen against the sky.

" Surely those are lights," said Hope. The little girl called out at the same moment, " See ! there are lanterns—they are coming to guide us."

Sure enough three lights could be seen coming down the hill ; they stopped at the shore.

" Shall we look now," said Matilde, " if we can venture ?"

" But how will you be able to know in the dark," asked Hope, " whether we can venture or not ?"

" If the passage where the gentleman carried me over is dry," said Matilde, " it will be safe to go ; but not till then."

" Let us see then how it is," said Hope, " for I shall not be sorry to leave our present quarters ; I own I never found time pass so slowly before."

It was now quite dark, and they stumbled more than ever in walking to the creek in the rocks which Matilde called the passage ; when they reached it, there was still a good deal of water running rapidly through, but it was not up to their knees in depth, and was running in the contrary direction to that in which it was raging when they passed it in the morning ; so they waded through and continued their course over the remainder of the rock, which they knew they had to pass before reaching the broad extent of sand which lay between them and the shore. Fear and daylight had made these rocks seem shorter than they now found them; and they had several more slips and tumbles to undergo before they reached the outer edge; when they got there the sand was not visible, but they had the pleasure of perceiving that the lights were advancing towards them.

"In for a penny, in for a pound," said Cross; "we are so wet we may as well walk at once; the water cannot be deep now." He slid into the water, which was but little above his knees; the rest followed, and they began their way rejoicing, stepping out towards the advancing lights; at each minute the water became more shallow, and when they joined the party who were carrying the lanterns, they were once more on dry ground. The party consisted of an old woman, a tall handsome girl, and a young man, each carrying a lantern; several other young men and girls were following. When the party from the rock came within range of the light, the old woman ran forward, embraced Matilde tenderly, then put down her lantern, cried violently, and ended by scolding her like a pickpocket.

Matilde bore these various paroxysms with great patience; we suppose she was used to them, but when the scolding had continued a moderate time she said—

"The gentlemen are wet, do not keep them waiting, mother; see how generous they have been to me;" and she put the two ends of her handkerchief with the contents into her mother's hand, who immediately ceased scolding, and began to bless her child and the two gentlemen.

The party then continued their course towards the shore, the young man leading the way. The tall girl fell back; she took off a coarse woollen shawl which she wore, and placed it on Matilde's shoulders. "Poor little one, you must be cold," she said.

"O Angela! how kind of you to come, and I not to see you," said Matilde, as she put her arms round her neck, and then she burst out laughing—"We have eaten all your oysters, and they were so good."

L

"You are welcome, little one," returned her companion, "although I did not eat your bread; I gave it to your mother."

"You are always good to me," said Matilde; "and these gentlemen have been so kind, they have given me all this money and this beautiful shawl; and listen," she whispered, "they have promised to give you one like it, to pay for your oysters, and to buy me a dress like your sister's."

"They are very good to think of me," said Angela; "but you saved them, and I am glad they are grateful, for you deserve it at their hands."

"Is that your friend Angela?" said Hope; "ask her to come to us this evening, we wish to speak to her. When you have got some dry clothes, you must come and get something to eat, and bring her and your mother with you. I hope," he continued to Cross, "we shall be able to get something for them when they come."

"No fear of that," said Cross, "with the Marquis to act as caterer we shall not want; but, poor man, what a state he will be in; no cook can forgive the person who is too late, and when a man is to eat, as well as to superintend the cooking of the dinner, to keep him waiting is a double crime. I suspect we shall find him in a very bad humour."

"We cannot help it," said Hope, "so we must do our best to soothe him when we meet. If eating what he has prepared will please him, I shall succeed, for I feel dreadfully wolfish. I wish I had my feet in a pail of hot water and his dinner before me, and I would astonish him."

"You propose two things in one sentence," said Cross, "not easily done—first, to get a foot-pail and hot water; secondly, to astonish the Marquis. But nothing is impossible, they say, to a willing hand. I will do my best to get you a foot-bath, and you must try what you can do yourself to eat up to our friend; for if you do you may astonish him."

This was the last thing like conversation that passed between any of the party till they reached their quarters, for as Cross

ceased to speak they arrived at the beach ; the ascent was heavy
through the loose sand, for they had to clamber up the steep
face of the rocky point, and then to walk along a narrow path
and a bad road for half a mile, before reaching their door.

Still with remaining wet for so many hours, Hope saw the
lights of the village with great satisfaction.   At the first turn
they came on a house better lighted than any other.   At the
door stood the Marquis in black trousers, silk stockings, a smart
silk waistcoat, a white neckcloth with very large bows, but a
linen coat like that of an English under-butler in the morning
when about to clean his plate.   He held a white apron in his
hand, which he began to tie round his waist the moment the
Englishmen and their party came in sight.   He was in a com-
miserative, not in an angry mood, which they learnt by his first
exclamation.

" Here you are at last, and alive, grâce à Dieu !   What you
must have suffered from hunger ; you must be famished !
Dinner late, and you three hours later.   I thought of you while
I ate my little morsel, and the thought was so painful, I could
not enjoy anything ; but now that you are here I feel my force
restored, and I hope I shall be able to do justice to the supper,
with which I trust you will be pleased ; for the news of your
situation arrived here in time to enable me to prevent the pans
being put to the fire, and the moment I heard the tide had
turned, and that you were safe, I made them put our roast in
order, and you see the fours are burning bright, and the casse-
roles are ready to be put down in a moment.   How long will
you be, that we may make our calculations ?"

While the Marquis was thus running on, Hope and Cross
had followed him into the apartment which, in fact, was both
the kitchen and dining-room of the little inn.   It was beautifully clean, and coming out of the dark, the light from the fire,
lamps, and candles, made it so bright, it was a moment before
they could see.   When their eyes became accustomed to the
brilliancy, which they did while the Marquis was speaking, they

saw the table spread on one side of the fireplace ; the cloth was
covered with several dishes, on which were piled pears of various
sorts, blue plums and greengages, apricots, two large pyramids
of prawns, and a huge melon. Round the fire were a number
of pots and pans, deep sunk in hot embers ; before it was a long
semicircular tin case, something between a plate-warmer and a
Dutch oven ; this case surrounded a spit, which was turning
merrily. All the little charcoal stoves were glowing bright ;
beside them stood some covered stew-pans and a frying-pan, and
at a little distance on either side were two of the beehive-looking
baskets. All this they saw at a glance, so that when the Marquis inquired when they could be ready, Cross answered, " In a
quarter of an hour or twenty minutes."

" Then let us say twenty minutes, and be exact," said the
Marquis, " and in that time all will be in order." He opened a
little trap-door in the top of the tin case, and showed a small
leg of mutton which had just been put down, lifted the baskets
and exhibited the fish, prepared for putting in the pots and
frying-pans, and pointed to the various other preparations which
were standing round the stoves. We forgot to mention that, in
addition to the many articles that were around and in front of
the fire, there hung above it one of the very large brass pans,
which they had seen used for making the cabbage soup. Their
attention was drawn to this by a question which Hope asked—
namely, whether there would be enough to give something to eat
to the little girl who had saved them, together with her mother
and friend ?

" The soup is excellent," said the Marquis, " and we shall
have plenty left from our dinner."

Cross looked into the large pan.

" Not that," said the Marquis, " but this," pointing to one of
the pots that was by the side of the fire ; " and I advise you to
take a small cup while you are dressing—it will warm you, and
prevent you being detained from the more solid nourishment
which I hope to offer you when you are dressed."

"Very good advice," said Cross ; "so away you go and get your wet things off. I will be after you in a minute, but I must see what I can do for your foot-bath."

Hope willingly followed this advice ; the warm room and the sight of the fire had made him feel even more chilly than when he was in the air. He followed the hostess, who led the way out of the house and up an outside stair into a large double-bedded room. There was a fire on the hearth, and the boy who had driven them was in attendance to offer his services—N.B., a most extraordinary instance of attention, for it is rare to find a Norman boy volunteer anything that will give him trouble.

The hostess offered to dry his feet, and produced a bundle of coarse white towels.

This service Hope refused with thanks, but expressed his great wish to have some hot water.

The hostess replied that she would see what could be done, took a small ewer out of another vessel that looked like a pie dish, and left the room. The said ewer and pie dish were the only preparations which the room afforded for washing.

Hope bade the boy unstrap and open his portmanteau, while he began to drag off the wet garments which were sticking to him. He was uncomfortable, and rather sulky at being disappointed in finding no means of washing off the clammy feeling of the salt water. At this moment the door opened, and Cross and the Marquis's servant made their appearance, carrying between them the identical large brass pan that had been hanging above the fire in the kitchen. In the other hand Cross bore a second pan of the same sort, only smaller, and behind him came the hostess with a bucket of cold water. She was laughing immoderately, and repeating, "They are a queer set these English lords."

Cross made her a number of fine speeches, and begged her to go to the Marquis, who would be in despair at her absence ; then poured a share of the hot water into the lesser pan, added cold till the heat was reduced to a bearable temperature, placed

the large pan before Hope, and the lesser in front of another
chair, and told him there was a bath fit for a king, and to make
the most of it.

Hope roared with laughing, but in half a minute he was
robed in his dressing-gown and sighing with the comfort of having his feet in this new-fangled foot-pail, which comfort was by
no means reduced by the re-entrance of the Marquis's boy with
two cups of excellent soup.

Cross did not allow his companion to luxuriate for any time
in his comforts; he urged haste, and so effectually that the
twenty minutes were very little exceeded when they again entered
the kitchen and dining-hall.

The Marquis was in all his glory. When they entered he
vanished for a moment, and then returned in a coat of the last
Paris cut, looking and acting the Marquis of the old school to
perfection, as he begged the friends to place themselves at table.
Hope, as he looked at him, saw that Cross had been right, for
he no longer recognised the ragged fisherman or the professed
cook in the highbred-looking gentleman before him. They had
brought down with them a couple of bottles of the wine which
Hope had stowed away in the seat of the carriage—one of champagne and one of sauterne—which they placed on the table.

"Ah! you have foresight, I see," said the Marquis; "this
white wine is an addition. I have been able to procure you a
bottle of Spanish wine, which you English like, and also a couple
of bottles of very superior Bordeaux from my friend the curé.
He is an excellent judge, and I can trust to his taste;—but here
comes our roast."

"Are we to have none of the fish?" asked Hope in a whisper.

"Yes, by and by," answered Cross, in the same tone; "but
you must eat according to the plan of our Amphitrion to-day;
if you don't like it, we will alter it to-morrow."

This whispered conversation was not heard or noticed by the
Marquis, for he was employed in cutting the melon into slices,
and his boy was placing on the table the plumpest but smallest

leg of mutton Hope had ever seen. The melon being cut up, the Marquis performed the same ceremony on the mutton, which the boy carried round to each of the party, who helped himself as he liked; the melon was then presented in like manner; Cross took a goodly slice, but Hope refused.

"My dear sir, you are wrong," said the Marquis; "I assure you the melon is a very good one, or perhaps you do not like to eat it with your roast? I have before met some of your countrymen who have the bad prejudice of not liking melon with their meat, and prefer to eat it with sugar at dessert; if you have this unfortunate predilection, my dear sir, let me pray you to give it up; melon after dinner is a villanous nutriment, it lies in a cold lump and never digests, but when eaten with your roast it gives zest to your food and adds strength and freshness to your stomach, preparing an excellent foundation for the rest of your meal."

Hope caught Cross's eye, so he helped himself to a slice of the rejected melon, followed the example of the Marquis by sprinkling it over with salt and pepper, and was surprised, on trying the mixture, to find that roast mutton and melon were very good together.

Cross, who remarked that the Marquis had given rather a contemptuous glance at Hope, thought it right to make an apology for his friend.

"My friend Mr. Hope," he said, "has not been long in this country, and, I grieve to say, for a man who is well instructed in other matters, he is sadly deficient in his duty to himself at table; but, as he is willing to learn, I hope, my dear Marquis, you will kindly give him your advice, and, in asking this favour at your hands, I am aware I do him a great service."

"It will give me very great pleasure," said the Marquis; "and I am glad to see that Mr. Hope already appreciates the only way of eating a melon; but now let us have our fish."

"My friend," said Hope, "has told you how ignorant I am; indeed, many of my countrymen are in the same state, for we begin with fish, then taste an entrée, and end with the roast ; we think that fish is apt to taste insipid after meat."

"You make a great mistake, my dear sir, by your arrangement ; you reserve your palate for the strong food to the last, eating your choicest plâts when the stomach is voracious, and you swallow the best exertions of your cook so quickly that you neither do justice to him nor to yourself. Now, by beginning with a small bit of roast, you imbibe the solid nutriment at a moment when you can best bear this coarser viand ; your fish follows, to fire the palate with its mild and delicate juices, and prepare you fully to feel and appreciate the exertions and talents of your cook." While he spoke he was cutting up the bass, which was served plain-boiled. "Let me call your attention to a sauce of shrimps which has been prepared, and which I can recommend to your notice ; it is more peppery than we generally like ; however, pepper in this case is not only excusable but laudable, as you will find."

Hope and Cross helped themselves to a portion of the fish, and to the sauce, and obtained a smile of approbation by praising it loudly ; the sauce was a compound of pounded shrimps stewed into a sort of paste.

The brill was carried round after the bass, and while they were eating it the sputtering sound of the frying-pan could be heard ; the Marquis rose from the table and went to the mistress of the house, who was busy at one of the little stoves ; some instructions were given and he returned.

"Let us," he said, "take a small glass of this Spanish wine, and then I must beg you to try the cuttle-fish ; I have taken them under my own special care, and I am anxious they should please you, for I can answer that the eyes were properly extracted, and every fish has been well hammered."

"Hammered !" said Hope ; "is that necessary ?"

"Not perhaps with these young ones ; but even with them it does no harm ; a few good taps with a hammer insure that there shall be no little hardness to give trouble in mastication."

The Spanish wine, as it was called, was handed round. It was hot, bad Madeira, but the friends had too much good tact to say what they thought of it, so they washed the fiery taste from their mouths with a tumbler of the weak claret and water, which Hope had already learnt it was etiquette to drink.

A dish was now brought forward ; it was divided in the centre by a slice of toast ; on one side of the toast was a mass of cuttle-fish stewed with a white sauce ; on the other a pile of them beautifully fried ; they were of a clear even colour, without the slightest appearance of grease.

The Englishmen helped themselves. Hope did not like the stewed portion, but both agreed that nothing in the shape of fish could be better than those that were fried ; they said so,— and Hope remarked on the total want of grease.

"Ah, my dear friends, I see that you are by no means so ignorant as you are pleased to say. You can judge of good frying. It is a great art, too often sadly neglected. Frying is, in fact, boiling in oleaginous matter ; but if there be too little liquid in your pan, only half your object is boiled ; the other is warmed into a greasy mass of half-done viand, by the drops that are thrown up and fall on the upper surface, there remaining to displease the eye and disgust the palate. To fry, the object must be totally immersed at once in the heated mass of liquid oleaginous matter ; for the rule is the same whether you use lard, butter, or olive-oil. The first and greatest care of the good cook is to see that there be plenty of liquid in the pan ; the second, that the liquid be of a proper temperament, and nothing, in fact, is easier if proper attention be paid to what you are about, and a fault-like negligence is inexcusable in so momentous a matter. Having seen that a proper quantity of oil, butter, or lard, as the case may be, is put into your pan, place it on the fire and let it heat till you have obtained the proper temperature. To learn when this has arrived, have ready several small sticks of bread, and dip them from time to time in the liquid. When the heat is enough, you will see

that the bread, on being held for a few seconds, becomes of a
clear brown colour. When you have a small object to fry,
now is your time ; plunge it in and lift the pan a little above
the fire, for the heat must not be allowed to increase, or your
object becomes too dark in colour—it is burnt in short. When
your object is large, then you must allow the colour of the
bread, when you withdraw it, to be more strongly pronounced ;
for the immersion of a large object—a sole for instance—will re-
duce the temperature to the proper tone, and at that you must
regulate it, neither allowing it to be too hot nor too cold. By
attending to this you will always find the colour clear and bright,
and not in the slightest degree greasy in appearance. You should
always take care, too, that the egg for your pané should be very
thinly and evenly laid on ; to insure this, the white only should
be used and beaten for a long time, and when spread it should
be allowed to dry for a little before adding your bread-crumbs
or flour. For myself, I always prefer what I have used to-day,
namely, the flour of the haricot-bean very finely ground."

Hope listened, and kept his countenance wonderfully during
this lecture on frying. Cross did still better, for he produced a
pencil, and pretended to take notes of the marked passages ;
when it was ended, they both returned thanks to the Marquis.
The entrées were then called for, and another glass of wine was
handed round ; while this was being drunk, the door opened,
and the party whom Hope had invited entered—Angela led.

"Will you allow them to come to our table ?" said Hope,
addressing the Marquis.

"By all means, ask them," he replied ; "but I doubt if they
will come, for they are modest, even the men are not presuming ;
in the interior, they would come without being invited."

Hope and Cross both rose and pressed the party to join
their table ; but they declined, and seated themselves at another
nearer the door, where the two Englishmen insisted on seeing
them served with soup and the remains of their mutton and
fish, before they seated themselves again at their table. The

Marquis was put out when they came back, which Cross saw.

"I am afraid," he said, "we have been indiscreet in asking these people to dine here, but I hope you will forgive the consumption of the mutton, which certainly would make a capital hash for breakfast, for that little girl saved our lives, and the other two are her mother and friend."

"They are welcome to the mutton," said the Marquis, "for I hate a hash even of the best materials; fortunately, when I knew you were to be here for a day or two, I saw the sheep from which that gigot was cut, and I bought the whole animal —at least, I made the host do so, which is the same thing. I was not thinking of the mutton, we shall be able to spare that, but our two plâts will be ruined by the delay, and that is mortifying."

The Englishmen sat down and renewed their apologies, till a dish of côtelettes was produced, which was replaced by a duck stuffed with olives. The Marquis recovered his good humour, for he declared both excellent; and the friends, to please him, ate of each, though they thought the duck and olives detestable. They were strong in hopes that they had then done enough, but the tin case before the fire was opened, and three quails rolled in bacon and vine-leaves made their appearance, and they were bound each to consume his bird, nor did they find it a difficult task; for, as Hope said, a man must be very far gone when he cannot eat a quail that has been roasted in a greatcoat of bacon. But this finished them, and the Marquis had to discuss alone three plates of dressed vegetables and a salad, which were produced in succession, and he ended with a compote of all sorts of fruit boiled in syrup, and a pot of strawberry jam.

This concluded the serious part of the dinner; dressed crab and the pyramids of prawns were then put down, and the Englishmen felt bound to taste of them as part of the day's sport; and in spite of all they had done before, they found them excellent. During dinner, though we have not mentioned it, both claret and sauterne made the round of the table. When the sweets appeared, the champagne was opened, and at the dessert the curé's claret was discussed with very little difficulty and no remark. It was first rate, and proved that in trusting to him the Marquis had not leant on a broken reed. Matilde and her party had eaten their dinner very quietly ; a bottle of wine and some cider had been sent them, a little of which they drank, and during the time the Marquis was finishing off his salad, the two friends had spoken to them ; but in spite of "liberté, égalité," they were shy and respectful, and as soon as they had finished eating, they rose, curtseyed, and left the room. As they were going, Cross told Matilde to return the next morning at ten, that they might arrange about her dress, and pay Angela for her oysters.

When the claret was finished, cups of excellent coffee were handed round, with the usual little glass of old brandy, and then the Marquis proposed cards. Both the friends hated play, so they begged to be excused on the score of fatigue after their long day. The Marquis looked vexed, but said that he too was so tired, that without a little lansquenet or écarté he could not keep his eyes open ; so in half an hour they all adjourned to their rooms.

"I don't think I shall sleep much," said Hope ; " or if I do I am sure of the nightmare ; such roughing as this would give any man a fit of apoplexy in a fortnight."

" You are not far wrong ; but everybody who comes here has not the Marquis for caterer and cook. Had we been alone, there would have been no fear of your getting a surfeit ; but as it is, he has shown that the material is in the country, and when aided by native talent, a man may live in a fishing village on the coast of Normandy."

" When do we breakfast ?" asked Hope, as he stepped into bed.

" You may get a cup of coffee and a bit of bread quietly here, whenever you like ; but if you wish to avoid giving deadly offence to our friend, you must hold yourself prepared to eat as much breakfast as you did dinner to-day ; and that not until twelve o'clock."

"Well, good-night," said Hope ; and in spite of his fears of the nightmare, in five minutes he was as fast as the seven sleepers. The beds were a perfect model of cleanliness and comfort.

Notwithstanding their fatigue, they were awake at an early hour, and talked for some little time as to what they could do that would be of more permanent advantage to Matilde than a dress. Cross proposed that he should get up and consult the master of the inn, who was an honest man, and knew all the people in the country, while Hope lay still and got a cup of coffee in his bed. The long time he had sat wet told more on him than on his younger companion, and he was not sorry to avail himself of the proposal. The tide would be later to-day, and they could not see the nets, lines, or stone fisheries till nearly two o'clock. The girl was not to come till ten, so till then he determined to lie still and read. Cross got up and dressed. An old tub had taken the place of the brass pan, and enabled him to make his ablutions with something like comfort.

Shortly before the hour Hope had fixed for rising, Cross returned with the landlady bearing a cup of coffee. When she had put the room in order and refilled the tub, which seemed to amuse her amazingly, she departed, and Cross then reported that he had found out that the small garden that lay close to the house where Matilde's mother lived, was for sale, and could be bought for a hundred and fifty francs—six pounds English— that the purchase was a great bargain, and would be quite a fortune to their little friend. Hope said he would willingly join in the purchase, so, while he was dressing, Cross again started to try and conclude the bargain, that everything might be arranged if possible by the time the girl and her mother came. The landlord undertook to be the agent, and the landlady to

give them their breakfast, and keep them engaged till Cross
came back, should any delay take place ; but he succeeded.
The owner was more anxious to sell than they to buy.   The
papers were all in order, and signed with a rapidity unknown to
Norman transactions ; and by a quarter past ten, Cross, Hope, the
landlord of the inn, and a notary, were standing in front of the
inn, with everything settled to enable them to give, possession
of the diminutive property, which would make the brave little
girl a proprietor.   As Cross had taken all the trouble, Hope insisted that he should also have the pleasure of being spokesman,
reserving to himself the giving of another of his silk handkerchiefs, and a five-franc piece to Angela, who was to be employed
to buy the dress they had promised to little Matilde.

When the old woman and the two girls arrived, all was done
as they had arranged ; the dress was to be procured, cross and
all, for fifty francs, and then Cross presented the deeds in his
own and his friend's name, making a short laudatory speech in
honour of their little friend's bravery and presence of mind.

At first she did not understand what had been done ; she
only knew that she had received praise and some bits of paper ;
she therefore smiled and blushed ; but when it was explained to
her that she was a landed proprietor—that the garden she had
hitherto assisted to till was now her own, and that her mother
must now pay rent to her and no one else, then indeed, she became wild with delight—she laughed, wept, danced, and clapped
her hands—asked every one if it was not too wonderful to be
true, and darting off, she seized the hands of her benefactors and
pressed them alternately to her lips, saying over and over again,
" How good ! how generous ! how magnificent you have been to
me !"

Hope had not been long enough on the Continent to relish
having his hand kissed—he withdrew it from her grasp, stooped
down, and pressed his lips to her forehead.   Cross took the
hand-kissing more as a matter of course ; but he too embraced
the little girl as Hope had done, and then gave his hand to her

mother, who first kissed her own, as a Highland peasant does, and then pressed alternately the hands of the two Englishmen.

Angela did the same, saying as she did so, " You are good and generous ; but Matilde deserves it." As for the mother, all her volubility was gone ; she only once said, " May Heaven bless you both."

A crowd began to gather ; it is wonderful how news flies in a small place. Hope hated a public scene ; more especially as he felt his heart shockingly soft, and was half inclined to weep. " Come away," he said to Cross, " tell them to get their breakfast, and to make the notary explain anything they may wish to know ; let us be off at any rate. I should like to go as far as the headland, and see our last night's post from thence." Hope turned away, and Cross did as he was requested, and followed the moment after. The two friends walked gently on for some little time in silence.

" Well, Cross," said Hope, breaking this silence, " my worm-hunting got us into a scrape, and has cost us five pounds apiece. I do not regret it, and I hope you do not either ; for, oh ! what a pleasure it is to make others so happy at so small a cost ; for to me the sight of that little girl's delight was worth five times the money."

" And to me also," said Cross ; " and yet if one thinks of it, it ought to make us sad and ashamed ; for what sums have I wasted in folly that might have made hundreds as happy as she is now !"

" Don't let us think of that," said Hope ; " my present pleasure is too great to allow me to look back on so sad a remembrance ; let the lesson be a guide for the future, not a punishment for the past."

They had cleared the village, and were then ascending the hill leading to the headland. Rather a handsome pointer and a little mongrel galloped past them, and a sharp whistle sounded behind ; on turning to see who it was, they recognised their

landlord, gun in hand, who was following them at a great pace.
They paused till he joined them.

" You are going shooting," said Cross, when he came up ;
" what do you expect to find ?"

" I may perhaps get a partridge or a hare, and I know
where there are some quails ; at all events, I have promised to
get a dish of white-tails (wheat-ears) for the Marquis, as he considers them worthy of being put before you, and he thinks you
have never tasted them."

" He is wrong there," said Hope, " for we have eaten them
often ; but in our country they are much more often caught
than shot."

" I should like to know how that is done," said the host ; " for,
to tell you the truth, when powder and shot are so dear, I do
not much like expending it on such small game,—you never can
get more than one at a shot."

" It is easily shown," said Hope ; " and I never saw a better
place to try for them than this hill ; there are so many lumps
of square slaty stones lying about, that you can never be at a
loss for a fall."

A peg and perch were cut from a dwarf bush, and with a
knife a hole was soon formed in the short turf, and then the
trap so well known on the Downs in the south of England was
set ; the landlord made another at a short distance, under Hope's
tuition, and they continued their walk, the sportsman abstaining
from firing, though the birds were numerous, at the recommen-
dation of Hope, who told him that he might shoot there on his
return, when he came to look at the traps, if nothing was caught.

The two friends then directed their course to the point, and
the landlord turned to the right, towards a hollow that ran more
to the northward, the sides of which were covered with scrubby
heath and dwarf whin, while the tops of the banks were sown
with corn and buckwheat.

When they reached the point, the view was most extensive,
too much so for beauty ; it was the same they had seen from the

lower ledge of the same point the day before, and, though interesting from its extent and variety, still, from the height where
they stood, it was too map-like to be altogether pleasing. Having
glanced around, the eyes of both fixed on the rock where they
had passed the disagreeable hours of the previous evening.

" Our kingdom was mighty small," said Hope.

" And it has got some other bipeds to reign over it to-day,"
said Cross. " Do you see what a flock of birds are sitting
where we did yesterday ?"

" I do," said Hope ; " they look like curlews."

" And so I believe they are," said Cross. " I have not seen
them here myself before, but I have heard that they come down
here in large flocks at this time of the year, and remain all the
winter."

" And where can they come from ?" said Hope ; " there are
no hills or moors for them to breed on that I know of near here."

" But there are plenty in Brittany," replied Cross ; " and I
have heard that they breed there. I believe it, because I have
myself seen large quantities of young broods on the great flat
near Dole. The sands there differ from those here, for they are
so quick that it is most dangerous to walk on them, and the
shore is a swamp. Early in August the young curlews go there,
and we may easily suppose that from thence they spread along
the coast as they gain strength of wing ; or one flock may drive
away another to seek more distant quarters, and so oblige them
to leave the flats at Dole and to come here ; added to which, I
suspect our friends the worms, that made us stay so long where
they now sit, may have some attraction for their long bills, as
well as for you."

" I think," said Hope, " it is the middle or latter end of
August before the curlews come down on our shores, and, by
what you say, they must be a fortnight or three weeks earlier in
this country."

" Just about it," said Cross ; " but I think that all birds that
are natives and bred in this country are about a fortnight in ad-

M

vance of us—except the birds of passage, and they arrive almost
on the same day here that they do with us—both those which
come to breed and those which come to hibernate. Of the first
of these I may mention the nightingale and the landrail, whose
voices may be heard almost on the same day that they are in
England. This very spring I received a letter from a friend, in
which it was said, ' There is a nightingale now singing under the
window ; it is the first time we have heard him this year.'
Now on the very day this letter was written, I was fishing up
the river at Ducie. In coming home late I heard a nightingale,
and remarked to a friend who was with me that I heard him
for the first time that year ;—clearly showing that they must
arrive at the same time in the two countries ; and the same rule
applies to the winter birds ; one instance of which I may tell
you, for it is very marked. I had the means of observing very
narrowly the arrival of the brent-geese—oie-cravant as they call
them here. It was in a bay in Scotland where I used to watch
them ; and for five successive years the first flock was seen on
the 16th of September. Well, last year, on the 18th of September, I went out in one of the trawling-boats, and took the
gun with me. We sailed through a flock of these birds and
put them up. I shot one, so that there could be no mistake. It
was lean and evidently tired ; for it sat so close as to allow me
to get within shot of it, proving that it was lately arrived ; but,
from the number in the flock, it was not the first. In the flock
I mention there were at least two hundred birds. Now, in all
the first flocks that I have seen arrive there never were more
than twenty birds, who seemed to be the advanced guard
of the great mass that came a few days later ; and, supposing
that the same thing happens in France and in Scotland, I should
say that the first oie-cravant arrives on the same day here that
the brent-goose does in the bays of Ireland and Scotland."

" That is curious," said Hope, " and as I am anxious to see
their method of trawling on this coast, if you will go with me
we will choose the 18th of September, for I should like

much to prove if these birds are as regular in their arrival here, as you have found them in Scotland."

The feathered bipeds had absorbed so much of the attention of the friends, that they had taken little notice of a large party of bathers who had been swimming below them. The sound of voices advancing up the hill now drew their observation to the path, where a number of people came in sight : among these was the Marquis. After an exchange of greeting, the Marquis pulled out his watch, and urged the Englishmen to remember that they had only half-an-hour to wait till breakfast would be served, and also reminded them that any delay or want of punctuality after bathing was a downright vice. They consequently turned towards the village, but as they had plenty of time they walked slowly, and made a slight detour to see what their host was about, having heard his gun several times. On reaching the edge of the hollow, they saw the pointer standing at a dead point. The sportsman was hastening up the bank towards the dog, but before he came within shot, the mongrel that was with him dashed forward and sprung a bevy of seven quails. The birds passed close by the two friends, and flew straight to the clump of brushwood and whin, where Hope had cut the pegs for the traps. There they lit ; the friends marked them to an inch ; and when the sportsman had mounted the hill, they showed him exactly where they were, and the whole three took their way towards the spot.

" What makes you take such a brute as that out with you ?" asked Hope, as he pointed to the mongrel. From the curl of his tail he certainly had in his blood a cross of the famille Trompette, and as a hunter of eels he might have distinguished himself ; but springing birds before a pointer, as he had just done, seemed to Hope's English notion of sporting a decided proof that he ought only to be allowed to hunt when a pickaxe, and not a gun, was in the hands of the sportsman. But this did not accord with the pot-hunting ideas of our Norman chasseur, for in answer to Hope's query he replied—

"He is no brute, he is an incomparable chien de chasse, as you will allow, when I show you that this very day he has caught me two landrails. Those birds, which are so good to eat, are very provoking, for they run away, and you can never see them to get a shot at them; but when my good little Favourite is with me they find themselves in a bad position, for if they fly I shoot them, and if they run he snaps them up, and either way they go into my bag. And then for a hare, if I have the good luck to find one, and do not kill him at once, you may believe me, that animal will chase him so long and so well, that he is forced to double. If he returns, as he is sure to do, on his own steps, I have him again, and I am certain not to miss twice. We have not found a hare to-day, but we put up two landrails in the bottom, and, thanks to him, they are now in my bag, and you will eat them for dinner. I have been very successful too, for I have shot three white-tails and a quail, so you will not want for game if I do not get any more to-day."

Hope was hardly able to resist bursting out into a roar of laughter at this description of a good sporting dog. Cross was not so much amused, as he had been longer in the country, and the merit of running a hare for half a day was not new to him; but when they were close to the spot where the quails had alighted, he suggested the propriety of tying up Favourite till they had been found by the pointer.

To this proposal mine host agreed, and owing to that arrangement the quails were sprung in detail, and out of five fair shots three birds were killed; the remaining four flew to a field of buckwheat, where they were safe from further pursuit for that day.

When they had started all the quails, they were close to the first trap. Hope saw that the fall was down, and pointed it out to the landlord, who ran up and gave a shout of pleasure, exclaiming, "It is something quite astonishing; by our Lady, here is one!"

Cross and Hope, who followed more slowly, came up to him,

and sure enough there lay a wheatear. The stone in falling had caught him by the head, and the bird was dead. The landlord was in a great state of excitement, declaring that it was astonishing, marvellous, and that Hope was a man of great talent.

"I am glad you are pleased," said Hope, "but we are in haste ; so set the trap yourself that I may see that you know how to do it ; then we will examine the other and go home to breakfast. We must not keep the Marquis waiting."

"True, true," said mine host ; "he would be in a sad state, for he would not know that I have learnt how to secure him a dish of white-tails at any time."

The trap was set, and they went to the second. It too was down, and the bird was alive within it. Hope showed his pupil how to take it out, and then with Cross they walked rapidly to their inn.

As they walked, Cross asked if it was not extraordinary luck to catch two birds in so short a time.

"No," answered Hope ; "the birds here are very numerous, and I have always found that the fresh-made traps catch the best. When I was a boy, I used to amuse myself often at this sport, and the new-made traps were always the most successful."

"But what induces the birds to go in ?" asked Cross, "for you put no bait."

"Why," replied Hope, "I suspect that wheat-ears, like your sea-loach and sea-perch, have an inquisitive turn of mind, and like to look under every stone they pass ; or perhaps, as they live on insects, the new-turned soil may lead them to examine it for food, and I am guided in the last supposition by finding that the fresh traps catch the most."

"That seems probable," said Cross, "and I have learnt something to-day, as well as our landlord. But I am surprised that he did not already know this mode of saving his powder and shot, for the French are a very ingenious people."

"Yes ; but what is more surprising," said Hope, "is, that

this most simple of all traps was unknown in Italy.   When I
was there some years ago I taught it to a man at Terracina, who
was even more delighted with the lesson than my pupil of to-day.
I don't think the people in this country trouble themselves much
with trapping birds ; whereas in Italy no bird can put his foot
down without the chance of finding himself fast by the leg in a
horse-hair noose.   My astonishment, when in Italy, was to see
so many birds ; for what with nets, nooses, and bird-lime, it is
quite marvellous that any escape.   But here we are, and what a
crowd !"

Sure enough, when they reached the house, half the village
was standing in front of the door.   The news of Matilde's good
fortune was known.

As they came forward a lane was opened for the two friends
to pass.   All hats were off, and when they had entered the
house the murmur of voices and the clapping of hands resounded :
they seldom cheer in France.

" Good, good !" said the Marquis ; " quite punctual, and they
are ready to serve ; but we must send the good people away, for
the most succulent meats cease to be nourishing if one is disturbed while eating."

He stepped to the door, bowed profoundly to the crowd, repeating exactly the same sentiment.

" My brave people," he said, " the gentlemen whose conduct
you are pleased to admire are going to breakfast.   The best of
food is no longer nutritious if it is not eaten in tranquillity ;
this is a point of consequence ; be considerate ; be French ; and
retire till they have finished their meal."

The matter of eating is a serious affair in France.   The Marquis's statement was of great force with his auditors, for they
immediately dispersed, and the two Englishmen obeyed the call
of the successful orator by placing themselves at table.

CHAPTER VII

A FRENCH breakfast was new to Hope. Cross was quite at home, for he had partaken of many : the first of these, therefore, only remarked that the table had no tablecloth, but otherwise that it was spread much as it had been for the late dinner of the night before. In the centre stood various fruits : there was no melon, but the apricots, plums, and pears were exactly the same. There were also piles of prawns and crabs dressed cold, as Cross had described them. In addition to all this, there were rolls, slices of bread and toast, and a large lump of butter. The toast attracted Cross's notice, and he complimented the Marquis on his attention in having ordered it.

"You see," said the Marquis, "that I understand the English taste. I know you cannot breakfast without your roasted bread, so I ordered it. For myself, I never inconvenience myself by eating it. It is dry food, and requires a great deal to make it tolerable. But here are our oysters."

Half a dozen, ready opened, were offered to each person, and Hope bolted his nearly as fast as the Marquis. He had determined to follow the lead of so able a guide, at all events as far as he was able. A plateful of eggs followed the oysters. The Marquis took two ; Hope contented himself with one. This was washed down with a little claret, largely diluted with water, and then a dish of côtelettes was handed round. The same proportions were continued by the two Englishmen ; that is to say, they helped themselves to one côtelette, the Frenchman to two. In the next dish were the sand-eels, fried according to the rules so clearly laid down by the Marquis, and of these Hope ate quite as many as his leader—indeed so amply, that when two roast chickens were put on the table, he could only venture on a very moderate portion, as he kept a small corner of his appetite for the crabs and prawns. These followed the chickens; then came a dish of fried potatoes, and after them two pots of preserves. Of all these the Marquis ate, helping himself to several spoonsful of the preserve, which he swallowed without bread. Some excellent bottled cider was produced, and drunk after the sweets; then the fruit and white wine, a sort of vin de Grave; and the breakfast at last concluded with coffee, and the usual glass of brandy. Hope found that breakfast was a matter of business, not of necessity. There was no hurry; everything was done deliberately, with a short pause between each dish, which pause was invariably filled up by a few remarks made by the Marquis on the merits of the last plât. He was eloquent in praise of the côtelettes; they were made out of the same little sheep whose leg had graced the table on the night before, and the Marquis enlarged on the merit of feeding sheep on salt marshes, adducing in proof the present côtelettes as an example. The eels also were praised, but the chickens were not so tender as they ought to have been. Altogether, however, his meal seemed to please him; and when he had concluded, and they rose from their long sitting, he declared that a man might contrive to live for a short time in a fishing village in Normandy, as the sea-air was excellent for the appetite; and, for the sake of obtaining one for his dinner, he should forthwith go and catch a few prawns.

Hope was anxious to see the remaining modes of fishing, so, when the Marquis went off to get his net, he started with Cross for the sands.

"This sort of morning dinner may be very well now and then," said Hope, "but it would bore me to death if it took place every day. It is such an endless affair; so many things, and such a long pause between each dish, with notes and annotations on them by the Marquis by the way of sauce; why, we

were an hour and a quarter at table, and I could have eaten all
I wanted comfortably in a fifth part of the time."

"I don't doubt it," answered Cross; "and an American would
do it in half the time you could; but if you consulted the Marquis
on this subject, he would tell you that you do ill, and the American worse. The French gourmand eats slowly on principle,
and they are not so far wrong; for, by thus taking their time
over their meals, they never feel uncomfortable, in spite of the
quantity they eat. For instance, if the Marquis had put his
huge breakfast into his stomach in ten or fifteen minutes, do you
think he could have started off at the rate of four miles an hour,
as he did just now? Or, to come nearer home, could you breast
this hill, at the pace we are now going, without being blown?"

"Very likely not," said Hope; "but to tell you the truth, I
still persist in thinking our arrangement the best, for I prefer
being obliged to walk a little slower at first starting to being
bored for an hour longer than is necessary in eating my breakfast;
and, since I have begun finding fault, there are two things that
go strangely against the grain with me in the table arrangements
of a people who consider themselves the most refined nation on
the earth. First, having no tablecloth at breakfast, and this
not from any want of linen, for I see that all the women here
make as much fuss about having a large stock of that article as
the old ladies do in Scotland. The want of a tablecloth at
breakfast is a custom, and a very nasty one; and, what is still
worse, never changing your fork—meat or fish, you must always
keep your fork, which is never changed till they begin eating
sweet things. I own I think this abominable."

"I agree with you," said Cross, "that having no tablecloth
is not a nice custom, but every country has its own ways; as for
not changing the forks, it is in fact a piece of refinement on their
part, and, in conjunction with their dinners, could hardly be
avoided. They have always a great many more dishes than we
have, a guest is expected to taste them all, the people are not
rich enough to have two dozen silver forks for every one at table,

and, as they like to eat with a silver fork, it is much better to
have your own than to give you that of another person wiped or
washed, which must be done if forks were changed with every fresh
dish that is handed round, and of which you are expected to eat."

"There is reason in what you say," answered Hope, laughing;
"and I confess myself to be a little John Bullish in growling
because everything is not exactly as we see it in England, where
we are now growing very pampered and apt to give ourselves airs,
although it is not so very long since our fine ladies brought their
own knives to dinner and ate with their fingers."

Thus talking they reached the steep path leading to the sea.
At the top they met their landlord, who was in great delight;
he had made a number of traps, and two more birds had been
caught.　He was there, waiting to beg them not to tell the
secret to any one else, for he considered the knowledge such a
treasure that he did not wish to share it with any one.

Hope made no answer to his request, but congratulated him
on his success. "Hang the fellow!" he said, when he was half
down the hill; "I am sorry I taught him, since he is so selfish."

"Phoo, nonsense," said Cross; "he is not worse than his
neighbours.　He keeps the inn and has to provide for our friend
the Marquis and such-like, so to him the lesson is invaluable,
while to others it is only the price they can get for what they
catch; and, if all of them took to trapping, they would soon
clear the coast.　But here is Matilde's mother; she is waiting
for us apparently."

She was so, for as soon as they approached her she joined
them.　She had on her shoulder one of the lesser prawn-nets
with the cross poles.

"I am waiting for you," she said, "and you are just in time;
it is my day for the fishing.　Matilde told me you wished to see
how we take the fish, so I sent her on, and waited to have the
pleasure of showing you myself."

"A thousand thanks," said Hope; "I do wish to see it, and
may I ask what you mean by your day at the fishing?"

"The fishery," answered Madame le Moine—for that was the old lady's name—"the fishery was made a great many years ago, and my father and his father before him had the right to fish it. When my father died my sister's husband and mine had some words about the right (they are both dead now—Heaven rest their souls!), but from words they came to blows, and it might have been serious if my sister and myself had not arrived in the nick of time. We soon settled them, the foolish fellows, and sent them home to wait till we came; and then my sister and I arranged that we should have the fishing every other day and pay between us the expense of retaining the walls when the sea makes them fall; and there has never been a word of dispute since. Yesterday was her day and to-day is mine; to-morrow it will be hers again, so this tide she has two good days, but next tide, perhaps, I shall have the two best days and she only one, so the arrangement is very fair, and we are quite satisfied."

"But does no one else dispute the right with you?" asked Cross.

"A year ago, some people did dispute our right, and one of them went and fished the fishery in spite of us; but we took her before the Juge de Paix, and proved that we had always built up the walls every spring, and that our fathers had done so before us; so the trespasser was fined, and no one has troubled us since."

"Is yours the only fishery?" asked Hope.

"O no, there are a great many more along the coast."

"And are they considered property too?"

"Yes, all of them; and since my dispute was settled, no one has interfered with any of those proprietors, who are known to have held the right of fishing from their fathers."

"Lucky for them," said Cross, "that Barbès and Raspail did not get their way, or there would have been a general partition at sea, as well as on land."

"Are these fisheries very productive?" asked Hope.

"Sometimes they are very good; but that is not often. I have had some excellent days; once I got six large carts full of herrings, and last year I caught two of great mackerel; but often we got very little. When the spring tides come, however, we always find something which helps to buy us bread when the tides are small, for then we cannot fish."

"Do you know," again asked Hope, "how long these fisheries have been made, or who invented them?"

"O no, we do not know how they were made; but some of them are older than others, and I have heard my father say that they were here when a people they call Romans and the French used to fight."

Thus discussing the antiquity of the fisheries, they advanced towards the one they were going to see. It was a very rude structure, being merely a long semicircular line of stones heaped on the sand, and stretching from one mass of rock to another; this wall, or rather mound of stones, was about four feet high at the ends nearest the shore, gradually increasing both in height and breadth as it reached the centre; there it was ten feet high, and about six feet broad on the top. The inside was built nearly perpendicular; the outside had a long slope, for the mound was nearly twenty feet broad at the bottom. On the inside there was something like regularity in the building; but the outside was merely composed of large blocks of stone tumbled carelessly together. Along the outside line there were apparently lumps of rocks rising from the sand and abutting against the structure; these, however, proved, when examined, to be only masses of spongy-looking substance formed by the same insect that had built on the rocks. Some of these masses had been broken in repairing the fishery, in different places; they were fully five feet thick, measuring from the sand, thereby showing that these insects must either work very fast, or that the fishery must be very old. Nearly in the centre there was an opening in the curved line of the building; and on either side of this opening, a better built wall projected about ten yards towards the sea. The space between these walls was rather more than four feet wide. At the end next the sea a strong wooden frame was

erected, and in the frame was fixed a sluice very neatly but
strongly made of wicker-work. When the party reached the
end of the mound nearest the land, they were obliged to mount
on the top of it and walk along its uneven and yet slippery
surface, towards the sluice, or killing-place. It was not an
easy job, for the stones were all covered with short sea-ware of
various sorts, but among these laver greatly preponderated. Any
one who has ever tried to walk on rocks where laver grows will
at once understand that there was some difficulty in progressing
fully three hundred yards along a mound of loose stones,
covered with this and other such marine herbs ; but difficult as
it was, they preferred this road to wading through the water.
Hope did not like remaining the whole day wet, and the top of
the dyke was the only dry road ; for, within the building, the
sea was dammed up, and looked like a very large pond ; while,
on the outside, the water was escaping through the apertures
between the stones, spouting out in every direction, and running
in rills towards the retiring sea. They did not hurry themselves,
for the old lady, when she saw the state of the tide, had told
them that nothing could be done for a quarter of an hour ; they
moved, therefore, gently along, picking their steps and pausing
occasionally to look at the heaps of shells, and cuttle-fish bones,
that lay scattered along the outside of their path. When they
had nearly reached the end of their journey, they saw a large
shoal of small fish dash out of the water, which was as clear as
crystal, and about five feet deep. When their attention was
drawn by the splash which the fish made in dashing out of the
water, they looked at the spot and saw that it appeared bright
green, from the shoal of little fish that were crowding together.

"We shall get something to-day," said Madame le Moine ;
"these must have been mackerel that were chasing the sardines."

Close to the edge, and on one side of the sluice, sat little
Matilde ; her friend Angela was on the other; by Angela sat the
same young man who had carried one of the lanterns the night

before.   Angela held in her hand a net like Madame le Moine's ;
the young man had two short poles, with very strong iron hooks at
the end, and close by Matilde lay a small bundle of nets with
corks to it.

Madame le Moine called to them, " Have you seen anything
to-day ?"

" Yes, yes ; we shall do well to-day," answered Angela ;
" there are mackerel, hole-fish (gar-fish), and a great many lançons (sand-eels) ; they will make poor work with the spade
to-day, for the lançons have not taken the sand this tide."

" That is good," said the old lady ; " what fortune you good
gentlemen bring us ; and Frederic is there, I see, so we shall get
those wicked beasts that are pulling down the fishery."

" Who is Frederic ?" asked Cross.

" He is a good young man, a relation of mine, and he has
come to help us to take the two minaurs that are destroying us."

" What is a minaur ?" asked Hope.

" You will see him," said Madame le Moine, " when we pull
him out.   He is an accursed beast, and there are two of them ;
but we cannot get them till the water falls."

" And is Frederic come to help you or Angela ?" asked
Cross.

The old woman looked at him and laughed.   " You have
found that out already, have you ?   Well, young men have
sharp eyes when a pretty girl is in the way ;" then lowering her
voice, she continued—" you are right ; Frederic is Angela's pre-
tender ; and they were to be married when he came back from
Newfoundland this autumn, but this 'maudite' Revolution prevented the fleet from sailing, and they must wait for a year, for
they are not rich enough to marry now.   Poor things ! they gain
what gives them bread, but they cannot furnish a house by
catching oysters, or working in a trawl-boat ; but they are good
and prudent, and they will wait.   The fleet will sail in the
spring, and then Frederic will gain good wages ; for he is to be
an officer next voyage ; and in the meantime he is not idle,

except when he comes to pay us a visit for a day or two ; and as
he was here, I have asked him to come and help us to take these
minaurs and mend the dyke.   We are not strong enough to do it
ourselves, and as we must pay somebody to assist us, I am glad
to choose Frederic, who will not work less hard when Angela is
with him."

This little confidence was delivered with great volubility.   If
a Frenchwoman were a hundred years old, she would always take
an interest in love, for when past the age of love herself, there
are still the loves of others to engage her attention and sympathy.

The two friends could not help looking at the couple.   The
young man was a very handsome dark youth, and looked like a
smart sailor.   He wore a dress like that of our sailors, which
showed his strong well-made figure to advantage.   Angela, as
we have already said, was a very handsome girl.   She was rather
pale in general, but when she saw the eyes of the two friends
fixed on her, while Madame le Moine was speaking, she probably
suspected what was being told, for her beauty was greatly increased by the bright blush that crossed her face.

" Change the subject, and look another way," said Hope ;
" the poor girl hears what the old lady is saying, and it frets her,
for she is blushing."

The small fish helped this intention, for they again made a
dash out of the water.   This time the friends saw a shoal of
larger fish swimming rapidly below the small ones.   A part of
them seemed to enter the outlet towards the sluice.

" See them ; they are mackerel," said Matilde.

The gentlemen hurried forward ; Angela stepped down on a
sort of landing-place ; she held her net by the upper end of the
handles, and plunged it in the water, then swept it towards the
sluice.   As soon as the bottom of the net touched the sluice, she
gave the net a shake and raised it.   The friends were then quite
close, and they could see that she had taken a quantity of fish
of some sort, which were springing and glancing in the bag.

The two girls had removed the baskets from their shoulders—

they were lying on the stones beside Matilde—to empty the net.
Angela held it across the stream ; Matilde took it, and, in her
turn, held it up to Hope and Cross, that they might see what
was taken. They looked, and saw forty or fifty mackerel,
about the size of small herrings.

"What beautiful little fish they are," said Hope ; "can
anything be more brilliant than the striped colours on their
backs, contrasted with the silvery white of their bellies !"

"And as they say in the North," continued Cross, "I will
warrant them to be as good as they are bonny. It does not
require a French Marquis to make these fellows eatable, as you
will allow at dinner to-day."

"Faith, then, they must be very good, for they are very
beautiful," said Hope. "Just look at the colour ; how it flashes
and changes between emerald green and sapphire blue ! They
look more like a mass of precious stones than live fish."

"They are not living," said Cross, "they are dying ; they
live a very short time out of the water, and as they die this
change of colour takes places. A mackerel is always a pretty
fish, but no one can have an idea of their beauty who has not
seen them caught ; so many of them together certainly adds to
the effect, and I can tell you, these little ones, for eating, are
as superior to the full-grown ones as it is possible for anything
to be—in no way are they so good as plain boiled in sea water ;
we must try and get a panful to let you taste them in full perfection. I have a friend at court here, and I will try and get
half a gallon of sea water up to our inn."

"Try to get some sea water ?" said Hope ; "one would think
that you were in the centre of Europe, instead of on the shores
of the Atlantic ! what is there to hinder your getting as much
as you please ?"

"Why, as I have no taste for picking oakum, or being shut
up in Mont St. Michel, or some less picturesque jail, I should
not like to be caught carrying sea water myself ; and I should
not like to bribe any one else to run the risk."

"What nonsense you talk," answered Hope; "sent to jail for carrying sea-water?"

"No less," said Cross; "don't you know that the duty on salt is enormous in France; so high that every art is employed to get hold of it; amongst others, if they were allowed, every man near the sea would make his own salt, by evaporating the water. To prevent this, all the salt-works swarm with excise officers, and the coast has guards and spies in every direction, who are ready to pounce on any one who attempts to carry off a single bottleful."

"Well, that is oppression!" exclaimed Hope; "and you really mean to say, that they would not allow you to carry off as much sea-water as would boil us a dish of fish?"

"I told you," answered Cross, "that I have a friend at court here; he can say—'How do you do,' and 'god-dam,' and thinks he can speak English. I have won his friendship by pretending to believe that he can. If he is on guard, and if I pledge my word to throw away the water as soon as our fish is boiled, he will let us have a gallon out of affection for us, who speak the same language that he does; but if he caught me taking it without leave, or without this promise, his friendship would not prevent his sending us to Granville, under the escort of half-a-dozen gentlemen with green coats, long muskets, and 'Douanier' cut out on a brass plate on their caps."

"That bangs Banagher!" said Hope; "and if people are governed by such a law as that, I don't wonder that they kick up a row now and then."

"They are coming in now, gentlemen," said Matilde; "if you will sit down you will not frighten them, and there is my petti-coat to sit on; I brought two to-day, for it was so cold last night."

"I beg your pardon," said Hope (who took the hint that he was scaring the fish); "but why should we make a cushion of your petticoat, and spoil it?"

"You will not spoil it, so pray use it," said the little girl.

The friends thanked her and sat down.

While they had been talking, the water had not ceased to flow, not only through the sluice, but through the crevices in the dyke ; the pond was therefore much reduced in size, and had fallen so much that it was not more than three feet deep. Madame le Moine had not crossed the sluice, and had walked for a considerable distance along the dyke on the other side. Angela was standing a little lower than when she made the first sweep her net was leaning against the side of the wall, one end resting on a stone, the other she held in her hand.

"Look out ! look out !" called the old woman ; "there is a fine lot of them."

The friends saw the wave which a body of fish made in moving through the water ; however, they did not enter the narrow neck, but turned along the side of the dyke in the direction in which the party had arrived.

"Run, Matilde," said Angela ; "turn them."

Matilde did as she was bid ; putting off her sabots, she ran quickly along the slippery stones, returning slowly, waving her arms in the air.

"Look, Angela," exclaimed both Cross and Hope at the same moment, for they caught sight below them of the large shoal entering the narrow. On the surface of the water they saw more than a hundred gar-fish dashing on with their shining green backs and long noses, and below them again was visible the glancing of ten times that number of other fish, also pressing forward in the same direction.

Angela remained quite still, leaning back against the wall for a moment ; then she dashed her net into the water, made her sweep, and raised it absolutely full of fish.

"Not bad," she said ; "there are always some that get away but there were not many this time. Help me, Frederic, for they are very heavy."

Frederic lifted the net and held it up, while Hope and Cross each took a basket and ran to cross the sluice by the wooden frame. When they came up to Frederic, they found that the net had taken all the gar-fish, and almost the whole of the shoal of mackerel.

"Empty the net, quick," said Angela; "the rest of the mackerel miss their friends. They have come again, and are rubbing their noses against the sluice."

The net was turned over, leaving the fish to kick their last among the stones, and was given to Angela, who repeated the same sweep she had before made, and this time not one of the remaining mackerel was missed. There were also six or eight very bright gray fish that looked like enormous dace.

"That is a beautiful sight," said Hope, as he again looked at the shining mass of changing colour, "and the mixture of other fish rather adds to their beauty. The gar-fish I know; but what is the name of that other fish? it is not a mullet."

"What do you call these?" asked Cross, pointing to the gray-looking fish, and speaking in French.

"Demoiselles," answered Angela.

"Yes, demoiselles; I remember," said Cross, "that is the name they go by here; but how are they called in the rest of France, or what is their scientific or English name, I cannot tell you. Sometimes they catch great shoals of them when they are about the quarter the size of these. I have seen great quantities of them in the markets early in the year."

"And are they a good fish?" asked Hope.

"Faith, I cannot say, for I have never eaten them; but these girls can tell you, or, rather, here comes Madame le Moine; she is an older, and therefore perhaps a better judge."

Hope put the question to the old lady.

"We poor people think them very good: but those who are rich enough to buy better, do not eat them; they have too many bones for people who are rich enough to like to eat their dinner without trouble."

"These," she continued, picking up a gar-fish, "are very good indeed; but I have seen people who even found fault with them as being too dry; and others again do not like to see their green bones ; some people are so fanciful, and because gar-fish have green bones, they think they must live upon copper."

" Are gar-fish common on this coast ?" asked Hope.

" O yes," answered Madame le Moine ; " we sometimes get a good many of them, and very large ones ; but they are much more common on the coast of Brittany."

" I know that," said Cross, " for they catch quantities off St. Malo, and farther down, with a white fly. They fish for them very much in the same manner as they catch seath and lythe on the coasts of Scotland."

" Which is not bad fun," said Hope, " on a summer evening. Have they any of those fish on these coasts ?"

" They have lythe, and call them by the same name. I will bet a trifle that we shall find one or two in the nets we are to see presently. But for the family of the stainlochs, I have never seen any of them. It was some time before I knew that stainloch, gray-fish, seath, cudding, and poddly, were all one fish at different ages ; and, knowing it now, I can tell you that hereabouts I have never seen any of the tribe."

" The water is low enough now," said Madame le Moine. " Now we have got the mackerel, there is no fear of these lançons taking the sand ; therefore we may as well drive them. And there are also a good many mullets, which the gentlemen may like to see, so let us put in the net, for they are much too cunning to drive, or to be taken with the hand-net."

Cross and Hope began to move with the rest of the party, but Madame le Moine stopped them.

" Stay where you are," she said ; " you will see better here than by moving ; and there you will see the place where those maudite minaurs are lying. Just look what a quantity of my wall they have pulled down."

The friends looked where the old woman pointed ; they saw several tons of stones lying a yard or two from the main wall, which at that place looked very ruinous and tumble-down.

" You don't mean," said Hope, " that a fish pulled that wall down ?"

" I do say so," replied she ; " and it is the truth. You shall see what an accursed beast he is, and what strength he has. Do you observe those two yellow marks on the sand ? Well, there is one at each of these places, for these are their holes. The one nearest us has the half of my clip in him, that I broke trying to haul him out last spring tide. But Frederic has brought two proper good ones, and a pickaxe ; so that, with the help of the Virgin, we will have them out to-day. But first we must clean the fishery, and if you stay, you will see everything ; or, if you would like to catch the lançons, you shall have the net when we drive them to the sluice."

Hope and Cross agreed to be guided by the old lady. They sat down on a large stone, while the rest of the party shouldered the nets, and slid down the dyke into the water. Frederic carried the net with the corks ; Angela and the old woman had each a pole-net ; and little Matilde held one of the poles with the iron hooks, which she called by the same name as the salmon-fisher in Scotland gives to his landing-hook— namely, a clip. The one Matilde carried was exactly of the same form as those used by the northern salmon-fisher, but was six times as strong, looking more like a short boat-hook, without the spike, than a clip. But a clip it was called. Once fairly in the water, the old lady led the way, keeping close to the side of the wall, the others following, till they reached the shallowest part of the water. There they spread out, and walked backwards and forwards, beating the water with the nets and poles. This they continued to do till they had traversed the larger half of the pond, and the water was then nearly up to their knees. Frederic then lowered the net which he carried into the water. It was a trois-mailles, about twenty yards long, and light, for though the meshes were very small, it was made of such fine thread that it could not be heavy. Angela took the other end of this net, first giving the pole-net to Matilde, and they walked

on, Frederic and Angela drawing the trois-mailles, Madame le
Moine and Matilde on either side of them, both striking the
water lightly with the poles of their nets, holding them by the
centre, so as to make the whole pole touch the water at once.
They came on quickly, till the ends of the trois-mailles touched
the dyke on each side of the sluice.

While they were thus advancing, a fish sprang over the net.
The moment it did so Angela and Frederic lifted the corks out
of the water.   A number of other fish sprang, but the net being
lifted a foot above the water, they struck against it, and failed
in their leap.

"Well done, my children," said Madame le Moine; "they
are safe enough, the cunning rogues; they are done for!"

The glistening of the fish, and the shaking of the corks,
showed that they were firmly fixed.

"There are some good mullet," said Cross: "they are well
bagged, and they shake the net so much that nothing else will
try to run back."

"I thought they were mullet," said Hope, "for I have seen
them play the same trick of jumping over the net in Scotland;
the fishermen there call them merry-fish. I have been told that
if they miss their first spring they never try it a second time,
and, to cheat them, Scotch fishermen draw two nets, one after
the other, so that if a lot get over the first net they are sure
to have them in the second. They are very numerous in the
muddy bays all round Britain. I have seen some very good
hauls taken myself, and a friend of mine told me he had
assisted in the taking upwards of fourteen hundred at one
sweep of a net."

"In the south of France," said Cross, "they would have
liked such a haul; for there they boil them down to make the
soup of a sort of water zoutchee, which they call bouillabaise;
but for myself, a little of them goes a long way.   Even when
dressed en fillet, with a rich sauce, by as good a cook as our
friend the Marquis, they have always a sort of leathery texture

which I do not like; but some people are very fond of them."

"Water zoutchee is a very good thing," said Hope. "I would like very well to taste their bouillabaise, to see if a Frenchman can improve on a Dutch dish."

"Well, it is not unlikely that you may do so to-day, for it is a favourite dish of the Marquis, and I saw all the soles and the rest of the fish we sent home yesterday in the act of going into a pot-au-feu, with sundry bundles of herbs. This, I am sure, is destined to be converted either into white-fish soup or bouillabaise."

"Are the lançons at the sluice?" asked Madame le Moine.

Cross and Hope had been watching the people, and had not looked towards the sluice for some time; but on hearing this question they turned their eyes in that direction, and saw hundreds of little fish with their heads against the wicker-work, and a great many more dashing up and down in the narrow space between the walls. They answered the question by describing what they saw.

"Take my net, then," said the old lady; and stepping across the trois-mailles, she handed it up to Hope, who took it, and stepped down on to the slope where Angela had stood when she took the mackerel.

He grasped the ends as he had seen her do, plunged it into the water, and tried to sweep it round as she had done, but he found that it was not such an easy job. The net twisted to one side as he was trying to give it the true scientific shake, and when he lifted it there were only three sand-eels in the bag.

"Confound the thing!" he said; "that girl must be as strong as a horse, for she moved the net with all the ease and grace of an opera-dancer, and here I have used all my strength and knocked the skin off three of my knuckles, and after all have only got a fish in exchange for each sample of my skin that I have left on these wretched stones."

The misfortunes of our friends, says the French cynic, are .

always pleasing to us.   Being in France, Cross seemed to agree
with the sentiment, for he only laughed at Hope's misfortune.
" Let me try," he said; " it is knack, and not strength, that is
required."

Hope gave him the net, and mounted again on to the top of
the dyke, where he employed himself in comforting his bleeding
fingers.

Cross took the net and the place which Hope had resigned ;
he got up the attitude, and tried to imitate Angela's graceful
sweep ; but the result was almost as great a failure as Hope's,
for when he raised the net he had only caught five.   It was
Hope's turn to laugh, and he did so, and when Cross turned to
the party, who were beating the water beside the net, he had the
mortification to see that they too were enjoying a comfortable
laugh.

" Everything requires practice," said Madame le Moine ;
" you cannot expect to learn a trade in a minute.   Have the
goodness," she said, addressing herself to Hope, " to give me
the net ; I will show you the safe way for old women and
beginners ; but you cannot do it without getting wet."

Hope gave her the net ; she held it by the centre, and laid
the length of the pole gently on the water, walking slowly towards the narrows.   The friends watched the water ; first came
the whole lot of sand-eels rushing against the sluice, and then
behind them the water was perfectly green, from the colour of
the backs of thousands of the little fish they had first seen, and
which they had heard called sardines.

Once within the narrow space between the two walls, the
old lady turned the net and walked on with it, pushing it before her, as if she was fishing for prawns ; when she reached
the end, she gave the same scientific shake, and raised it filled
with almost the whole of the shoals of both sand-eels and
sardines.

" Well done, madame !" exclaimed Hope, as he stooped to
look at this fish.

" Yes, we have done very well to-day," said the old dame, " and you have brought us our good fortune ; so, thanks to our Lady and you, we shall not want for many a day. Come on, my children, let us make an end, and then we have only to settle matters with those ugly minaurs."

Angela and Frederic drew the net on, till the two ends met ; they then kicked the bottom line into a bunch with their feet, then gathered the corks with their hands, and lifted up the whole in a mass to Madame le Moine and Matilde, who had scrambled on to the top of the wall to receive it. There were eight mullet, three or four more demoiselles, one little brill, and several small soles and brown-backed flounders.

" I am surprised," said Hope, " not to see more of the small soles, since they catch so many of them with the prawn nets ;" this remark was made in French to the old lady.

" It is not surprising," she replied, " if you consider where this fishery is ; flat fish hardly ever go on the rocks, and never cross the walls. All we get here, therefore, are only those which go near the shore, and forget their way back again when the tide turns. If they are inside the rocks, they come straight out and we get them ; but in general, they follow the great stream, which runs round, and not over the rocks. There are some fisheries beyond Granville that are built on the open sand, with no rocks near, and in them they catch a great many, and very fine flat fish ; but they do not get as many mackerel or herrings as we do."

" And these," said Hope, holding up a handful of the little fish that had just been caught ; " you call these sardines : are they the same as they catch in Italy, under that name, or are they only young herrings ?"

" I don't know anything about it," answered the old woman ; " we always call them sardines."

" Do you know, Cross ?" asked Hope, speaking in English.

" No, I do not," replied Cross, " for I never saw sardines before, except salted. I am no great naturalist ; what little I know, I have learnt more from observation than teaching ; but I think these fish are full grown, for the females have roes. I have also seen them cured, and they were quite as good as any Sicilian sardines ; and if we can only persuade our landlady to clean them, you shall try how they eat fresh. I will take home a basket of them and salt them slightly, to use for spinning for perch in the Mare de Bouillon. I had capital sport there with them once, and got some splendid perch."

"And I," said Hope, "cannot tell either what they are. I have seen and eaten thousands of sardines, both salt and fresh ; but when I was in Italy I thought more of fun and dancing than of natural history. It is pretty certain that these are full of roe, but I doubt much if that be any rule to mark the differ- ence between young and full-grown fish, for I have seen trout caught to stock a lake which were not longer than my finger when they were turned in, yet were quite full of spawn. I fished the same lake a few years after, and caught these trout there, weighing three pounds apiece. I am sure they were the same fish as those that were turned in, for none others were ever put there ; yet these fish which had grown to such a size were full of roe when they were not longer than my finger."

"That may be true enough," said Cross, " for the growth of fish is little known or understood ; I have seen trout turned into a large piece of artificial water which were caught in a stream not far from it ; in that stream (and I have fished it for miles) I never saw a trout that would weigh four ounces, and yet in the artificial pond I have caught them myself as large as those you mention. I made most particular inquiries, and can therefore say with confidence that every trout in the artificial water came from the stream where they were always small."

While the friends were thus discussing the sardines, the girls and Frederic had been arranging the fish in the baskets and clearing the nets ; the trois-mailles were laid on the stones to dry, and the pole-nets were stuck up, so as to let the wind blow through them. Angela and Madame le Moine each took one of the clips, Frederic took the pickaxe, and the whole party slid again into the water. Cross and Hope went to the place on the dyke, nearest to the spot that had been shown them as holding the minaurs.

Frederic began first by scraping a considerable hole in the sand with the pickaxe : he then took one of the clips, thrust it into the whole, and gave it a violent jerk ; it was drawn deeper into the sand after this jerk.

"That's into him !" he exclaimed, and he gave the end of the clip into Madame le Moine's hand ; little Matilde took hold of it also.

Frederic then took the other clip from Angela, and did the same with it as he had done with the first, returning the staff to Angela, when he felt that it was fast.

"Now haul away," he cried.

The three women pulled with all their force ; something white was seen, and then the water became black.

Frederic put down his pickaxe, and jerked violently ; something like a large eel appeared above the water, and Frederic nearly fell back from the force of his jerk.

"There is one of his arms," he said ; and he gave another blow with his pickaxe. After a number of jerks another arm showed above the water.

"Pull steady and let the water clear a little," said Frederic ; and he put out his hand to help Angela. The water running rapidly towards the sluice soon became clear. Hope and Cross, as they looked down from the more elevated station where they were standing, soon saw the state of matters below ; they could distinguish two white substances that were twisting in the water like two large eels ; several more could be partially seen half hid under the sand or large stones. The clips were fastened in a bag that looked like a man's cotton night-cap, for it was much the same shape, size, and colour. The colour, though white, was semi-transparent, and shone more brightly than a cotton night-cap would have done. It was evident that the cel-

looking branches which sprang from this bag were firmly fixed
to the stones under which they were hid, for many of the stones
had been moved from their places by the strain which the party
were giving to the clips. When the water became clear, Frederic
hooked his pickaxe into one of the half-hid branches, renewed
the jerks he had given to the other two with the same success,
for after shaking one of the large stones violently, something
seemed to give way, and another arm was twisting in the water.
The like process was repeated several times, always with the
same result; at last, bag, arms, and all, appeared above the
water, falling down into a lump; one arm only remained below
water, and that was fixed to a stone of about two or three
hundred-weight, which, in spite of its size, was dragged out of
its bed in the sand by the united strength of the old woman
and the two girls. Frederic hooked his pickaxe round this remaining arm, gave the usual jerks, it gave way, and a long mass
of nasty-looking stuff was lifted in the air.

"Well done!" said Madame le Moine; "the ugly beast, we
have settled him. He will pull down no more of the fishery,
nor swallow any more of my fish. Hook the other, Frederic,
while I put this one beside these gentlemen."

Saying this, one of the clips was unhooked from the creature
and given to Frederic, and the old woman clambered up the
dyke, holding the other in her hand, fast fixed in the fish;
when she was fairly up, she threw her burden with force on the
stones and withdrew the clip. "Is he not an ugly beast?" she
said, addressing the two friends.

"He is indeed," said Hope, who now could see it in all its
deformity. It looked like an enormous cuttle-fish. It had the
same form—the bag-looking body, the two huge eyes, and the
bunch of feelers springing from them; these feelers, however,
were far larger and longer than those of any cuttle-fish he had
ever seen before; they were fully as long as a man's arm, and
were covered on one side, from one end to the other, with lumps
rather bigger than a hazel-nut. As they examined it, and began

to stretch out these feelers to look at his size when spread out,
they observed a strong muscular action in them all, and the
lumps began to open and shut like so many mouths—opening
to the size of a shilling, and then again contracting till they
looked like warts.

"How disgustingly ugly and revolting it is!" said Hope;
"and if all those mouths eat, I don't wonder the old lady is glad
to get him out of her fishery. How would you like, Cross, to
have that brute clinging round you, sucking you in with all those
leech-looking mouths?"

"I don't believe they eat with those beastly-looking valves,"
said Cross; "they use them for clinging to the stones, or perhaps
for grasping their prey; but we will ask the old lady."

They put the question, and she confirmed what Cross had
said. "Yes," she answered, "they fasten themselves on the
stones, and tremendous strength they must have, to be able to
draw those large stones out of this wall, with such a weight resting above; you may suppose, when you saw how firmly they
grasp, that no fish could get away, if once seized hold of by
them."

"And do they eat fish?" asked Hope.

"Nothing comes amiss to them; they would eat a man if he
came in their way. I have seen oysters, shells and all, in them;
and in one, I found a large crab: oh, they are awful brutes; I hate
the sight of them."

"Perhaps they are not strictly pretty," said Cross; "but they
are interesting, as people say of young ladies. One fine calm sunny
day I organized a minaur-hunt with a fisher-girl at Granville, and
we started when the tide ebbed, armed with crook and knife.
After a scramble over the rocks, and a long search, my guide
pointed to a small pile of empty limpets, and freshly broken crab
shells and claws, at the bottom of a shallow rock-pool which glittered in the sun, with an endless play of bright colours, but was
unusually bare of living creatures. 'Behold, the minaur is here,'
she said; and forthwith began to beat the cover, while I looked

out for the game. The girl poked about with her crook under the sea-weed, at the deepest side of the pool, in the shadow of a bit of rock ; but I observed that she kept her feet out of the water. Presently she cried out—' There are two ;' and out they came, sailing over the bright shell-sand at the bottom, where I could see them as plainly as I see you. They looked like two small haggis-bags with the strings loose, or a couple of animated turnips, darting root-foremost through the water ; but they were complete, active, living creatures of sound understanding, in spite of their looks. Each squirted a small black cloud of sepia towards the danger, and then swam rapidly away from it behind the screen, jerking backwards by filling the bag with water and squeezing it out again. The pool was small, speed was of no avail, and they seemed to know it ; for they stopped suddenly near the shallow edge and disappeared. First the bag sat down and shrunk up, and then the long arms, which had trailed after it while swimming, spread out like a branching star, ploughed up the sand, dragged in stones and shells, buried the bag, and then, having stuck themselves all over with loose rubbish, by means of these glands the arms too wriggled out of sight, and nothing remained above ground but the open mouth of the bag, and bright eyes looking keenly up at the foe. The bulb had taken root, but it was watching, not vegetating ; for any sudden movement of ours was followed by a start, or some slight quiver amongst the shells as the creature shrunk deeper into his hole. My barefooted mermaiden stirred them up with her crook, and we watched them for a long time, till I came to the conclusion that they were very sagacious fierce little monsters, well able to take care of themselves, enormously strong, and with great appetites. If any big fish had pursued at first, he could hardly have got through the cloud till the cuttle had planted himself firmly ; and then he was more than a match for anything of his own size.

"At last we put them into an earthen jar, for I wanted to keep them alive, but they would not be quiet. They kicked, and twined, and struggled ; the long arms were thrust out like an elephant's trunk from his cage, and curled about, and stuck to everything within reach ; and so the arms dragged the bag out and dropped it with a flop upon the rock so often, that, in despair, I condemned my pets to death. They were executed on the spot, with a rusty knife, by the girl. I have often thought of their rigid, powerful, cold, sticky, clinging grasp upon my hand— especially when swimming near these rocks—and the thought was unpleasant, I can assure you.

"The fisher-girls dread them, and no wonder. As we walked home my companion told me that her hand was once grasped and held tight by a large minaur, when she was groping in a hole for crabs. The tide was rising, and she could neither free her arm nor drag the cuttle from his fortress. She had no weapons ; he was too tough to break by a steady pull, and he held on. She thought her last hour was come, and screamed for help. Fortunately a fisherman was within hail, who came to her and slew the brute ; but she had a very narrow escape, for the water was up to her waist before she got free."

"I have heard a similar story about a Highlander and a lobster," said Hope.

"The Granville story is true," said Cross, "for I took the trouble to ask the fish-wives about it, and they confirmed the girl's account of the matter ; and the lobster story may be true also. I wonder," he added, with a sly look, "what the author of the 'Vestiges' would say about a minaur. Perhaps he might argue that the first of the race was an uprooted bulb washed into the sea, and that our friend the Marquis was 'developed' from this type. Both are muscular provision-bags, armed with organs for filling them, and wit to use the means provided. The minaur was strongly attached to Marie when he sought her hand, and his thoughts must be in his inside, for all the head he has is there."

"Stuff and nonsense," said Hope. "Men alone are cooks, and the Marquis is a distinguished cook and a man ; one of the Breton branch of the old Macadam family. The minaur is of still older descent than he, and can point to the tombs of his ancestors amongst the old Welsh rocks ; but we have nothing to do with such speculations at present."

" Does anybody eat minaurs, Madame ?" he added in French.

" Yes," she answered ; " in the spring they are sometimes eaten ; but then they take more hammering and cooking than they are worth : but at this season they are so hard, that if you hammered them for one half the day, and stewed them for the other half, they would still eat like a mouthful of fiddle-strings ; but if you get them down, they tell me they are very nourishing, and that they are wonderful restorers of old men who have been rakes in their youth. They are a good bait for catching big cod, and they have one great advantage : if you once get the bait on to a hook, no fish can get it off again, so that one bait will last for a week."

" Just what I told you," said Cross, turning to Hope ; " and it is a great pity that they do not salt them down for this purpose. I will have a talk to Frederic about it as soon as they have hauled out the other."

The same process was pursued in taking the second monster as the first ; it was smaller, however, and did not give so much trouble. When fairly landed beside its companion on the dyke, Cross desired the old lady to leave a number of the mackerel and sardines at the inn, and, strange to say, he had considerable trouble in persuading her to receive payment for them. He then asked Frederic to go with them, to show them where the nets and lines of their yesterday's acquaintance were set, and they proceeded at a rapid pace across the sand, in the direction to which he pointed. As they walked, Cross spoke to him on the subject of salting minaurs and cuttle-fish.

Frederic was an intelligent fellow. He seemed to think that this idea might prove of value to his countrymen, for if there were any demand, a great many might be taken in a year. But he said that he had not thought on the subject, as he never had anything to do with catching the fish he brought back to

France, their trade being merely that of buying them in the
country and bringing them home. But in the course of their
conversation he mentioned a circumstance which interested his
hearers. He told them that he had once seen one of these
creatures four times larger than the one they had taken that
day ; that when he found this fish lying on the shore he was
walking with a Norwegian sailor, who had then told him that,
large as that one was, he had seen one far larger on the coast of
Norway—the feelers were nine feet long and as thick as his leg ;
and that he again had heard from his father that there were
monsters of the same sort in the sea that grasped ships and took
them under water ;—in short, that minaurs and krakens were
the same fish, only that on the coast of France they never came
to their full growth as they did on the coast of Norway.

As they walked fast, they were not long in coming up to
the party they had agreed to meet. They found the old man,
his two sons, and his wife, standing by the side of a very long
net ; it was shallow, and was lying with the corks towards the
sea, firmly anchored to the sand by the bottom line. We have
been so uncourteous as to mention the lady last, but, like the
chief personage in a state procession, she soon showed that she,
at all events, considered herself the leader.

"Here you are at last," she exclaimed ; " I was almost afraid
you had forgotten to come. My husband talked of emptying
the net and not waiting ; but I gave it to him. I sent him and
the boys to bait the lines and clean the other nets, but this one
I have kept for you to look at, because it has done very well ;
indeed, altogether it has been a great tide, and I am glad of it,
for you will see what our nets can do, and taste our best fish.
It is not often we get so many ; the tre-mailles (trois-mailles)
has done wonders—just look at it."

The two friends saw numbers of white specks and lumps
along the line of the net, but they were so much rolled up they
could not distinguish what they were ; but they now followed
in the wake of the old lady, who assumed her character of com-

manding officer, issuing her orders, which were promptly and
quietly obeyed. The husband and eldest son took their places,
one at the cork, the other at the bottom line. The sand was
perfectly smooth below the net, showing no mark of the holes
that had been dug to sink the straw anchors beneath it. The
action of the water had made them quite flat; all that could be
seen was about an inch of cord, holding the bottom of the net
firmly in its place. The father and son moved along, sorting
the middle fine-meshed net, and smoothing it between the two
outer nets, or walls. When they found the net all the corks
were towards the sea, being so drawn by the ebbing tide; this
was carefully reversed, the corks being laid towards the shore;
and the reason of this proceeding was explained by saying that
it was done to prevent any chance of the nets being entangled
when the sudden rush of the tide came on; for then the corks
would be carried before it till the straw holders held them, and
in passing over the net the corks might catch and so entangle it.
As the two fishermen moved along they came to the specks and
lumps that had been seen from the end. There were fish of
all sorts and sizes; every fish, whether large or small, had made
a bag for itself by drawing a portion of the fine middle net
through one of the large meshes in either of the outside walls.
We say either, for it was quite evident that the fish had been
caught in coming towards the shore, as well as in returning—
which fact was easily seen by observing that they had made bags
on both sides of the net. Hope was astonished to find the
variety of fish that one net had taken, and Cross was still more
so, for he had often seen the nets drawn before, and never with
such good success. There were two sorts of skate, the common
skate and the thornback; some very large gar-fish; a few very
fine mackerel; a quantity of soles, some of which were large; two
or three demoiselles; one turbot, not large, but very thick and firm;
five or six very fine brills; and a number of plaice and flounders.
    In the net these were all, but the lines had caught a great
number of skate; no difference was made in the varieties; all

were called raés. They had three bass, some conger-eels, and
two lythe that would weigh about seven pounds each. Hope
was glad to see these, for he at once knew them to be the same
fish which are caught in such quantities on the coasts of Scotland, where they bear the same name.

"We must have the turbot, and also the large soles, for our
bouillabaise," said Cross ; and he prepared himself for a wrangle
with the old lady ; but the price she asked was so very moderate that he gave it at once. He felt somewhat ashamed at
such unwonted moderation, and his surprise was expressed in
his face.

"I could not ask you more than they were worth," said she,
laughing, as she looked at Cross. "I heard what good gentlemen
you are, and how generous you have been to little Matilde. If
I were not so poor, I wished to give them to you ; but with
these boys and my husband, whom I must feed and clothe, I
cannot afford to give my fish for nothing ; but I have done
next thing to it, for I have sold them for the same price that
Marie de Coutance would pay for them."

"I thank you," said Cross ; "and as we kept you waiting so
long, you must take a franc apiece from my friend and me, to
drink little Matilde's health."

She made a most graceful curtsey, and rolled her money in
the corner of her handkerchief, promising to lose no time in
sending the fish to the inn ; and we may as well mention now,
that when the friends arrived there, they found not only the fish
they had paid for, but also the large mackerel and gar-fish : so
generosity breeds after its kind.

"The tide has turned," said the lady, "so we must not lose
time. Frederic, you must help to carry home our fish, for the
raés are too heavy for the boy."

Frederic was breaking in for a Granville husband, or he was
very good-natured, for he at once obeyed the imperious order,
and shouldering the heavy basket, they all took their way for
the shore.

We cannot say that Hope was exactly frightened, but there was undoubtedly a certain uncomfortable remembrance of the night before that made him feel rather unwilling to take a longer line than that chosen by the fishers; and when Cross explained that he wished to go to the rocky point to try and get permission to have some salt water, Hope agreed, though he certainly stepped out faster than he had ever before done in walking on the sand.

All the fishers were wending their way for the same end, and among the number they did not particularly remark two who were walking slowly before them; but on overtaking them, they discovered that one was the Marquis, the other his confederate prawn-fisher. Dressed like all the other fishermen, with their baskets on their backs, they had not distinguished them from the rest, for the Marquis did not wear his straw hat, and the gold band on the captain's cap had not caught their attention; but when they came in a line with them, they at once recognised the features of the one and the moustaches of the other.

The Marquis was in very bad humour, for he had had bad sport; and the Baron's net, near the rocks, had been more successful than his had been on the open sand. The same efflux of tide that had prevented the lançons from taking the sand, had swept the prawns out to sea from the open shore, and very few had been caught, except close under the shelter of the rocks. He must therefore eat prawns that had been twenty-four hours out of the water; added to the fact that the Baron had bragged awfully, these misfortunes had made him very sulky; but his good humour returned when he heard the excellent provision that had been made for dinner; and at the mention of the bouillabaise, he was again all smiles, and declared the willing pleasure he should have in taking care that the turbot should be properly cooked, and the soles converted into one of his favourite dishes.

"I have brought my friend," he said, as he stepped out before them, "who knows what is good, and he will make our fourth for a rubber this evening."

"Hang the fellow!" whispered Hope. "I hate playing cards all night; and I suppose these two Frenchmen mean to rook us."

"We must be good-natured," replied Cross, in the same low tone. "The Marquis is wretched without his cards at night; and if they do win, it is only paying him for his services, which are well worth all it will cost us should we lose every game. Since the Revolution they play for very low stakes—the question now being whether the points are five-and-twenty or fifty."

"Five-and-twenty francs!" said Hope; "that is a pound! They will not catch me playing for such high stakes."

"Who said it was francs, my dear fellow?—five-and-twenty or fifty centimes, I ought to have said—twopence halfpenny or fivepence—that is all you will be asked to risk. So you may save your virtuous indignation against gambling for a future occasion."

"If that is all, I do not mind boring myself for an hour or two by playing cards, if it will amuse our good-natured French friend."

The latter part of this conversation took place while they were crossing the rocky point where they had first seen little Matilde fall into the water in catching her spider-crab; they were then close under the extreme point, where the rocks rose more perpendicularly. Hope was rather startled by hearing a voice call out close above them—

"Who goes there? How you do? stand fast! god-dam!"

"O sir, there you are, speaking English as well as ever," said Cross, in French; "I was just looking for you."

"O yes, very good!" replied the voice; and then, being at the end of his English, he resumed his native tongue, declaring himself delighted to see Cross.

Hope was duly presented, and then Cross mentioned his wish for permission to have some sea-water to boil some fish, as his friend was a great gourmand.

The promise was exacted that the water should be thrown

away after the fish were cooked; and then the man in authority
promised to send one of his men with a greybeard of salt water.
After a proper exchange of thanks and compliments, Hope and
Cross took their way up a steep path in the rocks, and the
Douanier returned to a sort of hole where he had been sitting.
Against the back of this hole rested a musket ; the bottom had
an armful or two of straw spread over it.

"That must be cold quarters on a winter night," said Hope,
" if they have to stay there to look after sea-water at all seasons
of the year."

"Yet so it is," answered Cross ; " winter and summer these
poor devils have to watch along the coast ; and if some of our
Hampshire or Sussex fellows could speak French, I think they
would soon give the Government a practical lesson against high
duties and bad management. These people are ill-paid ; they
are on duty for twelve hours at a time, and their share of a
seizure is so small that I am only astonished any duty is ever
paid at all on tea, tobacco, salt, gunpowder, needles, earthen-
ware, or English woollen and cotton goods. At home, under
such duties and such protection, I suspect a ten-pound note
and a dark night would greatly lessen the revenue."

"You talk so con amore of smuggling," said Hope, "you
seem to have a taste for the pursuit."

"If I were not born a gentleman," said Cross, "I am afraid
I might have had a turn that way. There is a sort of romantic
danger about it that gives to smuggling the same sort of zest
that a keen sportsman must feel in tiger-hunting—that is to
say, not in the peddling way of sneaking a pound of tea through
the custom-house by hiding it in your pocket or your trunk.
That, in my idea, is like hunting rabbits with a ferret. My
fancy would be running cargoes on a wild night on a well-
guarded coast ; for that bears more resemblance to hunting
tigers—you have the excitement of danger and the triumph of
success, which must give the same sort of feeling as winning a
battle."

"I am ashamed of you," said Hope; "I rather suspect the feelings of a smuggler must be more like those of a successful gambler than a victorious general."

"Do you think so? well, perhaps you are right; and I should never make a smuggler, for I have lived for some years among people here who are awful gamblers, and have never yet taken to the trade. But here comes the man with the sea-water: we must step out to see that it is taken care of, and give the messenger something to drink."

CHAPTER VIII.

It would be only an idle repetition to describe the dinner of this day. It greatly resembled the supper of the night before; the dishes varied in the cooking, though not much in the materials; there were some additions, it is true—namely, the bouillabaise, and some bacon dressed according to a receipt of the Marquis. The first of these was, as we have already said, nothing more nor less than a very rich variety of water zoutchee; the latter was a piece of well-cured and well-smoked bacon, which, after being stuck full of cloves, had first been immersed in red wine for six or seven hours, and was then thickly pané'd and baked brown in the four de campagne. It was served with the chickens, which on this day were stewed in a white sauce, instead of being roasted. The two Englishmen took a note of this method of dressing bacon, as they found it excellent; but we do not allude to the dish out of sympathy with their improved perception of good things, but because, at a later hour of the night, this said bit of bacon led the observation of the friends to a curious fact in natural history. But when Frenchmen dine, the subject is too serious to allow of digression; so we postpone for a while the description of their discovery.

On this day there were two Frenchmen at dinner instead of one, both of whom were well and deeply read in the philosophie des gourmands. The proceedings therefore were far more methodical and slow than on the previous evening; there were long pauses between each dish, and a greater delay at table afterwards. But these pauses were not wearying, neither was the sederunt over the dessert; for while the Frenchmen ate, they talked, and talked well, on subjects that amused their more taciturn companions. The soldier was, like the Marquis, a complete royalist, detesting all republics. He narrated many interesting anecdotes regarding the late royal family, and spoke highly of their personal courage, as a proof of which, among other instances, he described the conduct of Louis Philippe when Fieschi fired at him with his infernal machine. This he could do accurately, for he had stood within ten paces of the king when the shot went off. He related the manner in which the various persons fell. The report, he said, was not loud, although so many barrels were discharged at once, but rather sounded as if a musket or two had been fired at some distance off, and this, he supposed, arose from the venetian blind, which deadened the noise, or drove it back into the room from whence the shot was fired; for it seemed by his account that the balls passed through a blind before striking any other object. "I heard," he said, "this deadened report, and at the same moment I felt something graze my arm, and immediately a little girl, who was standing behind me, fell forward and struck the street with her face. I heard a cry, and saw many more falling and fallen. I stooped to raise the girl, but she was dead; a ball had passed through her heart. Poor thing! she was young and very pretty, but I could do nothing for her—she was gone for ever! So I laid her down again. When I looked up, I saw the king's horse plunging violently, for it was badly wounded. Several of his court were trying to persuade the king to turn back, but this he would not do. I heard him give the word 'Forward' with a cool and determined voice—so much so, that all argument ceased, and the cortège advanced. I did not proceed with them, for my attention was rivetted on the convulsed faces of the wounded, who were being carried away for assistance, and I did not like to leave the body of the little girl, who had fallen by my side so instantaneously struck by death. A few seconds before she had been laughing and enjoying the gay scene; but she would laugh and smile no more. I believe," he con-

tinued, " I am as brave as another. I have seen my comrades
fall by my side from the balls of an enemy, and have thought
little of it. There was then strife and excitement; there was
war. I was anxious to destroy the lives of my country's enemies,
and willing to hazard my own. Those about me were actuated
by the same feelings, and when they fell, I said, 'Fortune of war,'
and all was over; but in the moment of peace and gaiety it is a
different thing. To see a man fall in battle is nothing; to stand
by the side of a fair young girl, who has come forth to seek pleasure and has met with death, gives a shock not easily told. I
am not ashamed to own that I was greatly affected. The people
began to bring the dead and lay them in a row close to the spot
where I was standing. I would let no one else touch my little
girl; I lifted her myself, and laid her with the rest, and stood
at her head till Louis Philippe returned. When he did so, he
paused before the line of bodies, and saluted each with his sword.
It was I who returned the salutation for the little girl, and as I
did so, I marked well the king's eye and expression; it was sad,
but there was no trace of fear. No, no, I tell you (and he raised
his voice); let them say what they will, our royal blood is brave.
They may make a mistake; they may want moral courage in a
great crisis; but no man can say with truth that they are deficient in personal bravery. If you want another instance, I can
give it you. People are not now afraid of the cholera, but in '32,
whenever the pestilence broke out, wives left their husbands, and
mothers their children. The very doctors were flying from the
hospitals; yet in that moment of universal panic the king restored their courage by going through the hospitals himself, and
speaking to the sick and dying. This, in my opinion, showed
greater nerve than riding calmly through the streets after an
escape from assassination; for I know that I would rather
face a battery of guns loaded with grape, than walk through a
pest-house."

" I remember," said Hope, " the sensation which this attempt
of Fieschi's made in London. We had exhibitions and models

of the infernal machine, and wax models of the heads of Fieschi
and his friends, which were wonderfully well done. Every little
trifle was copied : the wound on Fieschi's head, and the mark on
the noses of all, were accurately portrayed. The showman told
us that this mark on the nose was invariably found on the faces
of all criminals who suffered by the guillotine; but I never heard
why it should be so."

"The explanation is very simple," said the Marquis. "The
culprit is fixed to a frame that slides towards the place where the
knife falls. When the moment of execution arrives, this frame
is let down, the culprit remaining fastened to it with his face towards the floor of the scaffold. Then the frame is pushed forward,
and as the criminal lies, his head has to pass over the semicircular
groove on which his neck is to be secured. As he passes over,
his nose always strikes the edge, which leaves the mark you saw.
It is the only pain he suffers, for in half a second his head is in
the basket."

"That is an accurate description," said the Captain; "but this
gentleman gave a wrong name to Fieschi's fellow-conspirators
when he called them his friends. There is not a doubt that they
intended to kill him as well as the king. Several of the plugs in
the breeches of the muskets were made so as to be sure to fire
backwards. It was one of these that wounded Fieschi. He stood
a little on one side when he fired, and was only wounded. Had
he stood exactly behind, he must have been shot dead. Fieschi
himself was convinced of this evil intention on their part, or he
never would have given up the names of the others. This I know
to be the fact, for he told me so with his own lips."

The arrival of a fresh dish stopped all further conversation on
this topic. After the discussion of the plât and its merits, a new
subject was started.

"You English," observed the Marquis, "always converse on
politics. Hitherto the French, as a nation, have done so very
little ; but now all the world talk ; even the very gamins in the
street speak of governing the country, and finding out the defects

of our rulers. I remember the time when every man though
himself fit to be a general, and canvassed every battle that wa
fought, and every military movement that was made. Now, the
all begin to think themselves qualified to be prime ministers, an
talk of public men and public measures as they used to do o
generals and battles."

"And what are the grievances they principally complain of?
asked Hope.

"Every district has its own," answered the Marquis. "In thi
for instance, the people are fond of their money. Economy, tax
ation, and finance, are therefore the themes they dwell upon."

"Yes, a set of fools," said the Captain. "What do you thin
a farmer had the absurdity to tell me the other day? Why, h
said that two hundred thousand soldiers were quite enough t
protect France, and that three hundred thousand ought to b
forthwith disbanded. Did you ever hear of anything so absurd
Yet I assure you the fellow said so; and what most astonishe
me was, to hear anything so ridiculous come out of the mouth c
a man who had before spoken very sensibly."

"What had he said?" asked the Marquis.

"Why," replied the Captain, "he had been saying that th
industrious part of the population were eaten up by the useles
quantity of civil employés, and he enumerated a good many c
them that might, I allow, be very well dispensed with. I re
member one in particular—the Minister of Public Worship. H
is undoubtedly very useless, for the women could certainly go t
church without our paying a large sum to a minister to loo
after their worship. Let the priests do that, and save the salar
to the country. I am sure in Paris none of our acquaintanc
ever think of going to church, and it is very much the sam
here."

"Why, my dear friend," said the Marquis, "I go to churc
very often, and I have seen you there also."

"True, my dear fellow, I used to go, but I have left it ol
for I have some religion, and I was afraid I should lose wha

little I had by going to mass only to see you looking about at the women, and not listening to the priest.''

"No, no, my friend," said the Marquis ; "you do me injustice, for I go to mass here occasionally, and, generally speaking, all the women in Normandy are so plain that no man of taste would look at them twice. I present myself in church, and if I don't listen much, at all events I hear the sound of the priest's voice and the choir."

" What would our friends in Scotland say to such a method of performing our religious duties ?" whispered Cross.

" Why, they would wonder," returned Hope, " that the earth did not open and swallow them ; yet, strange to say, I once heard a worthy presbyterian Highland laird make a speech greatly resembling that which the Marquis has just made. My friend always went to church, at least once every Sunday, but in the hot summer weather, instead of entering the church, he always remained outside. Being asked his reason for this proceeding, he answered that the church was very warm and stuffy ; whereas, by staying in the churchyard, he could smell the flowers, feel the caller air, and hear the birds sing, while at the same time he got a *sough* of the gospel through the church-door."

These latter remarks and answers had been made in English, and spoken rapidly, so that they did not attract the attention of the Frenchmen, who were fully taken up with their own conversation and the sight of another dish, which was travelling from the stove to the table. While it was being devoured there was a pause, and for a time no one spoke ; but the same reflections, as was afterwards confessed, passed through the minds of the two friends ; namely, that although religion was at a very low ebb in France, yet there were many who perfectly understood the rule of " every one for himself and God for us all." The soldier considered folly that which the farmer and the civilian deemed wisdom, and *vice versa*, as each was swayed by interest.

" With interests so opposed, it will require a wise head and a strong arm to restore prosperity to this fine country," said Cross, when, at a later period, they compared their thoughts.

The longest dinner must have an end. The tables were at last cleared, after a long sederunt ; cards were produced, and the four were soon established at whist. The stakes were five sou a fish, or, what certainly sounds better than either, twopence halfpenny, or five sous ; they played for twenty-five centimes The Frenchmen were by way of being good players ; they wer undoubtedly in constant practice. The Englishmen seldon played ; yet such was the course of luck, that soon after elevei o'clock, when the party broke up, the Frenchmen were in ver; bad humour, being losers of thirty points. " You remember th Scotch proverb," said Hope, " ' The deil's good to beginners.'"

As they were passing through the house door to mount thei own outside stair, Cross stopped. " I remember, by the by, said he, " you doubted the strength of the jelly which could b made by boiling fish and fish-bones under pressure. Th remains of our bouillabaise will now be cold. Come into th larder and see how firm it becomes, and you will appreciat the use of confining the steam in the pot by laying a weigh on the lid."

" I should like well enough to see that," answered Hope So they turned back to ask permission of the landlady to ente her larder.

" Certainly, certainly," said she ; " here is a light. Th door at the end leads into the larder." She opened a bac door, and pointed down a short passage made of wood, leanin against the house, and leading to a detached building.

Cross took the light, and led the way. There were tw doors on one side, and one in front ; and when they came t the second, Cross opened it and walked in. He had fairl entered before he perceived that he was in a small bedroom not in a larder, and that the apartment was occupied. A ma was sitting at a table, with his back towards the door. On th

table were the remains of a supper, and a small lantern, which
threw a faint light over the room. The man had been leaning
his head on his hand, perhaps asleep ; but when the door opened,
and he heard the sound of footsteps, he sprang up evidently in
alarm. As he arose, he held a pocket-handkerchief to his face,
so that his features could not be seen. He wore a peasant's
blouse, and both it and his lower garments were covered with
mud.

" What may you please to want ?" said the man, after a
moment's pause, during which he had accurately surveyed
Cross.

" I beg your pardon," answered the latter ; " I thought
this was the larder."

The man recognised the accent of an Englishman, and
seemed reassured, for he removed the handkerchief from his
face as he replied, " The gentleman is mistaken ; this is my
room, not the larder."

Cross, while he spoke, was standing within the room ;
Hope was still in the passage. Cross carried the candle, so
that both the stranger and himself were in light ; while Hope
remained in the dark shadow of the door : he could thus see
them, but the stranger could not distinguish him.

Cross apologised for his intrusion, and was in the act of
closing the door, when the landlady rushed bustling into the
passage.

" Oh, mon Dieu !" she cried, " that is not the larder. It is
in front of you, at the end. How foolish he is ! Could he
not have the sense to bolt his door ?"

She followed close on the steps of the two friends, as they
walked into an apartment, built of wood, which opened at the
end of the passage, and closed the door behind her as soon as
they were all entered.

" You are so generous, you English," she said, " I am sure
you will not betray the poor gentleman or me. I was mad not
to show you the way, and he was worse not to fasten his door."

"Don't alarm yourself," answered both the friends together; "we shall never mention that we have seen any one here."

"Not even to the gentlemen with whom you dined?" said the landlady, looking anxiously in their faces.

"To no one, be assured," replied Hope; "for though we suspect him to be an *ouvrier* who has been concerned in the late outbreak at Paris, we shall not betray either him or you."

"He has been foolish, I am afraid," said the landlady, "but why or how I know not, for he is not an *ouvrier*, but a gentleman, who was once rich and liberal. My brother was servant in his house, so I could not refuse him shelter when he was in danger."

"And believe me," said Cross, "we respect your feelings. No one shall know from us that we have perceived any one in your house; so set your mind at ease, and show us what we came to see, namely, the cold soup from the bouillabaise."

The landlady produced a jar, in which stood a clear and very firm jelly. She was still slightly nervous, but in answer to questions put to her, she explained that this jelly would serve for another time by the addition of a little water; that it turned sour and bad if allowed to cool often; but when kept hot, and water added, it would be equally good for a long time. It was while Cross was talking to the woman, that Hope cast his eye round this apartment, half pantry, half dairy. The room, or rather shed, was divided into two parts by a canvas screen. On one side were ranged the milk vessels, on the other, cold meat and vegetables. A small quantity of raw meat hung from the roof. The milk vessels were as unlike those in an English dairy as possible; for instead of being large and flat, they were tall and round, looking like brown English beer-jugs without handles. Close to Hope was placed the remainder of the piece of bacon which they had thought so good at dinner. This caught his eye, for he thought he saw something move upon it, and when he stepped forward to ascertain what it could be, he was thunderstruck by perceiving an immense bright orange slug, having some small black spots on the back, which was busily engaged in devouring the bacon, in which it had already made a considerable hole.

"Hang it, Cross, look at this; here is something that will astonish you! a carnivorous snail! and not only eating meat, but salt meat. Why, I have always thought that a pinch of salt would kill any of the snail tribe; yet here is a fellow that has eaten a pretty good hole in this bacon, and is still going on with his meal."

"O the villanous beast!" cried the landlady, as she seized a wooden fork and jerked the slug on the earthen floor, where she crushed it with her sabot.

Hope made a dash to save its life, but was too late. "I am sorry you killed it," he said; "I should like to have kept it."

"Keep that vile creature!" exclaimed the landlady. "They are the plague of my life. I find them here constantly; sometimes eating the meat, and sometimes the bread. It was only two days ago that I found two of them eating a loaf of English bread that I had brought from Granville for Monsieur le Marquis; and how they get in, I cannot conceive, unless they come out of the ground."

"Most probably they do," said Cross; "for though the earth is hard and dry in the centre of the floor, it is quite soft round the edges, and I see several holes through which these creatures might come."

"Have you ever seen them eating meat before?" asked Hope.

"No, I have not," answered Cross; "but I have seen them eating filth on the road-side, and I have heard that they attack the fat of meat, especially when it has-been panéd as this bacon is."

"But salt meat!" said Hope; "to eat that is to me doubly surprising."

"I doubt," returned Cross, "if there is any salt left in this meat. What between soaking in water and simmering for so

P

many hours in wine, I suspect the salt must be all extracted ; and we are not the first to discover that snails are carnivorous."

" I am aware," said Hope, " that the garden snail, the Helix aspersa, eats insects in its native state, and meat in confinement. I know also that the Kensington slug devours worms and grubs ; but I never had the slightest idea that these large sleek-looking fellows ate anything but vegetables."

" I rather suspect," answered Cross, "that these orange-coloured slugs are a different variety from any we have in England. Works on natural history are not to be got here, and I have never met any of the natives who care the least about such studies. Observation is therefore all we have to trust to, unless you are in correspondence with any of your learned friends in Paris, who may help to enlighten us. Our friend the Marquis may be able to tell us if they are ever used as food. You know there is a variety of snail that is eaten both here and in Germany ; and I think I have been told that they make a sort of soup of slugs which is given to people in consumption."

" Yes," said Hope, " I know that to be a fact. I have heard of the same thing being done in England ; and it is said that soup made of the common black slug is one of the lightest and most nutritious kinds of food that can be given to an invalid. I have the means of knowing that slugs are very nutritious."

" How so ?" asked Cross. " Have you ever tasted them yourself ?"

" Not exactly," answered Hope ; " but I know that they were eaten to a great extent by an Irishwoman and her family. The circumstance is rather curious, and I will tell you about it. You may remember that my family lived for two years in Kent, near Sydenham. There was a large common near our house, greatly frequented by gypsies and tramps ; in a gravel-pit on this common, an Irishman and his family thought proper to squat. They built a hovel against the side of the gravel-pit, in which they lived ; and the man earned large wages as a gravel-digger. One unfortunate day, however, when the poor man was employed in cutting down a bank, the fall came before it was expected, and he was smothered. The widow and children still continued to live in the hut, and it was remarked that, although she had no visible means of earning her livelihood, both she and her children were more fat and rosy than any labourer's family in the parish. Now, several hen-roosts had been robbed and a great many sheep stolen in the neighbourhood. Suspicion fell on Widow Scudder, and a warrant was granted to search her house. I chanced to be walking on the common when these myrmidons of the law had completed their search, and I met them returning to the village. One of them had the poor widow in custody, and two others were carrying a good-sized cask on a hand-barrow; the children were following their mother, all weeping most bitterly. I was but a lad at the time, but I had taken an interest in this poor woman, as I had heard of her husband's death, and she had once given me a viper which she had killed on the common. She had shown me the folding teeth and the poison-bag at the root of the fangs; and this viper formed a very conspicuous feature in my boy's museum, where it hung in a bottle of spirits of wine, with its mouth open to show the fangs. I could do little in her behalf, excepting to use my tongue; but this I did exert to the best of my ability, remonstrating with the men, and asking what the poor woman had done that they should make a prisoner of her. One of the constables knew me, and so far condescended to sink his dignity as to inform me that they had plain proof that Widow Scudder was the person who had stolen all the sheep, for that they had found this cask which they were carrying full of the salted meat, which she had minced into little morsels. I looked to the poor widow to learn what she said to this accusation. 'Oh, darling, spake for me and the children,' she said; 'it's not mutton, though it's their meat and mine, and has kept death from our door this bitter winter!' 'What is it then, mother?' asked one of the constables. 'That's nothing to you, you

false-hearted blackguard,' roared the widow. 'The curse of
the Lord fall on you and yours, that would lay a hand on a
poor lone woman that never did hurt to you or your be-
longings.'

"I tried to persuade her to tell what was in the cask, but
she refused to speak before 'them blackguards,' as she called
the constables; and as no arguments could influence her, she
was taken before the magistrate, who was fortunately a very
kind-hearted man. I went with her. Mr. B. spoke mildly to
the woman; he examined the cask, which was half-full,
declared the contents were not mutton, and then asked the
widow to reveal to him what they were, as this information was
the best way to clear her from all suspicion. 'Send them fellows
away, and I will tell your honour,' replied the widow. The
constables were dismissed. I, as her friend, was allowed to
remain. She then told the magistrate that the cask contained
nothing more or less than salted slugs. She had seen them
given to a young man in Ireland supposed to be in a consumption, who had recovered his health, and got quite fat on this
food, and in consequence she had thought that what was so good
for him might be good for her children. She first tried them
fresh, and finding that her children throve, she then took to
salting them. Her mode was to drop the slugs into boiling
water, and afterwards lay them with salt in a cask. She and
her children had thus prepared two casks full, which had supported them all during the whole winter, and the cask then in
the room contained the remainder of her store. She besought
the magistrate not to reveal her confession to the constables,
which he promised not to do, and he kept his word; but he
told the story to a few of the gentry in the neighbourhood, who
joined him in a subscription, which enabled the widow in future
to have some bread to eat with her slugs. I too kept her
secret till she left the country; but I have never forgotten that
no one need starve where there are plenty of black slugs to be
got."

"I think," said Cross, "that I must be very far gone before I could eat a black slug. I am quite sure I would rather die than eat one of these orange ones, after what we see they feed on."

"Well," replied Hope, "I agree with you, and yet I am aware it is prejudice. We eat periwinkles, and think them very good, and they are nothing more nor less than sea-snails; and we have eaten this very day those spider-crabs, which are certainly more disgusting to look at, and quite as foul feeders. I wonder if an orange slug would eat a man as well as a bit of bacon! You know your friends the crabs would make no objections to such food."

This conversation had been carried on by the two gentlemen in English, the landlady looking on with curious eyes while they were speaking, as she did not understand a word of what they were saying. At last she showed what was passing in her mind by asking—

"Are you talking of the poor gentleman? Pray speak low if you are; for some one may hear you in the yard, and understand you, although I do not."

"O no," said Hope, "all the world might hear us without danger; we are only speaking of snails, and wondering if they are good as food. Can you tell us if the people about here ever eat them?"

"Yes," she answered; "they are sometimes used here, but only as a medicine. In La Vendée, and some other parts of France, they are eaten (the Lord defend me) from taste. When my husband was on service in the army he was a sous officier, and was caterer for their mess. Among the sous-officiers there was a sergeant who belonged to La Vendée with whom he had a quarrel, and they fought with sabres. Their dispute was about snails, for this man would always bring a capful of these creatures, which he cooked and ate at the table with my husband, though it made him sick to see them. Well, my husband desired him to give up such nasty tastes, which interference he

took much amiss, so they fought, and gave each other some very
pretty blows with the edge, and then they were good friends
again; only the Vendean agreed to eat his snails at another
mess. After this you would hardly believe that it was my
husband whom I first saw cooking snails; yet so it was. A girl
who was in our house as servant had a very bad illness of the
chest; she was constantly spitting blood, and all the doctors
said she must die. We were very sorry, for she was a good girl
and pleased us, when my husband remembered that he had
heard of such wonders being done for illnesses of the chest by
soup *au Limosin;* so he set to work to prepare some for the
poor girl as he had seen it made by the sergeant in La Vendée.
He gave it to her, and she had faith, for she got better. She
then learnt to cook it for herself, and took it twice a day, and
she got quite well and fat, and now she is married and has two
fine boys."

"Just your Irish widow over again," said Cross.

"Very like the way she learnt to eat snails, certainly,"
answered Hope. "And pray, madame," he continued to the
landlady, "can you tell us the manner in which they are
cooked?"

"With pleasure," she replied; "but you are not surely going
to try them?"

"Not at present," said Hope; "while we have the honour
of living with you we are quite contented with what you provide; but there is no knowing what may happen, and it is
always wise to take a lesson when we can."

"Very true, sir," said the landlady, who had curtsied low to
Hope's implied compliment on her cookery. "There are two
ways of cooking them. The snails with the shells are used in
the winter, for the slugs are not then to be found. These snails
with shells are found under ground at the foot of a wall, or in
holes in the walls. Those with stripes on them are not used,
because they have a bad taste and smell, but only those which
are of one colour. These are put for a minute into boiling

water, and then they come out of the shell quite easily. A little bit of hard matter is taken from the head, and afterwards they are stewed for a long time in milk. This is the winter soup, for at that season those snails are easily found and have no slime ; but in summer they use the slugs, and prepare them much in the same way, only with this difference, that the slugs are plunged into boiling water to kill them, and then they are washed in cold water, when a great deal of nasty slime comes off, after which they are stewed in water for a long time, and milk and seasoning added ; or they are stewed in milk in the same way as the snails with shells.'

"Thank you, madame," said Hope ; "and now we may go to bed, and let you go too. You may sleep soundly and without fear, for we shall never say one word to any person of the stranger to whom you are giving shelter."

The good woman thanked them and conducted them to the foot of their outside stair, where she handed a lantern to Cross, and bade them good-night.

"Well," said Cross, when they had entered their room, "that lady's receipt interested me, for her treatment of slugs was exactly similar to that followed by your Irish widow. The striped snails which she describes as being rejected are, I suppose, the Helix Nemoralis, or carnivorous snails of Sowerby. But what a fright she was in, poor woman, when she saw us in that man's room. I have a great fancy that he is one of the insurgents of Paris who has escaped, and has come down here to hide himself."

"And I am pretty sure that he is one," said Hope ; "I have seen him before, and not many weeks ago."

"Ah !" exclaimed Cross, "pray tell me about him. Was his one of the faces you saw grinning over a barricade ?"

"No," replied Hope ; "I never saw him at a barricade— though I have no doubt he was behind some of them—but I will tell you my story, and you shall judge. I was going into the Jardin des Plantes a few weeks ago with one of my learned friends, Monsieur G——, whose father is a banker. As we entered one of the walks we saw two good-looking young men sitting on one of the benches.

"They were dressed in rather shabby-genteel clothes. After we had passed, one of them, the very man now down stairs, followed us, and touched my friend on the shoulder. He stopped, and the intruder, addressing him by name, requested him to pause and speak with him. From the look he cast on me I saw I was not wanted, so I walked on, and waited for nearly a quarter of an hour before Monsieur G—— again joined me. When he did so, the first words he said were, 'How painful it is to be obliged to say 'no' when one would wish to say 'yes.' Did you ever find yourself in such a position?' I told him that few men reached my time of life without meeting with such an event. 'I am not as old as you are,' he said, 'and this has happened to me to-day for the first time. You saw those young men ; they are my juniors, it is true, yet we were at college together, and I protected the one who stopped me just now. I had a great liking for him, for he was full of talent, of good family, and not ill-off for money ; but he was very wild, and would never follow my advice. His present companion, Pierre B——, I knew less and liked less, for he was quite as wild, without the talent of my friend, Jules F——. With Pierre there was no reasoning ; he was as obstinate as an Austrian, and this obstinacy Jules F—— mistook for firmness, and allowed a man far his inferior in ability to lead him by the nose into all sorts of scrapes. After vainly endeavouring to draw Jules into steadier courses, I gave him up, and we ceased to be the intimate friends we had been, though I still met him in society, where he was running a reckless course of gambling, extravagance, and dissipation, spoiled by the admiration of the world, who helped him to his destruction by applauding his wit and never checking his vices. About two years ago, I heard he was ruined ; then I learnt that he had got some situation under government, and had gone to live in the country. Shortly after this I received a letter from him, asking me to assist him with a loan to establish him in his new situation, and telling me he was resolved to turn over a new leaf, as he deeply regretted not having followed my advice. I lent him the sum he requested, and he has repaid me nearly the whole amount, as he transmitted every quarter a portion of his salary. It unfortunately happened that the other young man whom we have just passed, Pierre B——, was also appointed to a situation in the same district where Jules F—— was placed, and I heard that they had got into several scrapes together before the Revolution. The interest of Jules saved him from dismissal; but with the Revolution came a change. Men in power, new men especially, always want to provide for their own friends and followers. Those who replaced the king were only too glad to take advantage of the faults of Jules F—— and his companion. They were summarily dismissed to make room for others, and I learn from him that they are both now absolutely in want of the necessaries of life. When Jules stopped me a minute ago, it was to show me a letter in which an editor of one of the papers offers him a situation, provided he will lodge five thousand francs in the concern as security for his good behaviour. He asked me to advance him this sum, or to persuade my father to do so. My father, I know, will not, and I cannot lend it. I was therefore obliged to say that painful word 'no,' and most painful I found it to do so; but I had no remedy. All the money I had in my pocket I lent him—some two hundred francs—and if he keeps clear of the gaming-table, that may give him food till he finds something to do; but that, alas! just now, is most difficult, for distress is universal, and who knows whether I may not in a week be as much in want of a few francs as he is to-day?'

"I told my friend Monsieur G——," continued Hope, "not to distress himself; but he was low and out of spirits during the remainder of our walk, and when we separated he was still depressed. A few days before the last outbreak I was again walking with this gentleman, when, at the corner of a street,

we came upon a considerable number of blackguard-looking men,
like the flash mob of Paris.   I saw one of these trying to avoid
us, and in another I recognised the elder of the two men whom
I had seen in the Jardin des Plantes, whom Monsieur G——
had named as Pierre B——.   He stared daringly at us from the
centre of this group.   We proceeded for about a hundred yards
in silence, when Monsieur G—— said, ' I had an anticipation
that this would be the case.   That young man is gone.   Nothing
can save him now.'   I asked for an explanation of these remarks,
and he told me that he had been making inquiries about the
young man Jules F——, to whom he had given the two hundred
francs, as his father had offered to take him as a clerk in his
bank till something better turned up ; but he learnt that his
exertions would now be of no avail, as Jules F—— had taken
his place in one of the clubs, and was already one of the most
admired orators and leaders in the communist department of the
Ateliers Nationaux.   ' I did not believe it,' he continued, ' but
I have just seen that it is too true.   Jules had the grace to try
and conceal himself, but I saw him in that group, many of whom
I know to be leaders of the very refuse of this city.'

   "Well, the outbreak took place.   I need not say anything
about that.   On the second day after it was put down I went
to call on Monsieur G——, and we set off together to look at
some of the districts where the fighting had been the hottest.
We were returning home again when we perceived a large crowd
advancing towards us.   There were a number of regular troops,
and a considerable body of the Garde Mobile, guarding about a
hundred prisoners ; and these again were followed by a crowd.
We drew on one side to let them pass.   As they came up we
could distinguish their faces.   In the front marched a prisoner
whose bearing struck me forcibly.   He had on neither hat nor
coat ; his face was black with powder, and he was evidently
wounded, for his shirt was stained with blood ; yet his hands
were tied behind him.   As he advanced he held his head very
high ; looking now up at the windows, now at the people in the

street, with the most daring bravado. The rest of the prisoners seemed so much depressed and wan that this man's conduct was the more striking. I own I did not recognise him, for his face was so begrimed with black that I could not distinguish his features. Monsieur G——, however, when they came near, got behind me and held down his head. 'It is as I expected,' he said in a low voice ; 'tell me when they are passed, and look for me, if you can see my poor friend Jules, for if he is not among them he has fallen !' Upon hearing this, I again looked at the leading prisoner, and then I knew him to be Pierre B——, the elder of the two men whom I had seen first in the Jardin des Plantes, and afterwards with the party in the street. I fixed my eyes on all the other prisoners as they passed ; Jules F—— was not among them. This I told to Monsieur G—— when they were all gone by. 'Then he has fallen !' he exclaimed : 'and perhaps it is as well ; better to die at once on the field, than perish on the scaffold, or pine away life in the Bagne !' He begged me, however, to follow the prisoners, which we did ; and we saw them all taken to their quarters. Here Monsieur G—— began to catechise one of the Garde Mobile, who gave us a graphic description of a hunt they had had after the flying insurgents, and for those who were hiding themselves in some of the woods round Paris. The horrors that had been committed by the insurgents on all the Garde Mobile who had fallen into their hands were universally known by the survivors of that corps, and they had been panting for revenge. By the description which this man gave us, they seemed to have glutted themselves pretty well with the blood of their adversaries ; for, by his account, their hunt had been a sort of battue, where men were the game, and not rabbits. 'When we had placed our posts,' said the Garde Mobile, 'at one end of the wood, to catch any stragglers, we spread out, completely surrounding the other three sides ; then the bugle sounded, and we advanced. Oh, it was grand sport to see them stepping from among the trees, and starting out of their lairs. The moment we got a glimpse of

one, if he ran, *plon!* down he came; if he stood still, we tied
his hands and drove him on; and indeed I am not sure that a
few of us did not take a sitting shot now and then. It was I
who dropped that fine fellow with his nose in the air; he was
mighty big when he got into the streets; but he sung very
small when he came to himself, and found his elbows fast in my
cord.'

"Monsieur G—— called me away, quite convinced that
Jules F—— was dead, and, truth to tell, so was I; and I was
therefore not a little astonished to-night when I looked over
your shoulder in the passage and recognised him still alive.
For Monsieur G——'s sake I will try and do something for
this unfortunate young man. At all events I may be able to
communicate with his friends, though he dare not do so himself.
In the meanwhile, let us to bed."

As the two friends had been undressing during the time that
Hope was speaking, it did not take them many minutes to conclude their preparations, and both stepped into bed at nearly
the same time. Silence followed, as far as words were concerned,
yet neither slept, and each heard the other turning and sighing,
by which the other knew that his companion was awake. This
had lasted nearly half-an-hour, when Hope sat up in his bed
and said softly—

"Are you awake, Cross?"

"Yes," answered he; "I am restless, and cannot sleep."

"And so am I," said Hope; "I hear a child crying that
annoys me terribly and makes me nervous. Listen! don't you
hear it? there again!"

A sound was heard very distinctly, and then Cross laughed.

"That is not a child crying," he said; "it is a number of
young cocks in coops in the yard below who are trying to crow."

"Cocks crowing!" exclaimed Hope, "impossible! why it is
barely midnight; there is no moon, and it is as dark as Erebus."

"All true," answered Cross; "nevertheless, what you hear
is nothing more nor less than cocks crowing. Open the window

if you doubt me, and listen ; you will hear the same sounds coming from every yard in the village."

Hope jumped out of bed, groped his way to the window, opened it, and leaned out.

"By Jove! you're right," he exclaimed ; "I hear cocks crowing distinctly all around me, both near and at a distance. It is very extraordinary, for the night is so dark I cannot see my hand a foot from my face."

"It struck me also as very singular when I first came here," said Cross, "but now I am used to it and forget to think that it is unusual, for every cock in this country crows half the night. I suspect they must dream, and do it while they sleep, for, dark or light, it is the same—the cocks are always crowing. I suppose the garrulity of the men descends to the feathered as well as to the unfeathered bipeds of the land. I have been told, however, that in the West Indies both dogs and poultry are mute during the day, but make up for their silence in daylight by barking and crowing all night."

"I have never met with this before," said Hope ; "or, if I have, it never struck me. I am glad, however, I have heard it, for it has changed the current of my thoughts, and I may now go to bed again and try to sleep."

He shut the window and groped his way back to bed.

"Neither am I sorry that you disturbed my thoughts," said Cross. "Our conversation about the cures wrought by eating snails called up some sad remembrances. I have been thinking that, had I thought of trying it, it might have saved my poor sister as effectually as it did the maid of an inn. With such well-authenticated cases, I wonder the remedy is not oftener tried. If the relations of an invalid were afraid of disgusting the sufferer by telling her that she was eating snail-soup, they might give it without letting her know how it was made, and mark the effect. They say it has no disagreeable taste, and looks like a white soup. A little parsley in summer, or celery in winter, might disguise it, even if there was any peculiar flavour."

"I have heard," said Hope, "that the cure has often beer tried, and with great success, among the lower classes in Britain The receipt is too simple, or the fare too disgusting, to be adopted by the upper classes ; but, do you know, since I have been told the way the soup is made, my own disgust is greatly diminished My horror was always at the idea of the slime, but when con vinced that this is got rid of by scalding and washing in cold water, I should not have any objections to trying it, were I ill and anxious to get well. Being, however, in good health, I own I should not like to eat snail-soup as a luxury, or to fight for my dish like the Vendean sergeant whom our hostess told us of. was very much interested certainly by our discovery of to-night namely, of a carnivorous slug ; but I was not kept awake by thinking of snails or slugs : the sight of that man down stair recalled to my remembrance the scenes I had witnessed in Paris and I was wondering to myself how many unfortunate people had been led by want to take a part in those deeds of blood Then followed the question, Whence came that want? and thought of this young man reduced to his present position of an outcast by that accursed love of gambling which is the bane of this country. One reflection called up another, and brough back the nervous, feverish sensation that oppressed me before left Paris. But now, thanks to those midnight crowers and the breath of fresh air which I got at the window, the feeling i gone and my eyes are heavy ; so, let us, as Richard says, 'once more try to sleep it unto morning '—good-night."

"Good-night" answered Cross.

The cocks in the yard continued to crow, but no one heard them ; certainly not the friends, for in two minutes it would have required a trumpet to awaken them.

CHAPTER IX.

A NORMAN BREAKFAST AND A STROLL.

THE morning was well advanced when they woke, but although the sun was high, the room still remained sombre and dark. Hope was the first to raise; he went to the window and threw back the curtains, meaning to look out; this, however, he found to be impossible, for a dense white fog was drifting slowly past the windows, and was so thick that it prevented his seeing anything twenty yards distant.

"Hallo, Cross!" he exclaimed, "look, here's a fog as dark as any I ever saw in London in December; is not such a thing extraordinary at this season of the year?"

"O no," replied Cross, "fogs are very common here. Remember we are on one side of the Channel and England on the other. With easterly winds the fogs which gather in the Channel fall on the English coast; with west and north-west winds they are drifted on to this coast. They gather in their passage from the ocean, first on the Channel Islands, and then pass on here, where they seem to accumulate and become more dense, being as it were dammed up in the large bay which is formed by the Norman coast and the long point of Brittany. Fog, as you know, thickens above wet ground."

"And yet," said Hope, "those two Frenchmen were joking us about English fogs, and asking on how many days in the year we saw the sun in Scotland."

"That is ignorance and prejudice," said Cross. "Fogs are rare in Paris, and it is the fashion for Frenchmen to talk of English fogs, and to boast of the clear sky of la belle France.

I never take the trouble of contradicting them, for no power on
earth could ever persuade a Frenchman to believe that there is
more ugly country in la belle France than in any other part in
Europe ; or that the fogs on the coast of Normandy are as frequent and as dense as they are in any part of England ;—nay,
more, that in Brittany they are even more frequent and more
dense, not to mention that more rain falls there than even at
Manchester in England, or at Greenock in Scotland, which are
supposed to be the two most rainy spots in the United Kingdom. Yet so it is."

    While Cross was speaking he had got out of bed, put on his
dressing-gown, and reached the window. The density of the
fog struck even him ; for he continued—" I have rarely seen
such a fog so early in the year. I suspect there must have been
a gale of wind out at sea, which has caused it, and this will explain the very high tide which so nearly washed us off the rock
the night before last. But I hear voices in the street, showing
that the world is awake ; so we may as well dress, although we
can do very little in the way of sport to-day. We must content
ourselves, I suspect, with a stroll round the country, and make
our arrangements for going to try what we may catch in the
Mare de Bouillon to-morrow. There will be no use in going to-
day, for I never saw fish rise in a foggy day. I have had good
sport in a bright sun and in heavy rain, but never in a dry fog."

    " I have had very good sport with bait in foggy days," said
Hope, " and once I had a remarkable day in the river Colun
by fishing with the live Mayfly during a very dense fog. The
morning was very bright, but about ten o'clock a thick fog came
on. While the day had been bright I had caught two or three
very good trout. The fly was rising very thick and the trout
were in full feed, but the moment the fog came on both trout
and flies ceased to show themselves. I changed my flies, and
tried every sort in my book, but not a fish would move. I was
just going to give up in despair, when I saw an old fellow
watching me whom I knew to be a regular poacher. I hailed

him, and after talking with him for a few minutes, I gave him
half-a-crown to drink, and began to wind up my line. 'I think
I could give you a wrinkle,' he said, 'that would make you stay
by the river.' I asked him to explain himself, and promised to
add another half-crown to the first if he told me anything that
would make it worth my while to stop at the river, instead of
going to kick my heels at my inn. 'Were not the fly rising
plaguy thick this morning?' said he, grinning. I told him that
they had been, and the trout also, but that since the fog had
come on neither fish nor fly had shown themselves. 'And don't
you guess why?' he asked. I answered that I supposed they
were frightened by the sudden change in the weather. 'Not
a bit,' he said; 'the fish be a-feeding below, and they don't
require to rise to the surface. The Mayfly be a-coming out of
their cases just now as fast as ever: when the sun is bright them
creturs is up and away in a jiffy; but when the day is dark, any
as does come out of his case either crawls up the reeds at the
side, or if they does rise in the stream, they gets on but slowly,
and the fish nabs them afore they reach the surface, as I will
soon show you.' He went to the bank, where there were a
number of flags growing in the water, and showed me a vast
quantity of Mayflies clustered round the stalks close to the edge
of the water. He collected several of these, and I saw that
their wings were quite soft and puckered. He then asked permission to arrange my line for me, to which I agreed. So he
set to work while I watched his proceedings. First he took off
my flies, and put on in their place two small bait-hooks, the one
about a foot above the other. Then he took two large split shot
out of his own pocket, and fastened them on the casting-line,
three feet above the upper hook. The two hooks were then
baited by running them through the tails of a couple of the Mayflies he had gathered from the flags. This done, he declared all
was ready. We then went to the head of a weir, where the
stream was very deep, but there was a rush of water through
two or three places where the sluice-boards were drawn. He

Q

bade me cast my line across one of these small rapids, allow i
to sink for a minute, and then draw it gently towards me throug]
the rush. I did as he directed me, and no sooner had the lin·
reached the rush than I felt the dash of a strong fish. 'Tha
be a good one,' said the old rascal, 'and when you lands hin
you owes me half-a-crown.' I did land a very fine trout, paic
my debt, and continued this newly-learnt practice, catching mor·
trout that day than ever I caught before or since in the sam·
river."

"Regular poaching," said Cross. "I wonder you are no
ashamed to acknowledge such deeds."

"I differ from you," returned Hope, "in calling it poaching
I thought it then, and I still think it, a very scientific mode o
fishing. Angling, after all, is the art of deceiving fish by pre
tending to feed them, in order that they may ultimately feed you
Skill consists in finding out the food that is the most tempt
ing, and placing it before the fish as near as possible in the way
that nature would present it; and I cannot think it mor·
poaching to play a fly below water than on the surface. B·
what I knew before, and by what my old man taught me, I ca·
show you that on a fine day the natural fly lights gently on th
water. You imitate this by throwing a fly as lightly as yo·
can, or by allowing the wind to blow it to the spot where yo·
see a trout rising. On a windy day the natural fly is blown o·
to the water, and struggles on the surface to escape drowning
This you imitate by drawing your artificial fly, and giving it a·
much as possible the action of the drowning reality. Neither c
these plans you call poaching; why, then, should you give tha
name to my old man's method? He showed me, and I felt h
was right, that a Mayfly changes from its pupa state into a pe·
fect creature, choosing a bright sunny day for the transformatio·
If the day be bright and warm, he rises at once from the botto·
and takes his flight, to fulfil his one day's destiny; but if th
weather changes, when these creatures have begun to cast thei
skin, they have no power of resuming their greatcoat with th

change of atmosphere. They must go on ; but they are weak. Deprived of the sun's rays, they cannot rush into life with the same speed and force. They struggle slowly to the surface, and, before they reach it, the fish, who has been previously dashing after the flying game, snaps them up with greater ease, and swallows them below water. My old man taught me to imitate these struggles ; for when the lure is thrown across the stream, it sinks. As you draw it gently towards you, the weight of the shot keeps the upper part very steady ; but when the force of the water catches the loose end to which your flies are fixed it makes it wave about in the stream, giving exactly the motion of a weak fly struggling into life and light. The fish are deceived by the cunning of man, who thus acts to them as Satan does to us. A fish is wiled to his own destruction by a fly ; the devil baits his hook with gold or a pretty face."

" What do you think of ambition or a French cook ?" said Cross ; " the last is the bait I should try for our friend the Marquis."

" You are right," answered Hope, laughing ; " and a pack of cards might do for the Captain. I am glad you have made me laugh, for I feel rather prosy and low. I have been dreaming all night of that poor devil down stairs, and I must see him as soon as possible. So let us dress ; you must kindly keep the people engaged while I slip away to him."

This arrangement was agreed to, and their toilet proceeded with all possible despatch. When dressed, they went down to-gether to the door of the inn, where a considerable party was congregated. There were also two horses with panniers on their backs. By one of these stood a man they had not seen before ; by the other was collected a group of fisherwomen. Hope did not pause to speak to either of these parties, but passed quietly into the kitchen, where only the landlady was to be found, en-gaged in arranging her implements for cookery. Hope whispered to her for a minute ; she looked round, and perceiving no one but Cross, who was standing at the front door, she led the way to the other, through which she had gone the night before, followed by Hope. The door was opened, and the moment after, it closed behind them both. Cross retained his place till she returned to the kitchen, and then advanced towards the group of fisherwomen. It was evident he had not been observed before, for when he was close to the party Marie hailed him.

"Ah!" she exclaimed, "here comes one of the good gentlemen; he will buy some of our fish. Look here, what beautiful gurnet! and think of our misfortune. We drew almost all the nets last night, and this morning the only one we had left set was full of these splendid fish. We have not had such a shoal on the coast for years, and only one net out! So you must give me a good price, or I shall break my heart."

To prevent such a catastrophe, Cross bought some of her fish, and sent them into the house. They certainly answered the description of "beautiful," as far as colour went, for they were brilliantly red, with the blue, green, and purple tints which shoot over them as they die. The red gurnet is a leaner-looking fish than the gray gurnet that is taken on the coast of Scotland, which makes the disproportionate size of the head the more striking. Still, the angular cut of the head, and the shape of the fins, give it a grotesque appearance that is by no means displeasing to the eye. Cross followed his fish to the door, and as soon as the landlady saw them she exclaimed—

"What made you buy any more? but it is my fault. I forgot to tell you that Matilde left a large basket of fish for you. They have had a great take at the fishery, and are gone off up the country with two carts to sell what they have got. Matilde and Angela came here before they started, and left some of the best for you two gentlemen; and I am ashamed that I forgot to tell you about them. The Marquis has been here, and has cut off their heads, and given directions for dressing them; so you had better take back these and recover your money."

"Never mind," replied Cross; "put these with the others, and cut off their heads also, if it be necessary and right. I suspect that will be an easier job than getting back money from Marie."

"I believe it will," said the landlady, laughing; "and when their heads are off, a gurnet is not a large fish."

"And why do you cut off their heads?" asked Cross.

"The Marquis will explain that better than I can," she answered. "He says it is to get rid of the oil; and I say, because there is nothing to eat on the head; and it takes a great deal of room in the pan, wasting the sauce for no use. But the Marquis is not far from the door, and if you ask him, he will tell you himself what he told me this morning about oil."

Cross went in search of the Marquis, whom he found standing near the man with the second horse, the panniers on whose back were filled, not with fish, but with a quantity of guillemots, commonly called marrots or sea-crows in Scotland. The present owner of the load honoured them with the name of *Canards noirs*. The Marquis was in the act of driving a bargain for a dozen of these birds. The owner was asking three sous apiece; the Marquis was offering a franc for the dozen.

"Don't buy those birds," said Cross; "they are carrion. It is impossible to eat them."

"Do you hear what this gentleman says?" asked the Marquis, addressing the owner of the birds; "you had better take what I offer. I said I would give you a franc, so I will not draw back."

The man cast a look of fury at Cross, packed up his property, and pretended to move off; but after vanishing in the fog, as no one called after him, he was no sooner out of sight than the sound of his horse's steps was heard returning; and when he again came into view, he had the twelve birds in his hand, which he presented to the Marquis, and demanded his franc.

"I knew I should get them," said the Marquis, "for I heard that a prodigious quantity had been taken in the stake nets at Mont St. Michel."

"I wish you joy of your purchase," returned Cross ; "but, for my part, I would not give a sou for the horse-load."

"My dear friend," said the Marquis, "forgive my observing that you display sad ignorance in saying so, and greatly neglect the bounty of nature. Ignorance in the culinary art is a great loss to many a clever man ; for instance, these birds, which you are pleased to despise, will, if properly treated, produce a salmi equal to woodcock, superior to hare. In the hands of an igno-ramus, I allow, they are not good eating ; but take away the whole back, cut up the remainder of your bird, place it in a casserole, and give it five minutes of the fire, empty your casse-role into a pan of boiling water, in which you must allow your viand to remain for a single minute, then remove it, replace it in a fresh casserole, and proceed as you would with a salmi of woodcock. The result is a dish which you shall this day taste, and which I am much mistaken in your judgment if you do not pronounce superior."

Cross expressed his gratitude for the lesson.

"Ah, my dear friend," said the Marquis, "I see you are worthy of a hint on these subjects ; but how many good things do we see thrown away and murdered from the want of a little attention to trifles. Now, for instance, many of the duck tribe in spring are sent to table not fit to be eaten, from neglect-ing to cut away the back of the birds. From this neglect an admirable viand is presented rancid to the taste and offensive to the smell : simply cut away the lower half of the back, and you at once get rid of the portion of the bird that contains the oil which melts before the fire and pollutes your food. Let me, my dear sir, impress strongly on your mind, that in almost all aquatic birds, especially towards the spring, you should invariably cut away the lower half of the back, not only before it is put to the fire, but immediately that you obtain them. I trust that if you remember this advice, I also shall leave a favourable impression on your memory, for there are situations and times when such knowledge merits gratitude."

Cross again declared his gratitude, and as there was no one near to make him laugh, he was extremely eloquent in his thanks. He had hardly concluded his peroration when he saw Hope coming to join them. They exchanged a glance, and then Cross asked the Marquis why he cut off the heads of the gurnet before cooking them.

"That is a similar case with that of the aquatic birds," answered the Marquis. "The head of the gurnet is charged with an oily matter which is somewhat rancid ; it taints the rest of the flesh in dressing, and thus a valuable frequenter of our coasts does not meet with the admiration it deserves.

"You astonish me," said Cross, "for we say in our country that all the meat on a gurnet's head is poison. This is said in jest, for there is nothing but bones in a gurnet's head."

"Very true ; but those bones are charged with the oil of which I complain, and which makes your proverb a truth and no jest ; for this oil, if it does not poison, at all events greatly deteriorates the rest of the animal."

"You are quite correct, sir," said Hope, "in what you say about the quantity of oil in the heads of these fish. The Highland poachers know it, and take advantage of the knowledge. They always cut off the heads of the gurnets which they catch, and pack them in very dry peat-dust. Late in the autumn, when they go to poach the rivers with leister and blaze, they arrange half-a-dozen of these heads in their hand-grating. All the crevices of the heads are by this time filled with the peat-dust, and a considerable quantity adheres to the outside, the whole of which has become saturated with oil—the heads being placed with the mouths upwards, and a small quantity of tow placed in each mouth. When they reach the stream where they are to leister the salmon the tow is lighted, the fire immediately communicates with the lips of the fish, and a beautiful clear light is emitted, which continues to burn for a considerable time. Sometimes also a single head, thus prepared and dried, is fixed at the end of a stick, and is used as a torch when a poacher

goes leistering single-handed. When the hand-grate is used, it
requires two people—one who carries the light, the other who
works the leister ; but with a torch, a man can carry the light in
one hand and use his leister with the other."

"I beg your pardon," said the Marquis, "but I do not understand what you have been describing. I hear you say that the
gurnets' heads, when dried, will burn either as fire or a torch,
and I am sure you are right ; but I do not understand what you
mean by a leister, nor catching fish with a blaze."

"It is I who should beg pardon," said Hope, "for using a
word which is not translatable into French, and for speaking of
a mode of fishing which is perhaps not known in this country.
A leister is a sort of three-pronged spear which is very much
used by poachers in the upper parts of the rivers in Scotland for
taking the salmon at the time they are spawning, during the
night. The salmon leave the deep pools, and come for the purpose of depositing their spawn on the gravelly shallows, where
the stream runs rapidly. The poachers know this ; so they wade
on to these shallows with a light and a spear. When the light
is thrown on the water every pebble at the bottom can be seen
and when it falls on the fish they seem to be dazzled or charmed
by the rays, for they lie still and allow their enemy to come close
to them. The common process in the Highlands of Scotland is
this :—When the poachers have reached the shallow at the head
of some deep pool which they know the salmon frequent, one
man holds the light high and casts the rays over every part of it
From the bank the fish may not at first be seen, but spots of
gravel are clearly visible, which are of a lighter colour than the
general surface of the bottom. This variety of colour the people
know to be caused by the male salmon, who digs holes of considerable depth, throwing out the gravel on either side. On
these heaps he rests, rubbing the gravel quite bright with his
belly, while the female deposits her spawn in the hole which he
has dug. Whenever this is effected she swims slowly away
The male then deposits his spawn on the eggs, and immediately

throws back the gravel he has before dug out, thus burying the spawn, and covering it with from six to twelve inches of gravel ; and here it remains till the warmer air of spring brings it to life, when all that the larvæ of the dragon-fly do not eat crawl through the gravel, and are known as parr. Before the actual deposit of spawn takes place there is a great deal of flirtation and toying between the fish. When the male begins to dig the hole the female remains beside him, resting on one or other of the banks he is throwing up. Suddenly she will dart off and rush back into the deep pool ; the male immediately pursues her, and they are then of course lost to sight ; but in a few minutes they return swimming close together. The female resumes her place on one of the heaps, and the male recommences digging, till the female thinks proper to make another start into the pool. This alternate digging, flight, and pursuit goes on for hours, till at last the female, instead of taking her position in one of the heaps of gravel, goes into the trench which the male has dug, and then the male takes his place on one of the heaps, where he remains till the female has spawned ; then he follows, as I have already told you. I have given you this explanation, somewhat out of place perhaps, for the purpose of making you understand why the poachers, before entering the water, hold up the light to mark the bright spots in the gravel. These being well noted, the poachers enter the water, wading towards the nearest spot, always choosing the one furthest down the stream, lest in wading they should disturb the lower fish by setting the gravel or sand in motion. When they come within spear-length of the fish, the person who carries the light keeps it very steady, while the one who is to work the leister or spear takes his aim. The rule is to calculate the depth of the water, and if it be eighteen inches deep he aims that distance lower than where the fish appears to be. If the water is two feet deep, he aims two feet below the fish. The spearman thus unknowingly allows for the refraction, and aims truly at the fish instead of over him ; he then dashes his spear forward, and the fish is struck. With a

large salmon there is sometimes a violent struggle between him
and the spearman, even after the prongs are through him,
before he yields himself up and receives the coup de grâce.
When fairly mastered and basketed the poacher still keeps his
place. If it should be the female that is struck, at the first
plunge and struggle the male dashes into the pool, but in less
than two minutes he will again return to look for his bride,
when he is pretty certain to share her fate, as her slayers are in
wait for him, and as soon as he is disposed of they move off to
the next bright spot, where they are sure to find another pair.
The great desideratum for this sport is a bright clear light; and
I have been told by some old hands at the work that the gurnets'
heads, prepared as I have described, are at once the best, the
cheapest, and the most lasting. The next best light is obtained
from the knots of bog-pine, which are dug out of the peat-mosses
and carefully dried for use."

"Monsieur describes the process so well," said Cross, turning
to the Marquis; "that I could almost persuade myself that he
has practised the occupation of *black-fisher* himself. Black-
fisher (he continued) is the name given to the poachers who kill
salmon when they are out of season."

"I hope not," said the Marquis; "for to kill those fine fish
when they are quite unfit to be eaten would be a great loss."

"It is not altogether a loss," said Hope; "although I allow
it is a great shame to kill them at that season; for in killing
one fish you destroy thousands. But when I was a boy I never
thought of this. I only knew that it was immense fun; and
many a hundred fish I have killed, and seen killed, in this way.
I am ashamed now to confess that I once leistered thirty-two
large salmon in one night. A good deal of what I have told
you, however, I have learned since I was older and wiser; and
when I knew that this sort of sport had absolutely nearly
destroyed the breed of salmon from some of the smaller rivers, I
then gave up the use of the leister; but I was curious to learn
the habits of these fish, and I still used a light to watch them.

Many a cold October night have I spent on the banks or in the water of some of our Highland rivers, observing the proceedings of the fish. It is from these vigils that I am now able to speak so decidedly about their proceedings when spawning."

"But, mon Dieu!" reiterated the Marquis; "what a pity to kill these fine creatures when they are not fit to be eaten!"

"There our friend Cross is wrong," said Hope; "for although, as an article of food, a salmon out of season is a very inferior creature, still, for the poor they are not to be despised. They are not, in general, used fresh, but are sometimes pickled with vinegar, or more frequently kippered; that is to say, they are cured with salt, sugar, and spice, and then dried in the smoke, which makes a very savoury morsel, a small bit of which will give zest and flavour to a large dish of potatoes."

"Ah! I remember I have tasted this kipper," said the Marquis, "and found it by no means bad. It was soaked in fresh water, torn to pieces with two forks, fried dry, and served in a napkin with the cheese. From my remembrance of that plât, I should have no objections to stick a salmon myself. I assure you I find your description valuable, and beg to thank you; but you must forgive me if I run away just now, for I have some birds that I must look after myself, as I have promised Mons. Cross that he shall taste them properly dressed. And besides the interest I take in your nourishment, I have a relation who is to breakfast with us this morning, who is a judge of what is good, so I should regret if he was disappointed when he came to visit me; therefore, with your permission, I will say adieu for the present."

The Marquis walked off to the kitchen, and the two friends remained.

"He has got a lot of marrots and beheaded gurnets that he is going to cook. He tells me that what we consider carrion at home is, by his magic touch, to be converted into something as good as woodcocks and better than hare."

"And I have little doubt he will keep his word," said

Hope; "for a Frenchman will live in luxury where our people would starve, merely from knowing how to make the most of what falls in his way. I confess I wish that our peasant women in Scotland knew something more of cookery than merely boiling a potato. Certainly our friend the Marquis errs quite as much in the one way as our Highland wives do in the other; still, if he can show us how to convert marrots into good food, the lesson is worth learning, for what myriads of them have I seen on the coasts of Scotland which might benefit our poor, instead of merely destroying the herring fry. So let us go and see how he gets on, and try to teach his method to some of the people at home."

"Tell me first," said Cross, "what you did with your insurgent."

"Oh, poor fellow! I gave him some little money, and have taken charge of a letter for him. I have promised also to procure him a passport to enable him to get over to Jersey; it seems that he has some relation there to whom he wishes to go whenever he receives an answer to his letter."

"And how did he escape the hunt which your Garde Mobile described?"

"He tells me that he was in the wood with the rest; but instead of rising to run away when he heard the troops advancing he lay flat down in a sort of ditch, and drew the grass and weeds over him. One of the Garde Mobile marched by within a yard without discovering him. He got up and ran back. He told me the number of people who were shot in the wood was very great, for that he had seen at least a hundred in the line he took. He began to tell me the escapes and sufferings he went through from that time till he reached his present hiding-place; but I could not stay to listen to him lest my absence might be discovered, and lead to inquiries. But I shall try to find some opportunity of hearing his adventures, for they seemed interesting, and narrating them may serve to lighten the poor fellow's confinement."

"His adventures would amuse me very much," said Cross; "so try and let me be present when he relates them; but in the meanwhile, if we are to have a lesson in cookery, we may as well go and join the Marquis. While we look at what he is doing we can ask him about snails, whether he thinks them eatable, and his mode of preparing them for table. I have no doubt he has some way; for a man that can make marrots good will not leave neglected these creatures, since it seems they are eaten in that part of the country from which he comes. I forgot, by the by, to point out to you that catching marrots so early in the year is another sign, in addition to the fog and high tide, that there must have been a heavy gale out at sea. I know that a considerable quantity of sea-fowl are taken near Mont St. Michel every year, but generally this takes place in October and November. I never heard of their being seen here so early in the autumn."

The two friends proceeded to the kitchen, where they found the Marquis dressed in his linen jacket and wearing an apron. Cross asked for an explanation of the mode of cooking the marrots, which the Marquis gave at length, but the Englishman found that he had little talent for this sublime art; and all he learnt was that the birds were cut up, partly dressed, then scalded in boiling water. The only description he could give of the after-proceedings was, that the bits of birds, with butter, gravy, red wine, and a very small quantity of herbs—he believed chives and rocamboles—were put into a flat pan, and were set on the charcoal stove to simmer to maturity. Perhaps the niceties were forgotten from listening to a dissertation on the merits of snails; for the moment they were mentioned the Marquis broke out into a strain of most eloquent laudation, and he seemed quite to take an affection for Cross for having named them.

"Ah, my dear friend!" said he, "I see that you are worthy to be a Frenchman; you have none of the absurd prejudices of your countrymen, who pretend to turn up their noses at this excellent article of nourishment. What a pity it is not winter, and I would myself dress some for you ; unhappily at present they are out of season—that is to say, those that have shells, which alone are worthy the notice of a man of taste. Slugs are very nourishing in soup, but I have no great affection for them. But the garden-snail is most excellent. There are many ways of dressing them, and if it was the season I would take them in hand for you myself; but as it is, we must wait, for now they might not please you. All I can say is, that you will find them not only good, but most highly nutritious. I have heard that in England you have a Dr. Saloman who makes a wine to renew the vigour of your old gentlemen. Well, send your old gentlemen to me, and with a plât of snails such as I can give them, in a month they will think themselves boys again."

"But could you not," said Cross, looking as grave as a judge, in spite of a most painful inclination to laugh ; "could you not mention one of the ways of dressing these valuable creatures which hitherto I have neglected ?"

"Even in the simplest way they are good," replied the Marquis. "Scald them, to get them from their shells, and then fry them with a few crumbs of bread and a little seasoning—pepper, salt, and a pinch of fine herbs—they will not disappoint you ; or they are excellent stewed either with a white or brown sauce ; in short, they are one of those things which you can hardly spoil. In choosing your viands, you should select those that are of a dark brown in the shell, heavy and well closed at the mouth ; these are in the best condition, and of course are the best ; for you may meet with lean snails as well as with lean mutton, and then you are naturally disappointed, for everything thin has an inclination to be hard."

Cross kept his gravity, not only during this part of the conversation, but during a great deal more that was said both on snails and slugs. Hope stood it very well for some time, but the glances which Cross cast at him from time to time made him feel so much inclined to misbehave, that at last he stole

away, and did not return till he saw the Comte M—— enter
the house ; he then followed, and was introduced in due form.
Cross was evidently in the highest possible favour ; for not only
was he presented to the Comte, with the greatest empressement,
but also during breakfast the Marquis insisted on his sitting
next to him, when he selected the bits, both of fish and flesh,
which he thought most choice, and presented them to him for
his eating.

Both Hope and Cross allowed that a marrot was an excellent
bird when cooked by a French Marquis ; what it might be
under the hands of a Highland wife remained another question.
The gurnets also were pronounced undeniable, whether from
the loss of their heads or the Marquis's sauce, we do not say.
Any further notice of the breakfast were useless, at least as to a
description of what was produced and eaten ; but we must
allude slightly to the new guest, as he was the cause of some
amusement. He was a gay little fellow, about sixty-five years
of age, but he looked much younger, and was so sprightly that
Cross whispered to Hope, " I suppose the Marquis must have
fed his relative upon snails, he is so young for his age ! If I
was sure of the fact, I certainly might make my fortune by
keeping a table-d'hôte for old gentlemen ; egad, I'll ask him."

" Do," said Hope.

" Your friend the Marquis," said Cross, looking extremely
grave, " has been explaining to us that snails are a highly nutritious food. Do you agree with him ?"

" Undoubtedly," answered the Comte ; " they are admirable,
and I am very fond of them ; but I have eaten in Martinique
another creature which I conceive to be fully better. I had
some little prejudices about them at first, which fortunately I
overcame, and found them excellent. The creature is not very
tempting in the raw state, being in fact a large white maggot
which the blacks gather from the palm trees ; but when dressed
it is very superior. You, my dear nephew," continued he, addressing the Marquis, " not having been in the West Indies,

have never met with this dish ; it is one that I am sure you
would approve of. I have never tasted the Beche de mer,
which is nothing else than a sea-slug dried. I had a great wish
to partake of them, but was always disappointed. I am told
they are highly restorative, and are justly valued by the wealthy
Chinese."

"I regret, indeed," said the Marquis, "that I have not tasted
them ; but we have a great deal in this country, if we make the
most of it."

" Indeed we have," replied the Comte ; "and talent is daily
discovering some new mode of presenting these in a more tempting form. For instance, what could be better than that lobster
à la broche which I tasted the other day ?"

"Cochonnerie !" exclaimed the Marquis, growing quite red
in the face.

The Comte turned at the sound of his nephew's voice,
looked at him for a moment, and then said, raising his voice—

"I am ashamed of you, and I pronounce that it was excellent."

"And I," said the Marquis, "that it was Cochonnerie."

"You make me blush for you," rejoined the Comte ; "you
have no magnanimity, no heroism. You did yourself a great
injustice in not tasting it ; and now, by abusing that plât, you
are unjust to my good friend who prepared it. I allow he was
wrong in his opinion of your pigeons ; but you ought to have
more heroism, more magnanimity, than to revenge yourself on
his error in judgment by condemning his lobster à la broche,
which every one else allowed to be excellent."

"Bah !" said the Marquis, "how could any man pretend to
be a cook, or a judge of what was good, who sent away those
pigeons which I had prepared with my own hands ? Anything
he could send up could not fail to be bad ; therefore I continue
to say that your friendship for that misguided person has led
you astray, for I repeat that his lobster à la broche was
Cochonnerie."

"But how obstinate you are !" interrupted the Comte, now quite in a rage. "You would not taste the fish ; I did, and I hope to obtain the receipt, which is still a secret. I only know at present that this creature being fixed on the spit, is placed before the fire, where he is basted continually with a sauce, the ingredients of which are as yet unknown to me."

"COCHONNERIE !" exclaimed the Marquis, which word he continued to repeat at the end of every sentence that the Comte uttered. He, however, took no notice of the interruption, but went on with his description, turning his back as much as possible on his nephew, and addressing his speech in turn to the rest of the party.

"As the heat touches the animal, the shell slightly opens, and through these cracks the rich sauce enters, and amalgamates with the"——

"Cochonnerie !"

"flesh within the shell. As the process advances, the flesh dilates, and these cracks become wider. To prevent which, or perhaps to prevent the"——

"Cochonnerie !"

"plât from being too rich, a choporline of champagne is poured over it. The wine flows into the dripping-pan, where it is well mixed with the first"——

"Cochonnerie !"

"sauce ; and the process of constantly basting is still kept up till the animal is thoroughly"——

"Cochonnerie !"

"done, when it is served as hot as possible, the sauce being strained and sent with it, although this is hardly necessary, for the great beauty of the dish is, that the sauce and the fish are so intimately amalgamated within the shell that it requires no addition whatever, being"——

"COCHONNERIE ! COCHONNERIE !" roared the Marquis ; "juicy, savoury, and, in spite of my nephew, super-excellent," screamed the Count.

" COCHONNERIE !   COCHONNERIE !   COCHONNERIE !"
shouted the Marquis, bounding in his seat.

This last interruption, which was louder than any of the
former, drove the little old gentleman quite furious.   A violen
altercation began, and was growing so loud that in a very littl
while the uncle and nephew would have come to blows, had no
the rest of the party interfered.

The Captain whispered to each alternately to remember tha
foreigners were present, but Hope was the most successful b
saying, that in cases of taste there was no disputing, and tha
the best way was to name a third party to act as referee, since i
was quite possible that a man might be ignorant in all matter
of flesh or fowl, and yet have some knowledge regarding fish an
crustacea.

The uncle was the first to recover his good humour.   H
related more at length the story of the dinner, where the quarre
had originally taken place.   It had been a sort of pic-nic o
gourmands, where each had ordered some dish of which h
thought highly.   The Marquis had produced what he considerec
a masterpiece, being some preparation of pigeons; this th
lobster-admirer had only tasted, and then sent away his plate
which the Marquis had considered to be such an insult that h
would not even look at the lobster, and very nearly called ou
his best friend for praising it ; indeed, he would have done sc
had not a third party soothed him with the assurance, tha
though the Comte had praised the lobster, he had certainl
helped himself twice to the pigeons.

"Two of a trade can never agree," whispered Cross.   Afte
a while, the Comte quite recovered his former gaiety.

" What an unfortunate fellow I am !" said he.   "No one o
earth hates émeutes and quarrels more than I do, and yet if ther
is a dispute in the country I am sure to get into it, and thoug
all the world should be at peace, some one is certain to fall ou
with me.   Here now is this ungrateful nephew of mine (whom
I mean to make my heir ; if he behaves well), he must need

quarrel with me, because I happen to like roasted lobster. The fact is, I am the fruit of an émeute, and into them I shall fall as long as I live. As I came into the world through one, I know that I shall go out of it by one."

The hint about the succession worked marvels ; the Marquis's face resumed its smiles, and he begged his uncle to tell the history of his early life, as he knew that this was what he took the greatest pleasure in recounting. The Captain had heard the story before, but he joined the two Englishmen in requesting the Comte to relate his pet story, to which he was nothing loath, and began—

"You must know that about seventy years ago there was a very bad harvest in France, which fell particularly hard on that part of the country where my grandmother's property was situated. The peasants, instead of blaming heaven for the unprosperous season, thought proper to abuse the landed proprietors and rich householders, and in consequence got up an émeute to revenge themselves on these innocent parties. This émeute became so serious that they were obliged to send for troops to put it down. Among those ordered on this service was one of the regiments of guards, the officers of which were men of the highest rank and fashion. Well, when the news arrived that this regiment was coming, a meeting of the proprietors was called to arrange how the officers were to be lodged, as it was considered quite impossible to allow such men to be billeted like ordinary soldiers. This question was soon settled by every one declaring that he would be delighted to quarter an officer. But out of this sprung another difficulty ; namely, who was to have the honour of lodging the Colonel. The Colonel was my excellent father, and I may say what I have heard of him, namely, that in addition to being rich and high-born, he was one of the handsomest and most agreeable men about the country. There was no wonder, therefore, that all the ladies were anxious to have him ; but the question still ran, who was to succeed ? At last it was proposed to settle

the matter by *doigt mouillé.** My grandmother's was the
fortunate name. In short, she hooked the Colonel, and accordingly he came to her house, where my mother saw him, and
what is more, he saw her, and became hooked a second time,
for they were married soon after, and as I am the produce of
that marriage, I am not far wrong in saying that I am the fruit
of an émeute, which fatality was proved very early in life, for I
was quite young when the great Revolution broke out. My poor
father was soon made an end of; they cut off his head among
the first. My grandmother, my mother, my aunt, my sister, and
myself, were sent to prison, and there we lay for some time.
Then our prison was changed, and we were put into another
where there was an immense number of prisoners. I believe
they forgot us owing to this alteration, for every day we saw
from fifteen to thirty of our companions led out to execution,
and as the windows of our prison looked out upon the Place,
we could hear the sound of the guillotine as the knife fell.
Young as I was, like those older than myself I became callous
to the fear of death. Indeed, our lives were so wretched that
they were not worth preserving.   I can remember now that all
the clothing I had on was a shirt and part of an old shawl of
my mother's. My poor sister was dressed in the same way.
My mother was a very clever woman ; she never asked for any
of the prison allowance of food, and I believe it was this precaution that saved us, since our names were thus forgotten. For
food, all we had for many a long day was merely cakes made of
buckwheat, or black bread, which was supplied by an excellent
creature who used to split our firewood when we were prosperous.
At last, however, when they had cut off the heads of almost
every one in our prison, an order arrived to send a special list

* *Doigt mouillé* is a method of drawing lots, something like *hide the
horse.* The two hands are held up ; one finger is marked by wetting, or
by fixing on it a bit of paper. One of the party then turns his back, and
another touches one of the fingers and asks, " For whom is this ?" Whenever the marked finger is touched the name given in answer wins the
prize.

of the names of any that might still remain. This brought
us to remembrance, and a second order came down for our
immediate execution. We were to suffer next morning. About
nine o'clock that night my grandmother and her two daughters
were at prayers ; my sister and myself were looking on. My
only remembrance of that night is, that I was more than usually
cold and hungry. Suddenly a noise was heard of shouting in
the streets, but that was nothing uncommon. Next, a noise
within the prison, ending in a shout of joy, which was *very* uncommon. Then the jailor entered, and told us that Robespierre
was dead. The next morning we were free, and took up our
quarters in the woodcutter's house, where we staid for some
time. Almost the whole of our estates had been confiscated.
They were gone ; but one small property remained in this
country, which ultimately my grandmother recovered. It is now
mine, and if this my good-for-nothing nephew behaves himself,
it will be his when I die. But to go on : the same fortune
which sent me to prison when I was a child sticks to me now.
Wherever there is an émeute there I am sure to be, whether it
be in Paris, Lyons, or anywhere else. If anybody is in a bad
humour and wants to pick a quarrel, he is sure to single me out
and vent his ill-temper on me, who only pray for peace and
quiet, a breath of air, a bit of dinner—well cooked if possible
—and a clean bed. But even this, you see, I cannot enjoy in
peace, for here is this fellow, who quarrels with me simply
because I approve of lobster à la broche."

The Marquis was now quite subdued ; so much so, that had
a roast lobster been placed on the table by his rival he would
have eaten the one and shaken hands with the other ; but as
this could not be, he contented himself with ample apologies to
his uncle, and the breakfast concluded by their embracing each
other. Since we shall see no more of the Comte, we now take
leave of him, as did the Englishmen when they went out to
walk. When they returned he was gone, and as the Marquis
was somewhat ashamed of the scene in the morning, very little

When the friends left the house they found that the fog was nearly gone ; the sun was still somewhat obscured, but an occasional glimpse of brighter light proved that he was soon likely to be the victor by dispelling any of the vapour that yet hung upon the land. Cross proposed that they should direct their steps towards the high ground to the southward, as from thence they could obtain a very extensive view of the country, which would not now be concealed by the fog. To this proposal Hope agreed, and they started in that direction. As they walked they talked over the events of the morning, and were able to enjoy unrestrained a hearty laugh at the scenes they had witnessed during breakfast. They then canvassed the merits of the marrots, and Hope again observed that something could be made out of the hint which might prove advantageous to the peasantry in Scotland.

"The sauce is a matter of luxury," said he, " but getting rid of the rancid oil by merely cutting away the back, and scalding off the remaining fat by plunging it into boiling water, is a process so simple that it might easily be learnt and practised by any one." He declared his intention of trying to make the process known. After talking of these birds for some time, the conversation turned to fish. Gurnets were first spoken of, and mentioning the oil contained in their heads led back to salmon and salmon-poaching.

"By the by," said Cross, after they had been awhile engaged on this subject, "you said this morning that all the salmon spawn that was left by the larvæ of the dragon-fly crawled through the ground as parr. What did you mean by the dragon-fly destroying the spawn?"

"Exactly what I said," answered Hope. "I believe a dragon-fly to be the greatest and most destructive enemy to fish —more especially to salmon. I know that a pair of these insects will do more harm to a river than a dozen otters, a flight of herons, or a shoal of trout."

. "How so?" asked Cross.

" By the number of eggs they lay. You may have often seen a dragon-fly in autumn resting on some weed that overhangs the water, beating its wings in an extraordinary manner. When you see this, you may know that she is laying her eggs ; these eggs soon become larvæ, and more voracious wretches there are not in existence. They will eat every living thing, but their favour ite food is the spawn of fish, more especially that of salmon. They seem to scent it out, and dig their way through the sand and gravel till they reach it. Fortunately the season is somewhat advanced before they have strength to accomplish this task, for if they could get near the spawn early in the winter, not a grain of it would ever come to life ; and such is their voracity that they will eat three or four times their own weight in a day. I have proved this by giving them that quantity of salmon spawn when I had them in confinement in a glass vessel, and they would eat the whole in a day. I have also given them a parr as long as my finger, and in twenty-four hours there was nothing left but the bones."

" What are these creatures like ?" asked Cross. " I never saw any of them."

" They are the most hideous of all larvæ ; and what is singular, in the pupa state they eat quite as much as when larvæ. It is difficult to describe them ; they are of a good size, something like a deformed shrimp, with a larger head, over which it folds a double set of jaws that form a kind of mask. At one period of the larva state they are so transparent in water that you can see the food passing along a tube in their bodies, which moves in a continuous stream through them as they eat. When they change into pupæ they become darker in colour, and are no longer transparent. The larvæ have lumps on the shoulder ; these lumps are larger in the pupæ, being the embryo wings. The larvæ move very rapidly, the pupæ move slowly, but are quite as voracious. The larva rushes at his prey at once ; the pupa throws out the double mask-like jaws, which are now much elongated and resemble two claws, draws himself to his prey,

and devours it. I have no doubt we shall find som
in this state on the weeds in the Mare de Bouillon.
be more difficult to show you the larvæ, but in the
in the west of Scotland, if any one can point out to
salmon spawn, you have only to dig it up and you
to find two or three of these creatures either in th
the gravel close by. The destruction they create n
thing incalculable. I suppose you have seen saln
all its stages, and are aware that as it comes to life
very much, and then a little head appears at one e
at the other; the egg gradually lengthens out and
body. I have taken them in this state, and have
glass globe where I kept my young dragon-fly. I
they in the water than the wretch rushes at them
and in five minutes they have passed through hir
pair of dragon-flies will generate an immensity of
demons, every one of which seeks for the spawn c
and if they find it they will eat at the rate of one hu
in twenty-four hours. Judge, then, if I am not ri
ing that these insects are the worst enemies that f
I have already said that in the larva state they
destructive to salmon, but they attack in like man
of trout or grayling; in short, of every fish down
gudgeon or minnow, if they deposit their spawn
gravel. The pupæ do not confine themselves to
when they have reached that state, they gradua
ground and crawl up the weeds, and there devour
those fish which deposit their eggs on the leaves
aquatic plants. They are horrid brutes, and I d
kill them whenever I meet with any. Many a cha
and shot have I sent after them, and thought the
well spent. I have heard a great deal of nonsense
the quantity of salmon-roe which is destroyed by t
folly; a trout will snap up a pea or two of spawn
to find any, but this does no harm, for these peas

portions of the mass which the male fish has failed to bury ; they are useless, as they would never come to life, and I would make the trout heartily welcome to them. But these brutes of dragonflies crawl into the beds where the spawn has survived the winter, and commence their work of destruction just at the moment that the young fish are about to enter into active life. Take my word for it, if you wish to increase the fish, either in pond or river, kill every dragon-fly you see."

" It is a pity," said Cross, " that what you say is not more generally known. I shall certainly in future kill every one I can find. They are very numerous here. I have amused myself by collecting as many varieties as possible, and I can testify that the common great-headed kind does not lose his appetite in his perfect state. I caught one last year in a butterfly net, and held him by the wings to watch his motions ; while in this position I held a small fly to his mouth, which he snapped up in a second. This struck me as so odd that I got a friend that was with me to catch a number more flies, and of those he ate eight, one after another. Not to spoil them as specimens, I always kill them by holding a feather, dipped in turpentine, to the mouth ; this they seize, and drink up the turpentine, which of course kills them, as it does every other insect, in a moment."

" I believe," said Hope, " it is the speediest mode of inflicting death on any insect, and I know that to rub a drop on your ears and brow is a way of giving comfort to man, if it gives death to insects. Many a brother of the angle has confessed this to me when I have given him a drop from my bottle, and shown him that rubbing it on his face will protect him from the attacks of those little torments, the midges. It is singular how little this is known. Many a man has been driven from the river-side after enduring martyrdom, when a single drop of turpentine would have protected him as effectually as a coat of mail, and allowed him to enjoy in peace a good day's fishing."

" That is true," said Cross. " An old friend of mine took it into his head to travel through Sweden last summer, and was

almost devoured by mosquitoes in the marshy forest tracts in the
north. He told me that the natives who distil ' Stockholm tar'
in these districts, and live in the wilds felling timber for great
part of the summer, smear their hands and faces with a substance
made from the pine which smelt of turpentine, and is called
pitch-oil. The woodmen and workmen, and those who work
the rafts of timber and floats of tar-barrels down the great rivers
to the Gulf of Bothnia, look like chimney-sweeps or smiths with
their leathern aprons and black faces, and each man carries at
his belt a small horn filled with this dark-coloured fluid, with
which he smears his skin wherever a mosquito can get at it. It
would be impossible for men to work in these regions without
some protection, for the big mosquitoes are more numerous and
vicious than Highland midges, and draw blood ; and the sand-
flies, though smaller, take the bit out. Even peasant girls wear
veils. My friend said that his own face was covered with red
marks, and he counted fifty-two bites on one hand. But for
spare diet he would have had a fever. Serious illness has been
caused by these bites ; but pitch-oil is as good as armour, and
might surely be made a cosmetic."

"You mentioned distilling tar," said Hope ; " did your friend
tell you how it was done ? I am always glad to pick up a
wrinkle."

"He told me what he had seen," replied Cross. "A tract is
selected in a pine forest, and the trees in it are barked all round
and hacked with an axe near the root. They cease to grow
leaves, and are half-killed ; and next year they are felled and
chopped up into short logs. A piece of ground is then chosen,
generally on the top of the bank of a rivulet, and a clay floor
sloping towards a centre is laid down. On this the logs are
piled up till a large mound is made ; this is covered with earth
and turf, and when all is ready it is set on fire. The burning
goes on for a long time, and is carefully regulated, and the tar
which distils from the pine flows from a duct which joins the
centre of the clay floor. It is caught in barrels, and these, when

full, are rolled to the nearest river, and floated down as great rafts. It must be curious to meet eight or ten tar-barrels fastened together, and rolling after a pony, led by a rough man with a dark streaky face, all covered with pitch-oil."

"They gather rosin in France," said Hope, "but on a different plan. At Arcachon, south of Bordeaux, and on the sandy coast lower down, great pine forests grow on the dunes. These yield turpentine, but the trees are not cut down. A perpendicular groove is cut deep into the wood, and the wound bleeds rosin ; the gum trickles down, and is caught in a bit of bark and hardens, and when the time comes the sticky harvest is gathered. When a wound heals, another is made ; and so it goes on year by year till an old tree becomes a fluted column for a height of twenty feet. The pines do not appear to suffer from this milking process, and the rosin is used in manufacturing turpentine."

"What a deal of work it takes to save fishermen from midges," said Cross gravely.

Thus conversing, they reached the top of the hill, where they paused to take breath and look about them.

CHAPTER X.

LOST ON THE GRÈVE.

AFTER drawing a few long breaths, the friends began to look about them. They were standing on a small open space on which masses of granite might be seen protruding through the green turf, which was composed of a short close herbage largely intermingled with wild thyme. From the sides of the granite rocks grew straggling bushes of whin, like advanced guards to a thick cover of the same shrub which covered the lower side of the hill, and which concealed the ground to the west. To the south, the whin was seen growing as under cover among the oak and chestnut coppice which grew in that direction, forming a foreground to the larger timber which they had formerly seen and admired around the old castle of St. Jean de Thomas. To the north was the more scattered underwood through which they had passed to their present station, and on the east was a continuation of the same sort of woodland ; but there it was fronted by a number of white and black thorn bushes, forming a kind of thicket not easily passed through. From their elevated position the view was very extensive, as they were able from the spot on which they stood to overlook the trees on all sides. Hope gave one general glance around, but that was all, for his attention was immediately rivetted on the south-westerly point of view by the very singular appearance which there caught his eye.

The sun had fairly mastered the fog, and was now shining brightly, obscured only now and then by puffs of vapour which occasionally floated by from the sea in small detached clouds. When Hope, therefore, turned towards the south-west to look at

Mont St. Michel, he was greatly struck by seeing nothing but the highest point of the building with the telegraph, the arms of which were then at work. This seemed to spring out of a plain of white cloud, the surface of which glistened in the sun's rays, looking more like silvery moonbeams on a placid lake than anything he had before seen in daylight. The portion of the building that was visible, and the arms of the telegraph, told hard and sharp against this shining plain, and were so distinctly seen that they looked close to them, although many miles of wooded plain and sand intervened between them and the fortress. After looking attentively for a minute at this singular appearance, he turned to Cross, who was examining with great earnestness the thicket of thorns on the other side.

"Bless me, man," said Hope, "what are you looking at there ? turn your eyes this way and tell me if you ever saw anything like this before ?"

Cross immediately turned, and he too looked for some seconds before he spoke.

"Well," repeated Hope ; "did you ever see anything like that before ?"

"Yes," answered Cross, "many a time ; but never perhaps so strongly marked as just now."

"And how do you account for it ?" asked Hope.

"It is the sea fog," replied Cross. "You must surely have seen something like it at home, when from the top of a mountain you have looked down in sunshine on a veil of mist or cloud hanging mid-way up the side. Don't you remember the lines—

'Though round his breast the rolling clouds are spread,
Eternal sunshine settles on his head ?'"

"To be sure I do," said Hope ; "but your quotation is hardly apropos ; for Mont St. Michel, though a very respectable rock, is scarcely entitled to the dignity of a mountain ; and these clouds do not roll, but lie like a quiet white sheet with all the apparent density of the waters of a lake. Indeed, my first impression, when it caught my eye, was that the place had been submerged. I have often seen what you allude to in Scotland ; but the cloud, or fog-bank, on which you looked down seemed gray, and you could partly see into it, and, as your poet says, it 'rolled' along, while this seems perfectly dense and stagnant."

"That is true," said Cross ; "in looking at it from this distance it seems perfectly still ; yet I suspect, if we were standing by the telegraph and looking down on the fog (for fog it is), we should see much the same effect as you describe, but with this difference, that in no part of Scotland did I ever see fogs so dense as those which frequently rest on this coast, especially on the Grève. But this fact, as I told you this morning, is a subject we may talk over among ourselves, when no Frenchman is by to hear us. Were any of them present it would be only waste of breath to tell them, for they would never believe such an assertion, or allow a comparison between savage Scotland and la belle France. I told you this morning that these fogs drift from the ocean, and seem to be dammed up between the coasts of Normandy and Brittany. Now, the Grève is exactly in the elbow of this great bay, where the fog is the most condensed ; and it strikes me that the vast plain of wet sand which is laid bare at low water adds to these moist vapours ; perhaps more so from the body of warm fresh water which flows into it from the two rivers Sée and Sélune. Professor Johnston has explained this by showing how you may account for the phenomenon so often seen in mountainous countries. I mean that a shower passing along a hill-side is always darker and heavier as it passes over particular places ; and on going to the places where this increase of darkness is observed, you will invariably find some small fresh-water loch or wet boggy land, the moist surface of which serves to surcharge the air and attract a greater discharge from the clouds as they pass over them. This is exactly the case on the Grève ; for both rain and fog fall heavier and thicker there than on the surrounding land, and I am very sure that the mist, which was thick enough with us this morning, was ten

times worse down there ; so that the sun's rays have not yet been
able to expand the air above the rivers and wet land.   As I have
seldom seen a thicker mist than we had this morning, so I think
that I never observed the strange effect of overlooking a cloud so
strongly marked.   It is these fogs which render the Grève so
very dangerous to the peasantry, who, while taking short cuts
across it, are often lost.   They are first caught in one of these
fogs, then lose their way and wander into the quicksands, where
they are swallowed up, leaving no trace behind them.   A quicksand is worse than the greedy sea, for the sea sometimes 'gives
back its dead,' but a quicksand never.   I can tell you, looking at
this sight makes my blood curdle, for it calls back the remembrance of the narrow escape I had last year, when four of us were
saved by God's mercy from that fate."

"Ah !" said Hope, " I should like to hear how this happened
You seem in luck on this coast, for, by what you say, you have
escaped smothering in the sand as well as drowning in the tide.
I hope it was not an old fool like myself that led you into this
scrape by looking for worms when he ought to have been striding
away for 'terra firma.'"

"In truth, my dear fellow, you make me blush," said Cross,
"by calling yourself an old fool and taking to yourself the blame
of our adventure on the rocks, when in reality the whole fault
lay with me.   You did not know anything about the rapid rise
of the tide, and I did ; therefore, for that cold sederunt I alone
am to blame ; but of the greater danger on the Grève I am innocent.   The hazard arose from the rattle of that young Irishman
we met the other day, and our safety was owing to his presence
of mind and sharp eyes."

"Your greater danger !" exclaimed Hope ; "you do not
mean to say that you were worse off in that bay than we were
the other night, when we were holding on to a few inches of
rock and the waves washing our shoes ?   If so, you must have
been, as a Yankee would say, in a considerable unhandsome fix."

"And I assure you," said Cross, " I thought myself a thousand times worse off.   On the rock I never felt any fear after little Matilde took us there, but on the Grève I went through all the stages, from the cold perspiration of good honest fear to the quiet resignation of despair ; and then felt again what I have heard described as the sensation of a condemned criminal who is reprieved at the gallows' foot : namely, a sickening feeling—first came joy and thankfulness for present safety, and then a more lively throbbing of fear and nervous agitation in remembering the past danger than I had felt when I had given myself up for lost, and had taken leave, in my own mind, of life and this world.   I can only tell you, that in spite of shame and exertion to hide my feelings, I should have fainted if I had not got a good pull at a bottle of brandy when we reached the carriage, and even the Irishman, who had shown the greatest presence of mind, and kept us all up by his jokes during the height of our danger, was as much in want of the brandy as myself.   As for the other two, they lay down with the guide the moment we were off the sand. They had been rather tipsy when we started from the rock, and when we went to get them into the carriage the wine or the fright had so floored them that we were obliged to help them into their places."

"You must tell me the whole adventure," said Hope.

"Well, I will, if it will amuse you," replied Cross ; "but the description of this sort of scene never gives any idea of the reality ; however, since you wish it, here goes.   Everybody knows about Mont St. Michel, for volumes have been written about it, and of course everybody who is near it goes to see it and to learn some fresh fable on the spot.   If you should meet a priest and choose him for your guide, he will tell you lies by the score about the archangel Michael ; if a soldier, he will be equally eloquent and false in relating the lickings that the French garrison have given to the English ; and if you should fall in with a savant, he will cram you with archæology ; if a geologist, he will talk of submerged land ; if a peasant, he will spin you a yarn about the knight who left the rock in a forest, and found it an island in a

quicksand. This, of course, you must bear with patience, and
you may do so with ease, for the place is well worth being seen,
in spite of its present use. The most splendid halls and apartments are cut up and subdivided into what, before this last revolution, were the prisons and workshops of the greatest ragga-
muffins in France. There is no use talking about these or the
place ; suffice it to say, I was asked to join a party going to see
all these wonders, and I agreed to go. We provided ourselves
with a hamper containing something to eat, and a few bottles of
wine, and started in a hired carriage to make a day of it. Paddy,
who was one of the party, kept us laughing all the drive ; and
after we got to the rock, he still kept up his jokes with a sort of
half gentleman, half guide, with whom he scraped acquaintance
on leaving the carriage. I know not what this man was, whether
priest, soldier, or savant, but he was well stocked with every
variety of marvels usually related by each of these professionals.
He firmly believed in the visits of the archangel, and that the
two large guns which are shown as trophies were taken from the
English by his countrymen, and not by the tide, although in all
other points he gave credit to the power and danger of a spring
tide on the Grève. After going over every part of the building,
from the entrance gate to the telegraph, we returned to the little
dirty inn where our hamper had been deposited. Paddy invited our guide to join our party, and amused himself and us
by plying his guest with wine, while he led him on to tell one
marvellous story after another. After exhausting his stock of
saintly and soldierly anecdotes, he persuaded him to describe the
many losses and escapes which had taken place at different times
on the sands. These were well told, and bore the stamp of truth ;
so much so, that we forgot the loss of time. When we had been
standing by the telegraph we had observed that the sea was
foggy ; but as the day was so bright and fine, we thought nothing
about a fog out at sea, till, in the middle of one of our guide's
best stories, our coachman came in to announce that the tide had
turned, and that as the fog was coming on, he wished to start

immediately. We suggested half-an-hour's delay, but coachy was imperative for an immediate departure, finishing by declaring that if we were unwilling to start then, he would go alone, and wait for us on the mainland; so that we might take our time and walk there, which, he added, we could do with safety, as we were not likely to lose the way on foot, although he might do so in driving, should the fog become much thicker. Some of us were for starting at once, but Paddy would not hear of such a proceeding till we had emptied the bottles and heard our guide's narratives to an end. His jokes and determination overruled our wiser scruples. The coachman was told to go or stay, as he chose. His choice was to go, and our glasses were barely filled to do honour to some toast which Paddy proposed when we heard the sound of the horse's feet clattering down the steep pavement. This was all one to Paddy; our guide was requested to go on with his story, and he was nothing loth, as each tale of peril ensured two glasses of champagne, which he swallowed like mother's milk. It was evident that he had the true Norman taste for good liquor, and plenty of it.

"The story he was telling when we were disturbed by the arrival of our coachman was one of a man that had been lost on the sands during a fog. Suddenly the day had cleared up before a rapidly-advancing tide, when he found himself about half-a-mile to the west of the Mount. Had he been acquainted with the sands, he would have known that he ought to make a circuit to avoid a branch of the river; but it seems he was not aware of this danger, for he ran straight to the rock till he was stopped by the deep water. He then turned and ran along the stream, sometimes one way, sometimes another, having seemingly lost his head. He was plainly seen from the rock, and the people who saw him shouted and waved to direct him which way to go; but he neither saw nor heard them. At last two or three of the fishermen ran down to help him, but they had a considerable distance to go before they could reach the place; and when they did get near him, the tide was advancing so rapidly that they were obliged to turn to save their own lives. The poor man then ran to a mound of sand which stood like an island surrounded by water. The fishermen were obliged to make the best of their way back to the rock, and from thence they saw the water rise around the unfortunate man they had gone forth to save. There was no boat ; inch by inch the water rose, till at length he was borne away. They saw him overwhelmed in the waves, and it was the last that was ever seen of him, for his body was never found. It was supposed that it had been swallowed up in some of the quicksands.

"The fellow told this story well ; much better than I can repeat it. He had a good deal of gesticulation and action, acting the different parts of the fishermen and the sufferer : shouting for the one, and running up and down the room and acting despair in imitation of the other. We forgot the coachman and the carriage ; the bottle went round, and as usual Paddy took care that his new friend should not be forgotten. In return for this the said friend began a new story, or rather an old one, for I think his next was the account of a governor being nearly lost, but fortunately saved by his wife."

"You may call it an old story," said Hope, " but it is new to me ; so let me hear it."

"Why," said Cross, " the adventure is told in every one of the many accounts which have been published about the Mount ; and I saw you reading one of the best the other day."

"The fact is," answered Hope, " I was not reading, I was only looking at the pictures, as the children say ; and as I did not read the tale, you may as well tell it to me."

"This is the story," replied Cross. " The Commandant of the Fort left it one day to go somewhere on the mainland, promising his wife to be back by a certain hour. One of these fogs came on, and as the husband did not arrive, his wife sent out the drummers to form a line, with directions to beat the drums as loudly as they could. It appeared that the husband had lost his way in returning, and was moving towards the

greatest danger, when the roll of the drums struck his ear. He
turned, and guided by the sound reached the first drummer.
With this drummer was his own faithful servant, who had also
gone out to search for him, and who had taken with him two
large glass lanterns, with two wax candles lighted in each ; in
short, a couple of those lanterns which you see carried before
the belles of the small Norman towns every evening when they
go out to visit. The fog was then so thick that no one could
see a yard before him ; and to prove this fact the story goes on
to say that the Commandant thanked his servant for coming
out to meet him, and then blew him up as a stupid fellow for not
bringing a light with him. Of course he was thunderstruck when
he found that the man had a lantern in each hand. The history
goes no further ; but it may be quoted as a rare instance of con-
jugal affection, as well as in proof of the density of Norman fogs.
Our friend, when he related the adventure, told us with a grin
that the Commandant and his wife had been very lately married.

"At the end of this anecdote of course there was more wine ;
then followed another story; then more wine; till, instead of half-
an-hour, we had passed upwards of an hour in listening and
drinking. The last history we heard in the room was that of a
vessel that had struck on the sand on some occasion when a gale
of wind and a fog had combined to mislead the sailors. The
crew were saved at low water, but the ship and cargo gradually
sank down into the sand. If I remember the story rightly, I
think it was on the fourth or fifth day after she struck that
nothing was to be seen of her but the truck of her mainmast,
and the next day that also had disappeared.

"As the story ended, the bottles were found to be empty. I
remember Paddy's last joke was bowing most respectfully to
the narrator, and calling him a confounded liar, in English,
which the honest man mistook for a compliment, as he did not
understand a word of our language. Our bill was paid, and, as
usual, we were called on to buy a number of the little articles
cut out of some hard foreign nut which are the work of the

prisoners. Paddy gave the word to move by saying, 'Shove ahead, old fellow, and show us the way; whether the sand swallowed the ship or not, you have swallowed our wine, and we have swallowed your bouncers, and we want a little exercise to digest them. So, *en avant.*'

"Down stairs we went, the guide leading, and I confess I felt rather a gasp when we got into the street and found it as dark as it was this morning. But our guide was quite comfortable; telling us to keep close to him and there was no fear, for that he could go the road blindfold, he knew it so well.

"We were soon on the sand, but the air apparently had an effect on our guide not quite to be desired, for he was evidently tipsy, and having already favoured us with so many stories, he then began to volunteer a song. His voice was bad, and his theme anything but decent. Paddy then ordered him to keep his eyes about him, and, by way of return, sang a capital comic Irish ditty. The rest of us marched on in silence, except that every now and then I asked our guide if he was quite sure he was in the right road. He always answered with confidence that we were. After a while, we came to a run of water, through which we waded ankle-deep. When we had passed this, and once more trod on dry sand, it struck me that it was lighter in colour than what I had before remarked. When passing in the morning I remembered that we had driven through several very shallow puddles of water; but as my impression and recollection of these puddles was that they would hardly cover the sole of the shoe, instead of being up to the ankle, I hailed our guide, and asked him more strictly than before if he was certain he was leading us right, drawing his attention to the last piece of water we had waded through and to the colour of the sand.

"The guide insisted he was right, and explained the deepness of the water by saying that the tide had turned, and asserted that the density of the fog deceived my eyes, for that the sand was exactly of the same colour as that over which we had been walking since we left the rock.

"This I felt might be true, for the fog was so dark that I could hardly distinguish the features of the speaker, though he was not six yards from me; so I told him to move on. He did so, but I observed that he often looked about him; and after another five minutes, he first slackened his pace, and then stopped.

"'Have any of you gentlemen seen a bush?' asked he.

"Paddy told him that he was a spalpeen, and that we had seen no bush since we left the mistletoe that was hanging above the inn door of the cabaret, at the Mount.

"'I am certain the fellow has lost his way,' said I; and, to confess the truth, I first got hot, and then broke out into a cold perspiration. The remembrance of all the stories we had been listening to rushed back on my mind with a most disagreeable distinctness.

"Paddy went up to the unfortunate guide, who was as white as a sheet, and taxed him with having lost his way. The poor devil confessed the fact, but declared that he could not be far wrong, and that he was sure he should find his track in a minute.

"On we moved again, the guide turning a little to the left. Paddy pulled out his cigar-case and a bunch of allumettes fixed on touch-paper. These were bad, and would not light. Paddy tried several before he got one to kindle; those that would not light he threw away, and these, in the end, were one great cause of our being saved.

"We walked on, our guide moving very slowly, and we not a yard behind him. One of the disastrous tales he had related to us in the morning, which I have forgotten to mention, was, that a marriage party were once crossing the sands; the bride and bridegroom were about ten yards in front of the rest of the party, when suddenly the happy pair vanished from their sight. They had slipped into one of the spring quicksands, and were engulfed in a moment, and of course never seen again. I know not why, but this story was constantly recurring to my mind. I had thought it a most improbable fiction when I heard it, and yet somehow or other it then always came back on me, and I dwelt on it more than on

any other he had told us. We had been walking at a slow pace
for more than ten minutes, this story still running in my head,
when of a sudden I saw the guide slowly sinking before me.
The poor devil screeched for help; without thinking, I rushed
forward, seized him by the collar, and threw him on his back a
yard behind me. At the same moment I felt as if something
gave a crack below my feet, and I felt myself slowly going down!
I own my heart leaped into my mouth; I had never felt anything like it. I have broken through many a bog, many a
trembling eye and *well-head* in the Highlands of Scotland, and
once or twice I have found that disagreeable and nervous
enough; but it is nothing to the horror of sinking into a quicksand. The sensation to me was as if a slight crust had broken
under my feet, through which they sank, and then something
seemed to suck or drag me down, leaving me not the slightest
power to assist myself. I did my best to raise one leg, but to
no purpose; the other only went deeper and faster down. In a
few seconds I was buried halfway up my thighs, and sinking
faster. I shouted for help! In a moment I felt Paddy's iron
grasp on my collar. The guide was a little man; it had required
no great strength to draw him out; but with me it was a different matter; a tall, heavy man, like myself, required no ordinary strength to lift. Fortunately, he who came to my assistance
was as strong as a horse, but it took his utmost exertion to raise
me. I felt two tremendous tugs, and then, oh happy sensation!
I found myself rolling on the hard sand beside the guide, who
was on his knees crossing himself with great devotion. It was
true I was without the collar of my coat; at least it was so torn
that a bit of red cloth, which had been inserted as stiffening,
was hanging out, and in my fall had wound round my face.
This I pulled off and threw on the sand.

"We took no long time to think or feel where we then stood,
for Paddy sprang back himself, and called on us all to do the
same. 'The ground is breaking under us," he cried; 'come
back, come back!' Our two friends, who were on their legs,

obeyed his call, and we who were on the ground were not long
in following their example, for we could see the sand as it were
cracking and flowing towards the spot where we had so nearly
sunk, which now looked as if the sand was rising out of it; as
you may have observed sand heaving in a strong spring. We
went back for about a hundred yards, and then paused, as the
sand was there quite hard, and so dry that it retained the marks
of our feet. This, I must tell you, had not been generally the
case, for in the greater part of our walk the moment we lifted
our feet the impression first filled with water, then the sand
seemed to slide into it, and all trace was obliterated.

"Our two friends had as yet made but few remarks. I believe the wine in their heads had lett little room for thought,
and up to that moment they had appeared unconscious of our
being in any danger; but then, of a sudden, they seemed to be
aware of our position, and to remember some of the stories we
had heard of the crust breaking under unfortunate wanderers on
the Grève, who immediately vanished into the bottomless abyss.
Of this I am certain, that they both became very much alarmed,
and one of them betrayed what was passing in his mind by
asking the guide if we were not on the top of one of the caldrons
which he had described in the morning as being bottomless, and
having only a thin crust of clay and sand resting on their surface. The guide had become so frightened that he was quite
stupified and unable to give any answer; but Paddy replied that
he believed, if we were not on the top of one of those caldrons,
we had been on the edge of one, for he had felt the ground
yield beneath him very like ice cracking, and that it was then
he had himself sprung back, and called to us to do the same.

"Our two friends became extremely frightened, and I honestly
confess I was so too. Paddy was no fool, and therefore, I am
sure, he shared our alarm; but he concealed the fear he must
have felt, and cut some joke about the appearance of our guide.
If fear is infectious, certainly courage is also; for Paddy's coolness gave me hope. I believe it was I who first tried to rouse

our guide. Paddy soon aided my endeavours, but it took some time before we could get him to give any rational account of where he thought we were. By dint of repeated questions we at last made out that he imagined we had gone too far to the left, and that we should then be near one or other of the rivers, as it was always close to the rivers that the danger was the greatest. Further questioning and drawing plans on the sand at length gave us to understand where our guide supposed us to be.

"Paddy, having acquired this information, insisted upon being our guide, for he said that by going to the right for a certain time, and then again easing off to the left, we should be sure to reach firm ground somewhere; and at all events, by bearing in that direction, if we went wrong we should walk into the sea, and drowning was a cleaner death than being smothered in sand.

"I thought his reasoning good, and did not oppose the proposal, but I suggested that we should all tie our handkerchiefs together, one end of which was to be fixed to his arm, and that I, as the strongest of the party, should walk behind Paddy and hold the other end, so that if he got into another quicksand I should be able to haul him out. The guide was now quite useless from fear; so our two friends undertook to bring him along between them, keeping close behind me. This, I must tell you, was absolutely necessary, for the fog was now so dense you could not see two yards before you.

"Our line was soon formed, and we started. After proceeding for some distance, Paddy stopped to hold, as he said, a council of war. His suggestion was, that we ought then to turn again to the left, and if the guide was right we must hit the land somewhere. We, as councillors, agreed, and the guide, who had partially recovered himself, joined in our opinion. I must tell you that in this walk we had been obliged to cross sundry strings of water, several of which took us up to the mid-leg. It was these bits of water that revived our guide, for he said they were the marks that showed we were going right.

"This news gave us fresh spirits, and we moved on at a

quicker pace and with lighter hearts, for we had again hope; but hope died gradually away, for after walking for a quarter of an hour, no land was to be found. Paddy shouted, 'Hurrah, boys! never say die, and never cry strike while there's a shot in the locker!' and on he marched for some minutes longer. Suddenly I heard him exclaim, 'All right! here's somebody's toggery.' He turned a little on one side and picked up something, what I could not distinguish till I stepped up to him, when—conceive my horror!—it was the lining of my collar which I had thrown away half an hour before. The fact was only too plain; we had been walking in a circle, and were on the same spot where Paddy had undertaken the duty of guide, and consequently within five yards of the quicksand into which both the guide and myself had so nearly gone down!

"It is quite impossible to describe accurately the sensation which this discovery created on the different individuals of the party. I can only tell you what I felt myself, and how the others acted. Our first movement, by one consent, was to rush from the place where we stood, and then our guide threw himself on the sand, began to bemoan himself, and to call on the saints for aid and protection. Our two friends said nothing, but both were very pale. Paddy ground his teeth and lit a fresh cigar. The effect on my nerves was singular. For some time before I had felt considerable agitation and anxiety; then I was convinced we had no chance. I knew that the tide was rising, and that before long we must be overwhelmed by the sea. I thought death inevitable, but the conviction made me perfectly calm, so that I looked about me, and was quite able to observe all that my companions did.

"Not a word was spoken for a minute or two by any of our party; the guide alone continued to moan, to wring his hands, and call on the saints. He was so fluent with his list that I am confident at some time or other he had been in some way connected with the priesthood. At last Paddy broke the silence by telling him to hold his blethers and let a gentleman speak. Then he turned to us and said, 'Well, boys, let's be moving; there's no good in standing still to be drowned; so at it again, and better luck this time !'

"He was beginning to move, when he again stopped and pulled a bundle of old letters out of his pocket, which he began to tear into little pieces. 'Dropping a bit of this as we walk along,' said he, 'may help to guide our eyes and keep us straight, if we spread out as far apart as we can, still keeping one another in view.' He asked me to go last, and call to him whenever he was swerving from a straight line, as the morsels of paper he would drop might, he thought, be seen even better than the figures before me. I at once agreed to take the place assigned me, and we were about to start for the second time when he again paused. 'Surely,' said he, 'some marks of our footsteps must still remain, and if we can trace them back, we shall be able to find out the spot where we first went wrong, especially if we can get that howling idiot to listen to reason.' He spoke to the guide, but the latter was quite incoherent from fear, and after a vain endeavour to recall him to his senses, he gave up the attempt. 'We must trust to Heaven and to ourselves,' said he; and turning to our friends, he asked them to take care of the poor man, and requested me to stand still, and answer him if he called out. He then walked in the direction where the lining of the collar of my coat had been found; he was out of sight in a moment, but I saw that he had dropped some morsels of paper to guide him in returning. After a second, I heard his voice hailing cheerfully, and calling on us to join him. We followed the line of scraps of paper, and were soon at his side. He told us that he could see the track we had come, and that he felt sure he could take us back on our former footsteps. I examined what he pointed out, and certainly thought there were marks, but so faint, I never should have discovered them if his sharper eyes had not first seen and pointed them out. I own I placed no confidence in them even then, but I agreed to the proposal he had previously made of taking the rearguard, and trying to direct a straight line by keeping one of my companions and the bits of paper in one. We started, Paddy first, then went one of our friends leading the guide, the second followed, and I brought up the rear, keeping my friend in view; but to do this, I could not allow him to be more than three or four steps in advance of me. Thus we marched on for several minutes without a sound being uttered by any of the party; for even our guide had ceased to moan aloud. I suspect we were all thinking, and thinking seriously. On a sudden, this silence was broken by a cheerful shout from our leader. 'Hurrah! never say die! there's life in a mussel!' said he; 'all right, and no mistake.' These were the words I heard; we all sprang forward, and a dozen steps brought me to his side. When I joined him, he was holding in his hand one of the allumettes which had failed to kindle, and which he had thrown away; this he had found lying on the sand, and it convinced us all that, so far at least, we had retraced our steps correctly. The guide was then again questioned—and, to say the truth, Paddy did not accost him with very gentle words, some of which, such as *spalpeen*, he might not understand, but poltroon and bête, together with a good shaking, seemed to rouse him, for by degrees he became more communicative, and gave us to understand that he was quite confident he had been in the right road till we entered the water, and that there, he now felt convinced, he had gone too much to the left. After clearly making this out, Paddy gave the word to start, but this time he himself took charge of the guide; the rest of us resumed our former positions. I soon saw by the bits of paper that we were leaning to the left, and I shouted to say so. I was answered, 'All right; I am doing it on purpose; but now keep me straight.' Thus we proceeded for some little time. I had again resumed my thoughts—not very lively ones, as you may suppose—when a fresh shout struck my ear, this time from the voice of the guide. I was soon by the side of my friends, who had rushed forward on hearing the cry; they were all standing by a sheet of water. Paddy stooped down and tasted it—it was salt! 'We've done

our best,' he said; 'but I fear it's all up with us.' Our guide
was tearing his hair; hope had revived in him for a while, and
then again despair completely overwhelmed him—indeed, he
seemed quite to have lost his reason. Paddy also appeared to
have entirely given up hope; he was perfectly calm in manner,
but very pale; our two companions were the same. One of them
said in a clear voice, 'The Lord have mercy upon us,' to which
we all with one accord responded, 'Amen.' As we uttered the
word a hollow sound was distinctly heard; it was the same
sort of moan which the sea gives, and which you heard the other
night just as we got on the rock: you then saw the manner in
which the tide, as it rises, comes gently on for a while, and afterwards rushes up in one great wave. There could be no doubt
that the sound we then heard was the roll of this fearful wave,
and if we had been uncertain about it our guide would soon
have enlightened us, for he redoubled his cries for mercy, and
shouted, 'The wave, the wave! we are drowned! we are gone!'"

"And what did you do?" exclaimed Hope.

"As I have told you," answered Cross, "I had given up all
expectation of safety some time before. I was therefore calm
and quite collected. I don't say this by way of boasting, but
simply because it was the case. I felt that death was inevitable,
and mine was the calmness of resignation to a certain fate which
I could not avert. Fear is most painful while there remains
any uncertainty; when doubt ceases, fear in a great measure
ceases also, and resignation takes its place. A man of courage
may meet death calmly when he can do nought to avert his
doom, for he knows that some day or other he must face that
dread conqueror. The struggle between courage and fear is only
agonising beyond endurance at the moment when despair is
crushing hope. I am sure it was so with me; I do not deny
that I felt that struggle painfully, and I think the feeling was
the same with us all. I looked at every countenance, and am
confident that, though they were calm, each was preparing for
certain death. We were all standing close together. I know

not who made the first movement, but we all pressed each other'ṣ
hands in silence. We did the same to the guide, which hac
the effect of setting him howling again. Through the noise hₑ
made we again heard the same hollow sound repeated, and wₑ
saw the water rising beside us, and running in an increasec
stream past us ; there was an air of wind also that came fron
the same quarter. Paddy said 'Whisht !' and turning to thₑ
guide, went on, 'God bless you, you poor creature, can't yoᵤ
hold your tongue and drown quietly ! I'm tired of your noise
If it was not for you we might perhaps guess where we are bᵧ
listening to the sea !'

"As he uttered these words a strong breath of air strucḷ
upon our right cheeks. We were then all facing the water
The breeze increased ; and in an instant the fog seemed to bₑ
lifted up, so that we could see for more than a hundred yards al
around us, and we perceived that, within ten yards of where wₑ
stood, a broken bush was firmly planted in the sand ; whilst iₙ
the water, not fifty yards from us, was the top of another whicḷ
could be clearly seen. Paddy shook the guide with no gentlₑ
hand as he pointed to them—'Do you see those, you spalpeen ?
said he ; 'and now can you tell where we are ?' The maₙ
looked for a moment, then sprang high from the ground, shout
ing, 'Saved ! saved !' In another second he was into the stream
wading as fast as he could move towards the more distant bush
The water was nearly up to his hips. We followed him withouₜ
exactly knowing why. We passed the bush, continuing to wadₑ
in the same line, and in two minutes more were again on drᵧ
sand : the marks of wheels, horses' and men's feet, were therₑ
visibly imprinted on a more muddy strand. A very few yardₛ
further a third bush was in sight. We were once more on thₑ
road ; we were indeed safe !

"I must now confess my folly. Up to that moment I hac
been calm, but then a revulsion came over my spirits. I felₜ
my ears ring ; a hot flush came over my face ; tears came intₒ
my eyes, and both my feet and hands had a tingling sensatioₙ

that deprived me of power; while my knees shook so much that I could scarcely walk. I was quite unable to see what my companions did. I heard Paddy's voice cheering on the guide, and mechanically I followed the sound. Fortunately we had not far to go. In less than five minutes we were treading on earth and stone instead of sand; in another minute we were beside the carriage. I clung to the side of it, and then I felt such an utter prostration of strength that, if I had not got hold of a bottle of brandy which was in the pocket, and swallowed a great gulp of the contents, I should have fainted.

"I do not think Paddy was much better than myself. He had shown great courage and presence of mind during the whole trial, but I think the reprieve from certain death had almost as great an effect on his iron nerves as on mine. He took a longer pull at the brandy than I did, and then pressed my hand, saying, as he raised his hat, 'Saved by God's mercy, my boy! and we may praise His name. If it had not been for that hole in the blanket we were gone coons!'

"After a while we looked round for the rest of the party, and, as I have already told you, found the three lying on the ground close to the sand. We administered a dose of the same comfort we had ourselves swallowed. The guide, who had betrayed the greatest cowardice during the danger, was the soonest recovered; he swallowed a goodly dose of the cordial, crossed himself, returned thanks to the Virgin and St. Michael, and then cut a caper, quite himself again. Our two friends were stupified, and what they drank seemed to make them worse; so we helped them into the carriage, and after slipping a couple of five-franc pieces into our guide's hand, which he willingly pocketed, we got into the carriage ourselves. He clambered up beside the coachman, and there, no doubt, he related our adventures, and made himself the hero and saviour of the party. This much I know, his voice never ceased for one moment from the time he mounted the box till we paused to set him down at a cabaret, about two miles on the road home; and the coachman congratulated us on our good fortune in having had such a man with us as a guide, for otherwise we must have perished! It was not worth our while to tell what a useless, cowardly fellow he had shown himself.

"We were half-way home before any of us spoke much, but then by degrees we began to talk over our adventures. I think the chief subject was the curious but well-known fact that people always have an inclination to walk in a circle instead of a straight line, either in the dark or with the eyes blindfolded; and since that time I have seen some very good fun and a considerable deal of money lost and won in bets as to whether a person could walk straight forward for a hundred yards with his eyes blindfolded; or better still, to see two people start together to try, for a wager, which could go the straightest."

Hope thanked Cross for his story, and allowed that the position he had then been in was far more critical than that in which they had been placed when surrounded by the water on the rock.

"I do not wonder," said he, "that you were alarmed, for the danger was truly frightful, and there certainly is something very appalling in being lost in a mist. I know that in such a situation everybody is oppressed with a feeling of dread which cannot be understood by those who have not undergone the trial; nor could any one who has not been so placed conceive the complete confusion of memory which attacks the coolest. People who have lived all their lives on a mountain-side may tell you that they know every stone and bush of heather within five miles of them, and yet will find themselves lost when almost close to their own homes. This I know to be true," he continued, "for I once wandered for several hours on a moor, every inch of which I thought I knew, and I was in company with a gamekeeper and a herd who had spent the greatest part of their lives within a mile of the place where we first went astray. They were as much puzzled as myself. We were returning home from shooting, when, just as it was growing dark, a thick fog came on. The keeper proposed that we should leave the track we were in to take a shorter cut over the shoulder of a hill, to which I at once agreed, as I knew that the line he suggested was shorter than the road we were following. We stepped out, and I remember at first that I only thought the hill rather longer and steeper than usual, but this I accounted for by recollecting I was somewhat tired, and when that is the case every one thinks a hill longer and steeper than when he is fresh. Now I know that years have the same effect as fatigue ; for I feel that as I grow older I find every mountain-side longer and more difficult to climb than I did twenty years ago. After walking for some time the hill seemed to get higher instead of becoming level and then falling off and descending. The long and short of it was, we were lost ; not one of us had a notion where we were. The ground was so marked in character, and we all knew the country so thoroughly, that I own when I found we had lost our way, I was half inclined to agree with the herd and think myself bewitched. Well, we wandered about for several hours without being able to make out where we were, till at last I was so tired I could go no longer ; so I desired the men to pull a lot of heather, and fairly made up my mind to sleep on the hill. We tried to make a fire, but the heather was wet and green, and we got little more than smoke for our pains. At ten o'clock we were still working away in this vain attempt when the moon arose. The fog was then gone, and to our astonishment we found ourselves not a quarter of a mile from the herd's house, and at least four miles from the place where we imagined ourselves to be. The line we thought we had been taking was to the south-west, but we discovered that we had gone exactly north-east, and to this hour I cannot understand how we wandered so far out of our course. The herd was afraid of fairies and witches, but no one else had the slightest fear, nor indeed was there any cause for alarm, as the worst that could befall us was a night on the hill ; and yet the effect of the mist was so confounding that three men, all skilled from our

T

habits in local memory, had strayed thus ridiculously out of our way, and this not in a strange country, but on ground that we had known all our lives. The dwellers in towns would never believe such a story, or if they did they would raise their hands and eyes, and say, 'What fools!'"

"A dweller in a country town might do so, but no inhabitant of London could think so with truth," answered Cross, "for I knew an honest Cockney who was nearly drowned by falling into the Thames at Hungerford market, when he imagined he was entering Hanover Square, which is quite as extraordinary as your wanderings on a Highland hill or ours on the Grève."

"That's true enough," said Hope; "and now you remind me of it, I have heard no end of queer stories relating to the adventures that have happened to people in a London fog; and these I can well believe, for nothing but Egyptian darkness could surpass two fogs I myself witnessed in that city. It was darkness that was absolutely felt."

While this conversation had been going on the two friends had seated themselves on one of the granite boulders. During the last minute Cross had risen from his seat, and though he still conversed, his attention was evidently fixed on something behind them. Hope rose also, and observed that Cross was again staring into the thicket on which his eyes had been so earnestly fixed when Hope first called his attention to the effect of the mist around Mont St. Michel.

"What the deuce are you looking at?" asked he; "it must be very attractive, to turn your thoughts and your eyes from what has so much interested me."

"And so it is," replied Cross. "There is a nest of shrikes among those bushes. Don't you hear them screaming? It is so very late in the season to find a nest of them just flown that I was very much taken up by the discovery, and I am now looking if I can get a sight of them: I was engaged in the same way when you first called to me. I have been trying all this season to get a young shrike, as I wish very much to tame one, and teach it to hawk small birds. Butcher-birds are common enough in this country, but I have never been fortunate enough to get a young one caught, and in despair I had given up all hopes of getting one for this year, when I heard those old birds scream-ing, and as there are young ones answering them, I am sure they may yet be taken. The old butcher-birds drive off their young the moment they are of an age to take care of themselves, but as these are still protecting their brood, I am certain that the young birds cannot be strong enough to fly far ; therefore, if you will help me, I may yet be able to catch one."

"With all my heart," said Hope. "Show me the birds, and I will do my best ; but I am afraid you will find me a very bad assistant, as I am rather too fat and stiff for running after any-thing that has wings or four legs. I remember when I was a boy that we often tried to rear these butcher-birds, and used to amuse ourselves by giving them large beetles, and watching the way they fixed them against the wires of the cage, and then tore them to pieces. You need not have come to France to seek for them, for there are numbers that breed all round Windsor—at least there were when I was a boy at Eton."

"You are thinking of the lesser butcher-bird," answered Cross ; "what the French call the écorcheur ; there are plenty of them in this country also. I have found several of their nests, and could have got as many young birds of that sort as I chose to take, but this is not what I am looking after. The birds you now hear are very scarce in England ; they are the great shrike, or butcher-bird, called by the French the pie grièche grise. It was once as much the fashion in France for the noble ladies to keep their pie grièches as it was for their lords to keep falcons. With the first they pursued their chasse au vol by hunting small birds in their gardens, while with falcons the sport was more fatiguing, for with them, as you know, they hunted herons, following the chase on horseback. Charles IX. was very fond both of falconry and of seeing the pie grièche attack the thrushes and blackbirds in his garden, and is said to

have enjoyed this smaller game as much as he did hunting
Huguenots or hanging heretics.   I once saw a curious old manuscript giving an account of the manner of educating the pie
grièche, and conducting this sport.   It was reading this work,
which was written during Charles IX.'s reign, that made me so
anxious to get some young birds, to try if I could train them in
the manner there described ; and as you have promised to help
me, do not let us lose any more time.   The only way to succeed
is to fix on one of the young birds and chase it till it is exhausted, and so tired that we can lay hold of it."

Hope laughed, but agreed.   " I hope no one will see us
' toodling,'" he said, " or they will think us mad ; two men, each
well on for six feet high, hunting an unfortunate bird by shying
stones and shouting to keep him on the wing, till he is no longer
able to fly at all ; but here goes, though I have not done such a
thing for forty years."

Away they went, and had any one been near to watch the
operation, they would doubtless have been highly amused.   The
two rushed into the thicket together, and having fixed on one of
the young birds, they commenced the chase.   Cross's longer and
younger legs gave him the start, and on he dashed, Hope following, and then only an occasional glimpse of them could be seen
from the open ground, but a listener might have heard their
voices as they called to each other ; first, Cross shouting, " Look
out Hope ! I've turned him," then a crash among the bushes, and
an answer from Hope of, " He is going to you now.   I've driven
him back again ;" and so on.   After a quarter of an hour of such
sounds, mixed with shouts and the rattling of sticks and stones
among the branches, Cross gave a cheer, and appeared again in
the open space, holding his hat in his hand with his neckcloth
tied over it ; Hope came crawling out shortly after with face
and hands scratched and bleeding, his coat torn in several places,
and streaming with perspiration.

Cross was much in the same state, but in high glee.
" Hurrah, my boy !" he exclaimed ; " I've got one, and if we

carry on, we may get the rest; there are certainly two more."

"No, I thank you," replied Hope; "I have done enough for to-day. Make the most of the one you have got, for he ought to be valuable, seeing he has ruined two coats, not to mention the skin I have sacrificed in his capture. The fact is, I am done up, and could not take such another run to save my life." He sat down on a stone and wiped his face.

Cross looked, and saw that he had no chance of persuading his friend to begin again, for crawling under one bush and squeezing through another is not an exercise that can be followed long by any man who has passed twenty years of age, more especially if the bushes chance to be covered with thorns, as they were in the present instance; and this even Cross felt, in spite of his desire to possess himself of the rest of the young shrikes.

"I believe you are right," said he; "this is no work for grown gentlemen; but if you do not mind going a little out of your way, as soon as you are rested, we may call at a farm-house not far from this, and try if we can get some boys to help me in catching another of these birds, and at the farm I may also procure something to make a better cage than my hat in which to confine my present captive."

"There is more sense in that proposal," answered Hope. "I wish I was a boy, and active enough to help you, but as it is, we must seek younger aid; so come along to your farm-house at once."

Cross was only too glad to begin the walk. The capture of the one bird had made him the more eager to get the others; so they took their way, returning through the wood along the same path by which they had come. When clear of the wood, all remembrance of mists, and perils from mists, was fairly forgotten; nothing was talked of but hawking, rearing hawks, and taming pie grièches, on which subject Cross was both eloquent and amusing, being well read in all the works written upon it, quot-

ing from many, especially from Campbell on Falconry, and from
the manuscript on the reclaiming of pie grièches which he had
lately seen, and which had so strongly excited his fancy as to
give him the desire to possess some of the birds on which he
might try his skill in rearing.

The walk was not long, and they reached the farm in less
than a quarter of an hour.   Like most of the farm-houses in
Normandy, there were ranges of ill-built out-houses, irregularly
planned, standing about the principal dwelling, with no sort of
order or method.   The whole crop, including hay, being always
stored in barns instead of in stacks, the farmer had built fresh
houses as his farm and crop increased.   An old château seemed
to have been the chief quarry from whence the stones had been
taken to erect these new buildings.   Of the château, one old
tower, with its steep roof and pepperbox corners, was still standing—the site being about a hundred yards in the rear of the present dwelling-house.   At one side of this tower were the remains
of the ruined walls of a large building ; on the other, a number of
low thatched buildings, above the roof of which a thick smoke
was rising ; and the sound of voices laughing and talking could
be heard in the same direction.

There was no one in the farm-house or in any of the buildings near it, so, after calling in vain at each, the two friends bent
their steps towards the old tower, the lower storey of which they
found was used as a stable and byre, for in it were standing two
horses and four working oxen ; such a number in one man's possession marked him as wealthy in his station.   The upper storeys
served as barns, and were then half full of hay and straw.   The
roof was evidently a pigeon-house, and a considerable number of
those birds were resting on the high ridge.   No person was to be
seen, so they turned to pass round the broken walls of the
château, and seek the parties whose voices were now much more
clearly heard.   It was impossible to tell what was said, for there
seemed to be about a dozen different voices, both male and
female, all talking together.

"This way," said Cross, as he directed his steps round the ruin. "We shall find the whole boiling of them here, and they are certainly settling something which they think of importance, for they are all talking at once—everybody speaking and no one listening, the invariable method of conducting a discussion in Normandy. I wish they had chosen some other day for their debate, for I am afraid I shall not be able to bribe a single boy to come and help me, though I can distinguish the young whelps' voices trying to out-scream the older men and women."

"I think they are fighting," said Hope. "There is a woman's voice that sounds most harsh and disagreeable ; she seems to be in an awful rage."

"Not a bit of it," answered Cross ; "it is only a friendly discussion. I recognise the voice you mean ; it is that of the mistress of the farm, a worthy old lady, and a great friend of mine."

The château must have been a large building when in its glory, for it took some minutes to walk round all the remains of ruined walls ; but at last the final corner was passed, and they came to a sort of enclosed yard in the rear of the tower, in the centre of which was a fire, with damp straw for fuel, that was blazing and smoking when they came in sight. Above this fire was formed a sort of triangle made by setting up a long pole and the trams of one of the country carts, and from this dangled the carcass of an immense long-sided pig. A dozen men, women, and boys, were employed around this arrangement, all roaring and giving orders, which no one seemed to obey.

"What are they doing there?" asked Hope.

"Singeing a pig," answered Cross ; "and as the animal is as black as my hat, the job, I suspect, is nearly done, and I may perhaps get the boys. But as the method of salting bacon among the common people in this country is rather curious, I advise you to stop and look at it while I return to seek after my butcher-birds. I will wait for you, or join you at the end of the wood."

Cross then joined the party. Hat he had none, but he

bowed profoundly to the old lady whose voice had been heard
the loudest. He made his wishes known, asked for the loan of
a cage, for permission that two or three of the boys should assist
him, and that she would show Hope her method of curing bacon.
To everything she consented with a good-natured smile, and as
the appearance of the strangers had caused a sudden silence, her
directions were listened to. The boys were sent off with Cross,
her husband was ordered to lower the pig, and she assured Hope
she should consider herself much honoured by his observing the
manner in which she cured her bacon.

While the old lady and Hope were making civil speeches to
each other, the pig was carried to a bank about ten yards distant
by the husband and the rest of the party, and as soon as Cross
and the boys departed the old lady led Hope to join this party.
There he found that the pig was laid on his back by the side of
a hole that looked very like a grave.

" What is that hole for ?" asked Hope.

" To put the pig into," answered the lady.

" Are you going to bury it ?" he again asked.

" Assuredly ; it would not take the salt in any other way,"
she replied.

" Why not cut it up and cure it in a salting tub ?" he inquired.

" Ah ! my good gentleman," she said, " you forget how dear
salt is. We should be ruined with your salt tubs. That may do
very well for rich people or town gourmands, but country people
must be economical. We can cure a pig in our way with less
than a quarter of the salt they use in the towns, which is a
serious consideration. Added to which, we may kill our animals
whenever they are fat, whereas with your tubs, you must wait
till the weather is cold before you can make bacon ; for, as you
see, we are now only in September, and our pig is fat, so we kill
it. In the towns they would wait till the end of November, and
thus undergo the expense of feeding an animal for nearly three
months longer than we do ; so that, what between extra food and

the additional quantity of salt, their bacon costs them five sous a pound more than ours."

" I shall like very much to see how you proceed," said Hope.

" That is soon done," replied the old lady ; and she issued her orders, upon which every one followed her example, and began to roar forth their own directions, so that it was quite impossible to understand what any one said. Nevertheless, while they talked they worked, and Hope was able to see, though he could not comprehend the orders given. A bucket was produced with a quantity of salt and saltpetre mixed in it ; every one took a handful of this; the pig was laid on a piece of coarse canvas, and the outside was rubbed with the mixture. The mouth, throat, and ears were then filled with the salt, and firmly tied up with string. A quantity was then put into the stomach, and it was also bound up with cord. The remainder of the salt was afterwards spread pretty evenly over the outside of the carcass, and the canvas was fastened over all ; which done, the whole animal was lowered into the grave, and the earth was thrown in, till the trench was filled up. Some bundles of straw were spread like thatch over the top, and the job was done.

" How long do you leave the animal there ?" asked Hope.

" About six weeks," was the reply.

" And do you do nothing else to it ?" he inquired.

" O yes ; when we take it out it is hung in the barn till the bad smell goes off; then it is cut up. Some of the pieces are hung in the kitchen to dry, and some are put into the chimney, where it dries faster, and the wood-smoke gives it a good flavour."

" Highly primitive," said Hope, as he made his bow ; " but," thought he to himself, " I will eat no more country cured bacon, now I know the way it is made." He then expressed his thanks, and was going away, but the farmer and his wife insisted so positively that he should taste their cider that he was obliged to yield, and he returned with them to the house.

A table was spread in a moment, with everything beautifully clean ; and Hope was struck by observing a similarity between the Norman and the Scottish housewife which Cross had formerly mentioned ; for here, as in Scotland, the old lady had a goodly stock of household linen, and was proud of her store.. She was washing her hands while her daughter was preparing the table, but she called Hope's attention to the piles of sheets, napkins, and table-cloths which were ranged in her walnut press ; not that they put any cloth on the table, but a napkin was laid in every plate.

Bread, butter, galettes of buckwheat, fruit of several kinds, lettuce, and *lait égoutté* (a preparation of sour milk), were set on the board ; jugs of cider were afterwards put down, and last of all the landlord produced two stone bottles.

Hope was kindly pressed to eat, and he did his best to please his entertainers by tasting of everything, even to the *lait égoutté*. The bottles were the last produced, and were the last opened ; but Hope allowed that " finis coronat opus," for never before had he tasted such cider. The draught cider in the jug was excellent, but that in bottle was nectar. He delighted his host and hostess by saying so, and was persuaded, as he took his leave, to drink a third tumbler, which was administered like " deoch an dorus" in the Highlands, with very muchthe same effect, for when he joined Cross at the end of the wood his eyes were dancing in his head, and the questions he put regarding the success of the hunt were not quite as clearly expressed as they would have been an hour before.

As for Cross, he was rather sulky, for though he had suc-ceeded in getting two young birds, one of them had been killed outright, and the other was in a bad way, his young assistants having shown their skill by knocking them down with stones, as the shortest way of catching them. The healthy bird first taken, and the invalid, were safe in a wicker cage, and one of the lads was in waiting to go with them and carry it to their inn.

As they walked back to the village Cross growled out the history of his *chasse au pie grièche*, and could not refrain from adding a few curses on French boys in general, and his late assistants in particular; after which he recovered his good humour, and began to question Hope as to what he had seen. He laughed heartily at the confession which his companion was obliged to make as an excuse for his confused answers; but after a while Hope found his head and speech grow clearer, for bottled cider is like champagne in its effects. It answers the Irishman's description, who said that champagne had but one fault, though that was a serious one, for when a man thought himself comfortably drunk on that liquor, he had the mortification to find himself sober again in half an hour.

When Hope had somewhat recovered, he, in his turn, began to catechise Cross, and to ask if the process of salting pigs which he had just witnessed was common in the country, and was surprised to hear that the practice was universal in almost all the farm-houses. "It is one of the consequences of the high price of salt," said Cross; "and it is astonishing the shifts the people undergo to save the use of that article."

"Well," said Hope, "I don't think I shall ever be able to eat any more bacon in this country; the idea of eating a bit of that black brute after he has been buried for six weeks gives me what the Scotch call 'a regular *scunner*.'"

"That is prejudice and nonsense," replied Cross; "you have eaten bacon so prepared several times, and thought it excellent. Seeing the process begun is nothing; if you had seen it dug up again I should not be so much surprised: then, I own, it is rather disgusting, for the smell is abominable. When it is first lifted out of the ground the odour is enough to knock you down, but after hanging in the air for a couple of days, that goes off. The animal is then cut up as the farmer's wife told you; a very little fresh salt is rubbed on to the pieces; the flitches are hung to the beams of the kitchen, and the hams and head are put up the chimney, where the pyrolignous acid of the wood-smoke soon finishes the curing. I confess I prefer our own method, but we might still take a lesson from what you have seen to-day, for what the old lady remarked to you is true enough. We always wait for cold weather to begin our operations; here, whenever the pig is fat enough he is killed. A great many of their animals are fatted at this season, for during the summer they have large quantities of damaged fruit, and vegetables running to seed, with the refuse of their kitchen and dairy ; and to this must be added the siftings of the buckwheat, and Siberian buckwheat, which, when mixed with damaged fruit and buttermilk, fattens their pigs astonishingly. The word *astonishingly* I use advisedly, for a worse breed of pigs is not to be found on the face of the earth than the slouch-eared, long-legged, and flat-sided brutes they keep in this country. When these get fat on the feeding they have to give, what might not be done if any one were to introduce some of our improved kinds! From what I have seen, I am sure they might feed three animals on the quantity now given to one. But this is not the point I wished to speak of. The plan of burying might be applied to the tubs as well as to the carcass. It is by thus placing their animal two or three feet under ground that they keep it cool, and enable it to absorb the salt. If our housewives would pay more attention to the placing of their salt tubs, we might be able, if we chose it, to cure either beef or pork all the year round."

"Very likely," said Hope ; "but I certainly shall not think it worth while to quote French curing as a model. The cider I tasted to-day is another thing ; how is that made ?"

"Very much as it is with us," answered Cross. "To make the best, the spoiled apples are carefully picked from the mass, which, after having lain in a heap for some time, are taken to the mill to make common cider. The apples are thrown on the ground and left there in large heaps exposed to wind and rain during a month or five weeks, by which, of course, a great deal of saccharine matter is lost, and to save trouble no selection is made, all sorts of apples being thrown together. But to make the quality of cider you tasted to-day, the best apples are first selected ; they are then thatched or laid in a heap under an open shed, and there left for a month to sweat, and before the mass is taken to the mill all the bad apples are carefully picked out. The mills in this country, as you know, are very primitive : a large circular stone trough receives the apples ; a stone roller is made to pass over and crush them. From the trough the fruit thus bruised is thrown on to the press, which is equally primitive. There is a strong floor of timber having a ledge six inches high round it, with pipes at one or two places. On this floor a straw mat is laid, and on the mat a quantity of the bruised fruit is thrown with wooden scoops ; another mat is then placed on the fruit, then more fruit on the second mat ; then a third mat ; and so on, alternate mats and layers of fruit till they have ten or twelve layers. A frame of wood is then brought down on the top of all ; to this frame is fixed a lever, which lever is brought under a screw ; whenever this screw is turned it presses down the end of the lever and gives a tremendous squeeze to the heap of mats and fruit. The press, in short, is like an enormous pair of nut-crackers, and the screw acts the part of a man's hand. In giving the pressure with a pair of nut-crackers, the hand gives the pressure and the nut is broken ; in a Norman cider-press the screw gives the squeeze and the juice flows through the mats. The pulp remains behind, the mats acting as a sort of filter. The juice, as it runs out, is retained by the ledge, and from thence runs off through one of the pipes into large receiving vessels. The use of having two pipes is this. When they wish to have very fine cider for bottling, the juice that runs off at the first slight pressure is led away by one pipe and is reserved as extra good. As the screw continues to turn, the pressure increases ; then the first pipe is stopped, and the juice is made to flow through a second pipe into another receiver : this is of inferior quality, and is kept by itself. The after-process is much the same as with all fermented liquors ; only with the finest quality, which is to be bottled, after the first fermentation and fining has taken place, it is run into a fresh cask, where a small quantity of the best brandy is sometimes added ; there it stands for some weeks, and is then put into bottles. It was some of this that you tasted to-day, and excellent it is, as I know by experience. The draught cider in the farms, where attention is paid to the manufacture, is quite different from the sour stuff which you buy at the cabarets in the towns, and no wonder, for it is better from the first, and water is not added to it. What you get in the towns is in general ill-made stuff, and that is largely diluted, and to my taste like bad vinegar. But habit is second nature ; the natives think it very good, for on this liquor, or apple brandy, most of the men, and women too, get drunk every market-day. If it is nasty, it is cheap ; so that in ordinary seasons a person may get very tolerably drunk for twopence."

"I never understood till to-day," said Hope, "how any one could get drunk on cider, but now I find it is very heady stuff, for I am sure the same quantity of strong ale would not have made me so giddy as I felt when I joined you ; but till to-day I never had an idea how excellent cider might be, as I neither fancied the liquor I have formerly tasted nor the earthen-ware cups."

"I thought you more a citizen of the world," said Cross, laughing, "than to find fault with a mere matter of form, though I have heard that Lord Byron, who drank out of a skull, was unwilling to eat a good dinner served up in Norman drinking-cups. However, here we are at the village, and as to-day's is the last dinner we shall eat dressed and inspected by a Marquis, I advise you to make the most of it, for to-morrow we must cater for ourselves, or trust to the discretion of a Granville host."

CHAPTER XI.

WHEN they reached the inn the Marquis was at his post, namely, beside the charcoal stoves. The Count was gone. Cross took possession of his birds, and as the invalid had considerably recovered from the blow of the stone that had secured him, the boy was well paid and dismissed. While Cross was preparing some bits of raw meat to feed his captives, the landlady whispered to Hope that the gentleman in her back-room wished to see him, and suggested that he could slip out as if he was going to the larder and see what he wanted. Hope did as he was requested; Cross saw him go, but made no remark, till in a few minutes he observed his friend again enter the kitchen, and in passing through make a signal that he should follow him.

When in their own room Hope told his companion that he had seen Jules F——, and had promised to go to him again whenever the Marquis was gone to bed; that the poor fellow was very low, and seemed anxious to tell his adventures, as an excuse, he believed, for getting some one to talk to. "To gratify him," continued Hope, "I have promised to go myself, and proposed bringing you with me, to which Jules has gladly assented." It was therefore arranged that the party should break up as early as possible without exciting suspicion, and that they should return to the back-room as soon as their companions had retired for the night.

Their toilette was made, and they went back to their French friends. Dinner passed as on the previous days, and they began their rubber. The Captain was very talkative, having drunk fully more wine than usual, and as they say *in vino veritas*, the worthy soldier showed a feeling unfortunately too common among the French families who claim a noble descent, namely, a sovereign contempt for mercantile pursuits, and for all who follow them. A reduced noble will not object to holding a place which no gentleman in England would like to hold, namely, that of a common custom-house officer, with a salary of eighty pounds a year ; but he would think he demeaned himself by entering into trade. Of this the Captain gave a strong proof that evening.

While the party were playing at cards, by some chance the name of a gentleman was mentioned who had passed through Normandy, and had become known and liked by many of the best families in the country. The Marquis asked if either of the Englishmen knew him.

Hope answered that he was well acquainted with him, and also with his brother, Lord ——.

" He is the brother of a peer, is he ?" said the Marquis ; " I did not know that ; I knew he was of a good family in your country. I also heard that he was rich ; that he was well-bred and an excellent fellow, we all found out for ourselves."

" Yes," replied Hope ; " he is an excellent fellow, and universally popular ; and he has great merit, for his means were originally small ; but by attention to business he has now realised a large fortune, and has been the principal means of raising the mercantile house of which he is a partner to its present high standing."

" What !" broke out the Captain ; " do you mean to say that an English noble, the brother of a peer, would demean himself by becoming a shopkeeper ?"

" Not exactly a shopkeeper," said Hope ; " but a merchant, which we consider a highly honourable position ; a station, in short, which no man of understanding in our country would despise."

" I beg your pardon," returned the Captain ; " I mean no

disrespect to your nation, for I know you have very strange notions on such subjects ; but for me, I would rather cut faggots than follow trade. Why, I had a cousin who demeaned himself by going into a bank, which, in my opinion, is only another sort of shop-keeping. In a bank they sell money, while in other shops they sell ribbons, cloths, or anything else that people want and that money will buy. Well, my cousin entered this bank. The head of it was his uncle by the mother's side ; for his father had made a més-alliance, which was partly excusable, for the lady was charming, and her father, who was a banker, gave her a large portion. When the father died, his son succeeded ; and as I tell you, my cousin went into the concern in some situation or other. His mother's blood preponderated in the fellow's veins, for he had a great taste for trade. He devoted himself to trade, and praised commerce as loudly as any Englishman could do. With all this, he was a very good fellow ; and when I was in Paris I saw a good deal of him. The old fellow, his uncle, kept a very good table, and I went every now and then to dine with him. We became intimate, and after some time my cousin, who lived with his uncle, would invite me without any notice to take my chance of a dinner ; to the credit of the old gentleman, I am bound to say, I never found a bad one.

"Well, upon one of these occasions there was no one at table but the old gentleman, my cousin, and myself. I was then on such terms that they did not mind talking of their matters before me ; indeed I never paid any attention in general to one word they said, for if I once heard the words scrip, stock, or bill mentioned, I closed my ears, and devoted my entire attention to the table. On the occasion to which I allude, however, it so happened that I did hear the commencement and end of the conversation that took my cousin out of this *mesquin* profession, and prevented my eating any more of the old gentleman's *dindon truffée*. The first of these consequences was an advantage to the honour of our house and name ; the last was, I own, rather a disagreeable loss to me. The conversation began by the old gentleman asking if my cousin had paid the fifty thousand francs ;—if the man had called himself, or who had called to draw the money ? I do not remember the whole answer ; but the money had been paid.

" The old gentleman then asked if the sum had been paid in bills or cash ; and if in cash, whether in gold or silver.

" The answer was, that forty thousand had been paid in gold, and ten in silver.

" ' You charged him the full price for the gold ?' the old gentleman asked.

" My cousin said he had, and mentioned the amount down to a centime.

" ' Did he take it away in one bag or in two ?' asked the banker.

" ' In two,' said my cousin.

" ' And who furnished the bags ?'

" ' He brought one with him, and I furnished the other,' replied my cousin.

" ' Have you a memorandum with you ?' asked the old man.

" ' Yes,' said my cousin ; and he handed over a small note-book which he took from his pocket.

" This the old man narrowly examined, making observations as he went along, such as ' All right, all right, not bad ;' but when he came to the bottom of the page he said, ' Did you not tell me we had provided a bag ?'

" ' Yes,' replied my cousin.

" ' I do not see the three sous marked,' said the banker.

" ' No ; they are not charged,' said my cousin.

" ' Paid in cash, I suppose ?' asked the uncle.

" ' No, sir,' said my cousin, ' they are neither charged in the note nor did he pay cash. In a transaction which has been so profitable to the bank I thought we might spare a bag ; seeing that a bag does not cost us one sou, though we charge three to our casual customers.'

"'What!' exclaimed the old man, 'do you mean to say that this is the way you attend to the interests of the firm? Have I placed you in a situation of trust and confidence to be thus deceived and robbed of my just profits? It is scandalous, and I am ashamed of you.'

"My cousin apologised, and said that really, under the circumstances, he thought the bank might well stand the loss. This made the old banker the more angry; he said my cousin would never make a man of business, and that allowing him to be thus robbed was as bad as robbing him.

"My cousin could keep his temper no longer—indeed I wonder he kept it so long; but when he was called a robber, the noble blood in his veins drowned the mercantile puddle that was mixed with it; he broke out on his uncle and told him some plain truths, calling him and his trade *mesquin* and sordid. Upon which the old boy seized the dish nearest to him. It happened to be spinach, with a white sauce. This he hurled at my cousin's head with such a good aim that the whole contents of the plate covered his face like a green plaster. You may well suppose the indignation which seized my cousin after such an insult. His noble Breton blood was evidently raised; whether it rushed into his face or not I could not tell, for the spinach completely masked it; but I am sure it must have done so, for the green seemed to smoke, as if it was undergoing a réchaufment on a stove. My cousin sprang from his chair, and I expected to see the old man exterminated, but a second thought seemed to strike him; he paused, clasped his two hands together, and rushed from the room. I followed him to his own apartment; he never said a word, nor did he seem to hear a syllable of what I said to him. He washed his face and changed his clothes in silence; and to tell you the truth, I had great difficulty in preventing myself from laughing outright at the sight of a human face served with a compôte of spinach, and as he washed it, it became more absurd. At every handful of water the green became brighter; so to prevent misbehaving, I looked out of the window till I heard the scratching of a pen; then I turned. My cousin was writing; it was only two or three lines that he wrote, which he folded up, put on his hat, and dashed down stairs. At the door of the house he gave the paper he had written to the porter, with orders that it should immediately be delivered to the banker, and in the next instant he was in the street and I was close at his heels. It was then that he spoke for the first time. 'Adieu for ever,' he said; 'we can never meet again. Thank God I did not kill him on the spot!'

"We walked about for some time, and by degrees my cousin was able to hear and to speak. The sum and amount of our conversation was, that he could not kill his mother's brother, but that he would never see him again.

"I applauded his resolution, and thus ended all connection of our family with trade; and much I rejoiced at the termination, for how can any gentleman endure such ignominy? A banker, you say, is the prince of tradesmen, and it may be so; for a kingdom of blind people, a man with one eye might be king. Here was an old fellow who, if all tales were true, had a fortune of nearly a million, who insulted the younger branch of a noble Breton house and his own nephew, about a wretched bag worth a sou, and of which he wanted to make a profit by cheating a customer and selling it at three sous. Yes, yes; trade is mesquin—at least," he continued, turning to the Englishmen, "in the eyes of a French gentleman—and I trust you will forgive me if you differ from me in opinion, for every country has its usages, and every gentleman has his own tastes. Mine, certainly, do not run towards commerce."

The two Englishmen laughed at the anecdote. Hope remarked that the scene must have been very ridiculous, but that it was hardly fair to condemn commerce and commercial men because you met with a banker who was an oddity and had a bad temper, or was a miser.

"But the man was no miser," said the Captain; "he bore the character of being very liberal, and ten minutes before he

quarrelled with his nephew about three sous he had helped me
to some slices of a dindon truffée which must have cost him
thirty francs."

" Yes," observed Cross ; " such a character is to be found
now and then in all grades of society.   I have heard of men in
our own country who would quarrel about an overcharge of a
sixpence and give away a thousand pounds directly after."

" And I will be bound," said the Captain, " that these people
were commercial."

" By no means," replied Cross ; " one of the people to whom I
allude is a member of one of the oldest families in our country."

" Contagion," said the Captain ; " you have so many shopkeepers in England that the air must be tainted.   Why, I see
in the extracts from your newspapers, which are republished in
ours, that there are a set of fellows who are attacking everything
that is great and noble in your land.   Your nobility, your landed
proprietors—nay, even your army and navy—are constantly abused
by people who, they tell me, are printers and spinners of cotton,
and you bear it.   If any cotton-spinning fellow in France were
to venture to say of the French army what they say of yours, his
life would not be worth an hour's purchase ; for one, I know I
would go a thousand leagues to pick a quarrel with him, and
run him through the body, and I would wash my sword well
after I had killed the fellow to free it from so foul a stain.   Bah !
bah ! I should like to see any man in France say that no man
was honest unless he was a printer or a dealer in greasy cotton."

Cross was looking a little fierce at this speech.   Hope, however, touched him before he spoke, and then answered—

" I do not think any one has ever said so in England."

" Not directly, perhaps," replied the Captain ; " but what
is worse, they have implied it, and so clearly, that no man can
mistake their meaning ; though, like assassins, they do not fire
openly ; but they call your landed proprietors and nobles robbers
of the poor and defrauders of the nation, because there is some
law about corn that prevents these manufacturers from reducing

the wages of their own workmen ; and they call your soldiers
and sailors I don't know what, because they use guns and swords
to defend the honour of your country, instead of blankets and
cotton thread, which these fellows are ready to sell, and which,
if you would buy them, would put more money in their own
pockets."

This last sally was too much for the friends ; they fairly
roared with laughter.

"What would the leaders of the League, say," exclaimed
Hope, " if they could hear the estimation in which this gentleman holds their exertions ? yet, strange to say, absurdly as he
states the case, there is some truth in what he says regarding
the way in which these free traders abuse every one who is not,
like themselves, connected with commerce. I have heard the
remark made before, and I am sure it has gone far to retard many
good measures."

" Hang your banker and his spinach !" said the Marquis ;
" you have revoked, and we have lost the rubber. There is no
use playing whist when people choose to talk ; so we may as
well retire."

Leave was taken, adieus were said, and the party broke up.
All retired to their rooms—the Frenchmen to sleep, the Englishmen to watch till the house was quiet.

In half an hour they returned. The door was ajar, and the
landlady in waiting, so that they were able to pass through the
kitchen without noise ; and in the next minute they entered
Jules' apartment.

He rose to receive them, and as he closed the door behind
them, he thanked them warmly for coming to see him.

" It is sadly triste," he said, " to sit here for hours and days
without seeing a human face except that of my kind protectress.
To reconcile myself to my present confinement, I am obliged to
remember how much more agreeable her face is than the one I
should see if I were taken, which reminds me that from hence I
have some chance of escape ; from a prison I should have none.

The only change from a prison would be to the Bagne either at
Cherbourg or Brest; but when I have comforted myself with
these thoughts, I have plenty of time to think of other things.
I have looked back on my past life, and oh! how I wish I could
live it over again.   I should not then dispute the advice of my
best friends, and follow the lead of every fool whose only merit
was that he was a greater *mauvais sujet* than his companions,
and was as unlike as possible, either in words or deeds, to my
father."

"That last reason," said Hope, "is rather a curious one for
the son of such a father to give.   I have always heard yours
spoken of with the highest respect."

"And I believe he deserved all the good that has been said
of him," answered Jules; "but he was too good; he could make
no allowance for faults in others, more especially in his son.
He was severe and harsh to me beyond what I could bear.
From him I only heard censure, never praise; while everybody
else flattered and spoiled me.   My mother and my nurse began
when I was a child; and as I grew older, the women, when I
entered their society, laughed at my jokes and applauded my
wit.   Some of my bon mots were repeated to my father.   He
thought them too free and libertine, and he forbade my entering
society at all.   He forced on me the driest studies, and kept me
chained to my desk, till I loathed both it and him.   Well, he
died, and I rejoiced at my freedom.   I rushed into dissipation,
and I tell you that I always loved the example best which dif-
fered the most from that which had been given by the father
who had taught me to think him a tyrant.   I feel now that his
advice was good, but ill-administered; and may my example
teach you, if ever you have children, to moderate your censure,
even of what is wrong, and mix with it some praise, even if not
well-deserved.   My father never praised me; but his censure
was unmeasured.   That I deserved reproof I know, but he overwhelmed me with more than I deserved; so I thought the whole
unjust, and became what I am.   Censure may be good; but like

water to the man that is perishing with thirst, it must be given
in moderation, or it does more harm than good. I once saw a
number of men lying dead and dying by the side of a small
stream in Brittany. I asked what was the matter with them, and
I was told they had come ashore from a vessel that had run short
of water. The officer in command had allowed them to drink
at discretion, and they had killed themselves by the quantity
they had taken. Well, as I sit here and look back at my past
life, every horror I have ever witnessed comes back on me with
redoubled force, and among the rest this scene of pain and
suffering strongly impresses me. I cannot help thinking that I
have perished from drinking too freely from pleasure's cup ; but it
was the total deprivation enforced by my father that gave the
thirst, and like these poor fellows I was maddened by too much
restraint, and when freed from the bonds that held me, I rushed
into the other extreme, and drank to my own destruction the
moment that I found myself free to taste of pleasure's stream, for
then it flowed uncontrolled before me—and see how it has
ended !"

"Never look back," said Cross ; "except as a warning for
the future. You have youth, and, with energy, the end may be
very different from what you expect."

"With life before you, you should never despair," said Hope.
"You told me that you had given yourself up for lost when the
troops surrounded you in the wood, and yet you escaped them.
Tell us what happened to you, and how you got here. The same
Providence that saved you then may raise you again to the posi-
tion from which you have fallen."

"Ah, what a thing it is to have a friend !" exclaimed Jules,
as he smiled and gave himself a shake. The change was extraordinary. The elasticity of his character at once showed itself ;
for from those few words of comfort, he seemed to throw off
the despondency that was oppressing him. His countenance
brightened up, and he continued—

"You are right ; you are a true friend. While there is life

there is hope, and fortune may smile on me when least expected, for she has done so before. You wish to hear my adventures? They are not worth listening to, but such as they are you shall know them. You remember the day I first saw you with Monsieur G——, in the Jardin des Plantes? Well, that generous friend lent me a small sum of money, but refused to lend me a larger that would have given me employment. I believe, now, that he spoke the truth when he said he could not do more; but at the time Pierre led me on, and urged me to think that he could have helped me, but would not. By talking to me, he excited my indignation against the man I now believe to be my best friend, and urged me to take a step he would the most have disapproved of. I heard afterwards what he had done for me with his father, but at the moment I believed him to be stingy and unkind, and I allowed Pierre to lead me where he chose.

" Monsieur G—— had lent me two hundred francs. With these in our pockets (for I gave the half to Pierre) we directed our steps to a house kept by a man named Sabroan. This man had several establishments in Paris, all of them disreputable. He had lodging-houses of various sorts, billiard-rooms, apartments where secret gambling was carried on; and last, but not least, a café, where there was a double entrance from two different streets, and divided into two sets of receiving-rooms. One of these apartments was appropriated to the reception of all the notorious characters of Paris; the other was frequented by wild young fellows like myself, when we went on any expedition which we wished to keep secret; and among other amusements, we had the power of seeing the people who frequented the back apartments, and by looking through a small concealed window we had the power of watching the proceedings of any notorious characters who might chance to be there; and thus, unseen ourselves, we could see these men, and women too, in all their glory.

" This man Sabroan I had known in my wildest days. I had lost large sums at his gaming-table; I had also spent much money in his house in suppers and other orgies; and as one of

his best customers I had free entrance to the room whence the
back apartments could be surveyed. Pierre proposed that we
should go to this man's house, to which I agreed, and off we
went. I must tell you that we were nearly famished with hunger, for we had hardly tasted food for several days. We had
now money in our pockets, and we resolved to make up for past
privations. We ordered dinner. Sabroan, who knew everything, had heard of our distress ; he insisted on pre-payment,
which certainly was the rule of the house, but as it had never
been mentioned to me before, I was indignant, and wished to
leave the place, but Pierre objected, and as he had produced a
handful of the five-franc pieces I had just given him, Sabroan
apologised so humbly that I yielded the point, and agreed to
remain. My ravenous hunger did more to soothe my pride than
either our landlord's excuses or Pierre's persuasions. Sabroan
seemed to have taken a second thought, and overwhelmed us with
his attentions. He sent us an excellent dinner with the least
possible delay, and when the dessert was served, he brought up
a couple of bottles of his best wine, and asked permission to join
us. He had often done so before when we had any mischief in
hand, so I could scarcely refuse him now. To do him justice,
he was a very clever fellow, and although I then thought him a
great rascal, I have now no right to say a word against him, for
it was he who saved me on that occasion. He was very enter-
taining, relating many curious anecdotes of scenes that had taken
place in his house. He did not drink much wine himself, but
pressed us to do so, and as the wine mounted into our heads, he
gradually began to speak of politics. He alluded to our dismissal, cursed the authorities, in which we joined, and then
abused the rich bankers, whose grasping avarice, he said, left
better men than themselves to pine in want while they were
rolling in affluence. How he touched on this latter subject I
know not ; he could not have known of Monsieur G———'s re-
fusal of a loan. He knew, however, of our dismissal from office,
and I doubt not, from our changed appearance, he guessed that

my wealthy friends had shown me the cold shoulder. Whatever
had guided him, he had made a good shot ; he had touched the
chord still vibrating in my brain, and bitterly did we join in the
cry he had raised. He then talked of the pleasure of revenge ;
and when he saw we were in the right tune, he mentioned his
secret window, and told us that from thence we might see and
hear a party of men who were then in discussion on the best
means of gaining the same end we had in view.

"Suffice it to say that he persuaded us to see and listen to
these men through the secret window. Heated with wine, we
listened with pleasure to proposals made by men whom we knew
by name, but never expected to see in such a place. They had
the power of great eloquence, and though they have kept aloof
in the day of trial, and therefore I despise them, yet when I
then heard them I was charmed by the powerful language that
gave promise of raising those who listened to wealth and power,
or of dragging the rich to the same state as ourselves.

"While our enthusiasm was at the highest, after one of these
speeches, Sabroan proposed that I should meet the men whom
he had just heard. We were introduced, and the result of that
introduction was, that I undertook to take a lead in several of
the clubs, and promised to address a great meeting the next
night. We separated then. Sabroan still stuck to us ; he proposed that we should adjourn to his gaming-house to meet some
of the parties who were to act with me the ensuing day. I
went, and was fairly committed, for I took the oaths they prescribed and learned their secrets. When told in plain words
what their object was, I was horridly startled, but I had gone
too far to draw back, and my brain was on fire with agitation
and with wine. As a distraction, I rushed to the gaming-table.
Fortune befriended me, and when in the gray of the morning I
returned to our lodgings, I was the winner of several thousand
francs. Pierre had left me in the course of the evening, and I
had not seen him for some hours. He came in a few minutes
after me, but he had lost every farthing I had given him. I

told him of my success. I gave him a thousand francs, and
then we went to bed. I awoke late ; then the scenes of the
past day came over me like a bad dream. I was greatly depressed. Pierre, on the contrary, was in high spirits. He
rallied me on my despondency, and told me, what I felt to be
true, that I must proceed, for I could not draw back. During
the course of the morning I went to the house of the only person in the world who, I believe, really loved me ;—it was my
old nurse. In her hands I deposited fifteen hundred francs,
begging her to take care of them for me till I asked for them.
I also gave her two hundred and eighty francs to repay Monsieur
G——, and then I rejoined Pierre at Sabroan's house. There
we again dined, and, to drown care, I again drank freely, and,
thus excited, at nine o'clock I joined the men I had met at the
gambling-house the night before. They, like myself, were to be
speakers at the meeting, and they conducted me to the place of
assembly.

" When it came to my turn to speak I rose. I have enjoyed
in society the credit of having the power of language. I hardly
know what I said, but my words pleased my auditors. I
warmed as I went on, and sat down amid a storm of applause,
and the declared leader of some hundreds of the greatest blackguards in Paris. I left the place ashamed and humbled by my
own success, and, as a distraction, once more rushed to the same
gaming-table. I was again successful, rising the winner of a
very considerable sum. I had again to supply Pierre, for he
had lost every farthing of the sum I had given him the night
before, and then we went to bed. I was too feverish to sleep,
and in the morning too ill to rise, and for the next day or two
I kept my room. As soon as I was well enough I a second
time took a portion of my winnings to my old nurse, and then
I found that I had omitted to give her G——'s address. I
did so then, and when I left her house I fell in with Pierre and
a number of the men who had been present at the meeting
where I had spoken. I heard from them—these were their

words—that my name was in every man's mouth, for that my
eloquence and sound sentiments had justly raised me to the
front place among the leaders of the ultra party—*the* party—
their party ! When I looked at the men I felt ashamed of
their praise, and felt a greater revulsion than ever against the
steps I had taken. I was now in a condition, without any
man's assistance, to obtain the situation I formerly had in view ;
but I could not take it—I was committed beyond redemption.
While these thoughts were passing through my mind, and
while I was surrounded by the companions I felt to be anything
but respectable, I saw you and Monsieur G——— close to us.
I tried to conceal myself, but I was convinced he saw me ; and
though I felt shame at the moment, I think that meeting
hardened me in my position. Had he spoken to me, I could
have struggled to be free, but as it was, I thought he passed by
me with scorn ; so I rushed still deeper into the mire. I attended the clubs, where I spoke every night ; and when the day
for the outbreak arrived I took the command of the men I had
been in the habit of addressing, and we fought together at the
barricades assigned to us. Before the outbreak I constantly met
the men who were the prime movers of the revolution. Every
evening there was an assembly of these men, who came in the
dusk to Sabroan's café. There I joined them. They praised,
applauded, and urged me on in my course. I admired their
eloquence and the fine sentiments they expressed so often and
so well, till in the end I thought I was wrong in having any
scruples. I thought they were true patriots, and admired them
as much then as I now despise them, for in the hour of danger
they were nowhere to be seen ; and now I hear that they are safe
while we are exiles, and I know that we were but the tools they
wished to wield for the advancement of their own interest, and
not the prosperity of their country. I have sworn never to
divulge their names, and I shall keep my oath. I wish I could
forget that I had ever known them.

" When the fighting first began I fought with all my soul,

for I thought the combat fair and legitimate ; but as the battle continued I saw dreadful atrocities committed, and I wished to withdraw, but I found that I had no choice.   I was a prisoner in the hands of the demons whom I was supposed to command, and then I felt the disgrace of the position in which I had placed myself, and wished to die.   I never fired another shot, but while the feeling of loathing was on me, I exposed myself on the top of the barricade in so reckless a manner that it is a miracle that I escaped the shower of balls that rattled round me.   This act of desperation had one good effect ; it again raised me in the estimation of the miscreants with whom I was associated, and gave me the power to control them and prevent their murdering the prisoners that fell into our hands.   The remembrance of that power has been my great, my only comfort, when I look back on those three days.

"Well, as you must know, at last they brought cannon against us ; why they had refrained so long I cannot understand, for the moment that was brought against us our posts were untenable.   The men who cared not for musketry fled like sheep before artillery.   I was carried away by the crowd till we reached the country, and then the love of life returned.   I fled to save it, and took up my abode in a wood which at first had but few fugitives concealed in it, but these rapidly increased till it was full. I had determined to seek some other place of shelter, and was waiting for night to conceal my departure, when I heard the sound of bugles and the tap of the drum.   I knew we were surrounded, but at the moment I was standing by the edge of a sort of ditch, the sides of which were covered with rank vegetation.   I laid myself down in it, and drew the weeds over me. Pierre did the same ; he was not ten yards from me.   As the troops advanced, I lay perfectly still, but I could hear and partly see ; and from what I witnessed, I can say that the Garde Mobile came on as if they were at a partie de chasse.   Every man as he was discovered was fired at ; if he was missed, he was taken prisoner ; but he was always fired at first.   I

do not think that Pierre was seen as he lay. I imagine that
he took fright and started from his lair, for I saw him run and
then fall to the shot of a Garde Mobile, who was not ten yards
from me. After firing, this fellow stopped to load his musket.
My eyes were fixed on Pierre, and so were his, for when Pierre
began to move and attempted to rise, the man rushed forward
and bound his elbows with one of several bits of rope which he
carried, and then he drove him on with his bayonet. It was
the last I saw of Pierre. I could do him no good, and by showing myself I knew I should only convert myself into a target
for one of those gamins to fire at ; so I lay still till I heard the
drums beating the recall a long way in advance of me. I then
rose and ran back in the line on which the troops had advanced ;
it was well marked, for it was thickly strewn with the dead and
dying. When clear of the wood I ran on as fast as I could,
hiding behind everything that could conceal my motions, till at
last I reached the open country. Here there was nothing to
conceal me, and I knew that if I attempted to cross this I
might be seen from a great distance. The only cover near me
was a pit, the edges of which were lined with brambles ; into
this I crawled, and through the leaves I saw several parties, both
on foot and horseback, scouring the country in search of flying
insurgents. I was dreadfully exhausted, both from fatigue and
hunger, and I believe I slept for some hours—how long I know
not—but my sleep must have been light, for I was wakened by
the sound of voices close to me. I heard every word that was
said, though I could only distinguish the speakers indistinctly,
for it was growing dusk ; but I saw enough to know that these
were two parties that had met, one of infantry, another of
cavalry. They were all saying that they were so much fatigued
that it was impossible to continue the search, and that they
must return to Paris. The officer in command of the cavalry
then declared that there was no use in seeking the country to the
west, for that he had scoured it for ten miles, and had not seen
a soul ; but that then both men and horses were so much

exhausted they could do no more. After some further conversation, the word was given to march, and to my joy I saw them move off. I lay still for half an hour, and by that time it was nearly dark. My sleep had refreshed me, but I was dreadfully hungry, and felt greatly exhausted when I tried to move, for I had eaten nothing for two days except some sorrel and the leaves of the brambles, which, while I lay in concealment, I had chewed and partly swallowed. I pushed on, however, as best I might, following the direction the officer had pointed out as that which he had searched without seeing any one. After continuing this course for about two hours, I could go no further. I felt so faint that I was obliged to lie down, but as I lay I saw something that looked like a cover, and I crawled towards it. When I reached it I found it was a field of early rye, which was still green, but the ears were fully formed. I pulled some, and found that the grains, when pressed, gave out a thick milky juice, and I immediately began to suck and bite them. Some of the beard got into my mouth and nearly choked me, and to obviate this, I rolled a number of the ears in my pocket-handkerchief, and sucked the juice through the cambric. Poor as this food was, it did me good, for I again found strength to move on. Hitherto I had avoided every house, but now I resolved to approach one that I saw near me. There was a light burning in one of the rooms, so I stole softly to the window and looked through. A candle was burning on the table, and by the side of it sat a soldier fast asleep. There must have been more of them in the house, for when this sight met my eye, and my disappointment was such that an involuntary groan escaped me, the cry of '*qui vive!*' from some one I did not see reminded me of my folly. I started back, and ran round the end of the house as fast as my weary limbs would carry me. I found myself in a small garden, where I immediately lay down. I was hardly ensconced among some tall plants when I heard the door open, and the same voice that had before spoken again called out the challenge. Of course there was no reply; he went round the building, passing through the garden, and then returned to the house, where for some minutes I heard the sound of voices, and then all was again still. I now found that I was lying in a bed of artichokes, on which the young flowers were forming. I pulled a number of them and put them in my pockets, and as I was stealing softly away, I could just distinguish that I was passing a bed of lettuce ; two or three of these I also took, and then crawled through the fence at the back of the garden, and moved on for another hour, eating the raw lettuce as I went. It is quite incredible how much this restored me. Still, I was obliged to rest, so I sat down and began upon my artichokes, which being quite young and soft, I was able to devour bodily. I ate all in my pockets, and the dreadful craving of my appetite was stayed. I knew that if the marks of my footsteps were seen in the garden I should be pursued in the morning, and feeling that I was still too near the cottages, I again got up to increase my distance. I walked as long as I could, and rested for a while ; then resumed my march, then rested again ; and thus, walking and resting, I continued till the morning was fast breaking. Through the faint light I saw that I was then close to some en-closures, and as I turned the corner of a ruined wall I found myself in front of a deserted château. It was in such a state of dilapidation that I did not think it could be inhabited, so I stole softly towards it, thinking that I might find some corner in which to hide myself during the day, and that at night I could continue my way. I went softly up to the house. The grass growing up to the door convinced me that it was uninhabited. However, the door was fastened with a padlock, and all the lower windows were closed with strong outside shutters. I passed round to the back, and here a number of ruined offices were standing round a sort of court. None of these were shut. Indeed few of them had either doors or windows. I entered the first, on which a door was hanging by one hinge. It had been the stable, for part of the stalls were still in existence, and in the corner of it stood a ladder leading up to a loft. To this

I directed my steps, and mounting as quietly as I could I peeped
into a long empty room. The roof was broken in several places,
but in one corner lay a quantity of half-rotten straw and some
broken implements of agriculture. On this I fixed as my resting-place. Some of the straw I arranged as a bed, and with the
remainder and a broken harrow I made a sort of wall, which,
when I lay down, would completely hide me should any one
look into the loft. These arrangements being made, I stole
down the ladder and cautiously examined all the other out-
buildings. I opened a door that was in the garden wall ; the
garden was uncultivated, and the general look of the whole place
convinced me that there was no one there, and that I was safe
for the time. I therefore returned to the loft, crawled into the
bed I had prepared, and, worn out with exhaustion, in two
minutes I was in most profound sleep. I had not long enjoyed
this blessed oblivion when I was roused in the most disagreeable
way, for at the same moment that I heard the sound of several
voices, I felt the weight of one man kneeling on my chest, and
I felt another binding my arms with a cord. The sounds that
struck my ear were all to the same tune, and that was to cut my
throat, for that I was an accursed spy. There is a strength in
despair that few men know they possess. I exerted it on this
occasion. With one tremendous jerk I threw off the man from
my chest, and freed my arms from the grasp of the other. My
wall of straw, together with the broken harrow, had been thrown
down. I saw an old spade with a long handle within my reach.
I seized it, sprang upon my feet, and stood on the defensive, like
a stag at bay, with my back resting against the wall. I then
discovered that the men who were attacking me were some of
those I had constantly met at the gaming-table and at the club.
The two who had been the most active in the assault were men
who had been the heroes of the club before I had joined it.
They had always shown a great dislike to me. I think they
were jealous of the success of my speeches. These were the
two who were trying to bind me when I woke ; and now that

I had thrown them off, the blood was in their eyes with rage. These left me no time to look about me. Both made a rush upon me at the same moment, while the other renewed the cries of 'Cut his throat! blow his brains out, the accursed spy!' As these men sprang at me, the one at my side tripped over the harrow and fell. The one in front of me I drove back with the spade; but the cries of the rest redoubled. They were all forming a ring to attack me at once, when another person entered on the scene. I did not see whence he came, but he dashed into the ring, crying, 'Silence, on your lives! there is a troop of cavalry advancing on the house. If they hear you, we are lost!" When I heard this voice I took another look at the speaker. It was Sabroan. I immediately addressed him, asking why I was thus assaulted. When Sabroan heard my question he came to my side. 'Are you wolves,' he said, 'that you eat one another? I am this man's friend—I am his guarantee;—but fly, for the supporters of the tyrants are upon us!'

" As he spoke we could hear the sound of horses' feet rattling on the paved court. The whole of my late assailants ran to the farther end of the loft, and clambered through a hole in the wall that I had not before observed. Sabroan followed, and led me in the same direction. He mounted himself, and gave me his hand to assist me in doing the same. He then filled up the hole by removing a prop and allowing a portion of the false roof to cover it. The light was then so faint that I could not for some time see where I was, or who was with me, but I could hear the breathing of several people, and I had no doubt that my late assailants were still with us. The sound of the horses' feet was so clearly heard that it was very certain that some of the troops were in the yard. With us the most profound silence reigned. The very breath was hushed, but I heard the throbbing of my own heart, it seemed to beat so loudly; for there is something very agitating in this sudden change from violent excitement to such profound quiet. However, this quiet did not last long, at least on the outside of the house, for we soon heard the sound of fresh horses galloping into the yard, and the voice of the officer in command, who was giving orders and asking questions. The first sentence we distinguished was, 'Have you surrounded the whole buildings ?' 'Yes, sir,' was the reply.

" ' Did you see any traces of people being here ?'

" ' I think not, sir. All the doors and windows of the house are fastened, and it is evident they have not been opened for long ; but we saw some traces of footmarks in the lane.'

" ' Those may have been made by the three fellows we have just taken. Have you searched the sheds ?'

" ' No, sir, not yet ; we waited for your orders.'

" We heard the order given for some of the men to dismount. ' And take your pistols with you,' said the officer in command. ' If you see any of these fellows, settle them at once ; it will save trouble.'

" In another minute the sounds of steps and the clink of swords were heard in the stable below. ' Here's a ladder,' said one. ' Well, up you go, and I will follow,' said a second. A shout from these two soon brought several of the other searchers to their aid, and then the voice of the same officer asked ' What is it ?'

" ' Some one has slept here last night, for we have found his lair,' answered a voice which seemed to speak through a hole in the roof.

" ' Wait till I come then,' said the officer.

" There was silence for a few seconds, and then we again heard the officer's voice, which rose above the hum of the others.

" ' Whoever he was, he is not here now. It is most probably the nest of the fellows we have caught ; the old woman told us she saw them coming from this direction. Look well round to see that there is no hiding-place, and then forward : we must not waste time.'

" Several footsteps resounded on the rotten floor, and we could hear the men striking the walls with the hilts of their swords. They came to the hole through which we had passed ;

involuntarily I raised the spade that I had brought with me. Sabroan laid his hand gently on my arm. My eyes had become accustomed to the darkness. I saw the blade of a sword pass two or three times through the mass of thatch that masked our place of entry, and then the voice of a man, apparently the corporal, called out, ' To horse, to horse ; there is no one here.' The steps moved off, and then a general sigh of relief was breathed from every corner of our hiding-place.

"I looked round, and was now able to perceive the men crouching in different attitudes round the walls of a loft, larger than the one in which I had made my bed. All were intently listening to the sounds of the troops who were filing out of the yard, and from this position no one moved for many minutes. At last some said, 'They are off, and we must not stay here any longer.'

"Sabroan ordered silence, and directed a boy whom he called Louis to take off his shoes and go and look out, to see that no one remained lurking about. He himself lifted the false roof that had saved us, and peeped into the other loft ; he then raised a small trap in the floor and looked into the barn below. ' There is Pot-de-vin's wife poking about the yard,' he said ; ' I have my suspicions of her ; so beware how you answer if she calls.'

There was a low growl of curses from those in hiding, and then again silence for nearly a quarter of an hour, for no one gave the slightest answer to various signals which were made by a woman's voice, who called out in the different offices below ; nay, she even took the trouble of mounting the ladder in the outer loft, and there renewed the same cry of ' Whist, friends, you are safe ; you may come out, it is only I.'

"As I have already told you, no one replied to these calls ; all lay still for a quarter of an hour, and then, on a sudden, I saw that the boy Louis had returned.

"'Gare Wolf,' he said, ' it is lucky you did not answer Pot-de-vin. I watched her go round the end of the garden wall and

speak to four of the soldiers who remained their in hiding. They
are gone now, and so is she ; but 'ware trap, she is a spy.'

"There was another volley of curses, and two men sprang on
their feet ; they were the same who were attacking me.

" 'Curses on her ! she shall rue it,' said one.

" 'Death to all spies,' exclaimed the other, and I could see
his eyes gleam as he advanced towards me.

"Sabroan asked whom he called a spy.

" 'The scoundrel beside you,' he answered ; 'it was he who
brought the troops upon us, and he shall die. I say he is a spy
and an aristocrat. Do I say well, or ill, my comrades ?'

" 'And I say that he is neither a spy nor an aristocrat, but
an honest lad and a brave comrade, and no one shall touch a hair
of his head,' answered Sabroan.

"There was a long discussion as to what I was, but as almost
all the party sided with Sabroan, the man who had shown himself so bitter against me was obliged to yield, though I saw that
he only hated me the more. Sabroan, after this discussion was
over, desired the men to move on, for that it was time to see
what they had to eat. The men went to the further end of the
loft, to a smaller room which had a sort of press in the corner ;
this was movable like a door, and behind it was a small staircase
which we ascended, and found ourselves in the roof of the château,
which, like many others, as you may know, was arranged as a
large store-room, with a number of casks placed round the sides,
and at one end were shelves for storing fruit. The stair by which
we had mounted was the private entrance used by the proprietors
for bringing in the various stores and grain, which were afterwards stowed in the now empty casks. There was another door
at the opposite side of the room which opened on a staircase
communicating with the interior of the château. This place was
perfectly well lighted by a number of small windows in the roof
and by slits in the wall, through which a very extensive view
could be obtained of the country on all sides. I was the last who
entered this grenier, and when I did so I found that some of the

men were placed at several of these openings, looking earnestly through them. The lad whom Sabroan had called Louis spoke to him as we came in. 'They are fairly off,' he said, 'and we may consider ourselves safe. Some infantry were coming this way, but they spoke to Pot-de-vin, and now they are turned in another direction.'

"'Well then, let us have something to eat,' said Sabroan, to my great joy, for I felt very faint. Two lettuces and a few raw artichokes was all I had eaten for two days. On Sabroan's speaking, several of the men began to busy themselves; a grate full of charcoal was pulled out of one cask, a pot full of half-made cabbage soup out of another; a frying-pan, some lard, several loaves of bread, and some cheese, were also produced from other hiding-places, together with a large packet of the same sort of young artichokes that I had eaten the night before. The sight of food made me feel so faint, that I am sure I could not have lasted many minutes, had not Sabroan observed my state, and given me a cup of wine and a large slice of bread. I cannot tell you how grateful I felt towards this man; I can never think ill of him again, for whatever he may have done, he twice saved my life that morning. The bread and wine quite set me up till the other articles of food were prepared, and these I thought delicious, though you may not think much of our bill of fare—cabbage soup, young onions and artichokes cut up and fried in hog's lard, some bread, cheese, and lettuce, was all we had; but never in my life before did I taste anything I thought so good. There was plenty of common wine and cider to wash down our meal, and of this many of our party drank to excess; but what took place during the greater part of the day is unknown to me, for no sooner had I eaten than I crawled behind some of the casks and slept a sleep like death.

" It must have been late in the day when I awoke. I sat up and looked around for some moments before I could remember where I was; but as my senses returned, memory returned also, and I looked to see what had become of the rest of the men.

Sabroan and the boy Louis were sitting by the side of the door by which we had entered ; they were whispering together, but so low, it was impossible to hear one word they said. The rest of the men were stretched on the floor at the other end of the place fast asleep. I moved softly, and stood up. Sabroan's back was towards me, but Louis saw me and touched him ; he turned round, laid his finger on his lips, and beckoned to me. I walked as softly as I could towards him, and sat down beside him ; he then continued to whisper to the boy. From their conversation I discovered that the men had drunk till they were intoxicated, and that the boy had overheard them settle that they would murder Pot-de-vin and his wife for being spies ; and as none of them had any money, they had also agreed to rob some houses in the neighbourhood, and afterwards to divide the spoil and separate. Sabroan had been called an old woman, and was not to be let into the secret, as he might object, lest his house should be burnt. By inquiries, I found out that the château in which we were was Sabroan's ; he had won it from the old proprietor, who had ruined himself by play, and had finally parted with this last remnant of his property. Sabroan had been in possession of it nearly two years, during which time it had been shut up, as he had only visited it twice with the boy Louis, who was in his service, and who knew every corner of the château, being the son of the confidential servant of the previous proprietor. Sabroan told me he had destined this place as a resort for any secret orgy, and had sent down some wine and cider, intending to despatch other supplies, but had neglected to do so till the defeat of the insurgents occurred, when he thought of it as a place of safety, and led the men then assembled to hide in it. They had entered the house by the way I had myself come, which was the reason no marks were seen around the building. Three of the party had taken fright and had left them before daylight that morning ; and those must have been the men who were seen and taken prisoners by the troops. 'And they will tell no tales,' said Louis, when he came to that part of the story ; 'for I am certain they were shot before the troops galloped off.'

"I also learnt, that as I approached the house, some of the men who were on guard, watching from the windows, had seen me, and had closely observed my after proceedings; and when they saw me enter the stable, they had stolen down to seize me, thinking me a spy; but on finding me asleep, they had recognised me, and would have taken me to their more secure hiding-place if the two men had not denounced me as an aristocrat and a police spy, who had pretended to join their meetings in order afterwards to give information against them. Had it not been for the timely arrival of Sabroan I should certainly have been murdered, and he cautioned me to be on my guard against my two fierce opponents, for that they detested me, not only because I had outshone them as an orator, but also because it was from them that I had won a great part of the money I had gained at play.

"I told you," continued Jules, after a slight pause, "that I had placed a considerable portion of my winnings in the hands of my nurse; a part I had also given to Pierre, but I still had nearly a thousand francs on my person. Five hundred of these were sewn up in the waistband of my trousers; the rest was in my neckcloth: this I told to Sabroan. 'That is good,' he said, 'and will help to rid us of these fellows who frighten me. Do not say a word about what you have got sewn up—that will make a purse for ourselves; but the remainder you must divide among them, and when they go out to forage to-night, they will commit some drollery which will make this place too hot to hold us; they will not come back, and we must be off; but we will take a route they are not likely to think of, and by that time,' he added, 'I hope the troops will think more of sleep than of hunting us.'

"I agreed to everything he proposed, and having settled his plans, we began to busy ourselves in cooking the remains of our provisions. The noise we made gradually roused the sleepers. We ate our meal, and when it was finished Sabroan addressed them. He said, 'You called my friend a spy; well, I prove that

he is a good communist; he has nearly five hundred francs,
which he wishes to divide amongst us. Some of you must go
out to forage, for we have nothing left to eat. Let those that
like take the money and buy us a good store, and bring it back
for the common good. Who will go?' All wished to go; so
Sabroan proposed that the money should be divided into three
parts, and that three parties should be formed, and in that way
one would be pretty sure to escape, if anything happened to the
others. The men jumped at the trap he set for them; they
whispered together for some time, and then made their parties,
scrupulously leaving us out of their arrangements. Sabroan
pretended to object to this at first, but allowed himself to be
overruled, and at last it was agreed that three parties were to
start in different directions, and that we were to remain to keep
guard in the house.

"As soon as it was dark they started. Sabroan then put
everything away, and in ten minutes after they were gone, we
too departed. He knew the country well, and took his line at
once, Louis and I following close at his heels. After walking
for about half an hour, we came near some enclosures. Here
Sabroan proceeded with great caution, and bade us tread lightly.
On a sudden we heard some loud shrieks; there were not many,
but they sounded like those of some one in despair or in mortal
agony.

"'I was sure of it,' exclaimed Sabroan; 'quick, quick, let us
be off, or they may see us.' He began to run and we kept close
to him. He continued this rapid pace till I was well-nigh exhausted, and then he began to walk. I asked what had alarmed
him. The only answer he gave me was, 'That was Pot-de-vin's
house. Poor devil! he has paid for his wife's peeping.'

"'And your friends have done it,' I said.

"'Our companions were all there,' he replied; 'some may
have worked and some watched, but I have no doubt the deed is
done.'

"'That is too horrible,' I exclaimed.

" 'They do not think so,' answered he. 'Pot-de-vin and his wife were spies of the police, and rich. Our companions have found both money and revenge at one blow, and although I would not have done it myself, I can hardly blame them—but no talking ; we are not far from the river now, and we may find more listeners than we think for, or would wish to meet ; so silence, and tread as lightly as you can.'

" In a few minutes I could see the water shining before us ; we were on the banks of the Seine. We skirted the shore, keeping about two hundred yards from the river, and advanced quickly, but silently, for rather more than a mile. Sabroan then stood still and bade us lie down and keep perfectly silent, answering no signal, till we heard a clap of the hands, followed by three low whistles, and he requested me during his absence to cut out some of my louis, as we should then be obliged to use them. He left us, and I immediately did as he wished with the money which I had concealed in the waistband of my trousers. A portion I put in my pocket, the rest I tied up in my neckcloth. I then lay down by the side of Louis, and began to question him as to where Sabroan had gone. He was a most intelligent boy. He told me that he could not answer my questions positively, but that he felt very sure Sabroan was gone to the house of some of the smugglers who lived on the banks of the river, and who introduced great quantities of contraband goods into Paris, by having secret places in their boats and barges ; and as he knew that Sabroan assisted these men in disposing of the goods they smuggled, he was confident he had gone to one of their houses. Louis was right in his conjecture, for in about an hour we heard Sabroan's signal, and we joined him. He led us into the back room of a small house close to the river-side, where I saw the clothes I now wear lying on a table ; a strong powerful-looking man was standing beside them. Sabroan bade this man bring the things he had ordered, and directed me to change my clothes as quickly as possible. I took off my coat, and the man left the room. The moment the door was shut

Sabroan whispered, 'Where is the money?'　I gave him all I had in my pocket, and pointed to my neckcloth.　He nodded, and said aloud, 'Dress quick.'　I did as he bid me, and was drawing on these boots when the man returned.　He brought with him three bottles and three packets of sailors' biscuits. Sabroan paid for them with my money, and divided them equally amongst us, telling me to stow them away in my pockets and take care of them, as I might find it dangerous to get any more food for some time to come.　Then turning to the man, he said, 'It is well understood; you are to have my friend's clothes and one hundred francs for those he now wears, and you are to take us to Rigot's in your boat.'　'Yes, yes,' replied the man; 'it is well understood; show me the money, and my boat and myself are ready.'　Sabroan produced the five louis, and the man without another word lifted my clothes from the floor, examined them, threw them on the bed, and led the way to the door. There he told us to pass him, and as soon as he had given a signal to some one in the house he again took the lead, directing us to a small creek where a boat was fastened.　This we entered; the boatman took the oars and began to pull stoutly down the river.　I observed that we frequently crossed to different sides of the river, and that on different occasions our boatman pulled his oars with great caution, and the cause of this I discovered by suddenly hearing a loud challenge and then a musket-shot from some sentinel on the side we had just left.　The boatman had desired us to lie down in the bottom of the boat before reaching this place.　The moment the shot was fired he started up and poured forth a stream of argot and abuse the like of which I had never heard before.　A loud laugh from several persons, and a cry of 'Oh! it is you, you old good-for-nothing! Why did you not hail as you passed?' showed me that we had just passed some post of river police, and I presumed that the frequent crossing of the river was to avoid others of the same character.　The boatman resumed his oars, but continued to pour forth the same volley of abuse and slang, till the laughter

of the people on shore sounded faint in the distance. 'That's
the last of them,' said the boatman, 'and the devil take that
fellow, and send him to sleep with a pickaxe for his bed-maker,
for nothing else will ever make him drowsy. Curse him, he
never sleeps himself or allows his men to do so ; though the
most of them on the other stations might beat a marmot, for
they could sleep through the summer as well as the winter !'
In a few minutes we entered a small stream on the southern
bank of the river, and rowed the boat into a little dock where
another boat was anchored. There we landed, and after a short
time we were admitted into Rigot's house. Here we had a full
meal ;—the last I had for fourteen days was in that house.
Sabroan gave me a little lard in a bladder to add to my stock of
provisions, and twice during my after wanderings I got some
eggs, and these were the only occasions on which I slept in a
bed till I reached this house ;—but I am forestalling. When
our meal was ended, Sabroan said, 'We must separate ;' and
asked if I would divide my money. I agreed, and having given
a third part to him and the same to the boy, we took leave of
each other, and began our journey, each taking his own line.
As I have already said, I wandered forward for fourteen days,
sleeping in sheds or in the open fields, except twice, when,
pressed by hunger, I entered two small cabarets. The price the
people made me pay for my shelter and for the provisions they
gave me greatly exhausted my small stock of money, and taught
me also that they knew I was a fugitive. At last I reached this
village. Worn out and wretched, I determined to take my
chance. I knew that the sister of my old servant lived near
here. I entered this house to ask where she could be found,
and you may judge my joy and relief when I beheld the excellent creature who has since concealed and tended me. For your
kindness," continued Jules, turning to Hope, " I must be for
ever grateful. If my old nurse is alive, I have enough to keep
me for years, for now I know the value of the money I formerly
squandered, and am not likely to fall again into the same folly.

I shall, if she lives, be able to repay the sum you have so gene-
rously advanced; if not, I must remain your debtor till better
times come."

"Cheer up," said Cross; "I hope those better times may
not be far off, and I do not see why you fear that the old lady,
your nurse, is dead."

"Alas! I fear it is so. She was very old, and may have died
a natural death; or she may have fallen by some chance ball;
or have been terrified to death; for the fighting was severe in
the street where she lived. Some accident, I am sure, must have
befallen her, or she would have paid my debt to Monsieur
G——; and if she had, he would have mentioned it when he
saw you after the struggle was over."

Both the friends felt that there was so much truth in these
words that they thought poor Jules' chance of getting back his
money a very poor one. They tried, however, to cheer him by
talking more hopefully than they felt, and pushed round the
bottle the while; but in vain; neither words nor wine seemed
to have any effect. A fit of despondency had come over him not
to be overcome. After pursuing their endeavours for some time
the friends became silent, and then Jules said—

"Good-night, good-night. You must not lose your rest in
trying to comfort a poor devil like me. A few days will bring
an answer to my letter, and whatever that answer be, while I
live I shall remember with gratitude the sympathy you have
shown for one who so little deserves kindness from any one.
Good-night."

Cross and Hope pressed the hands he held out, and slipping
softly through the kitchen, hurried to their beds. Cross was
rather inclined to talk over what they had heard, but Hope
stopped him, saying—

"We shall have plenty of time for discussion to-morrow;
so, in the meantime, sleep and do not talk, since you say we
must start at day-dawn."

CHAPTER XII.

SILENCE reigned in their room, and the friends disposed themselves to sleep as soundly as they could during the few hours
that remained till daylight. For a while a confusion of misty
dreams floated about both. Hope could not for some time avoid
starting up, fancying that he was sinking in a quicksand, for the
story he had heard from Cross haunted him with disagreeable
freshness, and in his dreamy fancy he was an actor in the scenes
he had heard described; while with Cross it was Jules' story
that returned on his brain, and mixed up with it was a confused
jumble of the Captain's indignation against merchants and mercantile pursuits. He had seen several members of the League,
and in his dreams he thought he was present in front of a barricade, on which were placed Jules and those gentlemen, while
a number of people were firing at them, all of whom bore a
striking resemblance to the Captain; but sounder sleep soon
banished these idle visions, and the entrance of their little attendant to call them was unheard, till he had thrown open the
curtains and knocked over a chair or two to let them know he
was there, and that it was time for them to rise. When dressing, they talked over their dreams, each relating his own; and
they were getting into a very learned disquisition on dreams in
general, when the boy again made his appearance with coffee
and the provisions they had ordered to be prepared for the day.

While they were discussing their breakfast the carriage was
brought round and packed, so that when they descended to the

street, they had only to take leave of their hostess and clamber into their places.

The landlord was up and in waiting at the door, and a lad was holding a horse all ready saddled for an expedition. The saddle was one of those huge masses of leather in general use among the Norman farmers, having a square ill-shaped demi-pique for the rider to sit on, with a large flap behind, covering the horse to the very tail, which flap is used as a pillion when the wife goes to market, and, on other occasions, serves as a resting-place for sacks of corn when the owner wishes to convey them either to the mill or for sale.

The landlord himself was dressed for a day's sport ; that is to say, he had a pair of leather gaiters buckled over his trousers, and wore a black velvet hunting-cap ; this last he doffed to the friends when they were seated in their conveyance, and inform-ing them that he proposed joining their fishing party, as he thought he might be of use, he asked permission to put his fishing-rods on to the top of the carriage. The two friends made him heartily welcome to put his tackle into the inside if he chose, to which he answered, that his rods would do very well on the top, and they might crowd the gentlemen if he tried to put them inside. He then vanished into the house, returning in a minute with a bundle that looked like a large baker's faggot ; with this he clambered up behind, and they felt the carriage shake as the burthen plumped on to the top ; the sound of a cord was heard for a minute as it grated in being fixed to the iron rim, and then mine host jumped down, took off his cap, said his thousand thanks, and bade the boy drive on.

"Fishing-rod !" said Hope to the boy ; "does the man call that a fishing-rod ? I have seen a bullock's liver tied up in a bundle of sticks like that, and set in the German rivers to catch cray-fish. Are there many of those fish here ?"

"I do not think there are many," replied the boy ; "but if there are, Monsieur Pinel will be able to catch them, for he is a fine fisherman."

"But for what purpose are all those sticks?" asked Hope.

"His fishing-rods," answered the boy. "Monsieur Pinel has a fine assortment of tackle."

Hope looked round at Cross, who was laughing. "It is not a fishing-rod," said the latter, "that we have the honour to be carrying for our friend, but five-and-twenty or thirty rods, all of which will be put into operation at once. Did you never see a Cockney fishing with half a dozen gudgeon-rods in a punt? Well, your Norman fisher is a regular Cockney. His object is not sport but fish, and he calculates by rule of three. Thus, if one rod and line will catch one fish, how many fish will thirty rods and lines catch; and catching the most fish is considered the sign of being the best fisherman; therefore, he who has the most tackle must (according to this calculation) be the best sportsman. But this you will see when we reach the Mare de Bouillon."

"With all my heart," said Hope, "I always like to see the manner in which people conduct the same sport in different countries, so I shall watch our companion's proceedings."

As he spoke, Monsieur Pinel came trotting up to them. He had on his back one of the baskets which are used by the shore-fishers. This was nearly full of bits of wood, round which lines were wound. These rattled and danced about as he trotted, making a considerable clatter. As he came alongside, the little horse in their gig, who was very fresh after his three days' rest, became either frightened by the noise, or unwilling to allow the other animal to pass him, so he set off at a gallop, unfortunately just at the moment they were entering on a part of the road, or rather track, worse, if possible, than anything they had gone through on their first journey. After dashing through holes and ruts for about a mile, without breaking down, the boy, in endeavouring to avoid a hole larger and deeper than any they had yet seen, went too much to one side; the wheel struck the bank, ran along it for a second, and then crash came the gig on its broadside. The boy lit on his legs like a cat, and ran to the

horse's head, who, fortunately, seemed satisfied with the mischief he had done, for he stood quite still, neither attempting to
kick nor run away.

Cross was undermost, and was not the least the worse for
the tumble. Not so Hope, however. The shock had thrown
him forward with a great jerk, striking his right arm and
shoulder violently against the hood. He said nothing about it
at first, but after crawling out, and once more on his legs in the
road, he felt so much pain that he was obliged to sit down on
the bank, feeling sick, and for a moment almost faint—so much
so, that Cross became alarmed at seeing him look so pale; but
after resting for a minute, the violence of the pain moderated,
and raising his arm sufficiently to ascertain that no bones were
broken, Hope declared it was nothing, but asked for some water.

Cross started off to look for some in the direction their
driver pointed out, and whilst he was gone, the boy kept up a
continued stream of curses on his own horse, on Monsieur Pinel,
on Monsieur Pinel's horse, and on the roads; but, as an extraordinary instance of forbearance, it is only fair to say that,
though he poured forth on all these every term of abuse in the
French language, he never once either struck or kicked his
horse. It is doubtful if any other driver in Normandy would
have so abstained.

Monsieur Pinel saw the accident from a distance, and had
the good sense to come gently forward, so as not again to
startle the horse. He joined them just as Cross returned with
the cup of his flask full of water, after drinking which Hope
declared himself better; "but," added he, "I fear my day's
fishing is spoilt, for my right arm is so stiff I shall never be
able to throw a line; however, as I have my left arm and the
use of my eyes, I can see what you do when we get to the water;
and in the meantime, I can hold the horses, if you will try and
put the gig on its wheels again."

There was not much difficulty in getting Blacky out of his
harness; he was placed under Hope's charge. Monsieur Pinel

tied his horse to a tree, and both of them stood as quietly as if there was no such thing as a runaway in France. Pinel, Cross, and the boy set to work with good will, and in two minutes the carriage was up and packed again, not one bit the worse for its overthrow ; indeed, if anything, the side that had been on the ground looked rather better than the other, for the scrape on the wet mud had scratched off some of the dirt with which it had been begrimed.

"There is nothing like a French carriage for a French road," said Cross. "A smart English turn-out would have been smashed to bits by such a crash ; but this old rattle-trap, as you see, is not a bit the worse, so we may as well pop the little rascal into the shafts again and be off."

Blacky was soon harnessed ; very little was broken, for everything fitted so loosely that the shaft had passed over his back, and the saddle had twisted under his belly as the carriage upset. Two or three bits of string made everything right again. The boy announced that all was ready, and pledged himself for Blacky's future good conduct. Good or bad, Hope was obliged to get in, for he did not feel able to undertake a walk to the lake. Monsieur Pinel held the horse's head ; Cross helped Hope to mount, and then jumped in himself, the boy standing by, repeating the same sentence over and over again, namely, "Soyez sage ! sac-r-r-r-e—b-r-r-r-i-gand !"

We do not pretend to say that the horse understood this admonition, but he started as quiet as a lamb, and they proceeded at a foot's pace, to avoid shaking Hope more than could be helped, and as they went on Hope felt less pain, and began to converse as gaily as ever.

"Our landlord is a civil fellow," said he, "and his wife seems to be an excellent creature. I have heard it asserted that your Norman peasant is a selfish animal, who never gives anything for nothing, and that their gratitude, like that of a political leader, is only shown in return for a lively expectation of services to come ; but our good hostess has proved that she,

at least, is free from such charges ; she can have little expectation of future benefit from poor Jules, yet has she resigned her
own safety, and given her property, in gratitude for services and
kindness shown to her brother."

"Yes," said Cross ; " she proves the injustice of sweeping
accusations.   I hope there are many more like her in this
district.   It is hardly fair to bring such a general charge against
a people, but I am sorry to say there are too many instances of
gross selfishness to be found, not only among the peasantry, but
also amongst the better class.   I have too often, to my great
disgust, heard those who ought to know better answer, ' But
what good will that do me ?' when a request for some assistance
or favour has been made to them by parties whom they call
their friends.   The love of self, I know, is too common a fault
all over the world ; but certainly there are few places where you
will find such an unblushing avowal of it as I have heard in
this fair district of Normandy.   There are exceptions, many I
hope, to this sweeping imputation ; still, most uncompromising
selfishness is the glaring fault of the country.   I cannot help
thinking that the perpetual ballot for the conscription has a
great deal to do in teaching the young men to consider the
golden rule for their guidance to be, ' Every man for himself,
and God for us all ;' at least, nine-tenths of them follow it."

Hope laughed.   " Bravo, Cross !" he said ; " you began by
trying to be good-natured and liberal, and you end by clinching
the nail that others have driven.   I have a great respect for
your opinion, because I know you are honest ; and the long and
the short of what you tell me is, that all Normans are not selfish
and ungrateful, but that you think nine-tenths of them are."

When Hope laughed, the boy looked round.

" I see you have forgiven poor Blacky and me.   It was not
his fault, poor beast.   If that accursed chestnut of Pinel's had
kept out of the way he would have gone as quiet as a lamb ;
and then these roads—the commune should be prosecuted ;
those holes are enough to spoil any horse's temper."

"Never mind, my little fellow," said Hope ; "nobody blames you. I quite agree that the roads are enough to try the temper of Job, so that no horse should be found fault with if he loses patience." Then speaking in English to Cross, he continued, "What passion guides this little Norman ? Is it affection for his horse or love for himself that makes him plead his excuse with such an anxious face."

"Both, perhaps," answered Cross, "with love of approbation added ; for though I think the selfishness of the people here makes them do many mean and paltry actions, yet they are brave and, generally speaking, kind-hearted and affectionate. The love of approbation, also, is strongly marked amongst the French. Many a man, for instance, who would neither lend his horse nor give five francs to oblige a friend, would risk his life to save him if he fell into the river, more especially if there were a good many eyes to see what he did. I do not say that they are very constant in their affections, but while they do love it is with their whole hearts, and they will fight like devils in defence of a lover or a friend ; anything, in short, but open their purse-strings. However, our little friend here is not a Norman. If you call him one he will tell you he is from Brittany, and no Norman, and will thank God and the Virgin on that account. The neighbouring districts know the foibles of the Normans ; for instance, if you are making a bargain with a Breton, he will take care to tell you the place of his birth, with a look that says as plain as look can speak, 'I am from Brittany, and therefore to be trusted.' But here we are in sight of the Mare de Bouillon. If you are still in pain, you can just see it, and then we can continue our road to Granville, and postpone our fishing for another day."

"Never mind me," answered Hope ; "if I cannot fish myself, I can, at all events, see what you and our host can do. I daresay I can get a little vinegar to rub my arm, and then I shall be quite fit for our day's amusement, which I should not like to postpone, as on another day I may not have an opportunity of seeing how a Frenchman contrives to use five-and-twenty or thirty rods at the same time."

"As you like," answered Cross. "And as the boy will be close at hand, we can go at any moment should you wish it."

In a quarter of an hour the boy pulled up at a house close to the lake. Some vinegar was procured, and while Cross assisted his friend to bind his shoulder and arm with handkerchiefs soaked in the acid, Monsieur Pinel shouldered his faggot-looking bundle of rods and went off with the man of the house to prepare the boat and begin his own operations. The friends followed in ten minutes, and although Hope was unable to use his arm, he felt greatly relieved by the cold applications. While Cross was arranging his own rod, Hope watched Monsieur Pinel's proceedings. This last had already put together about a dozen of his rods. They were of all lengths, from six feet long to sixteen, all equally rude in their construction—some jointed by splicing, some with sheet-iron. By the side lay two of a better make ; these were fitted with rings, and had small brass reels fixed on the butts.

Monsieur Pinel continued to put his rods together, till the greater part were in order ; he then tied them together and was about to move when Hope proposed to accompany him.

"I shall be back in an hour," said Pinel, "and then if you will do me the honour to come, I may be able to show you something ; but just now, as the boat is ready, you will be more amused there than with me. I shall leave these (pointing to his good rods and to some half-dozen of the rough ones, not yet put together) till I come back, and I shall be obliged if you will look this way now and then to see that no person takes them."

"Very well," said Cross. "Call us when you come back ;" then turning to Hope, he said in English, "Let him go ; you will see all you want to see by and by."

Monsieur Pinel walked off with a bundle of rods on each shoulder and his basket on his back.

"Norman to the backbone!" exclaimed Cross, as soon as he was off. "He is afraid if you go with him that you will get a share of some of the river. As soon as he has got rods baited, and set in all the best places, he will come and let you see what he is about."

"I would give five pounds to beat him, the selfish rascal," said Hope.

"And perhaps we may do so," answered Cross; "none of these fellows know anything about spinning. I have got some of the sardines and some beautiful spinning-tackle, and as the day is so bright, we have a better chance of getting sport with them than with the fly; at all events, let us try. There are some very fine perch in the water, and I have often observed that the hotter and brighter the day, the better the perch bite, provided you lead your line well, and spin deep. But don't let us loose time. If you could hold a rod over the stern of the boat, I will make this fellow pull us quietly along, and so give you a chance by trailing."

"I will try at all events; but I am so spiteful at that fellow I should not like him to learn how to spin, and if this man sees us, he will tell him."

"He is a stupid fellow, and I don't think he has the sense to understand what we are about; at any rate there are no such things as swivels in France, and without them no one can spin."

The rods were arranged, and they moved down to the boat. The Mare de Bouillon was a large piece of water, with banks of weeds surrounding the greater part of it.

"Where is the river?" asked Hope.

"There," replied Cross, pointing to the end of the lake, towards which Pinel had walked, "but it is more like a broad ditch than a river, and it is so closely lined with bushes on both sides that it is quite impossible to cast a fly. There are a good many fair trout in it, but there is no way of fishing for them except with bait, as you will see by and by when you go with Monsieur Pinel. If we had a little more wind we might pick up a good basketful in the lake ; but as it is, let us see what we can do with our sardines."

They got into the boat, and Cross directed the man to pull towards the river.   He arranged Hope's rod as soon as they were under weigh, and began himself to cast on either side of the boat.   He had not made above half a dozen casts before he called out " I have one !" and at the same moment Hope felt that he also had a fish.   Cross soon hauled up a fine perch, but Hope was only able to hold up his rod and wait till Cross came to help him to land the perch which he also had hooked, and in his haste he entangled his own line, so that it took some time to put on a fresh bait and get it again in order.

" Confound the roads and that little beast for running away," said Hope.   " I must give up all attempts at sport, for I can do nothing myself, and I only prevent you from beating Pinel ; so do your best and let me look on."

Cross remonstrated, but Hope stuck to his point, and insisted that no more time should be lost ; " for," said he, " I shall have quite as much pleasure in watching you, and it will be all the more glorious if you, with one rod, can beat that selfish fellow, with his whole bundle."   Cross yielded, and resumed his work. There was some delay before he was again successful ; but then he took two or three perch as fast as he could pull them out, and then again there was another long pause before he felt another bite.

" Make the fellow turn back," said Hope, " and stick to the two places where you have been successful.   You know that perch swim in shoals, especially in this warm weather, when they get into the deepest holes ; and if I remember right, it is old Isaac Walton who says ' that, like the wicked of this world, they do not mind seeing their companions carried off before their eyes ;' and he is right, for I have often proved it."

Orders were given to turn, and the plan was successful, for every time they passed the two places where the first fish were taken, they were quite sure to catch one or two more, and Cross had upwards of a dozen very fine perch in his basket before Monsieur Pinel came back.

"Put me on shore," said Hope; "don't say a word about what you have caught, and mind you do your best not to allow that Norman to beat you."

Cross laughed and replied, "I think you are growing somewhat Norman yourself by being so anxious to keep all the sport to ourselves."

"Not a bit," answered Hope; "I am only spiteful. If that fellow had not monopolised the whole river, I would have enjoyed his success as much as yours; but as it is, I must own, I would see him hanged before I would give him a line or a lesson; so put me on shore."

The boat touched the land, and getting out, he walked towards their companion, who was baiting one of his good rods; the remainder of the rough ones were put together and lying in a bundle.

"Come along," said Monsieur Pinel, "and you shall see what I have done. I was afraid you would find out one of my favourite places, so I put no rod there at first; but now that I have got a fair start, I don't mind your seeing it." He walked into the weeds and threw his line into the water. "There," continued he, "that is a famous place for bream; I have three hooks on that line, and when we come back, I shall have a fish on each, and by this time I hope some of my other lines have done something—so now, forward."

"Well, he is honest in his selfishness, at all events," thought Hope, as he followed his guide, feeling less angry with him than he had been five minutes before.

They soon came to the burn, which exactly answered Cross's description of it. It was narrow and sluggish wherever the water was deep; but every now and then there was a bit where the stream ran more rapidly over a shallow. Both sides were lined with trees or bushes, through which, in most places, you were obliged to force your way to reach the edge of the water;

here and there there was a break for a small space, and these
were the places which Monsieur Pinel now honestly confessed
he wished to keep to himself. "There are others," he said,
"that I know of which you would not so easily find out; but all
these opens are good for trout, and I was afraid, if you came with
me at first, you would have taken some of them and caught more
fish than I, for I know you Englishmen are fine fishermen."

"And perhaps you will be beat yet," said Hope.

"I do not think so," answered Pinel. "Your friend has
only one rod, and when I have set these I shall have thirty rods
and fifty hooks set in all the best places. Here, for instance,"
continued he, stopping and unwinding a short line from one of
the boards in his basket—"here is a place you would never
think of, and I always get some perch here. I like catching
them better than trout at this season, and when we come to
count what we have each got, I shall consider one perch better
than two fish of any other sort."

"You will, will you?" replied Hope. "I shall remind you
of this when the counting begins."

The line was baited with worms; Pinel pushed through the
bushes and dropped it into the water. In the same way he
baited and set his other rods, and then they came to the first of
those which he had set on his previous trip up the stream. It
was in one of the opens, and when pulled out it had a good
trout fast on the hook.

"Ha! ha!" said Pinel, "that is the third I have got; your
friend has not much chance." The hook was re-baited and again
set, and in like manner all the other rods were examined, both
in going up and returning down the stream. Two or three more
trout, and six or eight bream, were basketed—Pinel ha-ha-ing
most triumphantly as each was pulled out. When he came to
the hole where he expected to get perch, he crowed doubly loud,
for there he found that two small ones had taken his bait, but
on reaching the pet place for bream he was horribly disgusted to
find that his baits were gone, but no fish.

"I shall stop here for half an hour," he said, "and then examine my rods again; and as I am quite a sportsman I don't wish to take an unfair advantage of a stranger; pray tell your friend that at that place (pointing with his finger) there is a capital hole for bream; nobody can fish it from the shore."

"If they could, you would not have told him," said Hope.

"Well, perhaps not," answered Pinel; "at all events, I would have put a line there. When one has a name for being the best fisherman in the country, one does not wish any other person to catch as many fish as one does one's-self; but it is very strange that all my baits are gone and not a fish caught."

Hope looked at the hooks as Pinel was baiting them, and did not think it at all strange; the hooks were four times too big to enter the mouth of a bream, unless it was a great deal larger than any he had yet seen taken; but although in much better humour with him, he did not tell his discovery, for a thought had struck him, and he hurried away to call Cross.

"What sport?" said he, as soon as he was again in the boat.

"Very fair," answered Cross; "I have got six-and-twenty perch and one very small jack, but I think I have caught every fish, for I have not had a run for this last ten minutes; so we must try round and find a fresh place."

"No, no," exclaimed Hope, "come and torment that Frenchman a bit. He has got a pet place for bream, but he is fishing for them with large perch-hooks, and will not get one in an hour."

"Hang bream!" said Cross, "nasty, stringy, bony fish, that even a hungry pike will not eat. I am not fond of bait-fishing of any kind, and bobbing for bream with a worm is worse than fishing with a punt and rake for gudgeons."

"Stuff and nonsense!" said Hope. "I have no patience with you fellows who turn up your noses at everything but fly-fishing and salmon. Why, I have had many a pleasant day's

fishing with a paternoster* in the West India docks, sitting all
the while on a sugar hogshead, with my feet on a mahogany log,
and as I watched my line, baited with live shrimps, I could
cast my eye and my thoughts now and then towards Lovegrove's
and know that my wine was in ice, and that I was sure of
getting plenty of fish there, if the docks were unpropitious ; and
I am bound to say that the finest perch I ever saw in my life I
caught in those same docks. But that is nothing to the purpose just now ; you are fond of raising fish, and I want to give
you an opportunity of getting a rise out of a Norman, who will
give as much sport as a salmon. I have in my book a paternoster with beautiful small hooks tied on pig's bristles ; now,
though I cannot use my arm to throw, I can put my rod in
order and bait my pater; and when all is ready we will pull the
boat up to Pinel, and I shall have some fun watching his face if
you have any luck, and I think you will, for I see him raising
his rod every minute."

" I am ashamed of you !" said Cross.

" Gammon !" exclaimed Hope ; " ashamed, or not ashamed,
you must do it; so, like a good fellow, don't shake your head, for
I am sure it will be capital fun ! What do you think the
fellow told me a minute ago ? He said that, having a character
to lose, he did not wish any one to catch so many fish as he did !"

" Well, you old baby," said Cross, " I suppose we must do
as you wish; so arrange your tackle."

---

* For those who have never seen a paternoster, it may be as well to
explain that it is a line. The best are made of twisted gut, at the end of
which a plummet of lead is fixed. On the line itself small bits of bone or
ivory, in the shape of glass bugles, are placed between two knots in such
a way that they retain their places, but can twist round. These are fixed
at from three to six inches apart, and on each of them is fastened a hook,
tied either on pig's bristles or very strong stiff gut. By this arrangement
the bait stands out three or four inches from the main line. When baited
with small line bait they are able to move round and round the line,
which is kept perpendicular by a large float. When worms or grubs are
used they stand out all round. It is a poaching and deadly way of fishing
in still water.

Hope was not long in knotting the paternoster, float and all, on to his line. They had plenty of bait, for Cross, although he pretended to despise such sport, had not failed to provide both worms and gentles. The six hooks were baited, and they pulled slowly towards Pinel, stopping about twenty yards in front of him.

" I am afraid you will do nothing, gentlemen," said he, " for though the fish are biting every moment they will not take hold."

" Show him the difference, Cross," said Hope ; " if you get hold of one, don't pull up till you catch two or three—then astonish him."

Cross did as he was asked. The float, by good luck, was exactly right. In half a minute he had three fast, and pulled them out. Pinel swore, and Hope laughed.

" If I could only get my line out a little further," said Pinel.

" Pull a little nearer the shore," said Hope to the boatman ; " and you, Cross, like a good fellow, put your line close to his. Look how he is grinding his teeth ! You never had a better rise in your life than we shall have in five minutes; so fire away !"

Cross called his friend an old baby, but did as he was asked, and at every moment he pulled out two or three bream. " Nasty brutes !" he said : " I cannot bear to touch them ; and what a child you are to like to torment that poor devil. I will tell him to change his hooks."

" If you do I will never forgive you," said Hope ; " his face is worth any money. If you catch two or three more he will boil over, and then I shall be content."

Cross did not care for the sport of catching wretched little bream, and he thought tormenting Pinel childish, but he could not help being amused at the contortions Pinel made every time he hauled up his line with two or three bright little fish hanging to his hooks ; nor could he resist joining in the loud roar of

laughter in which Hope indulged when at last Pinel gave a
tremendous jerk to his rod, broke it in two, threw down the
bits, danced, swore, and finally kicked his hunting-cap into the
water.   As soon as he had recovered, he ran off, leaving his
broken rod behind him.

" Now I am content," said Hope ; and he shouted to Pinel
to come back ; but the discomfited fisherman either did not or
would not hear, for he continued his way without turning his
head.

" Never mind him," said Cross.   " If he finds fish on his
other lines, he will soon recover his good humour, for the
Normans are a good-natured people ; and though as hot as
cayenne when provoked, if you give them a little time or cut a
joke, they cool again as quickly as they warm ; and to tell you
the truth, I am tired of catching these creatures ; so let us try
round the lake for nobler sport."   He resumed his own rod,
ordered the man to pull on, and began again to spin his sardines.
" By the way," continued he, after taking a few casts, " did you
ever see the double worm, a sort of Siamese twins, that stick to
the gills of the bream ? if not, examine one of those fish ; you
will be sure to find some, and they are very curious-looking
creatures."

" I have heard of, but have never seen them," said Hope, as
he lifted one of the bream.   " Ah ! here they are," he exclaimed,
as soon as he had opened the gills ; " and now, as you are
a reasoner, can you account for them, or give as good an explanation of these parasites as of the worms and sea-lice that
torment the salmon ?"

" Indeed I cannot," replied Cross.   " A bream is not the
fish to excite my curiosity, and I never have watched them
sufficiently to discover the use of these curious-looking creatures.
I have examined them with a microscope, and they are certainly
most extraordinary ; and at this season and in this water they
are always to be found in the bream ; but I have not fished for
them at all times of the year, so as to find out if they are always

on their gills, or only to be found at times ; and without know-ing this fact, it is difficult to speculate on the use which nature may assign them. That they are of some use, there can be no doubt, for nature creates nothing without an end and a purpose ; and in these, her lower works, I suspect that the attacks of these insects, like those in the salmon, have something to do with the propagation of the fish. Several naturalists have observed these double worms on the bream, but I do not remember to have seen them mentioned as being found on any other fish ; so I may here remark that I have three or four times seen exactly the same shaped worm in the gills of whiting. The creature was of the same double form, joined in the middle like a capital H, only in the whiting it was of a redder colour, and four times as large as those you are now looking at."

"I shall examine the gills of every fish I catch in future," said Hope ; "these inquiries give a further zest to a pleasant sport, and these creatures are indeed very curious." He put a little water in the hollow of his hand, and allowed some of the worms to float in the water, the better to examine their form. Cross in the meantime continued to fish, and soon disturbed Hope's entomological studies by hooking a good trout.

It were useless to enumerate each fish that was taken. They rowed gently round the lake, and several trout, perch, and small pike were caught. In passing the weeds, some wild ducks were started, and Hope declared that the sight made him quite young again, for it recalled the remembrance of his early fishing days, when, as a boy, and on a Highland loch, he had been accustomed to see the ducks rise from the weeds, while the trout rose to his flies. They also searched the weeds in hopes of finding some larvæ of the dragon-flies not yet flown, but they were un-successful. Thousands of these insects of all colours were flying over the water, the weeds, and banks, and several of the small blue variety were already laying their eggs. These they watched, glistening in the sun, their glassy wings quivering like little gleams of light, as they flapped them with the rapidity of

lightning, while they hung on some leaf above the water,
making dragon-fly music, a sleepy sound between the hum of a
bee and the crackling of a dry leaf.

When they returned to the landing-place, they found Pinel,
who waved his cap to them as they came up. He was in high
good humour. He had changed his rods, and as he was then
fishing with smaller hooks, he had a good heap of bream lying
behind him. But this was not altogether the cause of his re-
storation. He had also caught a large tench on one of his lines,
and several more perch and trout; his bragging and exultation
were therefore nearly as amusing as his rage had been an hour
before.

Certain inward warnings had reminded both the friends that
they had breakfasted lightly at day-dawn, and that nature ab-
horred a vacuum, more especially when there was a well-stored
basket close at hand.

"Let us land and eat." The order to pull ashore and an
invitation to Pinel to join them was given by both at the same
moment, and Cross added, "Do not show our sport till after
luncheon, for Pinel is so excited that if we have caught more
than he has we shall spoil his meal." Hope nodded assent,
and they jumped on shore.

A dry bank was chosen, and Pinel, who seemed to think he
was doing the honours of his own table-d'hôte, ceased bragging
for a while, and made himself very useful in arranging the provisions, and sending for water from a spring close by; but no
sooner were their hands washed and they were fairly seated,
than he resumed his triumphant tone.

"Not bad, that pie," said he; "indeed, far worse than this
would be good in the eyes of a thorough sportsman. You
English, they say, know something of sport, and indeed I have
myself seen that you, gentlemen, are very successful in catching
bream; perhaps you know the satisfaction of taking a trout or
a perch? Did you ever catch a tench more than a pound
weight?"

"O yes," answered Hope, winking to Cross. "We have done such a thing sometimes, and I could teach you how to catch them, if you are fond of such sport; but we do not in general much care for taking any carp or tench."

"The gentleman is a little jealous," said Pinel, "and it is not surprising, for I have done wonders. I dare say he would have beat most people, but it is fair to say that I am famous for my skill and success. If it was not that I do not like to forfeit my fame as a fisherman, I almost wish he had been as fortunate as myself."

In the same strain did the worthy Norman run on during the whole time they were eating; nor did he stop, even when he had produced his pipe and stretched himself on the bank to enjoy it at his ease. The man who had rowed them was then summoned, and while he ate Hope proposed mounting a small elevation that lay behind them, so as to obtain a better view of the country before again entering the boat, to which Cross agreed, and they left Pinel to finish his pipe and do the honours of the remains of their pie to the boatman.

"What birds are those?" asked Hope. "They look like magpies, but there is such a flock of them it cannot be." He pointed as he spoke to a field about a quarter of a mile from the little height they had just reached.

"Magpies they are," said Cross. "I have never seen such a quantity of those birds anywhere as I have seen in this place. I counted upwards of fifty in that same field the last time I was here, and there seems to be at least that number there now."

"It is very curious," remarked Hope. "Have the country people the same superstition about them that they have in some parts of England and in the Highlands of Scotland? Do they consider them as birds of augury, and think that it is unfortunate to kill them? I do not wonder that game is scarce where so many of these pirates are allowed to exist."

"There are two reasons, I believe, why they are never killed," said Cross; "first, they consider it very unlucky to kill them,

and secondly, their flesh is bitter and not good to eat. Your
Norman sportsman will never waste his powder and shot by
firing at any thing that is not eatable ; and the birds seem to
know their safety, for they are as tame as barn-door fowls, and
will hardly take the trouble of hopping out of your way. My
Scandinavian traveller tells me that they are as common and as
tame all over the North. One morning he found six chattering
and dancing a war-dance round a salmon's head which he had
thrown away, and when he approached they only hopped a few
yards, and jerked their tails and chattered worse than ever.
There may be some old Norse superstition about them which has
survived. I do not know if they have the same rhymes about
them here that we have in England, but I know that they consider it fortunate to see an uneven number of them, and
unfortunate to see an even number. Let me see, how go the
lines ?—

> 'One is sorrow, two is mirth,
> Three's a wedding, four's a birth.'"

  " Ay, that is the English edition, and put together for the
sake of the rhyme ; but our Highland belief agrees with the Norman. We think that the uneven numbers are fortunate, and
the even unfortunate. In the Highlands the lines are—

> 'One is joy, two is grief,
> Three a wedding, four a death.'

And in the Highlands they go further, for they think that you
may calculate on the amount of joy or sorrow you are to meet
with by the way the birds fly. For instance, if one magpie
flies to the right, your good fortune is to be great ; if to the
left, it will be trifling. And again, if you see four magpies and
they go to the right, your sorrow will not be great ; if one flies
away and three remain, you will hear of a death and a legacy at
the same time. Now, as the 'land of the flood, the mountain,
and the mist,' is the true place for second sight and superstition,
I hold to the Highland version, and join with Rory O'More in
saying ' there's luck in odd numbers.' So, for the fun of the

thing, let us try and count these birds. I will count all that go
to the right, and you all that go to the left."

" We can try at all events to number them," said Cross, " for
it requires some one to vouch for the fact of seeing fifty magpies
in the same field. So come along."

They continued to mount the gentle ascent, till they reached
the corner of the high bank that surrounded the field, up which
they clambered, and saw from thence the magpies sitting all over
the field, more like a flock of rooks than of any other birds.
Some few were close to the bank as they mounted, and they did
not take the trouble of flying above twenty yards before they lit
again, and then hopped gently along, giving a twist to their heads
and a sly glance at the intruders, who were engaged in trying to
count them. One made the number fifty-two, the other fifty-
three."

" Well, it is a very curious sight," said Hope, "and talking
of superstition makes one feel superstitious. Do you see that
there are five parties, of four in each party, that keep separate
from the rest and always together ? I have five relations now in
Paris ; I hope I shall not hear of another émeute, and that the
insurgents have put them all to death."

" Should you be very sorry ?" said Cross, laughing, as he
clapped his hands and shouted, which put up the whole flight.

" To be sure I should," answered Hope.

" Then it is not their death that these augurs foretell," said
Cross, " for the whole party are off to the right, which, according
to your rule, proves that if you hear of five deaths, you will not
care much about the people who die."

" I wonder," said Hope, " if magpies could be caught as a
French postillion once taught me to catch jays."

" How was that ?" asked Cross ; "jays are very numerous
here, and their wings are worth having."

" My instructor," said Hope, " told me that he got a living
jay and took him to a field near some wood, where he knew that
there were plenty of wild jays. He then cut a couple of forked

sticks and fastened his decoy to the ground by pegging his wings to the earth. It is not painful, but it certainly must be very disagreeable to be thus spread-eagled, and the jay begins to scream and struggle when he is left alone. It seems to be the disposition of jays to hit a friend when he is down, for if there be one within hearing he is sure to attack the captive. He generally contrives to hook his claws into the assailant, and as the pegs hold him, so he holds the other till the sportsman comes in as umpire. Then jay number two is laid on his back, and the sport goes on till there are no more jays to be punished for cruelty to their kind."

" Serve them right," said Cross ; " but jays are not singular in this disposition. I once owned a family of terriers who lived in perfect friendship with each other and with a couple of big rough-haired deer-hounds, who generally took possession of the warmest arm-chairs in the drawing-room. This home pack did great execution amongst the hares and rabbits when we went out for a walk together in the woods. If one terrier started anything, he forthwith set up a vehement yelping, which the rest seemed to understand at once. Those who were behind yelped and ran as if for dear life, but those who were before crouched silently in the grass, while the long-legged hounds bounded to the outside with open eyes and cocked ears, to be ready for a fair race over the open. We once killed eight hares. As long as there was anything to run down, they were all of one mind, and when they came home they sat on the rug and blinked at the fire with sleepy eyes in peace and contentment. But one fine day one of the terriers trod in a trap, and yelped in a new key. We all ran, but with different aims, and the first up was the grandmother of the prisoner, who fell upon her and worried her, and there was a battle royal. I laid an ash stick about their ears, scattered them, freed the granddaughter, who was not much hurt, and then we continued our walk without more civil discord, and resumed offensive operations against the hares. Men are not much better at times ; see how Frenchmen are now worrying Frenchmen in France. But now, if you have seen enough of the magpies, let us go back, for I do not think we shall have much more fishing. Look out to sea ; do you observe how dark the sky is growing ? I should not be surprised if we had a gale of wind before long, for we may very probably get the tail of the bad weather which they must have had out at sea, to bring us such a fog as we had yesterday morning."

"It certainly looks like a change of weather," said Hope, " and I feel the wind rising—all the better for your sport, for I observe that there is a nice curl coming on the water ; so you may yet do something with your flies."

"I do not think we shall do any good," answered Cross. " You are an older sportsman than I am, and must have remarked what I have often seen, that just before a gale, as the change is coming on, no fish will move ; but let us try."

When they reached the lake-side they found Pinel looking very cross. He had lit a second pipe, and was puffing away with all his might as he stood by the side of the boat staring at the fish which Cross had caught—the boatman was washing them and laying them out in a row.

" Sacré ! mille tonnerre ! that is sport !" exclaimed Pinel ; "and you said nothing about it." He then seemed to recover his good humour, took off his cap, made Cross a bow, and went on, " You are my master, I must confess, but I do not think there is another man in France could do as much, or one I would ask to give me a lesson. Will the gentleman show me how he fishes ?"

" Well, as he eats humble pie," said Hope, " if you will show him how you spin, I will give him my receipt for making a paste that I believe to be the best in the world for catching tench and carp."

" Just to prove to him that we are not selfish, and therefore not like him," answered Cross—"so be it. Jump into the boat, and take him with you to the stern. I will take the bow, and while I spin you may write out your receipt. We have no

time to lose, for the sky is overcasting rapidly, and I am much
mistaken if we have not a dirty evening before us."

The boat was pushed off, and was pulled slowly to the upper
end of the lake, and then allowed to drift, broadside foremost,
along the edge of the weeds.   The sky soon became completely
overcast, and the wind began to rise, coming down in gusty
squalls, raising a strong curl on the water.   Nothing could look
more promising for fishing, and Cross tried his very best, first
with spinning-tackle and then with fly, but all in vain ; not a fish
would move ; and after persevering for nearly two hours, he proposed leaving the lake.

"There is a storm coming," said he, "and a bad one ; so we
may as well wind up and be off before it breaks, for we have
two miles of worse road than any you have yet seen, over which
we must pass before we reach the main Granville road, and it is
as well to do it in daylight."

"It does look rather bad," replied Hope, "so let us go : I
suppose it will be a mere summer squall, and be fine again to-
morrow."

"Worse than a squall, I'll answer for it," said Cross.   "The
fog of yesterday foretells more than that, and the fish are still
better barometers.   Nothing has moved since the change began,
which convinces me we shall have a severe storm.   So, to land,"
continued he, addressing the boatman ; "we shall be some time
packing up."

Hope had been writing out his promised receipt with a
pencil on a bit of paper, using his hat for a table.   "Here,"
called he to Pinel, "you are fond of catching tench ; here is a
receipt that you will find most deadly, and if one comes within
ten yards of this bait you are sure of him."

"Oh, that is delightful !" exclaimed Pinel ; "a tench is such
an excellent fish, and the skin is a delicious morsel.   Monsieur
le Marquis would tell you that for bouillabaise there is nothing
to equal tench.   He very nearly quarrelled seriously with a
gentleman, and has given up his acquaintance ever since, because

he did not eat the skin of two brace of tench which he had sent him as a present. Monsieur Montgomerie confessed, in my hearing, that he had thrown away the skin, and I never saw the Marquis so angry; indeed I heard him muttering to himself very often during the evening, and was tempted to listen to what he was saying. It was always the same sentence which he was repeating over and over again, namely, ' He did not eat the skin ! He did not eat the skin!' which proves that it must be very good, or so fine a judge would not have dwelt so much on the fact of Monsieur Montgomerie's neglecting to eat it."

"Well," said Hope, laughing, "I shall remember this in future. I am afraid I should have fallen into the same disgrace as Monsieur Montgomerie if I had eaten tench in the presence of the Marquis. But here is the receipt; and as you say there are very fine fish of that sort in this water, if you wish to please the Marquis when next he comes to your house, bait your ground a day or two before with a few handsful of small pills of this paste, and then either angle or set your lines when you wish to produce the fish. I will answer for it that you will not be disappointed ; but as the writing is probably not very legible, I may as well read what I have written."

He read, while Pinel looked over his shoulder : " First, Take the hard roe of a salmon (if you cannot get salmon-roe, the hard roe of any other fish will do, but that of the salmon is best); to every table-spoonful of roe add a bit of butter the size of a hazel nut, and put the whole before a gentle fire to warm slowly. When the heat is sufficient to melt the butter, the eggs of the roe become soft and burst, so that when the mass is well beaten with a wooden spoon, it will become of the consistency of pomatum.

" Secondly, For every spoonful of this roe pomatum add two spoonsful of finely-ground flour (bean-flour is best); beat the flour and the roe together, adding from time to time a drop or two of honey, and work up the mass with the hands till you have a firm paste of the consistency of baker's dough. A small quantity of finely-clipped wool may be worked into the paste to give it greater tenacity on the hook; but if the paste is well made this is not necessary. It is the best paste ever tried for carp or tench; indeed no leather-mouthed fish can withstand its temptations."

"There," said Hope, as he finished reading; "there is the receipt, and you are the only person in France who possesses it."

"I am so grateful," answered Pinel, "and I give you a thousand thanks. I hope you will never give it to any one else, for I shall take care to keep it to myself."

"Norman still," said Hope, as he exchanged a glance with Cross, who was busily employed in packing up his tackle.

"Shall I take the fish up to the carriage?" asked the boatman.

"Do so," replied Cross.

"You have such a quantity," said Pinel; "what will you do with all those fine perch? they will be spoilt before you can eat them."

"That is true," answered Cross; "and I suppose you would like to have some? Well, where is your basket? you are welcome to the half."

Pinel's eyes glistened with pleasure; his basket was taken off, and a full half of the day's sport was placed in it.

"They will be astonished when I get home."

"I will bet five francs he will say he caught them himself," said Hope, in English.

"Of course he will," answered Cross, laughing. "I fear, in our country, your fisherman often forgets what the keeper has done when he produces and brags of his basket; but come on— it is getting late, and it will be dark before we are out of that confounded lane."

"If the gentlemen will walk up the river with me," broke in Pinel, "I will show them all the best places. I am so much obliged to them that I will do for them what I would not do for any one else; there are two or three places for a night-line that nobody knows of except myself."

"It is too late, I fear," answered Cross. "You know the lane as well as I do, and another upset in the dark would not be agreeable."

"Send on the boy with the carriage," suggested Pinel. "It will be all the lighter, and you can join it at the cabaret in the hollow, where I propose to stop to-night."

"Not a bad plan," said Cross, "if you, Hope, are up to the walk; and to tell you the truth I recommend it, for the jolts will not do your shoulder much good."

Hope declared himself quite able for the walk, so they packed everything into the carriage, gave directions to the boy, and started. Their progress was slow, for they had to wait while Pinel wound up some of his lines and set others, which were to remain through the night and be lifted in the morning. The evening closed rapidly in; no rain fell, but the wind rose, and the clouds were so black that it was quite dark long before they reached the main road. They were also obliged to move slowly on account of Hope's helpless arm, which made him fear falling, and they therefore walked cautiously along the sort of path by the river-side. Hope, however, did not regret the delay, as he was delighted with watching the great number of glow-worms which were scattered in all directions up the little valley, and which seemed brighter than any of the same kind he had ever seen before. On remarking this to Cross, he told him he had made the same observation himself, never having seen glow-worms so bright as in that part of Normandy, and he pointed out the faint gleam of the males as they flew away from the females, when they passed.

"That is certainly very singular," said Hope, when Cross pointed out a male that rose from the grass, on which the gleam of light showed brighter than any they had before observed. "Fire-flies, of course, I have seen in millions at Naples, and more especially in the chestnut forests at Lucca Baths; but I never before saw the light on the male glow-worm. How do you account for this being the case here more than in hotter climates?"

"Glow-worms are carnivorous, and, like our friend the Marquis, they think snails excellent; at least I conclude so, for in confinement snails are the only food I can get them to eat. Now, as this country swarms with snails, glow-worms must have fine feeding, and being strong, I suppose, makes their light the brighter; added to which, I have always observed that these insects show a brighter ray before a storm; and if we required any further warning to get on, they now give it us, for I have never seen them brighter than to-night; and see," he continued, pointing to his feet, " here are a number of the luminous centipedes, who are, if possible, brighter than the glow-worms, for look, my shoes are quite covered with the shining liquid they have cast on them."

Hope looked at a large heap of rotten leaves which Cross had disturbed; several patches of phosphorescent light were flickering on the place, and the point of his friend's shoe was brighter than the leaves. The winter gales had drifted great quantities of dead leaves into the hollow where they were then standing, and there they had lain and rotted during the spring and summer. Hope began to kick at this mass, and at every kick he disturbed one of these centipedes (the Scolopendra electrica); the effect was most singular, for in a minute several yards of this mass of rotten leaves looked like a bank of pale blue fire."

" What an old baby you are!" exclaimed Cross. " You must have seen these creatures before; so do not dawdle any more; it is high time we were under cover, for it is growing darker and more stormy every moment."

"Baby, do you call me?" answered Hope; "I can tell you I consider my research to be highly scientific; I only wish my shoulder was not so painful, and I would stay here till the storm burst to see how long this light would last. It is true I have seen these insects often before, but almost always singly, and here I have kicked up more than a score of them in half a minute. The king of the Scolopendræ must give a court ball to-night to have such a gathering; for these centipedes are carnivorous, and they say in England pugnacious too, but there I never saw more than one or two together in the same spot, while here the place seems alive with them. Pray, how do you account for that?"

"Why, warmth, moisture—not too much of either—and plenty of food, I imagine, may lead them to congregate in such a spot as this; but now you make the remark, I think you are right, and that they are more numerous and more gregarious here than at home. I remember finding upwards of fifty of them on one evening, by stirring up a bank of dead leaves that had drifted along the outside of my garden hedge; but we can talk over this as well in the carriage as here, and seriously, we ought to be off, if we don't wish to be drowned, for the storm, when it does break, will be a snuffler."

This last appeal made Hope give up his examination. They moved off at a quicker pace, and did not again pause till they reached the cabaret, where they found the boy waiting. They took leave of their companion, clambered up into the carriage, and in a minute more were rattling along a broad excellent road at Blacky's best pace. The thunder began to growl in the west while they were still some distance from their journey's end; and as they advanced it came nearer and nearer, till just as they entered the town, a heavy peal rolled close to them, large drops of rain began to fall, and as they drove up to the inn the storm burst in all its fury. The rain fell in torrents, the wind howled, and peal upon peal of thunder made the very house shake. There were few guests in the inn, so that in less than five minutes their rooms were secured, and their portmanteaus placed in them. Cross undertook the ordering of supper, and Hope went to the window. The rain was falling in sheets, and the water was rushing down the street like a torrent; but he did not stop to look long, for a flash of lightning that nearly blinded him made him start back, and the roar of thunder which followed instantaneously made his heart jump. "We are lucky to be under cover," he exclaimed; "and thank God I am not at sea to-night."

In spite of the quantity of cold pie they had eaten at the lake, supper was not unwelcome. They consumed a good portion of their own fish, with other articles of food, and went to bed, where they soon fell fast asleep, although the wind howled round the house, shaking the crazy, ill-finished windows, in a way that would have kept most people wakeful. A long day, and but little sleep the night before, prevented the friends from being very delicate, so that the wind and thunder roared unheard by them five minutes after they were in bed.

CHAPTER XIII.

THE MOLE AFTER A GALE.

THE morning broke somewhat brighter; the rain had ceased, but the wind was still very high.

"We shall see the coast in all its glory this morning," said Cross, when they met; "and you may get a good look at the fishing-boats, for they are all sure to be in the harbour to-day; at least, if you are able to go out, for I see you have your arm in a sling."

"I can go out quite well," answered Hope; "for I have no pain, though my arm is as black as my hat, and so stiff I cannot lift it; but let us order breakfast, and then see what is to be seen."

Breakfast over, they started for the port; and as the day was still threatening, they each threw a cloak over their shoulders before they left the house. The streets were scoured by the rush of water that had flowed along them. Hope remarked on the fact, and found, from Cross, that these natural scourings were a blessing to the town, which without them would be neither clean nor sweet. As they turned into the main street several groups of women were seen clustered together, gazing at a straight canal-like river down which a great body of water was pouring. Their large dark eyes, handsome faces, and white oriental-looking caps, made these groups highly picturesque. Hope paused to look at them.

"What can have brought all these women together?" he said.

"They are the servants and washerwomen of the town, but

their occupation is gone for to-day. The rain of last night must
have been tremendous, for I never saw such a flood in this burn
before. Where you now see that mass of water rushing along
with such fury, there is in general a long quiet pool with a dam
at each end, and you may see many hundreds of women washing
the clothes and household linen of their masters and employers
in it ; but this to-day is impossible, for the place where they
usually kneel at their work is now two or three feet under water.
The grouping, as we now see it, is more picturesque ; but when
they are all at work the sight is very curious and striking to an
English eye, as we always connect washing clothes with the
adjuncts of a comfortable house, plenty of hot water, tubs, and
soap-suds ; but here, rain or fair, you see hundreds of women
kneeling in a row along the banks of that broad ditch, each
with a heavy mall pounding some unfortunate master's shirts
into ribands, or hammering his sheets and table-cloths into
holes by thumping them on a stone or lump of wood ; and that
operation they call washing. But this you can see at any time ;
so to-day we may as well move on to the port and look at the
sea in all its glory."

Hope said nothing, but walked on, while Cross led. One
broad street conducted to the harbour, which was crowded with
vessels and fishing-boats ; these were all aground, for the tide
was out, and many of them were leaning over in most picturesque irregularity, the masts and yards crossing in all directions,
but the hulls taking no harm as they lay in the soft muddy bed
of the basin. On each side of the old quay numbers of boats
were ranged in order ; these were all standing on their keels,
being properly shored up and secured ; and along the mole,
nearly a quarter of a mile in length, larger fishing-boats and
trading-vessels of all sorts were similarly arranged.

"You will have a famous opportunity for examining the
fishing-boats," said Cross, "and I wish you would do so carefully. You will see them here of all sorts and sizes, from five
tons burthen up to fifty ; but all are decked, the smallest as

well as the largest, and it is wonderful how very few lives are
lost on this coast. We never hear in this country, as with us
at home, of a whole fleet of boats being caught in a gale and the
half of them foundering in a heavy sea; and this I attribute to
the boats being all decked. Fain would I see the same practice
introduced on the coast of Scotland, as I am confident it would
prevent much of the dreadful suffering and misery which
periodically fall on our hardy fishermen. I shall never forget a
sight I once witnessed at ——. The day had been fine, and hundreds of boats went off to the herring-fishing. There were four
or five men in each boat, with their trains of nets. I stood on
the little jetty in the afternoon to watch these boats take their
departure for the fishing-ground. The great shoal of fish was
on a bank from seven to nine miles off the coast; and in this
direction all took their way, running before a gentle breeze, with
their many-coloured sails spread to the utmost, and looking like
a flight of butterflies as they faded in the distance. The air was
so soft and everything so beautiful that I lingered on the shore
till it was too dark to distinguish objects any longer, and then I
returned to the little inn where I had taken up my quarters.
Soon after I got there the wind began to moan slightly at intervals. About ten o'clock I was thinking of turning in when I
was startled by a rattling peal of thunder, and in a few minutes
more it was blowing a whole gale, the rain coming down as
heavily as it did last night. I was listening to the war of the
elements when gradually the voices of men and women became
mingled with the roar of the wind. I rang the bell several
times without being attended to, and at last I took my hat and
ran down stairs to learn the cause of the commotion which was
every moment increasing in the street. At the door of the
house I met the landlord entering; he was drenched to the
skin, as were also several tradesmen and curers who came
in immediately after him. In answer to my questions, I was
told that great alarm was felt for the herring-fishers, as, from
the quarter whence the gale was blowing, the boats would be

obliged to beat into the harbour, and the entrance was very dangerous, owing to reefs of rock which it would be difficult to avoid in such a night.

" Several gallant fellows, masters of smacks, had volunteered to go off in the lifeboat to carry lights to mark the end of the reef and to do their best to guide and assist the fishermen. The persons who had entered with the landlord had subscribed a sum of money to purchase spirits to give to the people when they came ashore, and for this they were then waiting. As soon as they had received their jars of whisky they again took their way to the shore. I joined them ; and oh, what a scene I beheld when I reached the little jetty ! what a change was there ! A few hours before all had been calm and beautiful ; now all was turmoil, terror, and despair. On the end of the quay a large bonfire had been made of old boats and herring-barrels. The oil and tar in the wood made it burn bright and clear, and the sparks were flying before the gale and casting a light for a long distance. When I reached this place the lifeboat had just pushed off ; there were five men in her, and they had a lantern hoisted on a short pole in the bow. As they crossed the fire-light I saw these five hardy fellows stript to their woollen shirts, and, as they bent to their oars, it was a pleasure to look at the cool determination of their countenances. A few strokes removed them from my sight, and then I turned to examine the faces of the crowd who had clustered to see the boat start. There had been a faint cheer as she pushed off ; and what a study for a painter did I see ? The greater part of that crowd was composed of women, some young and handsome, some old and decrepit ; some led weeping children by the hand, some held infants in their arms ; all were drenched with rain, and all were moved by one passion—that of intense anxiety and fear for some loved one who was braving the dangers of the sea on such a night. But, although one passion ruled all, how varied was the expression which it gave to the different countenances ! One stood with her face distorted by emotion, straining her eyes in looking seaward ; at her side another stood, the picture of despair, and her looks were to heaven. One woman pressed her infant to her breast, with her tears falling as fast as the rain ; while close before me one old woman struck a boy whom she held by the hand, and who was crying aloud by her side ; ' Whisht ye,' she said as she struck him, ' keep yer greeting till it's wanted ; Lord knows but ye may be a faitherless bairn afore morning, and I a bairnless mither !' This incident seemed to me a confirmation of the saying that all women are cross when they are frightened. The woman's face was the image of terror ; and she beat her grandson because he too was frightened ; and how often may you see a woman rush from her door to snatch up her child in the street and save it from being run over by some passing cart or carriage, while, if the danger be imminent, in nine cases out of ten the child gets a beating while the mother weeps."

" You are as bad as Pope," said Hope, " thus to interlard your story with strictures on woman."

" You wrong me," replied Cross. " I am no maligner of the fairer half of creation ; I give you but a sketch from nature ; but if it does not bore you, I must finish my story, for what I saw has happened scores of times, and will happen again and again, if our people do not learn to put a lid to the pot by decking their open boats."

" Pray go on," said Hope. " You were describing the looks of the people when the lifeboat pushed off."

" And I had plenty of time to do so," continued Cross ; " and plenty of faces to examine, for I do not believe there was a living soul in the village who was not on the shore that night ; the very collie dogs were wandering about, following the young things at whose feet they were accustomed to sleep. Sometimes the fire on the quay burnt low, and then I could distinguish a little glimmering light pitching fearfully out at sea ; it was the lantern in the lifeboat ; her gallant crew had reached the reef, and were lying on their oars in the surf, to watch the boats as they came in.

" I had been more than two hours on the shore when I heard
a faint shout, and observed a great commotion among the people.
I asked what it was. An old man to whom I spoke told me
that some of the boats were coming in. 'My eyes are too auld
to see myself,' said he ; 'but I hear those say so that have
keener eyesight.' The old man had been sitting down, wrapped
in his plaid, under the shelter of the parapet of the quay. I
too, for some while past, had sought the same cover, for though
I did not like to go home, I felt the wind bitterly cold as it
blew over my drenched clothes, and was glad to avail myself of
the warmth which the beacon fire and the low parapet afforded.
The old man, then, however, sprang up; I did the same; and we
went to the other side of the quay. Numbers of women were
pressing for the same point, and some of them looked nearly mad
with excitement. Several boats could now be seen, two of which
were close to the quay. I heard a scream, and a woman's voice
crying out, 'It's he ! it's he ! he's safe !' and in the next moment
I saw the old man dragging a young woman, who had fainted,
through the crowd. I lent my assistance, and together we
carried her under the shelter of the parapet. Some of the better
class joined us, bringing their whisky, which they presented as
a cure for every ill ; but some one said, 'It's Jemmy Ferguson's
wife, and he's safe, poor fellow. That's his boat just come in.'
The sound roused her, for she gave two or three gasps, and then
burst into hysterical weeping, which ceased, however, when a
tall handsome lad pushed through the crowd and took her in his
arms. He made no objections to the offered dram, and his wife
accepted some too from his hand. 'Keep your heart up, Mary,'
he said ; 'you will require it. I fear we are ruined, for we were
forced to leave the nets.' 'I care not,' she replied ; 'you are
safe, and I am thankful.' A number of people then pressed
round Ferguson, and began to question him. His young wife
half lay on his breast as he answered them. They learnt that
there was a tremendous sea running outside the reef and on the
bank ; the lifeboat had guided them in, and would be the means

of saving all who reached the mouth of the harbour; but he
reported that, when they cut their nets, several boats had already
foundered, as the sea had got up so quickly that the waves had
broken into some of those where the men, having their nets half
drawn, had not time to cut them away, and they had foundered
as they lay. Some of the unfortunate men had been picked up
by the other boats; but 'a hantle,' Jemmy said, 'must be
drowned.' Who they might be, he could not tell. He also
said that one boat had swamped close to them as they were
beating in; that his boat had made two or three tacks over
the ground where she went down, but they had not seen any
one floating, so that he feared they all sank with the boat!
The excitement that then took place was far too painful to be
witnessed; to describe it would be impossible; and as more
boats began to come in, each bringing worse news, the screams
of despair in some, and of hysterical joy in others, would have
melted a heart of stone. I know," continued Cross, "I could
not stand it, so I fairly turned tail and ran to my inn. Not a
soul was in the house; and after sitting a while to compose
myself, I became aware how cold and wet I was, so I changed
my clothes, and rolling myself in a blanket, lay down to recover
a little warmth. To sleep was impossible; therefore when day
dawned I arose and again returned to the shore. The rain had
ceased, and the wind, though still high, had shifted more to the
northward, so that nearly all the boats which had lived through
the night had run into harbour. The people were no longer
near the quay, they were now crowding together at a rocky
point about half a mile to the southward. Their occupation was
soon but too evident; two or three groups broke from the
general mass, and came towards the village. Each group was
the bearer of the body of some poor fellow who had gone on his
last long voyage. These were borne to a long shed used for
gutting herrings, and there they were laid out, side by side,
instead of being taken to their different homes. Why, I knew
not, but so it was; and the wails of mothers and widows that I

heard around that shed was a sound I shall never forget if I
live a thousand years.   Truly sings our Scottish bard when he
makes the fisherwoman say—

> ' Buy my caller herring;
> Though ye may ca' them vulgar faring,
> Wives and mothers, maist despairing,
>   Ca' them lives of men ;

and lives of men they cost that night, for thirty-two boats were
lost, and ninety-one poor fellows perished.   I saw sixty-three
laid out in the shed, and followed their bodies to the grave.
Some of the others were never seen again ; the rest were picked
up along the shore and among the rocks at different times during
the next fortnight.   And this was not all, for numbers of the
fishermen were ruined by the loss of their nets ; some, it is true,
recovered theirs, and found them filled with fish ; but in most
cases the herring were much damaged and torn by the dog-fish
which had got among them.   Amongst the fortunate few was
Ferguson's boat.   He had made fast a large buoy before cutting
loose, and this had guided them in their search.   But observe,
all this loss of life and property arose from the boats being
open ; for every boat that was lost either foundered at the nets,
or was swamped in the sea.   Had they been decked, the men
could have hung on and taken their nets on board without the
fear of foundering.   A few seas might break on board of them ;
but with a deck the boat would rise again as the sea rolled past ;
and with their nets on board, they might have beat back to their
own harbour, or run before the gale to some other.   They could
have carried on much longer, seeing that with a deck a plank or
two under water is of no consequence, whereas, in an open boat
the helmsman is obliged to luff up at every squall, deadening his
way ; or if water does come aboard, even though not enough to
swamp them, a moderate quantity spoils the sailing and the
buoyancy of the craft.   No, no ! give me a lid to the pot; and
I wish I could only persuade our countrymen to be of my
opinion on this subject, and copy the Frenchmen."

"But in a calm," asked Hope; "how do these Frenchmen get along?"

"Remarkably well," answered Cross; "in their larger boats they have sweeps, in the smaller ones they have oars, and they get along quite as well as our fellows do in the heavy wherries on the west coast, or even in the lighter and better built luggers on the east. But the best way is for you to come on board some of them and judge for yourself. I am bound, however, to say that these French boats are much more heavily manned than ours. Here, they generally have nine men for a crew; with us, rarely more than five, and often not so many; so that a French lugger with four sweeps, double-manned, and one to steer, can shove their craft along at a great pace."

While Cross was relating the latter part of his story they had been standing at the end of a slip where small craft were loading and unloading their cargoes. It was exactly where the old quay joined the mole, and no better place could be found for making the examination which Cross proposed. They walked down the incline towards some of the larger boats that were lying there, and in so doing they passed a man who was super-intending the unloading of a smack which was charged with a cargo of salt, and alongside of this vessel lay another of the same size, into which a number of carts were emptying loads of bullock's horns. "A curious trade they seem to carry on here," said Hope, "and not a very sweet one."

"But it is profitable, gentlemen," said the man to whom the first seemed to belong. His accent proved at once that he was an Englishman; but both Hope and Cross took a second look at the speaker to make sure that they were not mistaken, for he wore a mustache, a blouse, and a pair of sabots.

"Are you an Englishman?" asked Hope.

"Yes, sir," he said; "I am a Northumberland man. You are looking at my dress when you ask the question; but you

have heard the saying, ' when you are at Rome do as the Romans
do ;' so now that I am in France I do as Frenchmen do.   I have
married a Jersey woman, and own two or three of these craft,
with which I carry on a pretty brisk trade both here and at St.
Malo.   I am settled now, but I have seen a good deal of the
world, and tried my hand at many things.   My first lucky haul
was buying herrings in the North, and that makes me still like
to dabble a bit in fish."

    " Have you ever tried your hand at fishing yourself ?" asked
Cross.

    "Ay, ay, sir, at every sort—from trawling to long lines.   I
have tried curing too ; and to say the truth, the last trade is the
best, for a sharp fellow, with a little cash, can always get the
weather-gauge of the fishermen."

    "Then you know," said Hope, "the different modes of
fishing practised here, and on the coasts at home.   I should feel
greatly obliged if you would come down to one of these boats,
and show me in what they differ from ours in the north
country."

    " Willingly, sir.   My name is James Allan ; and you have a
bit of a burr on your tongue as you speak that makes me suspect
you to come from the North.   Shrimps and north countrymen,
they say, aye stick together ; and although I am half a Frenchman now, I have always a weak side to a countryman ; if I may
make so bold, I would ask your names, and whether I have
made a right guess in saying you hail from north of the Tyne ?"

    Hope told his own name and Cross's, and congratulated
Allan on the correctness of his ear, telling him that they were
both Scotchmen, and that the comparison he wished to make
was more as regarded the Scotch and French fishings than those
of the South.

    " There is hardly any comparison to make," answered Allan,
" for there is no herring or cod and ling fishing on this coast,
—that is to say, none to speak of ; the great fishing here is trawling for flat fish and dredging for oysters.   Some few boats

from here go as far as the Firth of Forth to the herring-fishing;
they carry great heavy trains of nets with them, but I suspect
they buy more than they catch. They have famous boats, strong
crews, and their nets are beautifully formed and fitted ; but,
after all, I do not think a Frenchman is a good fisherman. For
instance, their trawls are admirably made, better even than those
out of Torbay; but they never will stick to their own mode of
fishing, and in consequence it is astonishing how little they catch
in comparison with what they ought. When I was in a trawler
we always studied the run of the tide to an inch, and ran as
clear before it as we could ; we would have thought any man
mad who stood across the run of the tide when his trawl was
down, and the reason is plain enough. When you run fair with
the tide the trawl knocks up the sand and mud at the bottom,
and the tide sweeps it along faster than the net ; this, as a
matter of course, makes a cloud in the water and hides the net ;
the fish, when they are started and frightened, run into this
cloud to hide themselves, and they are hard and fast in the bag
before they know where they are. Whereas when you trawl
even one point off the run of the tide, the cloud of sand and
mud going with the stream leaves a part of the net bare, which
the fish see, and they dash clear of it. Any man who pretends
to trawl ought to know this, yet the fishermen here will take no
advice. They persist in dragging up and down the run of the
banks without paying the slightest attention to the tide ; and
as the greatest length of the banks is exactly across the general
run of the tide, the consequence of their plan is, that they take
mighty few fish, although, as I have already said, they have as
fine boats and nets as ever were put in the sea."

"And do the Scotch trawlers," asked Hope, "pay the same
attention to the tides that the south-country men do ?"

" In Scotland," answered Allan, "more's the pity, very little
attention is paid to trawling ; indeed, almost all the trawl-boats,
especially on the west coast, are from England or from the south
of Ireland ; the Irishmen in the north are as bad as Scotchmen

about this mode of fishing ; and it is a thousand pities that
nothing is done to stir them up a bit.   I once saw a trawl come
up after being down for an hour, and it was nearly full of turbot,
brill, and plaice.   This was on a bank at the north end of
Rachlin.   Our skipper put down the net for a trial ; but as we
were running at the time from Barra to Liverpool with a cargo
of live cod in the well, we had no time to waste, or, I am sure,
we could have filled our vessel by drifting over that bank for a
tide or two."

"And what is the difference in the nets ?" asked Hope.

"You can see," answered Allan ; and he pointed to a large
three-masted lugger by which they were standing.   The bag of
the trawl was hoisted to the mainmast ; the beam lay along the
deck.   There was little or no difference either in the net or the
beam from those used on the British coast ; but the bottom here
was of chain, and fitted in loops exactly as the double-handed
prawn-nets were, and this Allan pointed out, saying, "that it
was a very great improvement on the lead line in common use
with us ;" and he said that he believed this method was now
partially in use on the south coast in England, but that in
general the English fishermen still stick to the rope and lead.

From the net they proceeded to the examination of the boat.
The one they were then examining had three masts; her rig was
a jib and three huge lug-sails.   The hull was roughly built, but
Allan pointed out the excellence of her model.   She was decked
all over, having, however, a large hatchway amidships, which
was always closed in bad weather, leaving only a small scuttle
open abaft, by which the men could go below.   Allan pointed
out all the merits of the boat; but then he could not help
having a wipe at her imperfections.   "I wish you could just
see her jib," he said, "a beastly cut thing that would disgrace a
nigger; and then her lugs—they never dip them as we do ; they
are cut in such a fashion that if one is right, 'tother's wrong,
clapping against the mast in such a way, that on a wind I can
give them two points and a half, and beat them easy; although,

when going free, they go two lengths for my one. I assure you, gentlemen, it's a pity to see such nice bottoms so lubberly handled."

" And yet," said Hope, " I hear that very few of them are ever lost."

" True enough, sir," answered Allan ; " but for that you may thank the boat as much as the men. The boats are first-rate in a sea, and the people don't risk themselves more than is necessary. If they do get caught in a gale like last night, they have always cover to keep the sea out of them, and they reef as close as they like, and run for here or the rocks of Chausey without any fear of filling or swamping by the way."

" Ah ! there is the very point I wanted to get to," said Hope. " Do you think it an advantage or not that the fishing-boats on our coast should be decked as these are ?"

" An advantage !" cried Allan ; " to be sure I do. Just look at all those craft lying out in the mud there. How many of them would have got home, think you, in the gale of last night if they had been open ? Why, I stood at the end of the new quay to see some of them round the head, and I can tell you that they were taking in the green seas clean over all ; but then they were up again like a bung. In the nasty cross sea that was then running no boat could keep dry, and an open boat would have filled and gone down in five minutes ; whereas these fellows got their feet wet, and had to hold on now and then, and there was the worst of it. If they have had anything like this gale in the north, I suspect there will be bad news from the herring-fishers, and I am much afraid it will be so. We never have a snuffler here like that of last night and this morning without their catching it on the English and Scotch coasts ; and when it comes in the height of the fishing season, then a lot of poor fellows are sure to lose the number of their mess. Once every three or four years they get caught, and then widows are more plenty than fish."

" We are quite aware of that fact," said Hope, " but Mr.

Cross here thinks that if our boats were decked like these
Frenchmen, these wholesale losses would be greatly lessened,
if not completely prevented."

"I quite agree with the gentleman," said Allan. "In all
the great losses that I have heard of it is by the foundering of
the boats that lives are lost. Some of them, certainly, get driven
ashore, and the boats are smashed, but then the men are saved. A
Frenchman is precious pig-headed, but I suspect our own people
have a touch of the same nature too, for they will stick to the
open boats. They say the boats are lighter and more handy, if
they have to take to the oars, when they have no deck ; and no
doubt they are right in that, for a deck must always weigh something, be it ever so light. But these Frenchmen shove along
very well with their oars, and the devil's in it if a Scotchman
cannot do as well as a Frenchman. It's prejudice and laziness
combined that make them stick to a plan that risks their lives
and properties far more than they need to do. I think the
gentleman quite right," continued Allan, "and he will do a good
turn to the men's wives and bairns if he will persuade the
husbands to take a leaf out of the Frenchman's book. If you
come along the old quay you will be able to see a lot of the
smaller boats ; they are not so big as our boats, and yet they are
all decked, and fitted exactly like the one we are now looking at
—deck, hatchway, and all. The decks, to be sure, are light and
thin enough, but they keep the sea out as well as if they were
stronger.

On the strength of this proposal, they scrambled along the
old quay, and found that what Allan had said was quite true.
They examined several of the boats, looked at the shape of the
oars, and the way in which the rowlocks were fitted on raised
stanchions, so as to enable the men to pull ;—the only difference
between the larger and the lesser boats being that the largest
had three masts, three lug-sails and a jib, some of them carrying
a fourth lug as a topsail on the mainmast. The smaller had two
masts, two lugs ; and all carried the same ill-cut, triangular-look-

ing jib, on the unsightliness of which Allan was eloquently
abusive.

"Come to the end of the mole, gentlemen," said Allan ; "you
will get a good look at the.sort of sea these boats ran through
last night.   I daresay the sea is as wild, and the coast wilder,
in the north ; but you will be able to judge of what these boats
can do by seeing what an ugly breaking jabble gets up when it
blows hard, and meets the tide running over the sandbanks,
which you meet everywhere along this coast.   Harbours are not
very plenty on the east coast of Scotland, but they are still
scarcer here, and being all half-tide harbours, the boats are
sometimes obliged to stand off and on for hours before they dare
run in, and yet very few of them are ever lost."

As Hope was anxious to look at the sea outside of the mole,
they took their way along the splendid building.   It was a
curious sight to look down from the great height on the vessels
below.   The rise and fall of the tide being forty-four feet, and
it being dead low-water, they saw the whole height, upwards of
sixty feet, with a parapet to seaward seven feet high, the whole
built of large blocks of dressed granite.   When they reached the
platform at the end, they mounted on the carriages of the heavy
guns that were placed there, and looked down on the angry
waters.   It was still blowing very hard, and the spray dashed
in their faces as soon as they raised their heads above the parapet.
The sea itself had a yellowish tint, that, as Cross said, would
make drowning peculiarly disagreeable ; and as they looked
down on the raging waves that curled and broke in quick succession below them, it gave a strong and disagreeable impression
of danger for those who were obliged to encounter it, and yet it
was exciting to watch, and wonder at the power that gave such
motion to the elements.   They had stood for some time looking
and conversing with Allan on the greater or lesser danger of
navigating different parts of the ocean in different parts of the
world, when their attention was drawn to a number of people
who were hurrying along the rocky promontory which lay behind

them. Men and women could be seen clustering on its highest ridge ; all were apparently looking at some object that was hid from their eyes by the point of land which trended out for some distance to the westward.

"What can be happening there?" said Hope, turning to Allan.

"I suspect it must be some vessel," he answered, "that has got crippled in the gale, and is coming in here. They must be strangers on the coast, or they never would try to come in at this time of tide, for if they do they are sure to take the ground on some of the banks, and then nothing can save them."

"You are right," said Cross ; "is not that a vessel coming in sight at the point?"

"As sure as death it is," shouted Allan, as he sprang from the gun-carriage, "and if she is not warned to haul her wind, and stand for Chausey, every soul on board is doomed."

"But how can she be warned?" asked Hope. "No voice on earth could be heard ten yards off in such a gale."

"A boat must go to her," said Allan ; "it is the only chance."

"But no boat could live in that sea," said Cross.

"A good boat could get out, sir," answered Allan ; "the great danger would be in coming back ; but if the men got on board the vessel and went with her to Chausey they would be safe enough. They may lose the boat, but better that, though, than lose the men."

As he spoke, shouts were heard at the further end of the mole, and a crowd was seen hurrying towards them. As it approached, they saw that the leading man was an officer in the French naval service, who was closely followed by a number of smart active-looking lads, some of whom were evidently French men-of-warsmen ; others were the fishermen and sailors belonging to the vessels in the harbour. The crowd stopped when they came to a part of the mole about a hundred yards from where the friends were standing, and they heard the officer say, "Volunteers to man the boat!" A number of men started forward, and Allan ran towards them shouting that he for one was ready. Hope and Cross followed more slowly. When they joined the crowd the officer had made his selection. He had chosen eight men out of a great number of brave fellows who had come forward to volunteer their services. Allan was speaking to the officer as they came up. " I am obliged to you," was the answer that he made, " but this is a post of honour, and I must keep it for my own men. Now, now, be quick," he said ; " there is not a moment to lose." The men he had selected ran down a ladder made of copper wire, which was fixed to the side of the building, and jumped on board of a revenue cutter that was lying at the outside of the merchant vessels that lined the harbour. In another minute they were stripped, and on board of an excellent boat. The oars were out, and the men pulled gallantly for the head of the mole. Numbers of women came running up, and they cheered the men as they gave way. The men raised their faces to return the greeting, and as they did so Hope and Cross recognised Frederic, who was pulling one of the oars. They joined their voices to the shout, and then ran to take their former places on the gun-carriage. As the boat rounded the mole, a heavy breaking sea struck her, and for a moment they could hardly see the men ; but she went ahead, and though she pitched fearfully to each fresh wave, still she advanced. "She'll do," said Allan ; " she's through the worst of it. She'll get the sea fairer now that she's clear of the back surge. They're smart fellows those, and they have a first-rate boat, if she had but a sharp stern instead of that square one. There's no fear of them going out, but there are too many eyes looking on, and I fear they will try and come back for the sake of the brag ; and if they do, the Lord have mercy on them !"

" They are fine brave fellows," said Hope, "and they go to work like men who know what they are about. If there is real danger, they never will be so foolish as to run an unnecessary and useless risk."

" Look how many pairs of black eyes there are looking from

under white caps," answered Allan ; " there is no knowing what a sailor will not do for the sake of a petticoat ; our own people are foolish enough when women are in the way, and the French are ten times worse than we are. They are all young fellows in the boat, and I am sadly afraid they will come to some mishap by trying to get back, although I heard the officer warn them not to do so. A Norway skiff or a whale-boat might make it out, but that square stern will never rise to a following breaking sea, and, as sure as death, if they try it they will get pooped and swamp."

Hope and Cross, as they stood on the gun-carriage, grasped it hard, and held their breath, as each sea struck the boat, the white spray flying over the men. Numbers of women had joined them, and hung clustering round the guns ; and many more climbed on to the parapet, where they sat, careless of the spray, which must have wet them through. Numbers of men were there also, and the crowd was increasing every moment. Each party, as they arrived, and got a sight of the boat, gave a cheer, to which the first comers replied; so that a sort of perpetual running shout might be heard along the whole length of the mole. A gun was now fired from the hill, and the people on board the vessel seemed to have seen the boat pulling off to them, for they lay to, and the minute after they were pitching bows under, at a quarter of a mile from the point.

" She's very deep," said Allan, " and she makes such bad weather of it, she has either sprung a leak or shifted her cargo. The wind's getting a bit more to the north, which is lucky for her, or she would be pinched to make Chausey. After all, you may see she's drifting to leeward like a wash-tub."

The vessel was certainly in a very shattered-looking state, but as she drifted she approached the boat, which was pulling manfully towards her. As they advanced, the sea, though equally heavy, did not break so much, and they advanced more rapidly, so that, in half an hour from the time they rounded the mole, hundreds of anxious eyes had the pleasure of seeing them round to under the lee of the vessel.

"Thank goodness!" said Allan, "they are wiser fellows than I thought them; they are going aboard; they have got a line from the ship and are hauling up; and there goes one aboard—hurrah!"

This last exclamation was made as a man from the bow of the boat sprang into the vessel.

"By all that's good!" he said, "they're putting about, and the sloop has let down her foresail, and is standing on."

The women, when they saw this manœuvre, gave a loud shout.

"Fools! fools!" said Allan; "if you care for those men you would hold your skirling, for it's a hundred chances to one if ever you see them alive again."

Before the boat was a hundred yards clear of the shelter of the sloop, it was observed that they had met with some accident; two of the oars were stowed, the four upper ones only rowing.

"What is it?" asked Allan of a man who was standing on the gun-carriage near them, and who had a telescope, through which he was looking.

"A sea has broke into them," answered the man, "and they are baling; but they are getting on finely with the upper oars. Well done! they cleared that one well."

"He knows what he is about, the lad that is steering," said Allan; "or that last breaker would have done for them." He finished his speech with a groan, which was echoed by a hundred voices that ran along the whole length of the mole. A heavy sea had curled up just behind the boat, and had broken as it reached it. Boat, men, and all, were hid for a quarter of a minute in the white foam; but then again a shout was heard, for the boat reappeared. She was afloat, but that was all. Two men only were rowing; all the rest were baling with their caps. The boat had changed its direction, and instead of pulling for the head of the mole, they were now steering for a rocky point which lay at the back of the quay nearer the shore. There was a heavy surf breaking on the rocks, but still the sea was broken, and there was one small creek among the black points where it was possible the boat might be saved.

A number of people began to run along the mole towards these rocks. Cross was among them. Hope and Allan were so intensely attracted by the motions of the boat that they never missed him.

" It is the wisest thing they could do," said Allan. " But oh, I am wae for them ; if they get another breaker they are gone." The words were hardly out of his mouth when a wave curled high above them, and they were lost to sight. A groan louder than before echoed along the quay, and this time it was followed by no shout of joy. A babel of voices, crying, groaning, and screaming, sounded instead ; for when the wave had passed, the boat was gone, and the heads of the struggling crew alone were seen, as they struck out for the shore, or clung to the floating oars. The boat had been very rapidly driving before the wind and waves, so that when the final catastrophe took place, they were not many hundred yards from the shore ; but before reaching it the heaviest breakers were to be passed, and Hope felt that the men were gone.

" It is too painful to witness," he said, as he sprang from his elevated position, and ran with the crowd towards the shore. He was unable, however, to continue his pace for more than a minute, for in jumping down he had struck his injured arm. Such was his excitement, he did not feel any pain at the moment ; but after running a very short distance, he suddenly became so sick and faint he was unable to move his limbs ; his eyes swam, his head turned, and, in spite of himself, he sank down on some logs of wood that were piled against the parapet, and there for some time he lay almost insensible.

And while he is there let us follow Cross.

When he saw the boat upset he ran with all his speed to the end of the quay, where he turned sharp to the left through a break in the parapet, which led down a steep incline to the low rocks

which formed the back of the mole. He knew the place well,
for at these rocks boats were accustomed to take on board or
land passengers from the steamboats or packets when the tide
was so far out as to prevent these vessels from entering the
harbour. In ordinary weather there was a certain amount of
shelter at this place which rendered such a proceeding practi-
cable, although even in the finest weather it was a most disagreeable and uncomfortable proceeding. The rocks were of the same
coralline formation as those which they had examined at St.
Jean de Thomas, rising in ridges and lumps like huge sponges;
between these ridges were the same sort of hollows as on other
parts of the coast, but instead of being filled with water, as thay
are on the open shore, here they were filled with soft stinking
mud, the refuse from the harbour, which, drifting out with the
tide, is thrown back by the eddy caused by the mole. The rocks
themselves were partially covered with the same slimy substance
and with short green sea-ware, which rendered them extremely
slippery and difficult to walk on. With naked feet, or even with
thin shoes, it was a service of danger to cross them; for the soft
mud, yielding to the pressure of the foot, laid bare numberless
little sharp angles of the rock that cut like knives; but it was
over these rocks that Cross took his way with undiminished
speed. He was not alone or first, for some way before him ran
a girl, who had thrown off her gown, petticoat, and sabots, and
heedless of the pain she must have suffered from treading on
the rock, she rushed towards the mass that projected the furthest
into the sea. The breakers were striking heavily on this point,
casting high their spray, and then rolling back in masses of
white foam. Yet, unappalled by such a scene, the moment the
girl reached the edge she plunged headlong into the water, rose
again to the surface, and swam through the raging surf with a
strength that seemed almost superhuman. Cross's eyes were
rivetted on this girl; he forgot for a moment to look to his footsteps, and the consequence was a tremendous tumble. Before
he could rise, a number of female porters and some men over-

took and passed him, taking no notice of his misfortune, for all
eyes were fixed on the sea and on the girl.

When Cross rose with cut hands and knees, he continued
his way, limping, it is true, and therefore not so rapidly; but all
thought of his own pain vanished in a moment when, on looking
to the sea, he saw the gallant girl returning to the point,
struggling stoutly with the raging water, and supporting a man
with one hand while she struck out with the other. In a
moment he was by the edge of the rock, in another he was in
the sea, and several men with him. He struck out, striving to
help the girl, but the waves were too strong for him; one
heavier than the rest struck him before he had gone many yards,
and threw him back on the rocks. One of the Amazonian
porters seized him and pulled him out. "Stay where you are,
you fool! you are not able for this work," was the civil address
he received from the lady as she dashed off to assist in pulling
out the girl and the man. There was a shout as they were
drawn on the rocks, and a murmur of voices saying, "He is not
dead." But then there was a cry of despair from one voice, and
high above the rest Cross heard the words, "It is not he."
There was a dash into the water, and the same girl was again
forcing her way through the surge as if with magic strength.
In less than a minute she had grasped a second body; it was
clinging to a broken oar, which enabled her to raise the head as
she turned to the shore, and thus gave her some assistance. As
she proceeded, two of the young men joined her, and together
they were soon within reach of several men and women who
were holding on in a line as they stood up to their necks in the
water. All were soon on the rocks, where, by this time, a large
crowd had assembled. Some oars had been brought and a rope
twisted round them, to form stretchers. The first man who
landed had thrown off a great deal of the water he had swallowed;
he was groaning, but alive, and a number of hands soon placed
him on the rude bed prepared for him. The second man was
also disgorging the salt water, and his eyes opened for a moment;

but then they closed, and a livid hue as of death came over his features. " Poor boy, he is gone, I fear," said one of the women ; and a wild shriek was the response from a girl who threw herself on the body ; it was the same who had saved him—the same gallant girl who had made such marvellous and successful efforts in his behalf. " Lift up his heels, and let the water run out of him," said a number of voices, and they were in the act of executing their prescription when Cross ran forward. He had recognised the girl and the man she had saved as Angela and her betrothed Frederic. " For Heaven's sake do not lift his legs," he said ; " you will kill him ; life is not yet extinct, but it hangs by a thread. Angela, you know me ; keep up his head and get him to a bed as fast as you can, and he may yet be saved."

There was a murmur of discontent at this interference of Cross's, and some voices were heard saying "A bas les goddam." One woman, however—the same who had assisted Cross and then called him a fool—interfered on his side. " The Englishman is right," she said, " and he is not a bad fellow—he did his best— don't you see he is all wet ? He is right, I say ; lift him on to the stretcher, and keep his head up." " Oh, he is a good and a kind gentleman," said Angela ; " do as he bids you." There was a growl, but the order was obeyed. The stretcher was brought forward ; coats, petticoats, and shawls were thrown upon it. Poor inanimate Frederic was lifted up, and Cross and Angela supported his head ; more clothes were thrown on him, and Cross, as they advanced, picked up his cloak from the rock where he had thrown it, and laid it on the sufferer.

" Courage !" said Cross to Angela, as they began their march at as rapid a pace as the ground would permit. " Let some one run on and prepare a bed, and get as large a fire as you can." Two or three started to obey this order ; the rest of the crowd pressed round, each in turn lending a hand to carry the stretcher ; and thus they left the rocks, mounted the incline, and reached the break in the parapet that took them on to the quay, where they were joined by Hope ; so we may as well return to him also.

When he recovered, he found himself quite alone ; and after looking about for a moment, he rallied sufficiently to be able to move on. His motions, however, were slow ; and as he walked to the end of the mole, he was obliged again to sit down to recover from the giddiness which overcame him. This time he sat down on a block of granite, a number of which were lying at the extreme end of the parapet, exactly at the spot where the narrow road led down to the rocks at the back of the quay. The loud hum of voices soon drew his attention in that direction. He saw a number of people advancing up the slope ; they were bearing something on two oars. As they came near, he saw that it was the body of a man that was lying on the oars, which were used as a temporary stretcher. Some men walked on either side supporting his head, and a considerable crowd followed, the women moaning and wringing their hands. The man was alive, but that was all that could be said for him. To Hope's inquiries, the only answer he could get was that he was not dead yet. This party had hardly passed when he saw another following close behind. The crowd in this case was considerably larger than the first, and they pressed so closely together, it was not till they came to the narrow passage through the wall of the parapet that he saw that this party were surrounding a second body, on one side of which walked Cross, who was assisting a girl in supporting the head of a man, who, to all appearance, was quite dead. The eyes were closed, and the head lay without motion on the shoulder of the girl who walked beside him. A second look which he gave at the girl convinced him that he had seen her before ; and as she came close to him he recognised Angela. But there was such a look of despair in her face, it was painful to look at. Her long black hair hung dripping wet over her back and neck. Her feet were bare and streaming with blood, and she had nothing on but her stays and shift, from which the water was dripping as she passed. On the body lay Cross's cloak, and under it were seen a number of men's jackets and women's woollen shawls and petticoats. Hope ran forward to join this party. He took off his own cloak and threw it on Angela's shoulders, who seemed quite unaware of what had been done. She was bewildered with grief, nor did Hope wonder, for all was understood in a moment when he looked at the body they were carrying; and in the livid face he recognised the handsome features of Frederic. As he looked, he saw a slight motion in one of the hands, and a quiver in the lips.

"Keep up his head," he said; "and, quick, get him into the first bed you can reach. In the meantime, let me open a vein." He took from his pocket a case of lancets, bade the people stop for a moment with a voice and manner so commanding that he was obeyed. He immediately went to the body and opened the temporal artery, which was filled and swollen so as to be seen without difficulty. "Now forward," he said, "as fast as you can." At the first puncture of the artery, only a drop followed the lancet, but as the people advanced, the blood began to flow —first slowly, and then in little jets. Frederic began to gasp, and then to disgorge water in considerable quantities. His eyes opened, and he gazed around him for a moment, and then sank back with a heavy groan.

This took place just as they entered a street behind the custom-house.

"Cheer up, Angela," said Cross. "Thank God, he is safe. See how freely he bleeds. With care, there is no fear of him."

Angela heard the words, though the greater part of the crowd did not. Joy took the place of despair. It was too much for the poor girl; she gave a scream, and fell back into Cross's arms in strong hysterics, at the very moment the bearers turned into a door with their burden. Cross bore Angela in his arms, entering the house close behind the stretcher; and as soon as he had entered, an old man shut the door, and barred it.

"We must keep the crowd out," he said, "or those women will give the poor fellow no chance. Here, Marie, look after the girl."

It was fortunate that the old man had barred the door, for a

rush was made at it, and loud shouts and execrations were heard
against the English. When Angela fell back into Cross's arms,
the cloak fell off, and showed her white dress covered with the
blood which had flowed from Frederic's temple. A spirit of
anger had grown among the ignorant crowd. They had been
contradicted and commanded by two Englishmen—people whom
they considered to be the cause of the misfortune that had befallen them. They made no allowance for the braggadocio spirit
that had led their countrymen to try to return, contrary to the
advice of their own commanding officer and of common prudence ;
they only chose to remember that it was to save an English
vessel that the risk had been run. Five of their fellow-towns-
men had sunk before their eyes ; two had been landed, and these
two it was their good pleasure to think that the Englishmen on
shore had tried to murder. One of these offenders had prevented their hoisting the half-drowned man up by the heels to
let the water run out of him ; and another had stuck a knife in
him—for such was the term they gave to Hope's use of the
lancet. One stirred up the other. Each moment the crowd
increased in the street, and nothing could be heard but howls
and execrations against England and Englishmen. The principal
leaders of this commotion were the female porters, who, in the
port of Granville, do all those laborious duties which in our
own country we generally see discharged by the strongest men.
They form a sort of association among themselves, and, like our
navigators, allow none to join their body or ply their trade
without their special permission. If at any time a man should
presume to act, or offer his services to any new arrival, he is
threatened the first time ; if he transgresses again, he is
either thrown over the quay, rolled in the mud, or otherwise
ill-treated. In language and manners they greatly resemble
certain ladies who sell fish at Billingsgate market. But the porters of Granville have one advantage over the fishwives of Billingsgate, for among them may be seen many faces eminently handsome. These fair furies were the rulers of the storm that raged

in the street in front of the door where Frederic and Angela had been borne. One old woman, in particular, was in a frenzy of excitement. She acted as a sort of fugleman to the members of the society of porters. They echoed her cries, and from them it passed on to the dense crowd that nearly filled the street.

"Open the door, René," was the constant cry, "or we will knock it down. A bas les Anglais! turn out les sacr-r-r-é goddam, till we tear them in pieces, the assassins."

René, the owner of the house, was an old pilot; age and hard service had sobered him down, and quieted his national excitability. He stood at the back of his door, placing every now and then a fresh prop against it, to resist the blows and pushes which were made with the intention of forcing it open.

"The devil take me," he said, "but they are all gone mad; there will be no bearing these women soon; they grow worse and worse every day. But I must warn these Englishmen, or they will break in in spite of me; and if they get hold of them in their present humour, ill will come of it.

The house, fortunately, had no lower windows to the street. René's wife and daughter kept a sort of marine store. The room to the front was the principal receptacle of the ropes, iron, etc. etc., in which they dealt. The window had been built up to give more room for storing these heavy articles, leaving only a small grated aperture to give light and air to the place. The back room was the kitchen, in which the old man slept; and above was the state-room and sleeping apartment of the daughter. It was to this upper room that Angela had been taken by René's daughter Marie, who took off her wet and blood-stained coverings before she had recovered from her half-fainting state. Frederic had been carried into the kitchen, where he was stript by the man who carried him, assisted by old Madame René and by the same woman who had taken Cross's part. The bed had been dragged on to the floor close to the fire, and on this Frederic was laid.

Hope knelt by his side, keeping his finger on the artery to

stop the now profuse bleeding, while as many as could reach Frederic rubbed him with hot towels or bits of blanket which the others heated at the fire. He had begun to groan almost immediately after he was laid in bed, and after a while the gasping of his breathing became more regular and less convulsed. His eyes had opened several times, but without any return of consciousness.

"I wish to goodness we could get a surgeon," said Hope, looking up at Cross; "my arm is so painful, I can do nothing, and it is absolutely necessary to put a stitch in this artery, for I cannot stop the bleeding without."

Cross opened the door, wishing himself to run in search of the aid Hope required; but as soon as he was in the passage the roar of voices and the blows on the door sounded so formidable that he paused and looked towards the old man, who was standing guard at the back of his own door. While in the kitchen the sound had been partially deadened, and the attention of every one had been so riveted on what they were doing that little heed had been paid to the turmoil without; but now Cross was fully aware of the excitement in the street, as some of the exclamations against his country were too loud and distinct not to be heard.

"What is the matter?" he asked; "and what is the meaning of this disturbance?"

"Why, the devil's the matter," answered old René; "for he is the master at present, and he has got his own crew of those she-devils with him. I wish to heaven you and your friend were safely out of my house, for if they get in, there will be blood shed; I am afraid this old door won't stand much longer."

A tremendous clatter sounded on the door, which cracked under the blow, several splinters starting into the passage.

"Confound them!" he said, "they have got stones now; you must up stairs into my girl's room, we can keep them out of that for a bit."

Cross knew not exactly what to do; he was pausing, in some

anxiety, to consider how he could get out to get a medical man, when he felt some one touch him behind; he looked round; it was Allan.

"Run, sir, for Heaven's sake," he said; "they are bringing up an old top-mast, and the door will be down in a minute."

"But the poor fellow will bleed to death," said Cross, "if we do not get a doctor."

"We have got one," said Allan; "there is no fear for him, but there is for us—come." He caught Cross by the arm, and pulled him into the kitchen, closing the door behind him. A stranger was kneeling in the place where he had left Hope, and by his side knelt Angela with her hands clasped on her breast, and tears streaming down her cheeks. "He's safe, he's safe; he has spoken;" and there followed an incoherent flow of prayers, praises, and thanksgivings. But there was no time to look or listen more; another tremendous crack was heard against the outer door—so loud, indeed, that every one in the room started up.

"Fly for your lives," said Allan; "I know these devils better than you." He pushed Cross towards a second door which was standing open, and Hope was in front of it. This door led into a small court, into which Allan pushed the two friends, shut the door behind him, and pointed to a short ladder standing against the wall of the yard, underneath the window of a shed belonging to the next house. As the friends did not move, he renewed his cries. "Up," he said, "if you do not wish to be murdered, and to see me share your fate for helping you."

This was enough; on they dashed, ran up the ladder, and in a few seconds Allan was with them. He drew up the ladder, and closed the wooden shutter of the window.

"I'm glad you are well out of that," he said, as soon as he regained his breath. "They might be sorry for it afterwards; but had they got hold of us, they would have done for us all, as sure as death."

"And what for?" asked Hope.

"Just because their blood's up. Those poor fellows wished to make a sensation, as they call it, did a foolish and absurd act, and have got themselves drowned ; and because this misfortune happened when they went to help an English vessel, they will knock the brains out of any Englishman they catch during the next four or five hours. After that they will calm down again, if they have nothing else to start them, but till then we must keep out of sight if we wish to keep out of harm's way. I know them well, and I can tell you there are not such a set of devils on earth as these women, if they get their blood up."

"Hark !" said Hope, as a shout, louder than any they had heard reached them. It was followed by a dead silence ; and then the voice of a woman was audible, as if making a speech. The sound of the voice was clearly heard, but they could not distinguish the words.

"It is big Phrosyne," said Allan, "the woman that has been so useful. I know her voice; she is one of themselves, and a sort of leader. She'll do more good than a company of soldiers. We can slip down from here, and get into the next house ; the owner is a friend of mine. We may get a peep from one of the open windows, if you keep well out of sight, and then we shall know what is going on."

The friends were only too glad to agree to this proposal, for they felt both bored and ashamed of skulking in a hay-loft, hiding from a danger of which they were ignorant.

"Come along," said Hope, "it is absurd to be bullied by a pack of women ; come into the next house if you will, but no peeping ; we will show ourselves at once, and see whether they dare to touch us."

"I beg your pardon, sir," said Allan, "but I hope you will be prudent. You agree with me in saying those poor fellows lost their lives by bravado ; I hope you won't follow so bad an example. No mob is just ; men, when excited, are bad enough, but Granville women are the worst of all."

Hope felt his cheeks tingle ; he blushed with shame, for he

felt he had met with a just reproof, though administered gently, and by a man far below him in station. He held out his hand to Allan, and said—

"You are right, and I am wrong. I am old enough to be wiser, but years have not, and I fear never will, cool the hot blood that runs in my veins, which makes me always kick at anything like injustice ; but as you truly say there is no courage in running into useless danger, so I will be as prudent as you wish, and I see Mr. Cross quite agrees with you in thinking me an old fool."

"Not a bit," said Cross. "Mr. Allan and I have been longer among these people than you have, so we know them better, and I quite agree with him in thinking that we had better not show ourselves for some hours ; but that is no reason why we should not see them. After such a gale the outside shutters are sure to be closed in the upper rooms, and we can look through the openings and see all that is going on without the slightest chance of being seen ourselves. Come away then, Hope. Mr. Allan, will you lead the way ?"

Allan did as he was asked. He went down a small trap stair, through a cow-byre and a small yard, entered a house by the back door, and led the way up stairs to a good-sized room on the second floor. Several people were in the room, but these were not very clearly seen, as the room was nearly dark, the only light which entered being admitted through two small venetian blinds which were fixed in the strong outside shutters, which, as Cross had supposed, were closed and barred.

Allan went up to one of these people and spoke to him. He immediately came up to the friends and bade them welcome. He spoke to some young men who were standing at one of the windows, who immediately withdrew, making room for the friends to take their places. They held back, apologising for deranging them, but the first person who had met them insisted on their going forward. Hope and Cross expressed their thanks, and took the offered places.

The window at which they found themselves commanded a complete view of all that was going forward, for there was a slight turn in the street where the house stood, so that they could see not only the whole length of the street, but the door and windows of the house which they had lately left. The street was filled with people immediately in front of the house. The crowd was almost entirely composed of women. At a greater distance were men, some dressed in the blouses of countrymen, others in the round jackets of seamen. These last were laughing and cheering on the women, but they took no part themselves in the riot. Exactly in front of the door stood two rows of women holding bits of rope in their hands, and between these ranks lay the half of a broken mast. The shutters of the next house had been thrown open as well as the windows, and at one of them stood the old pilot René and his daughter, at the other the woman whom Allan had called " Big Phrosyne." M. Menard, the master of their present refuge, told them that the women holding the ropes had brought up the mast slung between them, and were going to use it as a battering-ram against the door, when big Phrosyne had thrown open the shutters and called to them to stop. Seeing her there, they had done so, and for a moment were silent. She had then made them a speech, telling them that one of the half-drowned men was in the house, and that if they made a noise they would kill him, whereas that if they were quiet there were hopes of him. There was a sort of cheer upon hearing this announce-ment, and a number of the people were beginning to go away, when the old woman who had been so conspicuous from the beginning stopped them, and insisted that the Englishmen should be turned out that they might throw them over the quay. Phrosyne told them there were no Englishmen in the house, which the old fury said was a lie, and she became very violent ; upon which several still wished to force the door, but the others would not let them, so the party was divided. " Phrosyne," said Monsieur Menard, " as you see, is mustering her forces from

777

the window, and you may observe the old woman bustling about among the rest, setting them on for a rush. And I fear," added their host, "that she will succeed, for the men are cheering them on from the sheer love of mischief. A message has gone to the barracks, but if they are not sharp, the soldiers will be too late."

As he spoke, the cries were renewed of "A bas les Anglais" —"Mort aux Anglais"—"Give us the goddams, and we will show them ros-beef; turn them out, or we will take them."

At the same time a rush was made from the back of the crowd, led on by the old woman, and the twenty or thirty girls who were standing by the broken mast shortened the ropes and lifted it from the ground.

"Shame! shame!" shouted Phrosyne; but the old woman carried the day. One of the drowned men had been cast on shore, and some of the people were bringing him up the street; at this sight the girls began to come forward with the mast, swinging it backwards and forwards as they came.

"There will be the devil to pay now, and no pitch hot," said Allan; "I am right glad we are in snug quarters, for the sight of that poor fellow's body has set them up again. Big Phrosyne has lost her power, and that old wretch has the best of it."

A new sound, however, now struck the ear; it was the rap-tap, rap-tap-tap of a drum; the men in the distance began to move, and in the next moment a body of soldiers charged into sight, driving the crowd before them with their bayonets.

The men yielded quietly; the women set up a screech of rage, and sent a volley of stones at the men, to which they paid not the least attention, but moved steadily forward, and drew up in front of René's house. The officer cut some joke which caused a roar of laughter, and in five minutes all was order. The crowd began rapidly to disperse; so that in ten minutes after the soldiers appeared the street was comparatively empty.

"I suppose we may go now," said Hope, addressing Allan.

Allan shook his head, and repeated Hope's proposal to the master of the house.

" O no, gentlemen," he said, "I hope you will not attempt to go. If you will do me the honour to remain here a little, I will send out to ascertain when the streets are quiet. To tell you the truth, I am not very anxious to show myself to-day, for I am not over popular among the Granvillaise. I have a great regard for your countrymen, for I find them excellent customers and honest. I do not belong to the town, but have settled here some years, and have been the means of scattering a great deal of English money in the neighbourhood; for I buy cattle, which I send every week to Jersey; eggs, wheat, and large quantities of potatoes, which I send to England; and I bring back coals, iron, and good English gold, the greatest part of which I spread through the country, in payment to the farmers for the articles I buy. This does a great deal of good to them; and I might do good to myself if these ladies would let me alone, but this very year they have cost me two thousand francs damages by throwing my potatoes into the sea and turning my cattle adrift, because they said that provisions were dear, and that I was the cause. Added to which, I have been twice stoned the whole length of the street, and once escaped as if by a miracle from being thrown over the quay. Whenever there is a disturbance in the town, if they see me, I am sure to come in for a share of their displeasure; so I take good care now to keep out of their sight, and I venture to advise you gentlemen to do the same. The wind is falling, and the sky looks so dark that I suspect we shall have some rain. If it comes down pretty heavy, you may go when you please, for a good heavy shower quiets these ladies better than anything else. But if it keeps dry, I recommend you to remain where you are till dusk, and then my young man can lend you a couple of blouses to disguise you as you go home."

"We would like very much," said Hope, "to see how poor Frederic is getting on. Can we not go out at your door and in at Monsieur René's?"

"Now that the soldiers are here, you can in safety; but if
any one sees you coming out of my house, they are sure to do me
some damage for sheltering you. I would therefore request that
you would do me the favour of going by the way you came. Mr.
Allan took the doctor that road when he went to fetch you
away."

This was too reasonable a proposal to be objected to. Hope
and Cross expressed their thanks; and, led by Allan, they took
their way down stairs, to clamber, by means of the ladder, again
into René's house. As they passed a door they looked into
a large shop. It was too dark to see the contents. Cross
asked Allan what Menard sold besides cattle and potatoes.

"He is a rich fellow," he answered, "and sells everything
from an anchor to a pocket-comb. If you want anything while
you are here, you will find him as reasonable as any one in the
country."

"And we certainly must buy something," said Hope, "whether
we want it or not, just to show our goodwill and gratitude for
his protection."

They mounted into the loft, lowered the ladder, and entered
René's kitchen. Frederic was sitting up in the bed, which still
lay on the floor. The surgeon was administering some hot soup
to his patient. Angela, Madame René, and her daughter, were
propping him up with pillows. The old man and big Phrosyne
were looking on. The other men were gone.

As soon as they were observed, Angela came up to them,
took their hands, one after the other, and pressed them to her
lips. "You, sir," she said, turning to Cross, "did your best to
save him—Phrosyne told me so; and the doctor tells me, sir
(turning to Hope), that to your presence of mind he owes his
recovery. May Heaven bless you both." The poor girl could
hardly speak, and tears ran fast down her cheeks as she strove to
do so.

Frederic tried to speak, but the doctor interfered. "No
speaking," he said; "you must take this soup and a little com-

posing draught I have sent for—then sleep. You will wake as
well as ever ; and Angela must do the same. She has done
more this day than would kill fifty girls. I have more fear for
her than you."

"I cannot leave him, sir ; I could not sleep," answered
Angela.

"But you must," said the doctor. "Here, Marie, take her
up stairs and put her to bed ; my bottle will do the rest and insure obedience—and here it comes." The doctor poured out a
small modicum for Frederic and a much larger dose for Angela.
"Now drink to each other," he said ; "and do as I bid you."

"Do," said Hope, "it is better for both. Let me see you
take your draught, and we will go."

"It is pouring of rain," said the messenger.

"So much the better," said the doctor ; "you will find the
streets quiet ; although I hope by this time the people know
what Frederic owes to this gentleman's skill. I took good care
to tell the men before they went out, and they promised to go
all over the town to make it known ; for I was deeply grieved
to hear of their injustice towards you."

"Oh, never mind us," said Cross. "This poor fellow is safe,
and Angela must take care of herself; so I will add my voice
to the doctor's to ask her to take his prescription, and then we
will all go together. Angela swallowed her portion, Frederic
his, and then held out his arms to Angela. She forgot all eyes,
and threw herself into them. She arose, blushing scarlet, but
no one even smiled. Hope led her to the door, where Marie
was waiting for her. "That's a good girl," said Hope, in a
whisper; "now take care of yourself. There is no fear for
Frederic ; the love of such a girl is worth all the doctor's stuff
in France."

Cross turned back to the doctor, and invited him to dine
with them at their hotel, to bring the news of his patients ;
"and come," he said, "half an hour before the dinner hour if
you can, for my friend has hurt himself, and though he pretends

to know something of your profession, I am a sad ignoramus, and I should like to have your advice."

When they were fairly in the passage they saw that all the props and barricades had been removed from the door ; it was standing open, but sadly shattered.

"It is raining very heavily, gentlemen," said old René ; "so you are quite safe ; but it may be as well to put on a couple of blouses—they will help to keep you dry, and prevent your being noticed."

This third allusion to the rain acting as a quietus on the excitability of a French mob made the friends laugh, but convinced them that there was some truth in it ; as the blouses were there, however, they thought it as well to put them on. Each slipped a douceur into the old man's hand as they donned their coverings, mentioning where they were staying, and observing that the door ought to be mended as soon as possible, and the bill sent to them.

Allan walked home with them, and at the door he wished to say good-bye ; but this they would not allow, and insisted that he should have one glass of grog there, and join them and the doctor at their late dinner. "We do not part with a countryman so easily," said Hope ; "so you must not refuse us."

"I am too much honoured to be so acknowledged," said Allan, "not gladly to accept so flattering an invitation, more especially from gentlemen so much above me in station." The speech and the bow that accompanied it showed that if Allan retained the honest integrity of his native land, he had profited by his residence in France to acquire some of its graces. And at dinner and during the evening he gave a marked example of the fact that it does not require to be high born to be high bred.

Education and his intercourse with different nations had given manner to this man born in a fisher's cottage ; modesty, and his desire to please, now gave him the indescribable tone of high breeding which all admire, yet very few possess. The doctor was clever and amusing ; he came at the appointed time ;

he prescribed for Hope's arm, ordering perfect quiet for a couple of days. He was all bows and parade, talked well, and told good professional anecdotes ; but how inferior was he to the more lowly-born guest who sat at the same table ! There is a manner in England, among a certain set of young men, known under the slang denomination of flash. English flash is bad enough ; but French is ten times worse ; and such was the doctor's manner. There was the presumption, the loud voice, the lay-down-the-law style, which makes an ill-bred Frenchman the most offensive of living beings ; and although he was amusing it was a relief when he made his bow. Allan smiled when Cross observed, " Now the doctor's gone, some of us may get in a word edgeways." Allan took his leave shortly after, and the two friends were not sorry to retire to their rooms.

The next morning all signs of the storm were past. The sun shone bright and clear; and when Cross opened his eyes, the busy hum of voices was heard in the street. Cross rose immediately ; but when he was dressed, he found that Hope had passed a feverish night, and was too unwell to rise. The doctor had promised to call early to see the one patient, and report on the state of the others. He kept his word. He was skilful in his profession, for Hope felt almost immediate relief from his external and internal prescriptions ; and he brought all the news which they were anxious to hear. Frederic was almost perfectly well, no bad symptom remaining except a partial loss of voice, with slight pain in the chest. He was extremely triumphant on this score, for the other poor fellow, who was attended by a brother practitioner, was a great deal worse, suffering from intense headache and almost total loss of voice. The day before he had given Hope the credit due to his bold practice of preventing apoplectic symptoms by opening the temporal artery ; that morning he seemed totally to forget to whom he was speaking, for he launched forth on the wisdom of such a proceeding in all cases of drowning ; but he took all the merit of the act to himself. Angela was well, except a great feeling of languor—"the natural consequence," said the doctor, "of the great excitement she had undergone, and of the strong opiate I administered; but you must content yourselves, gentlemen," he continued, "with my report, for whatever interest you may take in these young people, you must not think of going near the harbour to-day. All the bodies of the poor fellows have been found, and they are to be buried this afternoon; the excitement is therefore very great. All round the harbour, and in the old town, I regret to say, the same feeling of hatred exists against your country, and all that belongs to it, that you witnessed yesterday. It is as well, therefore, that Mr. Hope must keep his bed to-day; and I recommend you, sir" (turning to Cross), "not to go out either, or if you must, do not go farther than the Cabane, if you wish to avoid being insulted, or perhaps ill-treated."

"Well," said Cross, "that is no great punishment, and I suppose this feeling will not last long."

"O, no," answered the doctor; "in a couple of days they will have forgotten all about this misfortune. The funeral to-day keeps it alive, but as soon as that is over, there will come something else for them to think of. I will have the pleasure to call to-morrow; in the meantime I make my bow."

As soon as the doctor was gone, Hope said, "I was very feverish last night, and you will hardly guess what my thoughts were dwelling on."

"I suppose," answered Cross, "on some of the scenes you witnessed yesterday."

"Not exactly," said Hope; "do you remember the nonsense we were talking about the superstitions of the Highlanders, Normans, and Bretons, when we were looking at that congregation of magpies near the Mare de Bouillon?"

"Yes, perfectly," answered Cross.

"Well, then, all last night, when I was restless and tossing about, the thought would come over me of the five parties of four that we saw hopping about, and of what you said of them, —namely, that we should hear of five deaths, but none that we

would care about ; and thinks I to myself, I shall hate to look
at magpies again, for this is enough to make a low-countryman
superstitious, and doubly to confirm all the nonsense in which,
as a Highlander, I am bound to believe."

"It is curious," said Cross, "and is just one of those acci-
dents that create the superstitions at which we laugh.   Once
in a hundred or a thousand times some dream comes true, or
some birds show themselves as these have done.   Such an event
is mentioned, is marvelled at, and superstition is created or confirmed, because these rare occurrences are mentioned and remembered ; but the nine hundred and ninety-nine cases which
come wrong are never talked of, and therefore never thought of.
If you or I live to be as old as Methuselah, we shall never see
such augury prove true again ; indeed, I doubt if anywhere in
the world except in Normandy we shall ever see so many magpies together again.   But now go to sleep if you can.   After
breakfast, in spite of the doctor's warning, I shall go out as far
as the Cabane to see the newspapers, and I will try to find you
something to read whenever you have had your nap."

"There is nothing else for it, I suppose," said Hope, as he
turned on his side : "you have destroyed my romance, so I may
as well sleep."

Hope remained so unwell during the next two days, he was
unable to leave the house.   They received news of Frederic and
Angela from the doctor, but did not see them, as they had removed to their own homes, which Cross did not know.   They
heard, however, that they were quite recovered.   On the evening
of the third day Hope and Cross took their way to the Cabane,
where they could read the papers and breathe the sea-air, while
they watched the bathers from the windows ; the Cabane being
a sort of half coffee-house, half club, built of wood against the
rocks close to the sea where all the people bathed.   There were
in this building two good rooms ; in one were a number of
publications and newspapers, not to mention chess and card
tables ; the other was appropriated to the ladies in the morning

for music and work, and in the evening it was used as an assembly or ball-room. When the tide was high the ladies bathed within twenty yards of the windows, dressing and undressing in small portable canvas houses, and swimming in their blue dresses with the most perfect composure. Hope was much amused watching them, and quite agreed with Cross in saying that the French ladies had greatly the advantage of our countrywomen in this respect. The most fastidious could not find fault with their delicacy, for in their blue flannel blouses and trousers they were perfectly dressed, and in a dress in which they could learn to swim, of which power all seemed to have availed themselves, for there was not one in fifty who did not swim, and swim well.

They loitered thus till it was time to return for dinner; and Hope felt quite himself again from enjoying both the amusement and the fresh sea-breeze. As they passed through the rocky passage which leads from the shore to the town they saw a gaily-dressed group waiting in the road. As soon as they came in sight, two of the party came forward to meet them. One of these was Frederic; the other was little Matilde, dressed so gaily they did not at first recognise her. She had put on for the first time the dress which the friends had ordered for her, and was waiting to meet them as they came from the Cabane. Having first called at the inn, she had learnt where they were.

"Angela is to be married to-morrow," said little Matilde, as she came up to them; "and she has sent me with Frederic to say how much she would feel honoured if you would come to the dance in the evening."

"And so shall I, gentlemen," said Frederic. "Your presence will add one more to the great obligations I owe to you. I believe I owe my life to your skill, and I would fain desire that you should witness my happiness in joining my fate with the brave girl who gave you the power to save me."

"And we shall be most happy to come," answered Hope; "but you must tell us where."

"M. Menard has lent us his store," said Frederic. "Anybody can show it you."

"M. Menard, who lives next to René the pilot?"

"Yes, sir."

"Thanks," said Cross. "You may rely on seeing us to-morrow." They shook hands with Frederic, patted Matilde's cheek, and went on.

"We must go to M. Menard's to-morrow to buy some present for the bride ; for in this part of the country, when people in her station marry and give a dance, each guest brings an offering in his hand, which he presents to the nouvelle marieé—in short, the custom is one which resembles very much the old-fashioned penny-weddings of Scotland, where every friend brought something towards establishing the young couple. You and I must not be behind the rest of the guests, for, after her conduct of yesterday, I am much mistaken if we do not find a large assembly, each member of which will strain a point to make as liberal a gift as he can afford."

"It is curious," said Hope, "to see so many of the same customs and superstitions in this country as in Scotland ; for although England and Normandy are so closely allied, Scotland, whatever it has to do with Norsemen, has very little to do with the Normans ; and yet the habits and superstitions which I observe resemble much more those of Scottish Highlanders than of the English."

"You seem to forget," said Cross ; "it is true that the Normans never conquered Scotland, but many of our greatest families married Norman wives. France also was in close alliance with Scotland when at war with England ; but I suspect that the customs and superstitions which you have remarked here do not come directly either from conquest, marriage, or national alliance with Scotland, but have spread out of Brittany. The Bretons are distinctly Celts ; their language, habits, customs, fables, superstitions, songs, and dances, clearly mark the race. It is not therefore surprising that you should find some of these customs here, and that you should observe their greater resemblance to the habits of the Highland Celt than to those of the English Saxon. The Welsh, the Irish, the Scottish Highlander, and the Breton are all Celts, and all members of the same family. It is not therefore surprising that at every step in Brittany you trace the family resemblance, or that such close neighbours as the Normans should have, to a certain degree, followed their example, or adopted some of their customs. Whether the plan of the penny-wedding be originally French or originally Celtic, I will not pretend to say—you find it in both countries; and you and I must try and find something worthy of the bride's acceptance to-morrow, both out of respect for that brave girl and love for old Scotland."

"Most assuredly," said Hope; "and what sort of things should we get?"

"Let us dine as fast as we can," said Cross, "and go down and consult Allan—he will know; and if we cannot find him, we can speak to Monsieur Menard."

The plan was agreed to. The friends dined, and took their way immediately after to Menard's shop. Allan was on the quay in the act of starting one of his smacks, whose cargo of horns was completed, and which was about to sail for England; he at once came with them when he heard what they wanted. In moving from the quay to M. Menard's shop they were followed by several of the women who had been so furiously enraged against them three days before; but now they were all smiles and good humour. Allan quietly whispered to one of the women to go away, and not disturb the gentlemen, who were going to bring a present for Angela. This news was quickly communicated to the rest of the party, all which was unheard by the two friends, who were talking together at the time; they were therefore both startled and surprised when they heard a loud clapping of hands, and a shout of "Vivent les Anglais! vive Angela!" and on turning round they saw the party dispersing.

"Hang me, but they are a queer people!" said Hope; "they will cut your throat one day and cheer you the next."

"We need not care," said Cross, "so long as we only meet them on cheering days; and as this is one of them, let us make the most of our time."

On entering M. Menard's shop, they were cordially greeted by the owner. After returning renewed thanks for the shelter he had afforded them, they mentioned the object of their visit, and held a council with him and Allan on what would be the most desirable present to give to the bride.

"I know one thing, gentlemen," said Allan, "that Frederic would like to have and that Angela might like to give him, but I fear it is too expensive, and you might not wish to spend so much money." He pointed to a sextant which was lying in its box, with the brass shining brightly on the dark counter. "He is now first officer in a ship bound for Cadiz, and he can hardly sail without either a quadrant or a sextant; and unless Monsieur Menard trusts him, he is too poor to pay for one till he comes back."

Hope asked the price. "There is no necessity for either running in debt or sailing without one," he said, "for Angela shall give him this one if you tell me it is good."

"I have a much better," said Monsieur Menard; "indeed, a better never went out of France than one I can show you, and you can have it for the same price I first asked; for," said he, laughing, "there is no dealing in Normandy without bargaining; and though not a Norman myself, habit becomes second nature; so now I can never sell anything without asking at least one-third more than I mean to take; but as you gentlemen seem to forget where you are, I must not take advantage of you. As you are willing to spend a certain sum, you shall have your money's worth—and here it is." He went to a drawer and produced an instrument in a brass-bound case.

"Thank you," said Hope; "when I give a thing I like it to be good, and I feel fortunate, I assure you, in falling into such hands as yours."

"He is an honour to the country," said Allan, as he slapped his hands on the counter; "and he shall have the first offer of every cargo I bring, in remembrance of what I have just seen."

"But I don't promise not to have a wrangle with you," said Menard, "for you are half a Norman."

"I am not afraid," said Allan, "and as a proof, let me have six best checked shirts, and cloth to make a Sunday suit; you shall fix the price yourself."

"That's hardly fair, Mr. Allan," said Menard, "for I shall be obliged to give them at prime cost. But never mind, I'll make up for loss on the next cargo of coals I buy from you."

"And what am I to have?" said Cross; "come, advise me, Monsieur Menard; I will spend the same sum as Mr. Hope."

M. Menard thought for a moment. "I have it," he said; and he pulled out a drawer, and after searching for a moment, he produced a large umbrella in a cotton case. The case was taken off, and the umbrella opened. "There," he said; "there is the largest and the brightest red silk umbrella ever seen in Granville; that will win Angela's heart, and break those of every bride in the town for the next two years. I can sell it cheap, for no one has been rich enough to buy it; so I have had it some time, and if you must spend as much as your friend we may make up the difference with a blue silk handkerchief for Frederic, and some stockings for the bride."

Cross was quite delighted with the purchase. The price was paid, and Monsieur Menard was requested to send the things to their hotel.

"You had better leave them here, gentlemen," he said. "You are going to the ball, I suppose, and so am I. As it is to take place in my store, close to this, it may save you trouble if you call for them here. And if you will permit me, I will go with you, as I have a little offering to make also."

The friends gladly accepted the proposal, as it obviated all difficulty about finding their way. So they departed, leaving their purchases behind them.

Shortly after the appointed hour the two friends again knocked at M. Menard's door. Allan and he were in waiting ; their purchases were neatly packed up and ready for them, and each took his own.

Monsieur Menard lifted a tolerably heavy basket and followed ; less than a minute brought them to the store, which they entered. It was a large room with a boarded floor ; the walls were originally bare ; but the stones were nearly hid with wreaths of leaves, flowers, and moss, in the midst of which hung some lamps and candles, by which the place was tolerably lighted. In one corner of the room was a table on which sat three fiddlers. A man in the dress of a sailor was blowing an accompaniment on a cornet-a-piston. All the musicians were hard at work when the party entered, and the floor was covered with dancers.

" They are no great hand at it," said Hope, after watching them for a while ; " I thought all French people danced like ballet-masters."

" You are thinking of the grisettes of Paris," answered Cross, " who certainly answer your description ; but in the provinces, more especially in this part of the country, the people are fully more ungraceful than the veriest bumpkins in an English country village. The heavy wooden sabots they wear give an ugly manner of moving the limbs, even when, on an occasion like this, they exchange the sabot for the lighter shoe."

" There are some among them," said Hope ; " who are graceful enough."

" Yes," answered Cross ; " those are the fisher girls ; and they have the same freedom of motion which you see among the Highland lasses ; and for the same reason—namely, they generally go bare-footed. But here comes the bride to bid us welcome."

Angela came forward, followed by her sister, little Matilde, and a few of her more intimate friends ; she did the honours with a modest grace that was very taking. She led the party

THE BRIDE AND HER UMBRELLA.

to the upper end of the room near the musicians. On the opposite corner a table was placed which was quite covered with the
presents which had been made to the bride. Monsieur Menard
presented his offering. There was a loud murmur of approbation
when his basket was opened ; it contained a large brass pot for
making soup, there were four stewpans, shining like silver, and
half a dozen iron spoons ; these were looked at, admired, and laid
on the table. Allan came next and presented his offering ; there
was the same murmur of applause, the same examination, the
same thanks, and they were placed on the table with the rest.

Hope had watched the proceedings of his two companions ;
so he now came forward and presented his gift with a little
speech very well turned. Angela's eyes filled with tears as she
said her thanks, and when the box was opened and the shining
brass of the instrument was seen, the murmur of applause was
followed by a clapping of hands, during which Frederic found
time to say, " You are too generous, sir, and I cannot sufficiently
thank you. Your present is most magnificent, and gives me
what I so much required, yet knew not where to get." Hope
shook him by the hand, and the sextant was laid on the table.

It was now Cross's turn. He too presented his gift, and
made a little speech. All eyes were turned on the cotton bag
which contained the umbrella, and when it was opened, and
the brilliant red silk was seen within, the murmurs of admiration gradually increased till they ended in shouts of applause.
The women pressed forward, the umbrella was put up and held
for general inspection, amidst shouts of " Superbe ! magnifique !"
and " Vivent les Anglais !"

" I knew that would please them," said Monsieur Menard to
Hope. " Every bride must have a red umbrella as part of her
turn-out. To have a silk one is a mark of distinction ; but to
have so large and so red a one has done what I told you it
would. It has made every woman in the room break the tenth
commandment. Your more valuable present filled Angela's eyes
with tears of gratitude, but look at her now—all smiles, and

her eyes beaming with triumph. That umbrella has made her the greatest woman in the district for the next two months, and she knows it. You must content yourself by dancing second with the bride, for if you took the lead you would forfeit your present popularity among the women ; for with them the red silk takes decided precedence of your brilliant sextant."

[Here ends the manuscript.]

NOTES.

—o—

THE SOLAN GOOSE, Page 36.

The following communications may be of interest to naturalists :

My Dear Sir,—On referring to " Yarrell's Birds" for a confirmation of the statement regarding the solan goose, I did not find any allusion to the bird's peculiar mode of hatching ; and as I have watched these birds pretty closely for years, and have myself failed to notice the singular position of the foot, I thought it right to refer to the tacksman of the Bass, as the best possible authority. His reply is so much to the point, and is, at the same time, such a confirmation of the author's remark, that I send you the letter.

CANTY BAY, *November* 26, 1862.
Sir,—In reply to your note, the Solan Goose sits with one foot on the egg and takes one month to hatch ; then it takes three months before the young can fly. Also, it disgorges its food while on the nest at the approach of strangers coming too near ; then when left alone picks it up again. The Solan Goose egg is very good to eat. The Queen gets a dish every year, and is very fond of them. Some people like the young ones to eat and others do not; but there are different ways of cooking them. Yours respectfully—GEORGE ADAMS.

It is somewhat strange, in a work of such a high reputation as Yarrell's, to find it stated on the authority of Selby that the gannets are so tame when sitting in their nests as to " allow themselves to be stroked by the hand without resistance." Tame they certainly are, but woe betide the hand that ventures to touch them. I should not like to try it, as any time I have approached " the poultry yard" on the south-west face of the Bass, in the month of May, the old birds then shot most wicked glances from their sharp eyes, and snapped their long and strong beaks in a manner not to be mistaken ; while a never-ending chorus of hoarse screams, something like Grog,

Grog, issued from the throats of hundreds of angry and alarmed sitters. One day an unfortunate rabbit, chased by a terrier, threw himself upon the tender mercies of these birds. They made short work of him ; he was killed, and passed from bill to bill in a twinkling.

Sir Robert Sibbald, in his " History of Fife" (1710), was, as far as I am aware, the first to notice the position of the foot ; he says, " They put the sole of their foot upon it (the egg), and foment it so till the young one be hatched." A century later this was confirmed by Dr. Walker, Professor of Natural History in Edinburgh, who mentions the fact in his " Essays on Natural History," 1808. Dr. Fleming, the latest writer on the subject, appears to doubt the accuracy of the observation, and thinks it " probable that the gannet rests on the egg in the nest as other birds do ; but in preparing to move, especially in retiring from an intruder, it does not hesitate to set its foot on the egg, and hence it has been imagined to embrace it always throughout the whole process of incubation." *

D. D.

THE MINAUR, Pages 187-190.

The following description of the *Octopus vulgaris* is taken from Verany's " Mollusques Méditerranéens." I am not quite certain, however, that it represents the animal known on the coast of Normandy as *The Minaur*.

" The common Poulp is scattered throughout the Mediterranean, " and is found on the coast of the Atlantic at the Canaries. Ac- " cording to facts collected by M. D'Orbigny, it has been met with at " Hayti, Cuba, Bahia, the Isle of France, East Indies, and in the Red " Sea. It is caught on the rugged shores of Liguria in all seasons, but " more plentifully in summer. This cephalopod lives almost always " amongst rocks, and generally hides itself in the holes and crevices, " into which it penetrates with great ease, its body being very supple " and elastic.

" It is in these recesses that he lies watching for the animals on " which he lives. As soon as he perceives them, he cautiously " leaves his den, darts like an arrow on his victim, which he wraps

* *The Bass Rock*, 8vo, Edin. 1847.

" himself about, clasps in his serpent-like arms, and fixes by means of
" his suckers. When he darts on his prey, he starts with his body
" in front. When he comes near it he turns round, opens his arms,
" and fastens on it with such rapidity one has scarcely time to
" observe him.

" Sometimes he places himself upon a sandy ground at a short
" distance from rocks, and is careful to construct a hiding-place.
" For this purpose he brings together in the form of a circle a
" quantity of pebbles, which he carries by fixing them on his arms
" by means of his suckers. Then, having formed a sort of crater, he
" ensconces himself in it, and there waits patiently for some fish or
" crab to pass, which he skilfully seizes. I have several times had an
" opportunity of verifying this fact in the roadstead of Villafranca.

" In summer the young pöulps also come to the pebbly shores,
" and they are sometimes met with in muddy places, from which
" they are taken by the trawl, together with numbers of eledon.
" They are usually fished for with a line without a hook ; instead of
" which is substituted a piece of dog-fish, a bit of a cuttle-fish, a
" white fish, a bone, a piece of suet, or some attractive substance
" weighted with a small stone. The boatman, holding a line in each
" hand, draws them very slowly along the rocky bottom. Scarcely
" does the pöulp see them but he darts upon the bait, and rolls it
" up in his arms ; the fisher, feeling the resistance, gently draws the
" line towards him, and finally brings it into a little net with a
" wooden handle, which he holds with the other hand, and catches
" him.

" They are also caught with a small olive branch fixed at the end
" of a rod, and fitted with a hook, which is drawn backwards and
" forwards before the openings of the holes and crevices of the rocks.

" Some very large ones are caught by the fishermen with the
" *leister*, or trident. When the young pöulps spread themselves in
" summer over the pebbly coasts, they are caught by means of a line
" weighted with lead, and furnished with a cork fitted with several
" hooks, covered with pieces of scarlet cloth twisted into thongs,
" which are thrown out as far as possible, and afterwards drawn in
" very gently. The pöulp darts eagerly at it ; the fisher, warned by
" the motion and the resistance, gives a sharp jerk, and almost always
" hooks the fish, and draws it quickly out.

" This fish furnishes at Nice an agreeable pastime for the fine
" summer evenings. The pöulps live for some time out of the water ;
" the fishermen are consequently obliged, in order not to lose them,
" to kill them immediately. This they do by biting their heads, or
" by sticking a knife into the big ones. The common pöulp is much
" more plentiful in the market of Nice than in that of Genoa.

" When it is young and little, it is a dainty morsel. If it is of a
" middling size—weighing less than a pound—its flesh, still tender,
" is much esteemed by the common people ; but if it is larger it
" decreases in value, because the flesh is tough. Those who buy it
" take the precaution of hammering it for some time with a stick,
" before cooking it ; others, especially the Greeks, are careful to drag
" it for some time upon a stone, holding it by the opening in the
" body—and this probably to break the fibres of the flesh. The
" flesh has a peculiar and rather marked taste, for which reason that
" of the cuttle-fish, and especially of the common calamer, is pre-
" ferred to it, but it is more thought of than that of the eledon. At
" Naples shell-fish merchants of St. Lucia sell it cooked ; on the
" shores of Liguria it is prepared in different ways.

" The largest pöulp that I have ever seen was about three yards
" long, and weighed nearly half a cwt. A skilful and very intelli-
" gent old fisherman came across it at the head of the jetty in the
" harbour of Nice, seized it with his own hands, by leaning over his
" boat, turned it inside out, and mastered it at last, but not without
" a great deal of trouble.

" Pöulps of thirty pounds weight are not rare at Nice, and those
" of twenty pounds are common. The action of the suckers of the
" pöulp upon the skin when they fasten on it, the serpent-like
" movement of its arms, its muscular power, its hideous aspect, have,
" I think, caused the misdeeds of this cephalopod to be exaggerated,
" for it is stupid and incapable of injuring any one."

If the Octopus taken by the old fisherman in Nice harbour was
not torpid, he must have been a very good-natured member of the
family of which Madame le Moine's " ugly beast" was a formidable
representative. In Beale's *History of the Sperm Whale* there is an
anecdote showing, on the authority of Sir Grenville Temple, what
happened in the Mediterranean. " A Sardinian captain bathing at
" Jerbeh felt one of his feet in the grasp of one of these animals ;
" on this, with his other foot he tried to disengage himself, but his
" limb was immediately seized by another of the monster's arms.
" He then, with his hands, endeavoured to free himself, but these
" also, in succession, were firmly grasped by the polypus, and the
" poor man was shortly after found drowned, with all his limbs
" strongly bound together by the twining arms of the fish ; and it
" is extraordinary that when this happened the water was scarcely
" four feet in depth."* Another illustration is drawn from Mr.
Beale's own experience. He says :—" While upon the Bonin
" Islands, searching for shells on the rocks, which had just been left

* *Beale's Natural History of the Sperm Whale*, London, 1839, p. 65.

" by the receding sea-tide, I was much astonished at seeing at my
" feet a most extraordinary looking animal, crawling towards the
" surf, which had only just left it. I had never seen one like it
" under such circumstances before ; it therefore appeared the more
" remarkable. It was creeping on its eight legs, which, from their
" soft and flexible nature, bent considerably under the weight of its
" body, so that it was lifted by the efforts of its tentacula only a
" small distance from the rocks. It appeared much alarmed at
" seeing me, and made every effort to escape, while I was not much
" in the humour to endeavour to capture so ugly a customer, whose
" appearance excited a feeling of disgust, not unmixed with fear.
" I, however, endeavoured to prevent its career by pressing on one of
" its legs with my foot, but although I made use of considerable
" force for that purpose, its strength was so great that it several
" times quickly liberated its member, in spite of all the efforts I
" could employ in this way on wet slippery rocks. I now laid hold
" of one of the tentacles with my hand, and held it firmly, so that
" the limb appeared as if it would be torn asunder by our united
" strength. I soon gave it a powerful jerk, wishing to disengage it
" from the rocks to which it clung so forcibly by its suckers, which
" it effectually resisted ; but the moment after, the apparently enraged
" animal lifted its head, with its large eyes projecting from the middle
" of its body, and letting go its hold of the rocks, suddenly sprang
" upon my arm, which I had previously bared to my shoulder, for
" the purpose of thrusting it into holes in the rocks to discover
" shells, and clung with its suckers to it with great power, endea-
" vouring to get its beak, which I could now see between the roots
" of its arms, in a position to bite !
    " A sensation of horror pervaded my whole frame when I found
" this monstrous animal had affixed itself so firmly upon my arm.
" Its cold slimy grasp was extremely sickening, and I immediately
" called aloud to the captain, who was also searching for shells at
" some distance, to come and release me from my disgusting
" assailant. He quickly arrived, and taking me down to the boat,
" during which time I was employed in keeping the beak away
" from my hand, quickly released me by destroying my tormentor
" with the boat-knife, when I disengaged it by portions at a time.
" This animal must have measured, across its expanded arms, about
" four feet, while its body was not larger than a large clenched
" hand. It was that species of sepia which is called by whalers
" ' rock-squid.' " *

    Not to go back to the fables and exaggerations of the old mari-

* Beale's Sperm Whale, 8vo, London, pp. 67, 68.

ners regarding the Kraken—of which, by the way, a very good account is given in vol. ii. Blackwood's Magazine, in a paper written
by the late James Wilson—there are various well-authenticated
cases of large cuttle-fish having been seen.   One of the latest
(1862) was communicated by Dr. Spence of Lerwick to Dr. Allman,
Professor of Natural History in Edinburgh.   The animal was
thrown ashore somewhere on the Shetlands, its body measured 9
feet, and its arms were 16 feet in length.   It is evident that a
cuttle-fish of this size would be a dangerous adversary for an un-
armed man, either in or out of the water.

The young cuttles, I am told, are frequently eaten on the Firth
of Forth by the crews of the trawling sloops.

D. D.

EDINBURGH, *December* 6, 1862.

INDEX.

———

Printed by R. Clark, Edinburgh.

www.ingramcontent.com/pod-product-compliance
Lightning Source LLC
Chambersburg PA
CBHW032307280326
41932CB00009B/723